CURRENT ISSUES IN MONETARY ECONOMICS

CURRENT ISSUES IN MONETARY ECONOMICS

Edited by

Taradas Bandyopadhyay
University of California at Riverside, USA

and

Subrata Ghatak
University of Leicester, UK

HARVESTER WHEATSHEAF

New York London Toronto Sydney Tokyo

First published 1990 by
Harvester Wheatsheaf,
66 Wood Lane End, Hemel Hempstead
Hertfordshire, HP2 4RG
A division of
Simon & Schuster International Group

Typeset in 10/12pt Times
by Witwell Ltd, Southport

Printed and Bound in Great Britain by
BPCC Wheatons Ltd, Exeter

British Library Cataloguing-in-Publication Data

Current issues in monetary economics.
Bandyopadhyay.
1. Monetary system
I. Bandyopadhyay, Taradas II. Ghatak, Subrata, *1939–*
332.4

ISBN 0-7450-0128-9

1 2 3 4 5 93 92 91 90

To Bharati and Anita

CONTENTS

PREFACE

The main aim of this collection of survey articles is to provide an up-to-date and comprehensive account of some major issues in monetary economics. The literature on monetary economics is enormous; inevitably, our choice of topics has been selective. However, it is hoped that many important and topical issues have been covered in this volume. The primary objective of the collection is to make available, in a convenient form, a number of papers which are likely to be useful in the third-year undergraduate and postgraduate monetary economics courses of British, North American and other English-speaking universities and polytechnics. It is mainly intended to *complement* conventional textbooks, not to supplant them. The contributors to this volume are some of the leading experts in their fields, and are well known for their enrichment of the subject. Given a number of theoretical and institutional developments in the field of finance, we hope the selected papers in this book will help unravel some of the mysteries of monetary economics and indicate some guidelines for future research. The editors are very grateful to the contributors to this volume for writing the survey papers as well as acting, in some cases, as anonymous (!) referees. They are also indebted to Professor Milton Friedman and to their colleagues, J.C. Dow and Paul Herrington, for their very helpful comments on a number of papers. The usual disclaimer applies.

CONTRIBUTORS

Michael J. Artis is Professor of Economics at Manchester University. After graduating from Oxford University in 1959 he worked for a while at the Oxford University Institute of Economics and Statistics, then at Adelaide and Flinders Universities in Australia. He returned to become Editor of the National Institute of Economic and Social Research's *Economic Review* before moving to his first chair at Swansea University College. His principal professional interests and contributions lie in the fields of monetary and macroeconomics.

Taradas Bandyopadhyay is a Professor of Economics at the Graduate School of Management, University of California at Riverside, USA. He was Reader in Economics at Hull University in England. He has published many papers in leading economic journals including *Journal of Economic Theory, Review of Economic Studies, Economic Journal* and *Journal of Macroeconomics*. He has taught in English, Canadian, Indian and American Universities.

Jagdeep S. Bhandari is an economist at the European Department of the International Monetary Fund and was formerly in the Research Department of the Fund. He is also Professor of Economics at the West Virginia University.

M. H. L. Burstein is Professor of Economics at York University, Canada. He is the author of seven books on economic theory, most recently *The New Art of Central Banking* (Macmillan, 1990), and of a number of articles that have exercised influence, including 'A theory of full line forcing' and 'On the invariance of demand for cash and other assets' (with R. W. Clower). He has held chairs in Britain and Canada and has taught in the United States, notably at Northwestern University (1955–64).

Bernard Decaluwe is Professor of Economics at the University of Laval at Quebec, Canada.

Subrata Ghatak is a Senior Lecturer in Economics at Leicester University in England. He has taught in Universities in England, Canada and India. He has contributed numerous articles in leading economic journals and written six books, including *Monetary Economics in Developing Countries* (Macmillan) and *Development Economics* (Unwin Hyman).

Peter M. Jackson is Professor of Economics and Director of the Public Sector Economics Research Centre at Leicester University. He is author of *Public Sector Economics* (with C.V. Brown) (4th edition 1989); *The Political Economy of Bureaucracy* (1984) and numerous articles on public sector economics and management. His research interests are in the growth of the public sector; public sector debt; public sector efficiency and organisational analysis.

Kajal Lahiri, Professor of Economics at the State University of New York at Albany, is the author of *The Econometrics of Inflationary Expectations* (North-Holland, 1981) and numerous articles on econometrics and monetary economics. He is the co-editor (with Geoffrey Moore) of *Leading Economic Indicators: New Approaches and Forecasting Records* (Cambridge University Press, 1989).

Paul Levine is Professor of Economics at Leicester University and was formerly Senior Research Officer, Centre for Economic Forecasting, London Business School. His research interests include open economy macroeconomics, macroeconomic policy design, reputation and international macroeconomic policy co-ordination issues. He has many publications in leading journals in the above areas and is co-author of a forthcoming book (with David Currie), *Macroeconomic Policy Design in an Open Economy* (Cambridge University Press, 1990).

Mervyn K. Lewis is Midland Bank Professor of Money and Banking at the University of Nottingham, UK, and visiting professor in economics at Flinders University of South Australia. Recently he has been visiting scholar at the Bank of England, consultant to Australian Financial System Inquiry, and visiting professor at the University of Cambridge and the Business University of Vienna. He is a Fellow of the Academy of Social Sciences in Australia. He has published six books and numerous articles on monetary economics.

David T. Llewellyn holds the Chair of Money and Banking at Loughborough University and is Chairman of the Loughborough University Banking Centre. He has previously held posts at Unilever, HM Treasury, Nottingham University and the International Monetary Fund.

He has held consultancy posts at financial institutions and the OECD and the World Bank. He has written extensively in the areas of international finance, monetary policy and institutions and is currently researching in the area of competition, financial innovation and structural change in the financial system.

Patrick Minford has been Edward Gonner Professor of Applied Economics, University of Liverpool since 1976. He was formerly Economic Assistant to the Finance Director, Courtaulds Ltd; served as an economic adviser in Malawi and the UK; Editor of *Review of the National Institute for Economic and Social Research*, 1976; and started the Liverpool Research Group in Macroeconomics, 1979. He is author of *Substitution Effects, Speculation and Exchange Rate Stability*; *Unemployment: Cause and Cure*; *The Housing Morass*; a textbook on rational expectations (with David Peel); many publications on trade, international and monetary economics.

David A. Wilton is Professor and Chairperson of the Department of Economics at Waterloo University in Canada. After taking his PhD from the MIT in the USA, he worked for the Government of Canada in Ottawa. He taught at the Queen's University, Kingston, Ontario before joining the University of Guelph where he became a Professor of Economics. He has published numerous articles in the fields of macroeconomics and econometrics in all the leading journals. Recently, he has published the 2nd edition of (with D. Prescott) *Macroeconomics: Theory and Policy in Canada* (Addison-Wesley, 1987).

Mark Zaporowski is Assistant Professor of Economics and Finance at Canisius College in Buffalo, New York, USA. He received his PhD in Economics from SUNY at Albany in 1985. His research interests are in the areas of monetary economics, macroeconomics and applied econometrics, and he has published in many journals.

George Zis is Head of Department of Economics and Economic History at Manchester Polytechnic. In the early 1970s, as a member of the Inflation Workshop at Manchester University, he contributed to studies treating inflation as an international monetary problem which were collected in two volumes edited by M. Parkin and himself: *Inflation in the World Economy* and *Inflation in Open Economies*. His principal interest is in international monetary relations. He has written and co-authored a number of studies which have appeared in many leading journals.

INTRODUCTION

Taradas Bandyopadhyay and Subrata Ghatak

The eleven surveys selected here are among those that are regarded as important for understanding monetary theory and policy. At the outset, Michael Artis and Mervyn Lewis provide a comprehensive survey of money supply and demand analysis, mainly in the United States and the United Kingdom. Their analysis centres around the major determinants of money demand; the factors influencing supply; and the processes by which demand and supply are brought into equilibrium. The authors of this survey discover many differences between theoretical and the simple empirical money demand functions; between the conventional methods for determining money stock and the actual steps followed by the central banks in the United States, United Kingdom and some other countries; and between various existing channels for equating demand for and supply of money as compared with the stylized facts narrated in empirical investigations. Artis and Lewis note that Friedman's (1956) identification of the quantity theory with a stable money demand function, and the econometric evidence of the 1960s of a close and predictable relationship between the quantity of money and the major arguments in demand, e.g. income, prices and interest rates, often led to policies of monetary targeting in the 1970s. However, the apparent breakdown of this relationship during that decade led to a 'more eclectic approach to the formulation of monetary policy in the 1980s'. Instability could have occurred as a result of changes in the *arguments* of the money demand function rather than the function itself. Given the floating exchange rate regimes and the high rate of inflation in the 1970s, it is suggested that uncertainty might have been caused by inflation and disinflation during 1974 and 1985. The transition from commodity to fiat money could have enhanced uncertainty about future nominal values. Hence, expected inflation (or deflation) exerts a stronger impact on money demand.

Artis and Lewis then consider the adjustment lags and the buffer-stock models. With exogenous money, the presence of alternative channels of equilibrium (i.e. via interest rate, income or price effect) presents problems for the measurement of short-run money demand functions. Further, the instability in demand might be partly caused by Goodhart's Law, which states that any empirical regularity is likely to prove unreliable when it is leaned upon for policy purposes. If central banks did change from endogenous money in the 1960s to exogenous money in the 1970s and early 1980s, some disturbances in the stable demand function are not surprising. In any case, what is really important is the *reasonable* stability of the *long-run* money demand function. Despite some pitfalls in econometric methods employed (e.g. the use of 'too noisy' and highly collinear data and inappropriate model specification), most recent evidence suggests greater *long-run stability* in money demand than is evident in the short-run studies. In addition, recent deregulations, financial innovations and changing policy regimes could shift the demand function. Perhaps the function is still unaltered, but its arguments have changed due to recent high inflation and disinflation. Alternatively, it is suggested that instability may exist in the supply curve as a result of the move to fiat money with shifts regardless of demand. Appropriate policy responses could accordingly differ. But Artis and Lewis see no reason why all the above reasons might not have contributed to the final outcome and a faster rate of growth of bank deposits could be justified in a more competitive banking system. Thus although the stability of the money demand function is still an open issue, monetary authorities seem likely to adhere to open market operations to absorb any unexpected shifts in demand for money.

The important role of the market operations of the Bank of England and other financial institutions has been clearly highlighted in the chapter by David Llewellyn. In particular, he draws attention to the open market operations in the conduct of monetary policy, abstracting away from the discussion of the final objective of monetary policy and from the arguments about the most appropriate intermediate target of policy. 'Monetary policy cannot be conducted in an institutional vacuum', argues Llewellyn. Indeed, the nature of a sophisticated financial market, the role of the discount market, the different roles of the Bank of England and the different types of financial innovation can render the implementation of the monetary policy a very complex affair. The institutional arrangements in the London money market, described in detail by Llewellyn, are quite important in the determination of short-term interest rates as the supply and demand for bankers' *operational deposits* exert strong pressure on the movements of such rates. This is different from the conventional wisdom that the *supply of money*, along with its demand, determine interest rates. Short-term rates can change because of changes in administered discount rates, central bank dealing in markets, moral suasion exercised by the Bank, or changes in expectations. Thus, although Llewellyn allows market forces and expectations to play their role, he believes that the ability of the

Bank to determine the volume of banks' operational deposits, given the banks' inelastic demand, has a very significant effect in the determination of short-term rates. However, the power of the Bank declines as the maturity lengthens.

Lahiri and Zaporowski have carefully explored the impact of *expectations* on the determination of *real interest rates*. Fisher (1930) has argued that the nominal rate of interest should fully reflect the expected rate of inflation and the real rate of interest should remain constant. However, *ex ante* real interest rates do not remain constant. The estimation of such *ex ante* real rates has followed two alternative ways of modelling price expectations: the use of rational expectations hypothesis (REH); and the use of survey data. Under REH the *ex post* real interest rate is equal to the *ex ante* real rate *net* of a random inflation forecast error. The *ex ante* real rate is then estimated with the use of the *ex post* real rate as a proxy. The expected inflation rate is then the difference between the estimated nominal rate and the estimated *ex ante* real rate. In other studies, Livingston's survey data are used to assess the effect of price expectation, fiscal and monetary policies on the real rate in a reduced-form interest equation. But the estimated *ex ante* real rate here turns out to be very different from the same obtained from the use of the REH.

Lahiri and Zaporowski examine the nature of the differences in the estimated after-tax real rates and inflation expectations implied by the two different methods. This is accomplished by estimating two models in a more general econometric framework where the survey data are not used as an unbiased estimate of true price expectations and where the after-tax real rate is not regarded as a true random-walk process. They also use one-year-ahead predictions of inflation based upon Survey Research Center data. Where the nominal rate is adjusted for changes in the marginal tax rate on interest income, the Fisher coefficient turns out to be 0.25 in their extended model, which is rather low. This result is partly due to the fact that the American Statistical Association–National Bureau of Economic Research data set was the only one to result in unbiased estimates of true expectations. Thus, their estimated *ex-ante* real rates are different from those implied by other studies. A more flexible use of survey data by the authors significantly reduces the divergence of the estimated real interest and expected inflation rates suggested by the different approaches.

Given the belief in some quarters that the rate of growth of money supply depends upon the public sector borrowing requirement (PSBR), Peter Jackson carefully analyses the theoretical and empirical basis of such a relationship. His review of the literature shows the absence of an unambiguous set of correlations between the growth rate of money supply and PSBR. First, he shows that the monetization of public debt could occur when the debt is bought by the banks and they expand their lending due to a rise in their reserve assets. This view is regarded as too mechanistic as it washes out the complex realities of portfolio management of banks. Jackson argues that the cash–deposit ratios may not remain stable enough to give the authorities control of the money supply by changing the monetary base. Further, given the flow-of-funds accounting procedure, PSBR is given by the open market operations (OMO), non-marketable debt (NMD), use of funds to pay off maturity debt (MAT), finance obtained to accommodate external flows (ECF) and increase in high powered money (AB). Clearly, a very close relationship between AB and PSBR will imply that other factors in the identity account are insignificant. Jackson notes that in a developed financial system, it is less likely that PSBR will be monetized. With a well-developed financial system, OMO and NMD are high, thereby taking pressure off money supply. Further, the money base can be 'endogenous' if it responds to changes in interest rate differentials. Thus, the portfolio decisions of the different agents within the financial system could influence a simple accounting relationship between PSBR and money supply.

Jackson points out that the nature of monetization of debt depends upon one's view of the state of the world. In a 'Minnesota world' agents consider bond sales as deferred monetization. But in a Ricardian world, bond sales are simply regarded as deferred taxation. The empirical validity of these rival theories depends upon whether the economy is close to a critical value of its debt–income ratio. Unfortunately, there is little empirical evidence to suggest which theory is correct. In principle, if agents are willing to absorb additional debt, then the pressure to increase the monetary base or interest rate will diminish.

Jackson surveys a large number of econometric studies and concludes that the relationship between public sector deficits and money supply is not always positive or negative. The weight of the evidence seems to favour a positive but rather *weak* relationship. The time and place of study could seriously affect the final conclusion and this highlights the necessity to pay more attention to the understanding of the nature of the financial institutions of the economy.

George Zis has reviewed the literature on the main schools of thought on the causes of inflation, and argues that their relative adequacy could be measured by their ability to explain the international nature of inflation during the 1960s. He suggests that inflation is more an international monetary phenomenon than the product of a series of national sociological events. Such an explanation is regarded as satisfactory because channels of transmission of inflationary impulses across countries during the Bretton Woods period are well defined. Zis then discusses the failure of exchange rate flexibility to protect domestic economies from external monetary disturbances – a phenomenon which occurred contrary to what was predicted by supporters of flexible exchange rates. He then points out that it is only the nature of the transmission process that alternative exchange rate regimes can affect. Currency substitution has weakened the case for flexible exchange rates significantly. The only viable long-run basis for the creation of an international monetary system is supposed to be international monetary co-ordination.

In the 1970s and early 1980s, monetary theories of the balance of payments (MTBOP) merited considerable attention. In simple terms, they state that in fixed exchange rate regimes, an excess supply of money in the *j*th economy has direct absorption effects that drain monetary reserves. This dynamic process also leads to direct capital outflows. Without sterilization of the reserve inflows, there will be an expansion outside the *j*th economy.

Under floating exchange rate regimes, according to MTBOP, monetary balances (surplus or deficit) are quickly adjusted by changes in the exchange rates. With sticky prices and wages, an increase in money supply above the trend in the *j*th economy (i.e. an excess of money supply) first results in a more positive current account in the *j*th economy, to be followed by higher inflation and a consequent deficit in the current account. Before the eventual stabilization of the current account, the deficit in the current account could easily *overshoot* the equilibrium level.

In his critique of the MTBOP, Mayer Burstein argues that money *per se*, as an asset subset, has no special impact on changes in the current account of the balance of payments. 'All that survives of MTBOP are traces of a pseudo-monetary theory based on a broad spectrum of assets. Even these trace quantities are suspect.' With high elasticities of substitution among different types of financial assets, a change in asset preferences and central bank strategies is usually absorbed within the global financial sector without affecting the real economy. Besides, under modern conditions, when financial innovations occur regularly, the supply of money cannot be precisely defined. Such financial innovations include denationalization of monetary and quasi-monetary issues; interest on money; changes in the central bank lending and borrowing rates that could replace open market operations; and the growth of quasi-banking. Given such innovations, monetary disequilibrium can be corrected by changes in portfolios. The adjustment occurs within the financial sector without changing the balance of payments.

Bhandari and Decaluwe analyse the case of a stochastic equilibrium model of the open economy operating under two-tier exchange markets with incomplete segmentation. They show how a part of commercial trade transactions is settled in the financial market, due to both legally sanctioned 'leakage' and fraudulent transactions. Such modelling of the exchange markets seems to accord well with the current economic reality. The model has also been used to analyse the dynamic adjustments in such an economy in addition to the short- and long-run effects of different structural disturbances.

The model examines two sources of dynamic adjustment: reserve accumulation; and foreign asset accumulation. Changes in the stock of domestically-held foreign assets are a direct consequence of inter-market leakage. If the two exchange markets are completely segmented, the floating financial rates ensure no net movement in foreign asset stocks. With incomplete segmentation, it is the sum of the capital account *plus* the leakage that is equal to zero. The accumulation of foreign reserves is given by that part of total exports that is transacted in the commercial market. The authors then specify two necessary stochastic disturbances in the economy: foreign price disturbances; and domestic credit disturbances. They assume that continuous equilibrium prevails in all markets and that expectations are rational.

One of the results of the model is the presence of a kind of macroeconomic trade-off: while increased leakage 'insulates' the domestic price effects, it is gained at the cost of 'sharper' financial exchange rate and reserve stock alignment. If external price disturbances are unexpected such a trade-off ceases to exist. Other results suggest that domestic credit innovations are accompanied by generally weak effects upon the financial exchange rate, reserves and the price level. In general, increasing leakages are accompanied by reduced depreciation and higher inflation along with increased reserve accumulation. The authors also analyse the output and price effects of changing leakages as well as the necessary conditions to restore money market equilibrium. The final section of the chapter looks at the effects of the stationary state when both foreign assets and reserve accumulation have ceased. Here both anticipated and unexpected rises in the foreign price level lead to financial appreciation, reserve accumulation and price inflation. The authors conclude that cross-transactions between the segmented markets impose a dynamic cost on the economy due to an enhanced degree of 'persistence' in the adjustment of various macrovariables. But these costs are to be viewed against some potential benefits of leakage arising due to the reduced vulnerability of the domestic economy to external shocks and in terms of the possible rehabilitation of domestic credit policy in stabilization programmes.

Patrick Minford, in his survey, explains the implications of the rational expectations hypothesis (REH) for monetary policy in a closed economy. First, he shows how monetary shocks affect output. In an equilibrium model, a rise in money supply raises prices while wages rise with a lag due to slowly changing expectations. Real wages fall and output rises. In an equilibrium model, quantities are demand constrained; prices and wages are given by their expected values. Demand increases as money rises. Thus, output rises. Both these models are questioned by the emergence of the REH as they respond instantaneously to current availability of information.

Minford then defines monetary policy and its association with fiscal policy. The presence of a government budget constraint shows how instability could occur if monetary and fiscal policies are inconsistent, i.e. if money and bonds grew at different rates. Under the REH, the instability problem becomes an 'immediate' one: the impossibility of defining an equilibrium path at all. Hence, a policy of deficit imposes limits on the operation of monetary policy. Moreover, the *expected* avenues of monetary policy would affect *present* output and inflation.

As regards the role of monetary policy in stabilizing output fluctuations, Minford points out that provided the central bank has up-to-date information at least as good as that of the private sector, a good model of the economy, forecasting its future conditional paths, is efficient in implementing required monetary policy. The debate centred around the question whether the activist monetary policy would be at least as likely to increase as to dampen fluctuations. Now the debate is broadened since under REH economic agents include knowledge of the reactions of central banks into the calculation of their expectations. Given certain assumptions, Minford shows that such a phenomenon can offset the effects of monetary policy on output.

Naturally, the question of policy effectiveness has been discussed frequently in Western Europe and the United States in the context of the disinflationary fiscal and monetary policies pursued in the early 1980s. The adherence to such policies by different governments became a parameter of interest as the precommitment and reputation of a government's policy is supposed to depend on it. If private agents are forward-looking and believe in the credibility of future government policies, then the present can be affected. As shown by Kydland and Prescott (1977), 'optimal' policies designed today by minimizing some welfare loss function (whose arguments are, say, inflation and unemployment) can be sub-optimal in future. This is regarded as the 'time-inconsistency' property of an optimal policy. Paul Levine, in his chapter, surveys the large recent literature on this subject and points out that an incentive to renege on the time-inconsistent policy occurs in the absence of some institutional procedures which raise the real cost of changing policy rules. The credibility problem arises as the private agents with knowledge of the optimization problem can expect future reneging. Thus time-inconsistent policies lack credibility. Policies can be designed to be time-consistent, but they could be significantly sub-optimal in terms of inflation or unemployment costs.

The problem is whether planned 'optimal' policy can be self-enforcing without binding commitments. Levine argues that the answer depends on the information the private sector is supposed to have. He then analyses the problem in terms of a complete-information game suggested by Barro and Gordon (1983) between the policy-maker and the private sector. It is shown that the policy-maker's concern for his/her reputation for precommitment (e.g. 'the lady is not for turning') can, under certain conditions, sustain planned optimal policy, or at least policies superior to those which are time-consistent. The main limitations of such analysis are: the unravelling problem if the game has a finite time horizon; the multiple equilibria; the model specificity of the analysis; and the extreme assumption of complete information.

Levine then analyses the credibility problem with incomplete information. The major conclusion here is that uncertainty on the part of the private sector regarding the 'nature' of a ruling regime can be enough to sustain the planned optimal policy for much of the finite time for which the game is allowed to play. In other models, with imperfect monitoring of government policy and the policy-maker's knowledge of the random disturbance affecting money supply, it is shown that planned optimal policy can be sustained but periodic inflationary pressures can arise. Finally, he surveys the case where the policy-maker can control the random shock entering the instrument. The main result is that a low inflation rate (below the time-consistent rate) can be sustained and it may be in the interest of the government to confuse the private sector with loose control of monetary policy.

The rise of the doctrine of rational expectations has cast doubts about the role of the government in stabilizing the economy. David Wilton, in his chapter on 'Disinflation and wage–price controls', shows how a government can actually lower the rate of inflation by a judicious combination of a restrictive monetary policy and temporary wage–price controls. In the absence of wage–price controls, a disinflationary monetary policy is likely to impose significant costs on society because of lower output, higher unemployment and higher interest rates. Although the operation of an incomes policy in the form of wage–price controls imposes an administrative burden and some distortion in resource allocation costs, *temporary* controls can reduce some of the macrocosts to the society which usually follow the use of deflationary monetary policy. Wilton argues that should an incomes policy legislate the inflation rate down to a lower level and reduce high inflation expectations, the macroeconomic gains of temporary controls on prices and wages due to a rise in output and employment could be greater than their microeconomic costs, i.e. administrative and distortion costs.

After demonstrating the efficacy of the wage and price controls within an IS-LM-PEP (price-expectation-augmented Phillips curve), Wilton points out that the New Classical policy ineffectiveness proposition of a disinflationary monetary policy, i.e. deflation without a fall in output or employment, really requires the joint assumptions of rational expectations *and* continual market clearing. Despite the theoretical appeal of the assumption of rational expectations, Wilton cites a number of studies which have questioned the validity of the assumption of rational inflation expectations. Besides, the assumption of perfectly flexible prices and continuous market clearing of labour is treated as dubious due to the presence of (implicit and explicit) contracts in the labour market. In practice, a deliberate policy of monetary disinflation in the United Kingdom, United States and Canada did not instantly achieve a lower inflation rate without a 'deep and protracted recession'. Further, Wilton cites a number of econometric studies which have concluded that the Anti-Inflationary Board (AIB) exerted a substantial negative effect on Canadian wage increases. On the basis of his own research, he has shown that despite some small rise in administrative and other costs imposed by the AIB, the macroeconomic benefits of the imposition of wage–price controls in the late 1970s and early 1980s were about 600,000 more jobs for three years in Canada. He concludes that a monetary disinflation policy will reduce the long-run rate of inflation but at a very high short-run cost.

In the literature on money and economic growth, money is regarded as superneutral when steady-state real variables are independent of the rate of growth of money supply. In the basic neo-classical monetary growth models, as developed by Tobin (1965), comprising one good and two assets (money and capital), it is shown that capital intensity rises with the rate of inflation – a result which depends on both fixed savings and portfolio effects. In further extensions of the Tobin model, money enters the utility function as a consumer good or production function as a producer good. Here the steady-state real rate of return is independent of the rate of inflation and the capital–labour ratio changes if real balances affect marginal productivity of capital and labour differently – a conclusion which is supposed to emerge from dropping the assumption of fixed savings. In their chapter, Bandyopadhyay and Ghatak show that it is the form of the money demand function rather than the absence of a constant savings ratio or a different definition of disposable income (portfolio effect) which produces different results. The use of a variable Kaldorian savings function does not diminish the significance of the role of the money demand function. If money is a producer good, the neo-classical result that the steady-state capital intensity is lower in a monetary economy than in a barter economy holds. Further, a rise in the steady-state rate of inflation raises the steady-state capital intensity unambiguously if the nominal interest rate is greater than some critical value.

REFERENCES

Barro, R.J. and Gordon, D. (1983) 'Rules, discretion and reputation in a model of monetary policy', *Journal of Monetary Economics*, vol. 12, pp. 101–21.

Fisher, I. (1930) *The Theory of Interest*, New York: Macmillan.

Friedman, M. (1956) 'The quantity theory of money: a restatement' in M. Friedman (ed.), *Studies in the Quantity Theory of Money*, Chicago: University of Chicago Press.

Kydland, F.E. and Prescott, E.C. (1977) 'Rules rather than discretion: the inconsistency of optimal plans', *Journal of Political Economy*, vol. 85, pp. 473–91.

Tobin, J. (1965) 'Money and economic growth', *Econometrica*, vol. 33, pp. 671–84.

1 · MONEY SUPPLY AND DEMAND

M. J. Artis and M. K. Lewis

INTRODUCTION

The concepts of the supply of money and the demand for money lie at the heart of modern macroeconomics. In the popular IS–LM framework, for example, they trace out the LM curve and link the real and monetary sectors of Keynesian models. In monetarist analysis, the interaction of the supply of money – or its inverse, the velocity of circulation of money – with the demand for money forms the basis of models of price and/or exchange rate determination.

Both the Keynesian and monetarist frameworks can, in principle, accommodate many different hypotheses about the nature of the demand for and supply of money. Nevertheless, Friedman's (1956) identification of the quantity theory with a stable demand-for-money function has meant that the popularity of monetarist policy prescriptions and the success of econometric performance have gone hand in hand. Evidence in the 1960s of a close and predictable relationship between the quantity of money and the constituents of demand – income, prices and interest rates – was instrumental in the move to monetary targeting in the following decade. The apparent breakdown of that relationship during the course of the 1970s has seen instituted a more eclectic approach to the formulation of monetary policy in the 1980s.

In assessing what portents the current crop of demand-for-money regressions might hold for monetary policy during the 1990s, we begin by organizing our discussion around the determinants of the quantity of money outstanding; the determinants of the demand for money; and the reconciliation between demand and supply. This leads us into a consideration of the methods of monetary control in the United States and

---

Charles Goodhart, Milton Friedman, W. Allen and Subrata Ghatak kindly provided most helpful comments on the first draft of this chapter. Mrs J. Brown kindly typed the manuscript.

United Kingdom and a brief comment on long-run studies. We conclude with some observations about policy responses.

THE SUPPLY OF MONEY

By far the most usual situation in the past has been for the money supply to comprise, or be based upon, commodities such as silver or gold. Remnants of a gold standard carried through into the Bretton Woods system, for member countries of the International Monetary Fund (IMF) were required to define the parity of their currencies in terms of gold and to maintain convertibility into gold; the latter coming about indirectly by means of the maintenance of a fixed (but adjustable) parity with the US dollar, which was itself convertible into gold. It is only since 1971 that a system based entirely on fiat money – where the money supply comprises, or is based upon, inconvertible paper money, issued by national governments – has been in existence. This period of time is the first one for which there is virtually no prospect of or an intention of restoring commodity convertibility. Its uniqueness is an important factor which needs to be kept in mind when considering the apparent instability of monetary relationships.

For most countries the issues of fiat money do not constitute the major part of the money stock; what Keynes (1930) termed 'bank money', as opposed to 'state money', dominates. Money supply theories are thus concerned with the processes governing supply conditions in countries with extensive financial intermediation.

Three groups are involved in these processes, and the links between the three groups depend upon the institutions, regulations and financial technology which prevail in individual countries. The monetary authorities issue fiat money and determine the conditions under which the financial intermediaries operate. The public allocates its money holdings between fiat money and the claims of financial intermediaries. Financial intermediaries acquire securities issued by the public and the authorities, and supply their own liabilities in return.

Two basic approaches have been developed to analyse the interrelationships. Both are based on identities, yet are shaped by implicit hypotheses about the behaviour of the three participating groups. Those identities used in the United States, although they can be applied in any country with a fractional reserve banking system, are based around the quantity of base money or total reserves and a 'money multiplier'. Underlying them is the belief, explicitly stated by Brunner (1973), that the money supply process can be decomposed into two parts – one part being the exogenous input of the monetary authorities, the other representing the endogenous reaction of the banks and the public.

In other countries, such as the United Kingdom, Australia, France and Italy, the monetary environment has been seen to be less hospitable to such a strict division, because some part of the authorities' behaviour could be rendered endogenous due to a commitment to interest rate or exchange rate targets. It has been more usual in these countries to classify the sources of money supply change into 'credit counterparts' by means of the flow of funds without distinguishing the actions of the authorities from others.

Money multiplier approaches

Based on the writings of Friedman and Schwartz (1963) and Cagan (1965), the money multiplier approach builds on the standard analysis in money and banking textbooks, in which bank deposits, D, are derived as a multiple $(1/r)$ of banks' holdings of reserves, R. Reserve assets are the monetary liabilities of the central bank, i.e. base or high-powered money, H, divided among the alternative uses as bank reserves and the cash holdings of the non-bank public, C. Thus

$$H = C + R \tag{1.1}$$

The money supply is defined as

$$M = D + C \tag{1.2}$$

By denoting the ratios C/D and R/D as d and r respectively, one can derive

$$M = \frac{1 + d}{d + r} H = mH \tag{1.3}$$

which links the money supply to high-powered money.

The ratio $m = (1 + d)/(d + r)$ is referred to as the *money multiplier*, and under a system of fractional reserve banking (when $r < 1$) must be greater than 1. Part of bank reserves may be required by law or held by convention, with the remainder held voluntarily by banks in excess of the requirements. Accordingly,

$$R = RR + E \tag{1.4}$$

where RR is legal reserves and E is excess reserves, and

$$r = rr + e \tag{1.5}$$

where rr is the required reserve ratio and e is the excess reserve ratio, enabling us to rewrite the money multiplier[1] as

$$m = \frac{1 + d}{d + (rr + e)} \tag{1.6}$$

With rr a policy determined variable, control of the money supply might be achievable by H if the ratios d and $E/D = e$ are stable.

The question of the stability of the money supply processes arises because H, d and e are, in the words of Friedman and Schwartz, 'proximate determinants' in the sense that they are in turn governed by more fundamental factors. The ratios d and e are the outcome of portfolio decisions of the non-bank public and bank sectors, respectively, in response to relative interest rates, summarized by a vector of relevant rates, $\mathbf{i}$. If attention is focused on the authorities' actions in supplying base money by means of open market operations altering the central banks' holdings of securities, S, a relationship of the form

$$M = h\,(S, \mathbf{i}, rr) \tag{1.7}$$

can be substituted for Equation (1.3), along the lines of Sims and Takayama (1985). Where open market operations themselves respond to variables such as income or prices by means of a policy reaction function, Equation (1.7) can be decomposed further.[2] The reader may note that many of the variables which would then enter the right-hand side of Equation (1.7) are the same as those which feature in demand-for-money models.

It is fair to say, however, that proponents of the money multiplier identity typically hold to a particular view of the money supply process (Andersen, 1967; Jordan, 1969). This is one in which the monetary authorities provide a particular quantity of base money, from which the banks must meet reserve requirements and obtain their desired holdings of excess reserves and from which the public acquires its currency holdings. Thus the two groups are in competition for a limited amount of base money, with the entire quantity always claimed. Changes in the quantity of the monetary base will create discrepancies between desired and actual reserves of banks, leading to alterations in the banks' acquisition of earning assets and thus their deposits.[3]

This idea is carried through into the *reserves available* approach which focuses upon that part of the monetary base which remains after the public's currency requirements are met. It is a special case of the money base–money multiplier model in which the reserves available to the banking system are treated as exogenous. With total reserves treated as the control variable, we have

$$M = \frac{1 + d}{rr + e} \cdot R \tag{1.8}$$

The sources of total reserves are member bank borrowings (BR) from the Reserve Banks and non-borrowed reserves (NBR), the latter arising mainly from system open market operations (along with Federal Reserve float and

Treasury currency outstanding). Thus we can rewrite Equation (1.4) as

$$\begin{aligned} R &= NBR + BR \\ &= RR \quad + E \end{aligned} \tag{1.4a}$$

Frequently, reserves required to be held against government demand deposits and time and savings deposits are deducted from the total reserves figure to focus upon the reserves available for private sector demand deposits (and desired excess reserves).

Support for these interpretations of a process running from the quantity of reserves or high-powered money via a money multiplier to the quantity of money is offered from examinations of the relative importance of the public's, banks' and monetary authorities' behaviour in the money supply process for the United States (Brunner, 1986). Variations in the multiplier are prominent in the short run, whereas the behaviour of the authorities dominates longer-run movements. When considering short-run movements, it must be remembered that the multiplier models are based on ratios which summarise underlying portfolio equilibrium relationships. Unexpected disturbances create deviations of actual asset ratios from their equilibrium values which are only rectified over time. A decrease in base money, for instance, must instantaneously reduce banks' excess reserve ratios. Variations in asset ratios may then reflect a lag in portfolio adjustment, signalling not the inappropriate nature of the behavioural assumptions, but simply their inapplicability to short-run situations. Of course, finding that H or R is strongly correlated with M does not establish exogeneity, a question taken up later.

Evidence for the United Kingdom is different. Figure 1.1 shows a remarkable change in the multiplier; after having fluctuated within a narrow band in the 100 years from 1871 to 1971, it has soared in the ten years since then (from around 4 to nearly 10), the combination of a sharply declining ratio of currency to deposits and a greatly reduced reserve ratio. Much of the latter can be attributed to the ending under Competition and Credit Control in 1971 of the conventional minimum 8 per cent cash ratio which the clearing banks maintained by agreement with the Bank of England. But the years since 1971 have seen a rapid growth of, and British banks' participation in, wholesale markets for liabilities and bought funds.[4] These markets largely obviate the need for a bank to provide for its own cash liquidity needs. Instead, banks can seek out lending opportunities secure in the knowledge that they can buy in reserves to support their loan book – what is known as 'liability management'. Such developments suggest the desirability of a money stock formation approach which focuses upon bank lending and its contribution to the quantity of money. The alternative credit counterparts approach does so.

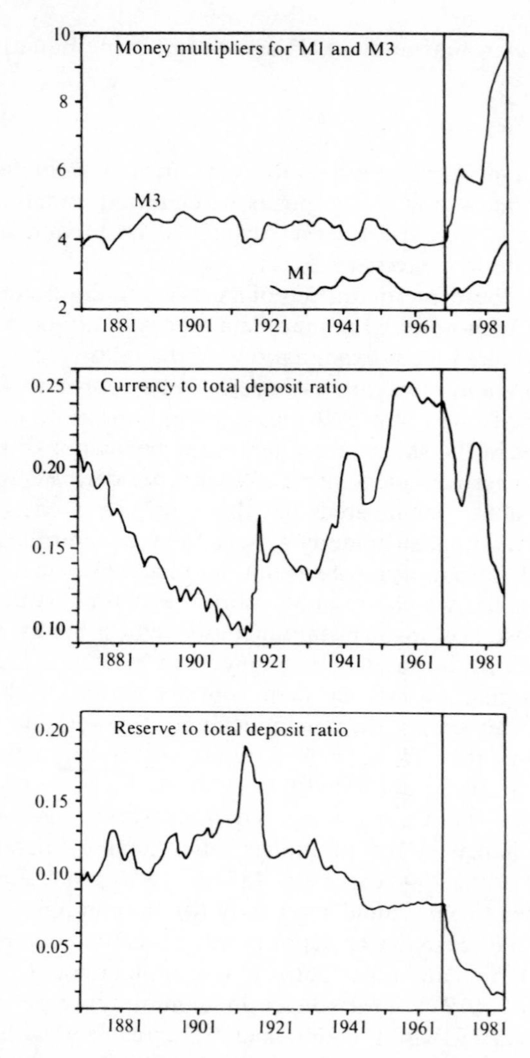

Figure 1.1 Money multipliers, United Kingdom, 1871–1985 (*Source*: Capie and Rodrik-Bali 1986)

Credit counterparts approach

This approach, also involving identities, is derived from the flow of funds. Table 1.1 is a simplified four-sector version in which the central bank and the government are aggregated into an official sector, along with the foreign sector, private non-financial sector and the financial sector (comprising in this case only the banks). Columns (i) and (ii) give the

Table 1.1 Simplified flow-of-funds account

	(i) Income	(ii) Expenditure	(iii) Deposits	(iv) Non-deposit liabilities	(v) High-powered money	(vi) Govt securities	(vii) Domestic lending	(viii) Foreign lending
1. Official	T	G			$-\Delta H$	$-\Delta GS$		ΔRes
2. Foreign	Z	X						$K - \Delta Res$
3. Private non-financial	S	I	ΔD	ΔNDL	ΔC	ΔGS_p	$-\Delta A$	$-K$
4. Financial			$-\Delta D$	$-\Delta NDL$	ΔR	ΔGS_B	ΔA	
Total	$S+Z+T$	$I+X+G$	0	0	0	0	0	0

income and expenditure items, showing, for each of the four sectors, how funds have been derived through the earning of revenue and used for expenditures, with any difference constituting the particular sector's net borrowing or net lending (along with unidentified items). The remaining columns (iii)–(viii) show how the net borrowing or lending gives rise to changes in financial assets and liabilities.

The requirement that total income equals total expenditures is simply the familiar national income identity:

$$S + T = I + G + (X - Z) \tag{1.9}$$

This can be rearranged to give the parallel financing requirement, for the flow of funds provides the financial counterparts of the income and expenditure items which appear in the national accounts:

$$S - I = (X - Z) + (G - T) \tag{1.10}$$

In this form the identity says that borrowing by the overseas sector to finance an excess of home exports (X) over home imports (Z), together with borrowing by the government sector to finance an excess of its expenditure (G) over its revenue (T) must be matched by net lending by the non-financial private sector of the economy arising from its surplus of savings (S) over capital formation (I). The financial sector is assumed to have no net saving.

Net lending by the non-financial private sector results in its acquiring more financial assets than it issues by incurring liabilities, corresponding to its increase in net financial wealth. The assets may be acquired directly from the overseas and official sectors in the form of capital outflow ($-K$) or additional holdings of official debt issued as cash or bonds ($\Delta C + \Delta GS_p$). Alternatively, the acquisition may occur indirectly via the banks (the private financial sector) by savers adding to deposits (ΔD) and net non-deposit liabilities (ΔNDL) in excess of the loans obtained by investors (ΔA). From row 3 we see how the net surplus is allocated across the portfolio, i.e.

$$S - I = \Delta D + \Delta NDL + \Delta C + \Delta GS_p - K - \Delta A \tag{1.11}$$

By equating Equations (1.10) and (1.11) and rearranging, we obtain

$$\Delta D + \Delta C = (G - T) - \Delta GS_p + (X - Z + K) + \Delta A - \Delta NDL \tag{1.12}$$

The left-hand side is simply the increase in money supply (sterling M3). The first term on the right-hand side corresponds to the public sector borrowing requirement (or budget deficit). The second is the net sales of government interest-bearing debt to the non-bank private sector. The third term is the net external flows from the balance of payments identity, as given in row 2 (which includes changes in official reserves along with

Table 1.2 Counterparts to growth in sterling M3, 1987 (£ million)

Public sector borrowing requirement	–1,391
Sales of public sector debt to non-bank private sector	–569
External influences	3,027
Sterling lending by banking sector to private sector	38,571
Non-deposit liabilities	–4,923
Total = increase in sterling M3	34,715

various short-term bank flows, e.g. non-resident transactions in sterling deposits and assets and the banks' switched position between sterling and foreign currency). The fourth term is bank lending to the private sector, while the last is the increase in net non-deposit liabilities (bank share capital and internal funds less non-financial assets such as bank premises along with any errors and omissions).

Thus, we have the credit counterparts by which, in the case of the United Kingdom, a change in sterling M3 equals the public sector borrowing requirement *less* sales of gilts to the non-bank private sector *plus* external influences *plus* increase in bank lending to the private sector *less* increase in net non-deposit liabilities. The empirical counterparts for 1987 are shown in Table 1.2.

Comparing the two approaches

Both approaches are based on identities, and in that sense are equally correct. Why, then, is the money multiplier identity favoured in the United States and the credit counterparts identity preferred in the United Kingdom and Australia? Our contention is that long-outstanding institutional differences between the countries have shaped the approach to the analysis of the money supply.

We first note that the link between the two can be made from row 1 of Table 1.1 where

$$\Delta H + \Delta GS = G - T + \Delta Res \tag{1.13}$$

That is, if the official sector is running a deficit and/or adding to international reserves then it must be issuing high-powered money and interest-bearing government securities. The latter can be acquired by either banks or the non-bank private sector so that

$$\Delta H - \Delta GS_B = G - T - \Delta GS_p + \Delta Res \tag{1.14}$$

Substituting the right-hand side of Equation (1.14) into Equation (1.12) gives

$$\Delta M = \Delta H + \Delta GS_B + \Delta A - \Delta NDL \quad (1.15)$$

The last three items on the right-hand side of Equation (1.15) can be described loosely as the net non-cash assets of the banks and, from the balance sheet of the banking sector in row 4,

$$\Delta GS_B + \Delta A - \Delta NDL = \Delta D - \Delta R \quad (1.16)$$

Using Equations (1.3) and (1.5) we can rewrite Equation (1.15) as

$$\Delta M = \Delta H + \frac{1-r}{d+r} \cdot \Delta H = \frac{1+d}{d+rr+e} \Delta H \quad (1.17)$$

This derivation immediately suggests one reason why the counterparts framework is preferred in the United Kingdom. As noted previously, an implicit hypothesis underlying Equation (1.17) is that banks' acquisition of non-cash assets is governed by the availability of cash reserves. In short, a supply mechanism determines changes in banks' earning assets. However suitable this assumption is for the United States, it is less applicable for the case of bank lending in the United Kingdom, where the widespread use of the overdraft system means that the usage made of lending limits is largely at the customers' volition. An analysis based on the demand for credit rather than the supply of reserves makes more sense, and behavioural relationships about the demand for advances can be slotted readily into a framework such as Equation (1.12). In addition, bank lending has long been a special focus of monetary policy in the United Kingdom, and this is a second reason why the counterparts framework is preferred.

Third, bank lending to the government sector in the United Kingdom has frequently been determined more by the fiscal than by the monetary authorities. 'From the point of view of the monetary authorities, the size of the deficit to be financed is an external parameter which they have to accept' (Goodhart, 1975). Unlike the position in the United States, the central bank is not an independent authority but rather one component of a co-ordinated centralized policy-making machinery. One advantage claimed for the counterparts method is that the components can be identified, respectively, with fiscal policy ($G–T$), debt management policy (ΔGS_p), exchange rate policy ($X–Z+K$), and monetary policy ($\Delta A–\Delta NDL$).

Fourth, the counterparts framework can be readily applied to aggregates which embrace the whole of the banking sector (e.g. sterling M3) and is less readily applicable to the M1 aggregate preferred in the United States. Finally, the money multiplier has the advantage of isolating the impact of reserve requirements (*rr*) on the money supply. Since required reserves do not play a role as a policy tool in its monetary policy formulation, this feature is unimportant for the UK system.

Many of these long-standing institutional differences between the United States and the United Kingdom have been eroded. M1 is no longer the dominant aggregate in the United States, and the broader aggregates are now accorded greater emphasis. Paradoxically, this has coincided with a move in the opposite direction, away from broad to narrow aggregates, in the United Kingdom. Likewise, less lending in the United Kingdom is now by means of overdraft than was formerly the case, while more lending in the United States is under loan commitments, both formal and informal. Since 1985, the UK government has followed the practice of fully funding its deficit by sales of securities. Consequently, for the time being, the link between monetary and fiscal policy in the United Kingdom has been severed, albeit informally. And in terms of the adoption of base money (termed M0) as one of the targeted monetary aggregates, the United Kingdom would seem to have moved closer to US practice.

Reconciliation of supply and demand

Irrespective of the method used to analyse the sources of changes in the money supply, there is still the question of how we are to interpret the results.

A common approach followed in econometric models in both the United Kingdom and Australia involves modelling elements on the right-hand side of Equation (1.12) above. The quantity of money can be made as broad as is desired merely by altering the range of financial institutions considered and the definitions of bank and non-bank private sector accordingly. However, for the magnitude to be narrower than M3, which corresponds to the banks' domestic currency balance sheet, it is necessary to estimate separate functions for the deposit aggregates which are to be excluded.

On one interpretation the observations of the quantity of money trace out a demand-for-money function. Although the demand for money is not being estimated directly in terms of variables such as income, wealth and interest rates, essentially equivalent variables feature among the determinants of credit demands. If the financial sector is appropriately seen as an equilibrium system, with the balance sheet identities implying overall equality between the demand for and supply of financial assets, Walras's Law can be invoked to show that there must also be equality between the demand for and supply of money. It does not matter whether the demand for money is modelled directly, with some other asset the residual (bonds, government securities, overseas assets), or estimated indirectly. Although residual, the amounts so supplied must be willingly held in full equilibrium.

Accordingly, on this equilibrium view, the counterparts merely show how the various components add up to the total increase in the amount of money demanded. Use, instead, of the money multiplier method would not alter this interpretation in any fundamental respect. It is only necessary to read Equation (1.3) with the causation running from *M* to *H*. Given the money multiplier, the equation then indicates how the quantity of high-powered money responds endogenously to demand. In a similar vein, Equation (1.8) would show how total reserves respond to demand.

On an alternative disequilibrium view, the amounts of money are supplied, but they need not be demanded, at least initially, as part of longer-run desired money holdings. A basic characteristic of money balances is that they are acceptable in exchange for goods, rising temporarily in response to an unbalanced flow of transactions in goods or assets, and held to exchange for goods as a means of payment. In a money-using economy, these discrepancies between purchases and sales of goods and assets can occur sequentially. Money enables transactors to defer transactions by selling goods or assets for generalized purchasing power which can be exercised later: the money balances are accepted now and spent later. Conversely, acquisition of goods and assets can be brought forward by running down cash balances. This means that money absorbs any differences in the timing and value of transactions by serving temporarily as a store of purchasing power. The means-of-payment function and the store-of-value functions necessarily overlap.

As we have described it, this distinction between the 'accepting' and 'demanding' of money, which is the basis of the 'buffer-stock' theory of money, has always been part of the quantity theory tradition (Friedman, 1987). This same tradition provides an analysis that can readily be used to support the idea of an 'exogenous' money supply. The essentials are the distinctions between nominal money balances and real money balances and the argument that substantial changes in the supply of nominal money can occur independently of demand. In the limiting case the entire nominal supply of money can be regarded as determined by the authorities. Should this quantity fail to accord with the real amount that people wish to hold at existing prices, then the price level is bid up as unwanted balances are spent or bid down as expenditures are reduced, both lines of action bringing real balances to the level desired.

It is useful to keep these equilibrium and disequilibrium alternatives in mind when we consider the various approaches adopted to the measurement of the demand for money.

MEASUREMENT OF THE DEMAND FOR MONEY

Few of the empirical studies of the demand for money are predicated on a particular model of the demand for money and thus on a distinctive conception of the role of money in the economy. Most draw upon the literature of the demand for money to suggest a list of potential regressors, allowing the data both to select from among this listing and to determine the specific functional form.

Keynesian analysis

One starting point is provided by the transactions motive for holding money, stemming from money's use as a medium of exchange, along with the asset or portfolio motive, deriving from money as a store of value. While prompted by the transactions, precautionary and speculative motives for holding money suggested by Keynes (1936, chapters 13 and 15) – his finance motive is generally ignored[5] – the antecedents of this approach can be traced to Irving Fisher and the Cambridge school (Patinkin, 1976; Eshag, 1963).

These early accounts assumed that balances held for transactions increase in proportion to money incomes and consist entirely of money. Baumol (1952) and Tobin (1956) allowed balances set aside as working funds to be invested as well in securities, and applied inventory theory to determine the amount held as cash. For them, the 'motive' for holding transactions balances is to reduce the transactions costs of realizing income-earning assets when cash is required for transactions. Determinants of the demand for money are the flow of transactions, interest forgone by holding money balances instead of securities, and the costs – brokerage charges and inconvenience – of effecting transfers between the two assets. The idea is that, given the pattern of payments and payments habits, transactors choose that frequency of transfers and average level of money balances which maximises interest income net of the transactions costs.

By making specific assumptions about the above determinants it is possible to derive from these models precise hypotheses about the response of money balances to potential explanatory variables (Niehans, 1978, chapter 3). Working balances are usually assumed to follow a regular 'sawtooth' pattern as income is received at regular intervals and expenditures occur at a steady rate. Transactions costs (in terms of pecuniary charges or the time, effort or 'shoe leather' involved) can be fixed, i.e. equal in amount for each purchase or sale of bonds, and also variable, in the form of brokerage fees and interest penalties which depend on the value of the securities encashed. The predictions are as follows:

1. The elasticity of money balances with respect to real income lies between 0.5 (fixed transactions costs) and 1.0 (proportionate transactions costs).
2. The interest rate elasticity ranges from –0.5 (fixed costs) to –2.0 (proportionate costs).

3. Nominal money balances increase proportionately with prices.

In very broad terms these predictions have been confirmed by the mainstream empirical studies described below. Nevertheless, a number of theoretical qualifications need to be borne in mind, and these provide some stepping-stones to recent ideas. First, in a money-using economy in which a form of Clower's (1967) 'cash-in-advance' constraint applies – income being received in monetary form and payments made only by using money – the existence of fixed transactions costs makes it possible for 'corner solutions' to arise. An individual will not hold securities as part of working balances unless the interest income exceeds the cost of the return trip into the securities market. This may give rise to discontinuities in the response of individual money holdings to alterations in interest rates and transactions costs.

Second, the models rely on a lack of synchronization between receipts and payments existing, but do not let the payment habits which bring this about adapt to economic incentives. As argued by Niehans (1978, chapter 2), the holding of money enables a more attractive pattern of transactions to occur, and rising interest rates and inflation seem likely to bring about rearrangements to purchases and sales. Payment practices, treated as exogenous in the standard models, seem likely to be a complex mix of autonomous developments arising from scientific advances in information technology and those induced by factors such as changes in interest rates.

Third, limitations come from the deterministic nature of the models. While an irregular pattern of purchases and sales seems unlikely to alter the main conclusions of the Baumol–Tobin models, an uncertain cash flow overlaps the transactions demands with the precautionary motive. An early, but remarkably prescient account, by Miller and Orr (1966) showed that quite different decision rules can result. Instead of regular transfers being made to bring money balances to the desired level (m_t^*) there is implied a range for an individual's money holdings with adjustments occurring in a lumpy, discontinuous fashion when balances hit the upper and lower bounds. As shown in Figure 1.2, securities are acquired when balances accumulate to the upper limit (U) and are sold when balances hit the lower limit, which in their model is zero. This idea of an upper and lower threshold was explored later by Akerlof and Milbourne (1980) in a transactions-demand context[6] and underlies the buffer-stock approach, about which more later.

Keynes' speculative motive for holding money as an asset was to take advantage of expected declines in the prices of securities due to anticipated future movements of interest rates. This was generalized by Tobin (1958) and Markowitz (1959) into a portfolio approach in which the motive for holding money balances is the avoidance of capital losses when there is

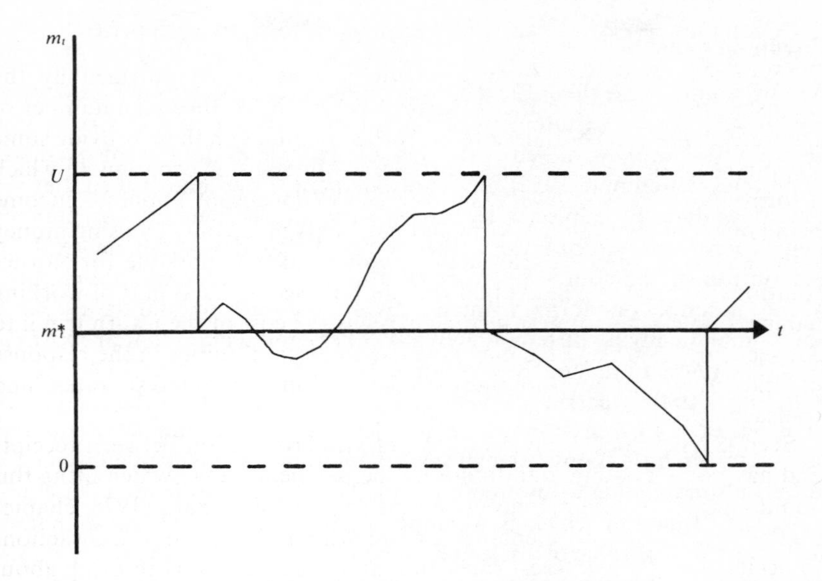

Figure 1.2 Individual money holdings in a Miller–Orr framework

uncertainty about the direction and extent of future interest rate changes. Each individual is confronted by a choice of holding a portion of wealth in money, offering low risk and low return, and a proportion in securities, promising a higher return but greater risk, and can hold various mixtures of the two depending on the mean and variance of expected returns and preferences for risk-taking. This general approach yields predictions that the desired holdings of money will depend on wealth, the expected return from money (including non-pecuniary benefits such as liquidity services) and the expected returns (and variances) of alternative wealth-holding forms.

Ambiguities arise about the definition of money in this framework. If considered narrowly as a cash and transactions medium, then money is likely to be dominated by savings, time and other deposits, which can also avert the uncertainties of holding assets with variable capital value, yet bear interest. A theory of money as an asset possessing the unique characteristic of being generally accepted as a means of payment in the community dissolves into a general theory of those assets which have the feature of being fixed in nominal capital value. On the other hand, if we make our focus money as an exchange medium we have the difficulty of determining whether 'money' embraces claims such as money market funds, against which cheques can be written yet which do not legally guarantee convertibility at par into currency.

Friedman's analysis

A way around these theoretical conundrums was suggested by Friedman's (1956) well-known restatement of the quantity theory as a theory of the demand for money, allied with his earlier methodology of positive economics (Friedman, 1953). In the restatement, Friedman argued that no special analytic principles were needed to study the demand for money. The general concepts of value theory can be used without an explicit description of the source of money's utility to an individual demander. Money is simply one form in which individuals choose to hold their wealth and is analytically no different from any other capital good that produces a flow of services to its holders over time.

In line with the doctrine of positive economics, the aim of the exercise is to produce a formulation which predicts much (the course of money income) from little (knowledge of the behaviour of the quantity of money – indeed ultimately high-powered money). The link comes from a demand-for-money function which is a simple aggregate of individual demands such that the real value of a selected monetary total bears a relatively stable relation to a measure of the aggregate budget constraint (wealth or permanent income) and opportunity cost variables (interest on bonds, dividends on equities, the anticipated inflation of commodity prices). What particular variables are selected is itself a matter for empirical investigation. Friedman and Schwartz (1970) eschew a definition of money based on grounds of principle in favour of one based on grounds of usefulness – i.e. the aggregate which yields the most accurate predictions. Interest rate and income elasticities are responses which remain to be revealed by the data as would be the case if one were examining the demand for motor-cars or refrigerators. Here we have a blueprint which equates theoretical advances with econometric success: a blueprint which has guided the course of research into the demand for money over the last three decades.

While the operational attractions of such an empirically based approach are obvious, it is clear that the separation of empirics from explicit modelling can give rise to problems. Two studies – one long-run and the other short-run – illustrate the point. On the strength of the decline in the velocity of money in the United States from 1869 to 1957, Friedman (1959) estimated the income elasticity of money (M2) as 1.8, much higher than the elasticity revealed by other studies yet entirely possible if one merely concludes that money services 'must' be a luxury. Later evidence made it apparent that Friedman attributed to a high income elasticity variations in the velocity of money due to other influences such as interest rates and the growth of banking. In similar vein, Price (1972) estimated income elasticities for M3 in the United Kingdom of 2.3 to 2.8 over the period 1964–70, again well in excess of other estimates (which ranged from 0.96 to 1.54). This result implied that this monetary aggregate should be allowed to expand at a much more rapid rate than real income. When M3 in fact did so in 1972 and 1973, it was difficult to judge initially whether the expansion was excessive, holding future portents for inflation, or was simply in line with demand; in retrospect the former proved to be the case (Artis and Lewis, 1981). An empirically based approach can also leave researchers adrift should the empirical stability – which provides the major justification for the functional form – disappear. This was the position which arose in the 1970s.

Empirical studies before 1974

The earliest empirical studies of the demand for money were based around the velocity of money (see Latane, 1954; and a survey of earlier studies by Selden, 1956) or sought to separate out the transactions and asset components by estimates of 'active' and 'idle' balances (Brown, 1939; Tobin, 1947; Bronfrenbrenner and Mayer, 1960). Following Friedman (1956) and the associated upsurge of interest in monetary economics, the empirical studies drew more generally upon the theoretical studies to suggest three groups of determinants.

First, since money is used for transactions purposes, the amount that people and business firms wish to hold (M^*) is expected to be related directly to real income (y), reflecting either expected transactions or proxying for wealth. Second, since M^* refers to nominal money balances, the price level (P) is included as a scale variable, normally with unit elasticity to indicate an absence of money illusion. Third, because money is only one among many assets in which wealth may be held and because transactions balances have an opportunity cost, desired holdings are expected to vary inversely with interest rates on other assets (r), the anticipated rate of inflation (p^e), and possibly directly with the own rate paid on money balances (r_m). These considerations lead to a relationship of the form:

$$M^* = Pf(y, p^e, r, r_m) \qquad f_y > 0; \quad f_r, f_{p^e} < 0; \quad f_{r_m} > 0 \tag{1.18}$$

or

$$M^* / P = f(y, p^e, r, r_m) \tag{1.19}$$

so that the relationship is explicitly one between desired real money balances and the governing variables on the assumption that the demand function exhibits homogeneity, i.e. is unit-elastic with respect to prices. If we further suppose that the demand for real money balances is proportional to real income, nominal income can be used as the scale variable and Equation (1.19) simplifies to

$$M^*/Y = f(p^e, r, r_m) \tag{1.20}$$

In this case the dependent variable is the desired ratio of money to nominal income, i.e. the Cambridge k. If Equation (1.20) is inverted we have a *velocity function*, relating the desired income velocity of money to measures of the cost of holding money. All three functional relationships (1.18)–(1.20) have formed the basis of empirical work undertaken in the United Kingdom and the United States.

Much work has been done to find the precise empirical counterparts of these theoretical variables by transforming actual magnitudes into expected variables, experimenting with various functional forms, and using different measures of the budget constraint and the opportunity cost of holding money. In terms of scale variables, existence of both transactions and asset theories of the demand for money means that it is not immediately apparent whether it is wealth or income which should enter the demand function, but the absence of adequate wealth figures has meant that most studies have employed some measure of income. In some cases, a permanent income measure forms the basis for the equation, but given the lack of reliable means of estimating this subjective concept, its inclusion can be seen to be achieved by appropriate transformations which yield an equation containing current income and lagged money stock values (see below).

Portfolio approaches to the demand for money emphasize that wealth-holders have a choice of holding money or a variety of financial and real assets – bills, bonds, equities and commodities. In an open economy without exchange control, foreigners hold domestic currency in the form of bank deposits and other short-term paper, while domestic residents hold foreign currency claims in equivalent forms, so that interest rates on foreign securities also influence the demand for money. However, in most instances selection of one representative rate, such as the yield on long-term securities or short-term securities has proven to be adequate.

The impact of inflation expectations on the demand for money has never been resolved theoretically (Steindl, 1973). Friedman (1956) has money substituting for both securities and real assets, so that both nominal interest rates and the anticipated rate of change of prices (p^e) enter the demand function, as in the equations above. By contrast, in the analysis of Mundell (1963), inflation expectations are incorporated into nominal interest rates (but only partially in the short run), so that the cost of holding money relative to securities is the real rate of interest plus the anticipated decline in the purchasing power of money. The Mundell approach allows the impact of p^e to be taken up by the nominal rate of interest, and this is the approach followed in most empirical work.

Finally, most of the empirical studies left out the variable r_m (Klein, 1977, was an important exception). Since the cost of holding money depends on the *difference* between market rates of interest (r) and the own rate (r_m) use of r alone is predicated on the assumption that the own rate adjusts sluggishly to market forces. Such rigidity was to be expected from the cartel arrangements which marked the UK clearing banks' interest rate setting prior to Competition and Credit Control in 1971 and from the ceilings on time and savings deposits in the United States before the deregulation of bank interest rates in the 1980s.

Having thus simplified the demand function down to four variables – money, prices, real income and an interest rate – there is then the question of how the resulting equation is to be estimated, for desired money balances cannot be observed directly. In retrospect, this question did not receive the attention that it deserved in the early studies. In the United Kingdom, as in the United States, research into the demand-for-money function proceeded at two levels, one concerned with an examination of long-run trends, the other dealing with short-run dynamics. For both sets of analyses, there was assumed, simply, equality of actual with desired balances, that is:

$$M = M^*; \qquad M/P = M^*/P; \qquad M/Y = M^*/Y \qquad (1.21)$$

When used with annual data over long periods of time, equations produced by combining Equation (1.21) with Equations (1.18)–(1.20) gave reasonable results, summarized in Table 1.3. Studies by Latane, Meltzer, Laidler, Chow, Khan, Laumas and Mehra for the United States provided relatively consistent estimates, when allowance is made for different time periods and different opportunity cost variables. Elasticities with respect to income, permanent income or wealth ranged from 0.65 to 1.51 but most estimates were just above unity, while the impact of interest rates was clearly established. For the United Kingdom, studies by Kavanagh and Walters and Laidler, following graphical analyses of Paish (1959; 1960) and Dow (1960), suggested a much greater stability of the demand for money than many had thought existed. Moreover, as Laidler noted, the demand for money function for the United Kingdom over the long run did not look very different from that for the United States, an observation taken up later by Friedman and Schwartz (1982) when they estimated a combined demand function for both the United States and the United Kingdom.

These investigations did not establish whether the relationships could be relied upon for shorter periods of time. For this purpose an examination of quarterly data was required. Heller (1965) and later Hamburger (1977) obtained estimates by fitting long-run functions to quarterly data, but most other studies found that sensible results depended upon introducing

Table 1.3 Summary of selected studies of the long-run demand for money

Study	Data	Money variable	Income variable	Interest rate	Elasticity with respect to: Income	Interest rate	Comments
United States							
Latane (1954)	1919–52	M1	GNP	Long term Corporate bond yield	1.00	–0.70	Velocity measure used Income elasticity constrained to unity
Meltzer (1963)	1900–58	M1	NNP	✓ ✓	1.05	–0.79	Compares income, wealth
		M2	Wealth	✓ ✓	1.32	–0.50	and permanent income
Laidler (1966)	1919–60	M2	Permanent income	✓ ✓	1.15	–0.72	Also uses first differences
	1892–1960	M2	✓	✓ ✓	1.51	–0.25	
Chow (1966)	1897–1958	M1	✓	✓ ✓	1.06	–0.74	
	excl. war years	M1	✓	✓ ✓	0.93	–0.79	Using lagged money stock
Laidler (1971)	1900–65 excl. war years	M2	Permanent income	Long term Corporate bond yield	1.31	–0.39	
				CP rate	1.26	–0.19	
Khan (1974)	1901–65	M1	✓	Corporate bond yield	0.65	–0.30	Evidence of some instability
			✓	Commercial paper rate	1.09	–0.12	when short-term rate used
Gandolfi and Lothian (1976)	1929–68	M2	✓	Bond rate less own rate on deposits	1.20	–0.42	Instability reflected in changes in intercepts
Laumas and Mehra (1977)	1900–74	M1	✓	Long-term bond rate	0.90	–0.46	No evidence of change in
		M2	✓	✓ ✓	1.07	–0.28	parameters

Friedman and Schwartz (1982)	1873–1975 cycle average data	M2	NNP	Difference of commercial paper rate over own rate	1.15	–0.19	Dummy variable to allow functions to shift during inter-war and at end of war
Lucas (1987)	1900–85	M1	Permanent NNP	CP rate	0.97	–0.07	Instability unless income elasticity is constrained to unity
Wenninger (1988)	1915–87 quarterly	M1	GNP	CP rate	0.86	–0.36	Persistent pattern of instability for M1, less so for M2
		M2	✓	✓ ✓	1.04	–0.14	
United Kingdom							
Kavanagh and Walters (1966)	1880–1961	M1	National income	Consol rate	1.15	–0.31	
		M2	✓	✓	1.27	–0.46	
	1926–60	M1	✓	✓	0.96	–0.50	
Laidler (1971)	1900–65 excl. war years	M2	Permanent income	Consol rate	0.80	–0.57	
				Treasury bill rate	0.67	–0.15	
Graves (1980)	1911–66	M1	National income	Commercial bill rate	0.30	–0.10	Instability in standard equations includes variable for urbanization and age distribution of populations
Friedman and Schwartz (1982)	1874–1975	M2/M3	Net national product	Commercial bill rate less own rate	0.88	–0.19	Dummy variables for inter-war and post-war shifts
Batts and Dowling (1984)	1880–1975	M1	✓	Commercial bill rate	0.57	–0.07	Instability evident around war years and possibly 1970s
		M2	✓	✓	0.47	–0.08	
Artis and Lewis (1984)	1920–81 excl. 1973–6	M2	GDP	Consol rate	1.00	–0.59	Possible shift during war years
Longbottom and Holly (1985)	1878–1975	M2/M3	NNP	Commercial bill less own rate	1.08	–0.09	Dummy variables for shift war years. Possible instability in 1930s. Inclusion of CDs gives instability in 1970s

lags into the equations estimated. Substitution of expected for actual magnitudes into Equations (1.18)–(1.20) is one method of doing so and Feige (1967) showed that the usual Koyck distribution lag formulation, by which expected values of income and interest rates are approximated by geometrically declining lags on present and actual past values, gives rise to an equation with lagged monetary variables. More usually, however, the hypothesis of 'partial adjustment' was incorporated: that people will not move to their desired long-run money holding immediately, but will take time to do so, either through inertia or because it is too costly to move instantaneously. Like the demand function itself, this idea, too, was borrowed from general value theory on the basis that individuals would adjust their actual real money balances to desired levels along much the same lines as they would bring stocks of consumer durables to their desired levels (Chow, 1966).[7]

With the addition of the partial adjustment assumption, the standard functions which featured in empirical work on the short-run demand for money can be derived. With all variables transformed to natural logarithms, the simplified long-run demand function can be written as

$$M^*_t - P_t = a + by_t + cr_t + u_t \tag{1.22}$$

where u_t is a random variable. Some studies (Chow, 1966; Laidler and Parkin, 1970; Goldfeld, 1976) employed what is now called the real adjustment hypothesis

$$m_t - m_{t-1} = \lambda(m^*_t = m_{t-1}) \tag{1.23}$$

where m represents real money balances ($M - P$). This gives

$$M_t - P_t = a\lambda + b\lambda\, y_t + c\lambda r_t + \lambda u_t + (1-\lambda)\,(M_{t-1} - P_{t-1}) \tag{1.24}$$

While actual real balances in any quarter are not at the desired long-run level (assuming $0 < \lambda < 1$), their movement is always towards the desired level. In that way all of the quarterly observations of real balances are capable of tracing out the long-run demand function once allowance is made for the estimated speed of adjustment, λ.

A peculiarity of Equation (1.24) is the asymmetric speed of response of nominal money balances to the arguments of the demand function. The speed of adjustment is an aggregate of individual responses. However, prices, interest rates and, for quarterly observations, even income must be seen as given to the individual, leaving nominal balances as the only magnitude which can be adjusted. The partial adjustment hypothesis recognizes that adjustment costs prevent individuals from speedily bringing money holdings to the desired levels. Yet, the formulation above carries the implication that nominal money holdings adjust fully and instantaneously to prices while responding only partially to movements in interest rates and real income. This can be seen by rewriting Equation (1.23) as

$$M_t - M_{t-1} = \lambda\,(m^*_t - m_{t-1}) + \Delta P_t \tag{1.25}$$

and noting that the coefficient on ΔP_t is unity.

Other studies (Goodhart and Crockett, 1970; Goldfeld, 1976) accordingly preferred the nominal adjustment hypothesis

$$M_t - M_{t-1} = \lambda(M^*_t - M_{t-1}) \tag{1.26}$$

which, when combined with Equation (1.22), gives

$$M_t = a\lambda + b\lambda y_t + c\lambda r_t + \lambda u_t + \lambda P_t + (1-\lambda)\, M_{t-1} \tag{1.27}$$

or, if estimated in real terms,

$$M_t - P_t = a\lambda + b\lambda y_t + c\lambda r_t + \lambda u_t + (1-\lambda)\,(M_{t-1} - P_t) \tag{1.28}$$

It is apparent that Equation (1.28) is similar to Equation (1.24), differing only in the replacement of $(M_{t-1} - P_{t-1})$ by $(M_{t-1} - P_t)$, and most likely in practice the two formulations would yield similar results.[8]

Table 1.4 summarizes selected short-run studies for the United Kingdom and United States. Notwithstanding some of the ambiguities noted below, the quarterly results until the mid-1970s were sufficiently consistent with the long-run examinations for some important implications for monetary policy to be drawn:

1. If a stable demand function containing a limited number of explanatory variables exists, policy actions which alter the money stock can be expected eventually to have predictable effects on ultimate goal variables. A fairly general form of the demand-for-money function – encompassing ideas drawn from major theories – seemed capable of explaining the course of monetary behaviour in the United States and United Kingdom (and other countries). In most cases, the variables influencing the aggregate demand function could be limited to income and one or two interest rates.
2. Knowledge of the income elasticity of the demand for money is needed by those who advocate the adoption of monetary rules aimed at a constant rate of monetary growth. A fairly clear picture emerged from the earlier studies, with the long-run income elasticities of fixed deposits and savings bank deposits greater than unity, that of current deposits or M1 of around or slightly less than unity, with broad money sometimes well over unity.
3. At least one interest rate had a significant negative impact upon the demand for money. The nature of the response of money balances to interest rates is important for monetary policy. Within the IS–LM

Table 1.4 Summary of selected studies of the short-run demand for money function

Study	Data	Money variable	Income variable	Interest rate	Long-run elasticity with respect to: Income	Interest rate	Comments
United States							
Heller (1965)	1954–59	M1	GNP	Commercial paper rate	1.08	–0.10	No adjustment lags
		M2	GNP	Commercial paper rate	1.41	–0.18	
Goldfeld (1973)	1955–72	M1	GNP	✓ ✓ ✓	0.53	–0.05	Nominal adjustment
				Time deposit rate		–0.12	
Garcia-Pak (1979)	1952–76	M1	GNP	Commercial paper rate	1.26	–0.96	Implausibly long lags
Boughton (1979)	1960–77	M1	GNP	Commercial paper rate Time deposit rate	*	*	Lagged coefficient exceeds unity; instability after 1973
		M2		Commercial paper rate	1.20	–0.11	
Gordon (1984)	1956–72	M1	✓	Savings deposit rate	0.43	–0.03	Instability offer 1972; need to add supply shocks
Anderson (1975)	1960–83	M1	✓	90-day bankers' acceptances	(1) 0.83	–0.24	(1) Standard equation. Long lags found (4-year average lag)
					(2) 0.86	–0.64	(2) Interest rate adjustment. Average lag 3 quarters
United Kingdom							
Laidler and Parkin (1970)	1955–67	M2	GDP	Treasury bill	0.59	–0.02	
Goodhart and Crockett (1970)	1955(3)–69(3)	M1	GDP	3mo LA	1.25	–1.05	
				Consol	1.09	–0.00	
	1963(2)–69(3)	M3	GDP	3mo LA	1.41	–0.21	
				Consol	1.54	–0.51	

Price (1972)	1964(1)–70(4)	M3	GDP	Consol	(1) 2.29	–0.37	(1) Personal sector
				3mo LA	(2) 2.77	–0.36	(2) Corporate sector
Hacche (1974)	1963(4)–72(4)	M1	TFE	3mo LA	0.70	–0.06	
				Consol		–0.21	
	1963(4)–72(4)	M3	TFE	3mo LA	*	*	
					1.00	–0.25	(2) Inserting interest rate variable for shift after 1971
Artis and	1963(2)–73(1)	M1	GDP	Consol	1.24	–0.66	Instability in 1971
Lewis (1976)	1963(2)–73(1)	M3	GDP	Consol	(1) 3.89	–1.46	(1) Standard equation
					(2) 1.21	–0.34	(2) Interest rate adjustment equation
Hamburger (1977)	1963(1)–70(4)	M1	GDP	3mo Eurodollar	0.67	–1.07	No adjustment lags in model. Instability in 1972
Coghlan (1978)	1964(1)–76(4)	M1	TFE	3mo LA	1.01	–0.30	Complex adjustment lags. No instability
Boughton (1979)	1963(2)–77(3)	M1	GDP	3mo LA	1.32	–0.51	Instability in 1971
	1963(2)–77(3)	M3	GDP	Consol	*	*	Instability evident
Grice and Bennett (1984)	1963–78	M3	TFE	Return on gilts	0.32	0	Dynamic instability present; dummy variable added
Anderson (1985)	1960–83	M1	GDP	(1) Treasury bill rate	0.68	–0.45	(1) Standard equation
				(2) ✓	0.70	–0.49	(2) Interest rate adjustment

framework, this elasticity is one of the crucial parameters for assessing the relative efficacy of fiscal and monetary policy, a low elasticity signifying a greater potency of monetary policy and a lesser potency of fiscal policy. A considerable measure of agreement existed about the elasticity. In most cases, the response was found to be inelastic, often less than (–)0.50.

Evidence of instability

This unanimity began to break down in the 1970s as evidence mounted that demand functions of the type surveyed above exhibited instability.[9] By 'instability' we refer to three interrelated features.

First, when equations estimated with data for the 1950s and 1960s were used to predict the behaviour of real or nominal money balances in the 1970s, errors of prediction occurred. Clear evidence of this instability exists for the United Kingdom, where Artis and Lewis (1974; 1976) and Hacche (1974) show that the Bank of England's demand-for-money functions seriously underpredicted monetary growth in the 1971–3 period. In the United States, instability is evident for 1974 and 1975 in studies by Pierce (1975), Enzler *et al.* (1976), Goldfeld (1976) and Meyer (1976).

Second, when data for the 1970s are incorporated into the sample used for estimating the equations, the coefficient on the lagged dependent variable varies, suggesting that there has been some change in the nature of the adjustment process. In some work the coefficient on the lagged variable consistently exceeded unity, indicating an explosive time path (see studies in Table 1.4).

Third, in order to accommodate the additional data from the 1970s, some studies have found that the goodness of fit is improved by adding variables which previous researchers had not found it necessary to incorporate (Goldfeld, 1976) or by including dummy variables (Thornton, 1985; Grice and Bennett, 1984).

Looking back at the short-run studies, there are some ambiguities present concerning the lags of adjustment and interest rate responses which have not been satisfactorily resolved. An inconsistency exists between quarterly and annual studies of the demand for money. The annual studies assume implicitly that any adjustments in the monetary sector are completed within the year. When quarterly data are used, this assumption is tested explicitly by allowing for balances to be in the process of adjusting to equilibrium. Almost invariably the speeds of adjustment which are estimated indicate that less than 50 per cent, and sometimes as little as 15 per cent, of the difference between actual and desired money balances is eliminated in one year, and that in consequence many years elapse before the adjustment of balances is, say, 90 per cent completed. For the United States, De Leeuw (1965), Modigliani, Rasche and Cooper (1970) and Cagan and Schwartz (1975) find that only 4–10 per cent of the difference is eliminated within the first quarter; for the United Kingdom, Goodhart and Crockett (1970) report adjustment coefficients ranging from 0.04 to 0.15. Lags of such length have surprised many economists, and as such these sluggish responses do not sit easily with views that money markets facilitate rapid adjustment within the hour, let alone the quarter or the year. Their inconsistency with the results from annual studies remains a puzzle.

A peculiarity also exists with respect to the measured interest rate elasticities. It would seem likely that high interest elasticities would be found for assets which are the closest substitutes for money, since then only a slight change in yield should induce a large reshuffle of portfolios (that is, a relatively 'flat' demand for money schedule). In fact, the reverse is found, with higher elasticities suggesting that long-term securities are closer substitutes for money than shorter-term ones. Arithmetically, the estimates follow directly from the lower amplitude of cyclical fluctuations of long rates *vis-à-vis* short rates. While expectations of future short-term rates seem likely to be the major influence upon the yield curve, the authorities' practice of effecting transactions in securities at the short end of the market might have some influence upon yields. If so, the specification which sees interest rates as exogenously determining money balances, with a long lag, must be called into question. The nature of adjustments to monetary disturbances is examined further in the following section.

ADJUSTMENTS IN THE FINANCIAL SECTOR

Many factors may have contributed to the poor predictive performance of the models. The prior stability of the demand for money may have been exaggerated. A large number of complex and special factors can interact to generate the aggregate demand for money, and the search for a simple successfully aggregated function may be too ambitious. Perhaps the econometric estimation procedures are at fault; altering the functional form, refining autocorrelation procedures and using different lag estimators might all help. These seem unlikely to hold the complete answer, for the pattern of the errors is common to subsequent studies employing different estimating forms, which points to some other systematic factors at work.

We are led to look more closely at the model being tested. The usual approach is to treat the observations of nominal or real money balances as movements along a (short-run) demand function induced by changes in the nominated variables. This interpretation is justifiable only if we can exclude the possibilities that the demand schedule itself may have shifted and/or changed unpredictably, or that actual real balances may have differed from the public's desired holdings. The choice between these interpretations is central to an assessment of monetary management. Consider a large expansion of money as occurred in the United Kingdom in 1972–3. If some factor(s) peculiar to this period produced successive shifts of the demand function, the contribution of the money balances themselves to economic instability would seem to be minor. On the alternative interpretation, monetary growth was presumably in excess of demand, producing subsequent pressures on asset prices, output, incomes and ultimately the rate of inflation.

Given the simple form of the estimated demand functions there is a real possibility that some important variables have been omitted. Transactions costs, the pattern of monetary payments, and the own rate of interest on money were all assumed constant and asset variance (*à la* Tobin–Markowitz) ignored when deriving the standard function form, and these all seem likely to have been influenced by the substantial innovation and deregulation which have occurred in the financial sectors since the early 1970s. Both of these themes have been explored in re-examinations of the demand for money in the United Kingdom and the United States.

Innovation and deregulation

Emphasis in the United Kingdom has been upon deregulation and the institutional changes which then resulted. Underprediction of monetary growth in 1971–3 coincided with the release of lending controls, alterations to required reserve ratios, and the ending of the clearing banks' interest rate cartel arrangements. Reimposition of controls in 1974 saw the money supply begin to move back towards the predicted path. Even greater and persistent underprediction in the 1980s seemed to be associated with the removal of exchange controls and the remaining direct monetary controls.

Factors like the own rate of interest, 'roundtripping' via certificates of deposit, greater volatility of bond prices, and dummy variables to allow for policy and regulatory changes have been added to standard equations (Hacche, 1974; Artis and Lewis, 1976; Grice and Bennett, 1984) but they are unable to account satisfactorily for the experience. Some of these items reflect, although they may not fully capture, the switch by banks from asset to liability management, a process whereby banks competitively bid for and increase their interest-bearing deposits to sustain lending rather than adjust assets in line with predetermined levels of deposits. Less easy to proxy is any process of 'reintermediation' set in train by deregulation due to an improvement in banks' non-price competitiveness. It is also far from clear whether reintermediation should be thought of as a once-for-all stock adjustment or as a new growth path for monetary aggregates.

Financial innovations were explored in US studies of the demand for money when the standard functions overpredicted money balances in the mid-1970s. It seemed that the US economy was making do with less money relative to income and interest rates (so that the income velocity of money rose faster than expected), and a number of developments were seen to have facilitated this trend. Cash management services and new financial instruments such as Eurodollar accounts and repurchase agreements were seen as allowing firms to economize on money balances and hold more of their working needs for funds in interest-earning securities. In terms of the Baumol–Tobin type models, the developments may have reduced the transactions costs of converting securities into money and hence desired money holdings. Carried through to the Miller–Orr model, innovations in money management techniques can be viewed as reducing the uncertainty of receipts and payments, and thus the precautionary demand for money.

A survey of the empirical manifestations of these ideas can be found in Judd and Scadding (1982). Overall, the results must be judged less than successful, for a number of reasons. While the additional variables and proxies succeeded in patching up or helping identify factors which may have caused the demand for money to shift in the mid-1970s, the new equations have proven to be no more durable than the old when confronted with later data.

Adding new elements to the right-hand side of the standard equations begs the question whether the innovations are correctly seen as autonomous technological developments or as induced consequences of rising interest rates and inflationary expectations (and thus already incorporated into the coefficients of these variables) as firms invest in new ways of reducing the opportunity cost of money holdings. In the latter case, the responses may already be incorporated into the coefficients on interest rates and inflation, although the lumpy and discontinuous process of innovation suggests difficulties in adequately identifying the effects. An examination of some of the specific instruments such as money-market mutual funds and the cash management account points to the importance of induced responses, for the products were invented and lay largely unused for years until high interest rates encouraged their widespread use (Lewis, 1986).

Financial innovations also are not much help in explaining the course of monetary developments in the 1980s. Income velocity in the United States (and also the United Kingdom) fell sharply after 1981 and neither the standard equations nor the previously modified specifications were able to track this new trend. While it might be argued that lower interest rates and inflation brought about an unwinding of cash management techniques and a turning away from the new financial instruments, these possibilities seem unlikely when account is taken of the nature of financial innovations.

Money-saving devices should perhaps be thought of as similar in their operation to labour-saving devices in that there are presumably high costs of seeking out the new devices and putting them into place. Cost increases due to interest rates need to pass through some threshold before it is worthwhile doing so. Once in operation, however, the new instruments will remain in use after interest rates fall.[10] Much the same points can be made about regulatory changes, for these both influence and are influenced by the economic and financial environment. The scramble to lift interest rate ceilings on US depository institutions in the years 1980–2 was itself an induced response to high interest rates as consumers withdrew savings deposits and placed them with money market funds. Deregulation was also not reversed when interest rates later declined. Indeed, the more attractive deposit instruments on offer at banks presumably contributed to the declining path of velocity after 1981.

Some downplaying of the role of both financial innovations and regulation is suggested by the appearance of parallel trends in a number of other countries – Japan, West Germany, France, Italy and Canada. Figure 1.3 shows, although the timing is far from uniform, that velocity rose (absolutely or at a faster rate) in all of these countries in the early 1970s and declined from around 1982, in many cases much faster than predicted from standard demand for money equations. Deregulation has been of minor importance in West Germany and, until recently, France and Japan, and so has financial innovation. But whether, and how, a common thread is to be drawn through this similar cross-country experience remains an open question.

Inflation and disinflation

Rather than look to new factors which might have shifted the demand function or to changes which might have altered the pecuniary or non-pecuniary returns from holding deposits in ways such as to produce a complete change in the parameters of demand, an alternative might be sought in terms of movements within the standard function. Atkinson and Chouraqui (1987) argue that the instability may come from the arguments of the demand-for-money function rather than from the function itself. Uncertainty introduced by the process of inflation and disinflation seems the most likely candidate.

Klein (1977) defined the quality of money balances as the flow of monetary services yielded per real dollar, which we can assume to be positively related to the degree of price predictability as certainty about the future purchasing power of money enhances the usefulness of holding

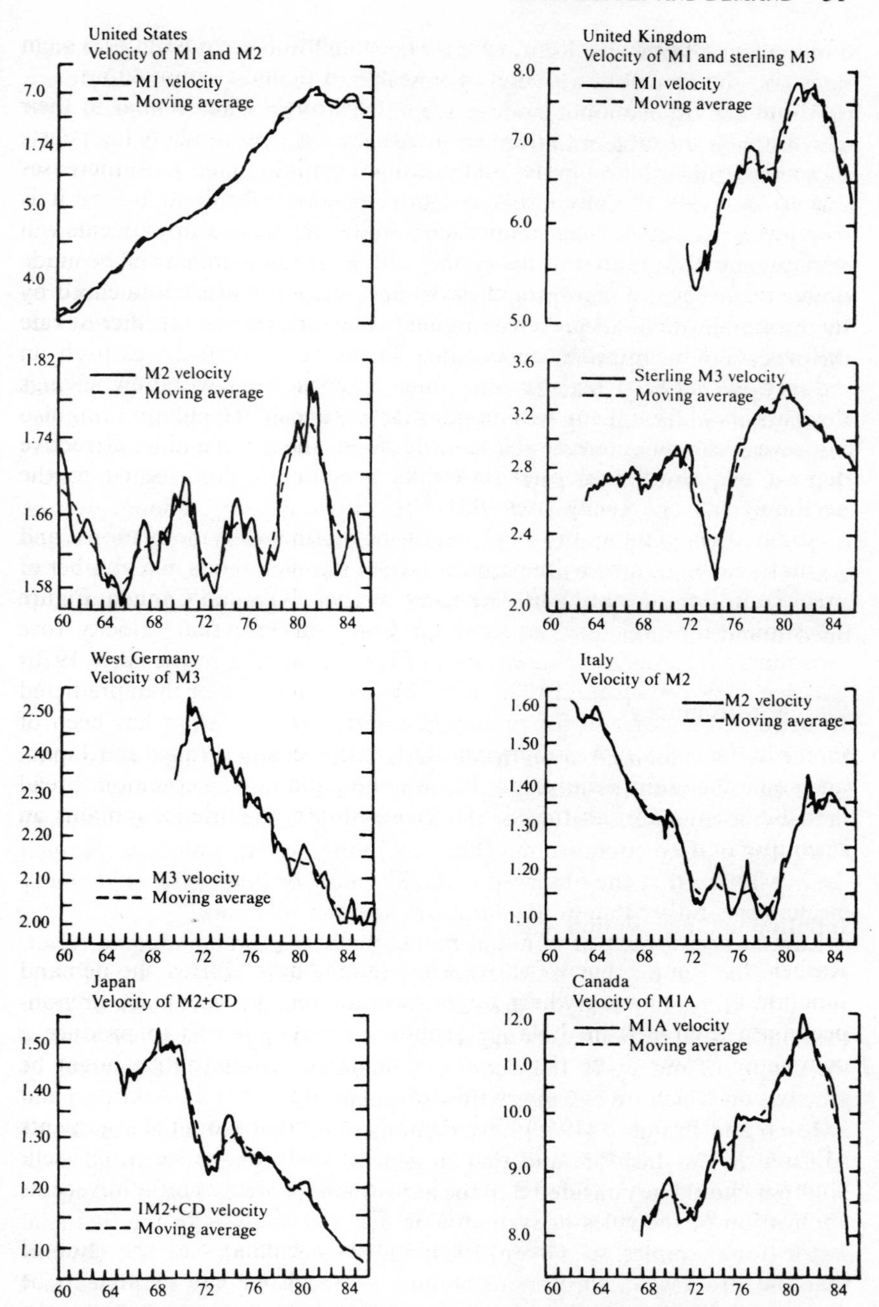

Figure 1.3 Income velocity of money in selected OECD countries (*Source*: Atkinson and Chouraqui 1987)

nominal claims (see also Kent, 1985). The abandonment of fixed exchange rates and the arrival of a period of unstable exchanges, commodity price rises and activist economic policies seem likely to have led to expectations of rising and unstable inflation, so increasing velocity in the early 1970s. Conversely, disinflation in the 1980s should see the demand for money rise and velocity fall. Both hypothesized movements are in the right direction to explain velocity movements in each decade; are presumably common to experiences in a number of countries; and, if the adjustments of expectations are sufficiently abrupt and ill-defined, seem unlikely to be captured by the standard equations which ought, nevertheless, to settle down once the process of disinflation is concluded.

Friedman (1988) reaches the same conclusion as Atkinson and Chouraqui, while starting from a quite different tack. His paper examines the impact of stock market prices upon the demand for money and finds that the response in the period 1974–85 is markedly different from that measured for the years 1886–1973. He attributes this change to the transition from commodity to fiat money, ushering in an era of increased uncertainty about future nominal values. As a consequence, he argues that anticipated inflation and deflation came to assume greater significance for the demand for money.

Endogenous money?

So far we have focused upon the demand function and its arguments. The short-run demand-for-money function, however, embraces two hypotheses: one about the nature of the long-run demand function, the other about the path to equilibrium. These are jointly tested, which leaves open the possibility that the observed instability may be due to the adjustment mechanisms rather than to the long-run demand function.

Lagged adjustment of nominal money balances to demand, we recall, rests on the notion that transactors are individually slow to adjust their actual holdings of money to desired levels due to adjustment costs. When these individual responses are aggregated we obtain a partial adjustment of the supply of money to the quantity demanded. There are a number of grounds on which we can query this formulation.

Tobin and Brainard (1968) have demonstrated that not all assets can be adjusted in this fashion, and that in general the discrepancy in all asset holdings should be considered in the adjustment process. This is merely an application of the rules of system-wide demand analysis to the financial sector (for examples, see Green, 1984; and Weale, 1986). Nor is it obvious that the process of adjustment should be the same for increases and decreases of money. Consumption habits formed may make it easier for some people to reduce money balances by spending in excess of their income than to attempt to increase them by saving. Finally, and this is our main concern, while such adjustment can occur at a micro level, it is not clear that it survives the aggregation procedure. Here we query the almost universal practice of reconciling the short-run to the long-run demand by means of a passive supply of nominal balances. One individual may augment his/her money holdings in this way but it is far from clear that the economy as whole can do so; one individual's accretion of money may be someone else's loss.

There are circumstances in which the economy as a whole can adjust its money balances. One is when the central bank stabilizes interest rates and allows the quantity of money to respond to demand. Another is maintenance of a fixed exchange rate which enables money balances to be replenished via overseas transactions. With a fixed rate of exchange and interest rate pegging policies, transactors are afforded some implicit guarantees about their freedom to exchange bonds or foreign securities on demand for money; to this extent (and the account is obviously a highly stylized one) the argument runs that the amount of money actually in existence is determined by *demand*, as excess supplies can be instantaneously liquidated and excess demands satisfied without repercussions for the arguments of the demand function.

However accurate this description is of the 1960s, and we have reasons to question it, clearly different institutional arrangements operated later on in the 1970s. Monetary authorities moved away from interest rate setting to monetary targets, and from fixed to floating exchange rates. Activist monetary policies were followed. All of these are circumstances in which discrepancies between actual and desired money holdings might arise. By the same token, of course, monetary policies in the mid- and late 1980s have seen some movement back towards previous arrangements. Putting to one side for the moment the question of changing policy regimes, we wish to focus upon the portfolio reallocations which result from a disequilibrium between desired and actual money holdings. How long the discrepancy exists and the means by which it is removed become vital questions. By assuming the nominal money stock to be demand-determined, the answers to these questions were effectively prejudged by the earlier researchers.

Buffer stocks

A useful starting point is the Miller–Orr model referred to earlier (page 14), and in particular Figure 1.2. Only when money balances reach the upper threshold, U, are actions taken by the individual to bring the quantity of money back to the desired level. These actions involve increased purchases of assets and/or goods. Sales of goods or assets are made only when money balances fall to the lower limit. By these means, an individual's actual money holdings will rise and fall, gravitating over time around an average or desired level, m_t^*. In the short run, however, an increase (or decrease) in balances can be accommodated without provoking any immediate reaction from the individual. When considering an expansion of the aggregate money stock distributed across a number of individuals, the overall position seems likely to be muddied. Some individuals will be pushed immediately to their upper threshold, others will absorb the increase, while money spent by the first group could end up in someone else's *U*–0 range. But it is apparent that some part can be willingly held – even if not demanded as part of desired holdings – at unchanged levels of expenditures and asset prices. Here we have a representation of the *buffer-stock* function of money.

Central to the buffer-stock approach is the idea that a disequilibrium in the financial sector can be met by a temporary deviation of the buffer stock from its desired level. When considering the implications which then follow for modelling the demand for money, the question is not *whether* money acts as a buffer (for it is inherent in the role of money in straddling the means-of-exchange and store-of-value functions that money balances will temporarily rise and fall), but *over what time period* it acts as a buffer. If the discrepancy in money balances is offset more or less instantaneously, then other assets (or even expenditure flows) serve as the main cushion preliminary to a major reshuffling of portfolios. Alternatively, the drop in money balances may, if money is held as a buffer, simply be maintained until transitory inflows of money restore cash balances to their initial (desired) level. The cost of transacting into and out of the buffer-stock asset appears critical in this. If, for example, it is relatively easy to transact from narrow money to the interest-bearing component of broad money, but somewhat more difficult and costly to transact from broad money to other assets, then we might expect to find that broad, rather than narrow, money would be the buffer. Paradoxically, while other assets would be a poor buffer because of the costs of investment and disinvestment, narrow money would be a poor candidate because, *ex hypothesi*, it is so *easy* to transact out of this aggregate.

These possible responses indicate the various roles of money as a buffer stock. When transactors move to offset the discrepancy quickly, the buffering role of money is the same as that envisaged by Friedman and others analysing exogenous monetary disturbances in a simple quantity theory, with money serving as a temporary store of value. The case in which the discrepancy is allowed to persist corresponds in broad terms with the 'shock-absorber' models of Carr and Darby (1981). Somewhere in between the 'taut' and 'slack' responses we have the role for money envisaged in most of the buffer-stock models (for surveys of the concept, see Laidler, 1984; Goodhart, 1984; and Knoester, 1984; and for an examination of the empirical work which has resulted, see Cuthbertson and Taylor, 1987).

Different implications flow from these formulations for the dynamic process by which equilibrium is restored in the money market. Equating expressions (1.3) and (1.18) enables us to define monetary equilibrium as

$$M = mH = Pf(y, p^e, r, r_m). \qquad (1.29)$$

Suppose further that the equilibrium is disturbed by an increased growth rate of the nominal money supply. Immediately after the change, $M_t > M^*_t$, and restoration of quality requires that over time the growth rate of the money supply (M) falls, or the demand for money (M^*) grows at a faster rate, or some combination of these.

A feature of almost all the models is that the role of adjustment *within* the monetary sector itself is ignored or downplayed. Own rates of interest on monetary assets (r_m) are assumed either to be invariant or tied to market rates of interest (r) by supposing that competition forces banks to pay deposit rates which move in harmony with market offerings (Davis and Lewis, 1982). Impacts upon the components of the money multiplier also feature little in the empirical work. Consequently there is no direct mechanism in the money market by which a disequilibrium between the demand and supply of money is extinguished.[11] Rather, the adjustment is assumed to occur in the markets for *other* commodities or assets. Suppose that the growth rate of M falls. With no elasticity allowed for in the money multiplier, the quantity of money must be extinguished (or augmented) via the quantity of high-powered money involving transactions in other markets, particularly the bond market or markets for foreign goods or assets. If the growth rate of M^* rises however, in the absence of autonomous or induced shifts in the function f (such as might come from financial innovations or deregulation), adjustment in terms of the quantity of money demanded necessitates changes in one or more of the variables P, y, p^e and r on the right-hand side of Equation (1.29), as monetary disequilibrium induces price or quantity adjustments in other markets.

It is the last scenario which fits in most readily with the quantity theory framework. With the money supply exogenously determined, the burden of adjustment falls upon the demand for money. Although some lag may be implied by the role of money as a temporary store of purchasing power, the adjustment process begins more or less immediately. Some longer delay in the disposal of excess money follows when money serves as a buffer asset in portfolios, but the 'shock-absorber' idea is different again. It does not carry with it any presumption that monetary disequilibrium will influence the arguments of the demand for money function. Standard models of estimation can, with appropriate modification, be retained, so that the quantity of money is still determined by demand, but the adjustment process is interrupted briefly by supply shocks. Carr and Darby's model is of this genre, with the additional twist that the supply disturbances take the form of money-supply changes which are unexpected. That part of the increase in the money stock which is anticipated is assumed, with perfectly clearing markets and rational expectations, to be fully and instantaneously written up into prices, price expectations and thus the demand for money. The unanticipated changes are absorbed voluntarily into monetary balances, without triggering portfolio adjustments. Carr and Darby's formulation (with all variables in logarithmic form) is

$$m_t = \alpha \boldsymbol{x}_t + \beta (M - M^a)_t + U_t \tag{1.30}$$

where m_t is real money balances ($M_t - P_t$); $\boldsymbol{x}_t$ is a vector representing the arguments of the demand for money function; M_t is the nominal money stock; and M_t^a is the anticipated part of the money stock.[12]

Exogenous money

If supply disturbances play a more dominant role than is assumed in the 'shock-absorber' models, alternative procedures are required. This is because attempts by individuals to acquire or dispose of money balances by transactions in financial or real assets do not change the stock of money but instead alter the arguments of the demand function until equilibrium is restored. In a Sargent–Lucas world of rational expectations, of perfectly flexible clearing markets and of no long-term contracts, an immediate response of wages and prices would occur. Suppose that the original growth rate of the money supply (and that of the demand for money) was g_0, and that the new growth rate is g_1. So long as this growth rate is sustained and does not revert to g_0, the demand for money must adjust such that it grows at the same rate. Referring to Equation (1.29), and dropping r_m which is assumed not to adjust, the growth rate of M^*, denoted as $\dot{M}^*$, can be written as

$$\dot{M}^* = \dot{P} + E_y \dot{y} + E_r \dot{r} + \mathrm{E}_p^{\mathrm{e}} (\dot{p}^{\mathrm{e}}) + E_u \dot{u} \tag{1.31}$$

where E stands for the elasticity of M^* with respect to the relevant constituent of the demand function. In a stationary economy, with $\dot{y}$=0, $\dot{r}$=0, for M^* to grow at a rate of g_1 and satisfy the rational expectations equilibrium it is necessary that prices move instantaneously so as to satisfy the condition[13]

$$\dot{P} = \dot{p}^{\mathrm{e}} = \dot{M} = g_1 \tag{1.32}$$

In an open economy, where world prices are growing at the old equilibrium rate of g_0, maintenance of Equation (1.32) will necessitate a continuous depreciation of the exchange rate at the rate (g_1-g_0). Inflationary expectations and nominal interest rates will adjust to the new higher rate of inflation, and the same is true of exchange rate expectations, all three producing once-and-for-all reductions in the demand for money. Equilibrium requires at the same time a once-and-for-all rise in P so as to bring about a reduction in the equilibrium stock of real money balances.

Were this rational expectations scenario to be acted out in reality, it would be necessary only to estimate equations like (1.22), in which real balances are the dependent variable, even with quarterly data. This does not seem to be the case, which we can attribute to a combination of unanticipated monetary developments, absorption of monetary changes in buffer stocks, and the existence of price stickiness. A number of implications then follow. Stickiness of prices means that neither individual inertia nor buffer-stock money are needed in order for monetary disequilibria in aggregate to occur. Each individual may move to dispose of his/her nominal money balances promptly (but only to another individual), yet until prices rise real balances will in aggregate still exceed the desired level. It seems likely in consequence that this disequilibrium will be worked out in the meantime in terms of adjustments to interest rates and output – the other arguments of the demand-for-money function.

Thus, in the case of exogenous money, three channels exist for the resolution of the monetary disequilibrium.

1. An interest rate effect bringing money demand temporarily or permanently into line with the new supply.
2. An income effect, involving changes in real income (y) and the demand for money induced by the monetary disturbance.
3. A price change to restore real money balances to the new equilibrium level.

In asking which of these adjustments is the most likely to occur, consideration needs to be given to the period of time under examination, the size of the supply disturbance and the transmission mechanism envisaged. Most econometric models in the Keynesian tradition have visualized the adjustment proceeding in a particular way. Asset markets are typically seen to respond first. Adjustments in goods markets then follow. Variations in interest rates and output both have consequences for the balance of payments (and thus the exchange rate), but in addition feed through to prices via excess demand for goods and labour and as expectations of inflation are revised. It is here that the institutions of a particular economy may be important. Some short-circuiting of the money–interest rates–output–prices sequence will occur if expectations of inflation are 'forward-looking' rather than 'backward-looking'. Also in the asset theory of exchange rates, exchange rates and interest rates are seen as being jointly determined by monetary changes, so that exchange rates will also form part of the transmission mechanism of monetary impulses. Nevertheless, it seems most likely that the initial impact will be upon r and y, and the ultimate effect predominantly upon P.

Second, perceptions of the transmission mechanism are influenced by what is meant by 'asset' markets. If portfolios comprise only the money and bonds of Keynesian analysis, imbalances can initially be resolved only by a change in the price of bonds, i.e. 'the' rate of interest. Should asset portfolios be made up of many assets, ranging from money through to consumer durables and even real estate, a monetary disturbance will have direct implications for the demand for existing and newly produced goods.

Finally, a distinction needs to be drawn in a growth context between two types of equilibrium. A *temporary* or *quasi-equilibrium* exists when $M=M^*$, and a *long-run* or *full* equilibrium when both $M=M^*$ and $\dot{M}=\dot{M}^*$. Assuming once again a constant change in the growth rate of the money stock of g, the former can be achieved by 'one-off' changes in the variables on the right-hand side of Equation (1.31), but the latter requires them to be continuously changing. For M^* to grow at the rate of g, either $\dot{P}=g_1$ (prices grow at a rate of g_1) or the other determinants are continuously changing. Considering these other variables, few would argue that monetary expansion generates enduring increases in the growth rate of real income. While most would contemplate some change in the level of interest rates and inflation expectations, none would suggest that they are continuously changing in long-run equilibrium. Among the other possible determinants, exchange rate expectations may undergo a change in level (for, as we have seen, the exchange rate may fall continuously) but as they relate to the expected rate of exchange rate change, they do not change continuously. Consequently, among the arguments of the demand for money, prices seem the most likely element to adjust the demand for money to the supply and satisfy the requirement $\dot{M}=\dot{M}^*$ for long-run equilibrium. Reaction in terms of interest rates seems more appropriate for examinations of temporary equilibria.

The existence of these three channels of equilibration poses some difficulties for measurement of the short-run demand for money when the money supply is exogenous. Generally, r, y, and P can be expected to share in the adjustment process, but all three cannot be put onto the left-hand side of a simple equation. A number of small-scale buffer-stock models have been built (Jonson, *et al.*, 1977; Coghlan, 1979; Laidler and Bentley, 1983) in which an exogenous monetary disturbance will initially be absorbed in portfolios and partially removed in each period through a variety of transactions, some of which involve adjustments to the money stock itself and some of which alter the arguments of the demand function.

Elements of all three adjustment mechanisms we have discussed for exogenous money are incorporated along with portfolio reallocations which directly reduce the money supply, particularly purchases of foreign assets, bond purchases from the authorities or reductions in bank advances. A demand-for-money function can be estimated implicitly in the process.

Use of single-equation methods seems justifiable only if one of the arguments of the demand-for-money function bears the brunt of adjusting demand to supply disturbances. In the short run, interest rates seem to be the likeliest candidate, and Artis and Lewis (1976) proposed interest rate adjustment equations for an examination of states of temporary equilibria. These equations took the form

$$\Delta r_t = \alpha(r^*_t - r_{t-1}) \qquad (1.33)$$

which allows for the actual rate of interest to adjust partially to the market clearing value (r^*_t) required to equilibrate the demand for money (Equation (1.22)) and the current supply, viz.

$$r^* = (1/c)\,(m_t - by_t - a - u_t) \qquad (1.34)$$

Combining the two gives an equation for estimation:

$$r_t = \beta_0 + \beta_1 y_t + \beta_2 m_t + \beta_3 r_{t-1} + U_t \qquad (1.35)$$

where

$$\beta_0 = -\alpha a/c,\ \beta_1 = -\alpha b/c,\ \beta_2 = \alpha/c,\ \beta_3 = (1-\alpha) \text{ and } U_t = -\alpha u_t/c.$$

Comparing Equations (1.24) and (1.35), we can see that by having M rather than either r or Y on the left-hand side, the conventional functions are the 'wrong way round'. In this sense they mis-specify the adjustments in the monetary sector. We also expect $0 < \alpha < 1$, whereas when the standard model is used continuous equilibrium is assumed. Not surprisingly, quite different adjustments are specified; specifically, there is no overshooting mechanism here, in contrast with the implication of conventional analysis. According to that analysis the short-run response of interest rates to a change in the money supply will overshoot the long-run response. We can see this by solving Equation (1.27) for r_t:

$$r_t = -\left(\frac{a}{c} + \frac{by_t}{c} + \frac{P_t}{c} - \frac{M_t}{\lambda c} + (1-\lambda)\frac{M_{t-1}}{\lambda c} + \frac{U_t}{c}\right) \qquad (1.36)$$

Note that here the immediate response of the rate of interest to changes in the money supply, $1/\lambda c$ (the coefficient of M_t), *exceeds* the long-run response, $1/c$ (obtained by setting $M_t = M_{t-1}$).

It is this *overshooting* feature which forms the basis of Tucker's (1966) paradoxical contention that the long lags in the demand-for-money function speed up the transmission of monetary impulses. His idea was that the lags would induce overshooting in the interest rate which would compensate for the long lagged effects of interest rates themselves on the real economy. But Tucker's argument assumes what is obviously illicit, namely that it is safe to take a behavioural equation which assumes an endogenous money supply and simply to invert it to derive the effect of exogenous money supply changes.

Andersen (1985) compares the performance of equations like (1.35) with the standard equations, and finds that in four of the seven countries studied – the United States, Japan, the United Kingdom and Italy – the alternative procedure provides more stable estimates of the underlying demand for money function in the 1970s and 1980s. As would be expected, relatively short lags are estimated (one to three quarters at most). But so long as interest rates carry implications for the subsequent course of expenditures, these responses cannot measure more than quasi-equilibrium in the monetary sector.

For an analysis of the longer-run situation analogous modelling gives a price adjustment equation

$$\Delta P_t = \gamma(P_t^* - P_{t-1}) \tag{1.36}$$

with P_t^* being the price level which brings real money balances to the desired level m_t^* as defined in Equation (1.22). While one could then solve through to obtain an equation in which P_t appears on the left-hand side, Laidler (1982) notes that if instead M_t is added to both sides of the resulting equation, what results is

$$M_t - P_t = \gamma a + \gamma b y_t + \gamma c r_t + \gamma u_t + (1-\gamma)(M_t - P_{t-1}) \tag{1.37}$$

This expression is similar to Equation (1.24) except for the last term, in which M_t replaces M_{t-1}.

Despite this apparent similarity with the real adjustment hypothesis examined earlier, the interpretation of Equation (1.37) is different. Lags arise not from within the demand for money due to individuals' response to the costs of rapid adjustment, or even within the financial sector, but from production lags or institutional impediments in wage- and price-setting mechanisms in the economy as a whole. Considered in conjunction with the relatively short lags suggested by the interest rate equations – which might give an indication of sluggish adjustment due to buffer stock money and inertia in portfolio behaviour – a more plausible explanation is thereby provided for the long lags found in conventional studies.

These are some of the implications of treating the money stock as exogenous, as in Friedman's (1969) 'helicopter money' model. In those models, the essence of the story revolves around the distinction between nominal and real money balances. Nominal balances come about like 'manna from heaven', and people bid the price level up and down to ensure that, in the long-run equilibrium, real money balances accord with desired levels. In short, the nominal stock of money is determined by supply while the real stock is governed by demand.

When we move outside such simple models, 'supply' need not imply that the nominal money supply is determined by factors which are distinct from demand. One of the merits of the 'money multiplier' or 'reserves available' approaches over the 'credit counterparts' approach is in breaking the money stock into a number of components, reflecting respectively the behaviour of the non-bank public; the actions of banks; and, finally, that of the monetary authorities. Interactions between demand and supply can occur through any of the three group's responses, but we concentrate in the next section only on the authorities' policies.

CHANGING REGIMES OF MONETARY POLICY

It has not been lost on some observers that the apparent instability in the demand-for-money function coincided with the institution by major central banks of policies aiming at achieving targeted ranges of money-supply aggregates – ironically a policy switch which had been prompted in large part by evidence of a stable short-run demand-for-money function. According to 'Goodhart's Law' this correlation is not coincidental: Goodhart (1979) argued that any empirical regularity is likely to prove unreliable when it is leaned upon for policy purposes. An argument along much the same lines advanced earlier by Kaldor (1970) suggests another explanation. Kaldor argued that the apparent stability of monetarist empirical relationships came about because money is a residual in the economy without any causal significance: the authorities had passively supplied money in response to contemporaneous and prior movements in income and thus the demand for money. Clearly, if central banks did switch from endogenous money in the 1960s to exogenous money in the late 1970s (and perhaps back again during the mid-1980s), the tenor of the arguments above is that some distortion to previously estimated functional relationships between money, interest rates, output and prices was only to be expected.

If such a policy change had occurred it should be possible to set up a model which pooled periods for which money is presumed to be endogenous and periods during which it is supposed to be exogenous. In practice, neither of the positions we have sketched out of endogenous and exogenous money can be seen as other than caricatures. No central bank has rigidly controlled the stock of money as a policy variable. None has passively ladled out money on demand, other than perhaps in the very short run.

As we noted on pages 9–11, not all central banks are able to exercise control over the amount of high-powered money and must residually fund the government deficit and the net balance on private sector foreign exchange transactions. When they do have control, they typically have used it not to force a contraction or expansion of banks' balance sheets via a textbook money multiplier, but to bring about a structure of short-term interest rates consistent with maintenance of exchange rate parity, or economic growth or bank lending or even the growth rate of the money supply. In the case of the Bank of England and the Federal Reserve, the market procedures by which interest rate objectives are achieved have remained largely unchanged in their essentials over a number of decades.

But these institutional characteristics do not warrant our going to the other extreme and supposing that interest rate or exchange rate targeting, as it actually has operated, implies strict endogeneity of the money stock. Institutional arrangements were never in fact quite so clear-cut as implied. Foreign exchange controls flanked the fixed exchange rate in the United Kingdom and many other countries, affording some room for the exercise of domestic monetary policy. Exchange rate expectations undoubtedly alter foreigners' demand for securities and domestic borrowing from overseas, and are associated (under fixed exchange rates unless sterilized) with a variation in the *supply* of money. That they necessarily alter the *demand* for money by an exactly equivalent amount is disputable. Much the same comments apply to an interaction between the demand for credit and the demand for money, as is clear in Brunner and Meltzer's (1976) distinction between credit-market and money-market hypotheses. When interest rates are being stabilized, many short-run increases in the money stock derive from variations in bank lending (as highlighted in the credit counterparts approach). These increases in money may not be demanded, but will always be accepted and willingly held as a store of purchasing power for later spending. Finally, interest rates have never been pegged outright. To enforce a new interest rate peg, the central bank must alter the money supply; in this instance, the money supply is instigating the change, not adapting itself passively to prior events.

Consequently the dichotomy between the maintained view in studies of the demand for money, i.e. that money is endogenously determined, and that in the textbook accounts based around a policy-determined, i.e. exogenous, quantity of high-powered money or base money has been drawn too sharply. This becomes apparent when we consider actual policies. Whether central banks could or should operate monetary base control raises a set of different issues, but does serve to lead us into the subsequent discussion.

Reserves base control

Equation (1.4), on page 3, can be interpreted as defining an equilibrium condition for the 'reserves market' in which the supply of reserves, the left-hand side, is equated with the demand for reserves accruing on the right-hand side, from required and desired excess reserves. Given reasonable stability in the latter it follows that variations in the demand for reserves are likely to be dominated by movements in required reserves. With lagged or contemporaneous reserves accounting, these are in turn a reflection of current movements in bank deposits. Central banks argue that they have no alternative but to supply banks with the reserves needed to validate deposit growth if stability of the banking system is to be ensured. All they can do is to influence the cost at which cash is made available to the system, and even here their effective discretionary power is limited. Considering the margin of excess reserves which banks normally hold in modern-day financial systems, the demand for total reserves is highly inelastic with respect to relevant interest rates. Moreover, now that banks practice liability management, they react to any reserve deficiency by bidding more aggressively for deposits and reserves in the wholesale funding markets to support their lending rather than disposing of assets. Any failure of reserves to keep pace with deposit expansion will merely see interest rates spiral upwards seemingly without limit rather than directly impelling banks to contract their lending.

Such considerations prompted 'overfunding' in the United Kingdom as a means of monetary control. Following the removal of lending controls in 1981, a number of special factors have combined to boost demands for bank credit to levels incompatible with the targeted growth of sterling M3 (which effectively encompasses the whole of banks' sterling balance sheets). Under the new procedures, the banks have become almost passive intermediaries in the process of monetary control. The 'job' is to raise loan rates in line with market rates, but if borrowers are not daunted by higher interest rates, the banks bid for deposits and reserves to sustain any expansion of advances. In this case, the authorities must either wait for credit demands to subside, raise rates further, or seek means other than reducing bank advances to restrict the rate of growth of the quantity of money. The alternatives suggested by the counterparts identity (1.12) were reducing the government budget deficit (G–T) and, latterly, larger sales of public sector debt to the non-bank private sector (GS_p). Frequently the removal of cash by sales of gilts exceeded the injections of cash from the budget deficit, i.e. overfunding occurred, and the authorities purchased short-term bills to relieve banks' cash shortage.[14]

Conditions in the United Kingdom in the early 1980s were admittedly rather special because by 1981 UK banks had reduced government bonds and bills to a minimum, and the ability to sell off part of their loan book did not exist. It is possible to visualize events proceeding differently in normal times. Liability management enables banks to 'run but not hide' (Dewald, 1975) from system-wide reserve deficiencies, since with flexible exchange rates and full funding of the government budget, extra issues of deposits by banks cannot pull in more cash to the system as a whole. Banks usually have the alternative of disposing of earning assets to the non-bank private sector, leaving total deposits unchanged. The idea that there is some new breed of banker who will always eschew asset management for liability management is patently false. If interbank rates are bid up high enough, it would pay some banks to sell bills and bonds to the private sector in order to obtain funds for lending out in the interbank market. Liability management is allowed to succeed because the central bank always provides the reserves needed to validate deposit expansion from bank lending. The deposit increase, in turn, provides the non-bank private sector with funds with which to buy the gilts sold by the monetary authorities. Indeed, firms may even borrow from the banks in order to buy the gilts – this being one possible hedging strategy should interest rates be expected to fall.

Implications could follow for behaviour 'next time round'. If banks are able to get cash, and at a price not always penal, they are unlikely to rearrange affairs so as to avoid putting themselves into the position of having to seek out cash in the future. Were the consequences of interest rate changes allowed to proceed under alternative arrangements (such as shifting penalty borrowing costs to the banks), behaviour next time around might well be different. After being forced to make up reserve shortages at penalty rates, banks would likely exercise much greater care in future when granting overdraft facilities and open credit lines. There would be an incentive for banks individually to refrain from lending and build up reserves when cash shortages are anticipated. Surges in monetary growth may be less likely to occur.

However, this is perhaps to confuse what could be with what is. Goodhart (1986, p. 50), argues that:

> Central Banks have historically been at some pains to assure the banking system that the institutional structure is such that the system as a whole can *always* obtain access to whatever cash the system may require in order to meet its needs, though at a price of the Central Banks's choosing: and there has been a further, implicit corollary that that interest rate will not be varied capriciously. The whole structure of the monetary system has evolved on this latter basis, that is, that the untrammelled force of the monetary base multiplier will *never* be unleashed.

One way in which this is achieved in practice is by the presence of various 'safety valves' which allow banks and the financial system generally access

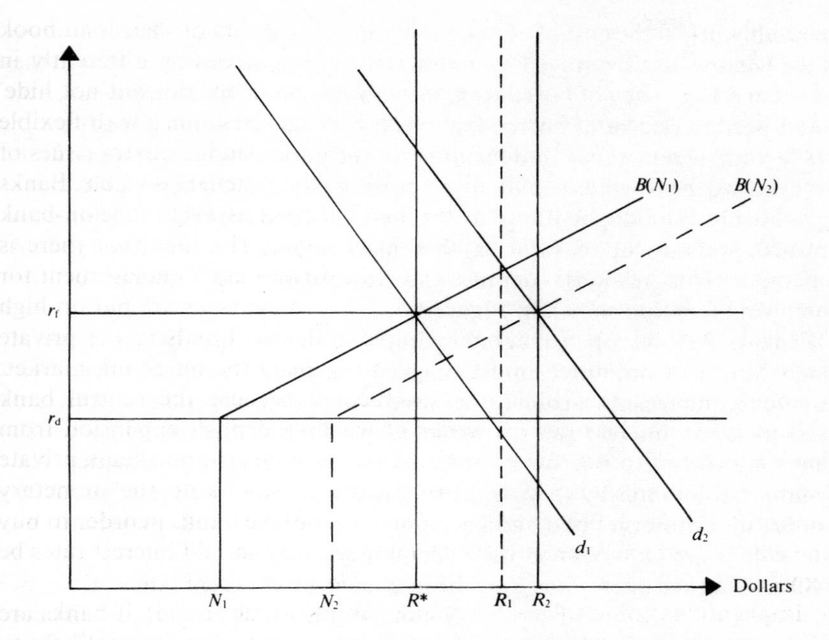

Figure 1.4 Representation of the reserves market (r_f=federal funds rate; r_d=discount rate; R^*=total reserves; N=non-borrowed reserves; R^*-N=borrowed reserves; B=borrowing function)

to high-powered money.[15] In the United Kingdom the safety valves operate through the discount houses (official money market dealers) at penal rates (see below). In the United States, the same effect works through the discount window, but at non-penal rates. We consider the US case first.

Federal Reserve policies[16]

Our discussion of US procedures is based on the 'reserves available' approach (Equation (1.8)). Figure 1.4 is a representation of the demand and supply of reserves. Required reserves in the United States may be held in vault cash as well as in bankers' balances (called Federal funds) with the Federal Reserve system. Because reserve requirements are met primarily by adjustments to Federal funds, the market for these funds is the focal point of monetary policy. However, reserves need only meet the minimum required level on average over a two-week statement period, which in itself acts as a safety valve for the system since banks need be less concerned about day-to-day cash flows than is the case in the United Kingdom.

US banks typically meet part of their reserve requirement by borrowing directly through the discount window facility. Such borrowing is invariably below the cost of comparable funds in the market. Excessive use of the window is discouraged by 'moral suasion', i.e. rules which govern the extent and frequency of borrowing, the application of which can be seen as a non-pecuniary cost of borrowing which rises with volume (Goodfriend, 1987). Banks' reluctance to depend upon the good graces of the discount window, when the volume of their borrowing rises, leads them to bid more aggressively for bought funds in the Federal funds market, which puts upward pressure upon rates in that market and the financial system generally. This response defines the upward-sloping segment of the borrowing function shown in Figure 1.4.

Federal Reserve open market operations, determined by the Federal Open Market Committee, must balance the banks' need to meet their reserve requirements against the needs of monetary policy. Upward pressure upon interest rates is achieved by altering the extent to which banks are forced to borrow in order to satisfy reserve requirements. The Committee does this by varying the supply of non-borrowed reserves. With a demand for reserves of d_1, and a supply of non-borrowed reserves of N_1, borrowings are (R^*-N_1) and the Federal funds rate is r_f.

These market operations have been guided by different conceptions of the needs of policy, and most US commentators identify three distinct phases. The first, from around 1970 (when targeting of the money stock began) until September 1979, accords most closely to that of endogenous money. At each of the eight meetings each year, the Committee would specify a target rate for the Federal funds rate and a range for the rate until the next scheduled meeting. The trading desk at the Federal Reserve Bank of New York would then supply non-borrowed reserves consistent with that target. In the face of an increase in the demand for reserves from d_1 to d_2, due perhaps to an increase in the quantity of (demand for ?) money, interest rates could be allowed to rise to the higher end of the range, but thereafter the increased demand would be accommodated at unchanged interest rates. This is the position illustrated in Figure 1.4, where r_f is the higher end of the target range and additional reserves of (R_2-R^*) are supplied by open market operations which increase non-borrowed reserves from N_1 to N_2.

However, the situation was never as rigid as that just sketched out. If the expansion of money prompting the increased reserves demanded was judged to be excessive, the interest rate target could be lifted at the next meeting. Or, if deemed desirable, an amendment to the target range could be made in between meetings, by means of a telephone link-up of the Reserve banks with Washington. Nevertheless, the arrangements clearly had the potential to let through expansions of the money stock in excess of targeted magnitudes.

Accordingly, tactics switched in October 1979 from targeting interest rates to targeting reserves, specifically the amount of non-borrowed reserves. Suppose that N_1 is the targeted quantity. An increase in the demand for reserves from d_1 to d_2 no longer elicits an accompanying increase in non-borrowed reserves. There is nevertheless an increase in total reserves from R^* to R_1, but because the addition is borrowed, the funds rate and other rates are pushed up. This feature was seen (e.g. Wallich, 1984) as a self-regulating mechanism, for the higher rates would tend to push the money supply back over time towards target.

From this description, it is apparent that the new system was not simply one of monetary base control, for the safety valve of the discount window remained in place. Monetary base control would imply fixing R^*, and in this respect the system was a compromise between one of reserves and interest rate targets. Also, due to the borrowed reserves slippage, and the negligible elasticity of the demand for reserves under lagged reserve accounting, the initial equilibrium between the demand and supply of reserves is again brought about through variations in supply. But unlike in the previous regime, the interest rate consequences of the change in supply will presumably reduce bank lending and the quantity of money and eventually feed back onto the demand for reserves.

Despite this softening of the consequences of a policy of strict reserves control, the interest rate fluctuations experienced were violent enough to be uncomfortable and alongside other considerations, e.g. falling inflation and the advent of the LDC debt crisis in the summer of 1982, led to some retreat from the system in October 1982. Under the new arrangements, borrowed reserves (R^*-N_1) are targeted. An increase in the quantity of money, due perhaps to an increase in the demand for money, which raises the demand for reserves from d_1 to d_2, would cause borrowed reserves to rise in excess of the quantity targeted. This creates the presumption that non-borrowed reserves should be expanded to N_2 so as to keep borrowed reserves unchanged at R_2-N_2 ($=R^*-N_1$) at the ruling Federal funds rate r_f.

As such a response is the same as that under the policy which operated prior to October 1979, critics have argued that if this is not interest rate targeting, then it is a close relation. Yet it would seem that the new system is more flexible. The Federal funds rate fluctuates far more on a day-to-day basis, and the Committee operates on a much more judgemental footing. Rather than supply reserves automatically, and correct the position later, an assessment is taken of the circumstances behind the expansion of the money stock. If the increase is undesired, then non-borrowed reserves would be expanded by less than (N_2-N_1), allowing interest rates to rise above r_f.

Bank of England policies[17]

A similarly eclectic policy is being practised by the Bank of England, despite the fact that it, like the Federal Reserve, is ostensibly operating a system of monetary targets, though both the aggregates targeted, e.g. M3, M1, PSL2, M0, and the centrality given to the achievement of such targets have varied considerably in recent years. Moreover, while the institutional arrangements are different, the two systems appear to work along similar lines.

Although not formally subject to reserve requirements, all banks in the United Kingdom must nevertheless hold 0.5 per cent of their deposits with the Bank of England in non-interest-bearing form. It is a constant sum revised every six months in order to emphasize that this represents a 'tax' to provide funds for the Bank of England and is not intended as a reserve ratio. Separate operational accounts are kept for the clearing of funds through the payments system. Although the government budget deficit is generally funded fully over the financial year (overfunding was stopped in 1985) there are substantial day-to-day alterations in the cash position. Banks collectively gain cash when the Exchequer has a deficit, and lose cash when it has a surplus. These daily losses frequently exceed the small operational balances (excess reserves) held by the banks at the Bank. Open market operations undertaken by the Bank of England, mainly in eligible bank accepted commercial bills, have the aim of providing banks with their cash needs at the end of the day, in the light of their estimates of the budget deficit, flows over the foreign exchanges and gilts markets (which are settled on subsequent days) and shifts in the public's currency holdings (which have large intra-week fluctuations) (see Bank of England, 1988).

Inevitably, these estimates are often incorrect, and there are net drains or additions to the cash position. Yet banks are obliged to keep their operational accounts at the Bank in credit and are unable to borrow reserves through the discount window as in the United States. Instead, two other safety valves come into play. One is inherent in the Bank's transactions. Dealing to maintain the desired cash position occurs twice daily, enabling some intra-day reaction to contrary trends. The other is the borrowing facility held by the discount houses. They are the chosen intermediaries between the central bank and the rest of the banking system. Because of this facility, banks are willing to hold most of their excess reserves in the form of deposits with the discount houses instead of in the form of operational balances at the Bank despite the fact that the banks' accounts at the Bank of England must be settled up each day. By means of this mechanism, the system works much like the borrowed reserves system in the United States.

When it seeks to influence market conditions, the Bank of England does not try to alter the supply of reserves, as would be expected from the 'money multiplier' or 'reserves available' formulae. Rather, like the Federal Reserve, it alters the form of and cost at which reserves are supplied, although procedures have altered somewhat over time and depend on whether the authorities wish to send an overt or explicit signal to the markets. In the past, in order to tighten conditions, less of the banks' cash needs were met through open market operations and more came from borrowings when the discount houses were forced 'into the Bank'. Unlike banks' borrowing at the discount window of the Federal Reserve, the discount houses almost always have to pay a rate at or above the comparable market rate. Access to the borrowing facility is thus rationed by price (rather than non-pecuniary cost), and usage of it sent a direct signal for bill rates, interbank rates and bank base (prime) rates to follow. Nowadays, unless an overt signalling is preferred, the Bank tends to slightly over- or underdo its assistance to the money market, and shift its time of open market operations, early or late in the day, in order to 'nudge' interest rates in the direction desired.

Such market operations in bills to make effective an appropriate level of short-term interest rates has lain at the heart of the Bank of England's operations for the last 120 years. Since the end of 1973, the Bank has generally sought to set interest rates with regard to achieving the growth rate of one or more monetary aggregates. Initially, the Bank related its daily dealings to a particular level of rates, which tended to be tied rather rigidly to its posted discount rate (bank rate). From August 1981, the more market-related techniques have been used to achieve a particular level of short rates, again with specific monetary targets in mind, although with the breakdown of demand-for-money relationships there has been no mechanical link between the growth of the aggregates, relative to target, and the setting of interest rates. In recent years, and certainly since 1985 when overfunding was abandoned (see pages 43–4 above), an essentially pragmatic policy has guided market operations, in which exchange rates have featured along with a number of monetary aggregates.

Some implications

Our examination has revealed that the actual methods of monetary control in the United States and United Kingdom bear little resemblance to the money multiplier approaches which feature in money and banking textbooks. In both countries there now exists sufficient separation of monetary policy from debt management and exchange rate management to give the central banks the technical ability to control the quantity of high-powered money quite closely. Neither central bank has used that potential to enforce strict control over the quantity of reserves. Both allow the supply of reserves to respond to demand in the short run, partly out of adherence to traditional operating procedures, but mainly to ensure that banks do not run out of cash and with an eye to avoiding violent fluctuations in interest rates. Instead, they determine how much of that supply of cash comes from market operations and how much is contributed (actually or potentially) by borrowings. This breakdown has implications for the structure of short-term interest rates which feed through the economy and back upon the demand for reserves. Consequently, within each policy regime, there is a complex interaction of exogenous and endogenous elements which the simple demand-for-money functions, based upon either endogenous money (as in the maintained approach) or exogenous money (as in the interest rate and price adjustment models), simply do not, and perhaps cannot, capture.

Conceivably, these difficulties could be overcome by a simultaneous equations system in which the quantity of money would emerge from the interaction of demand and supply as part of a more complete system. Realistically, the frequency with which the strategies have altered in what is a relatively short space of time, and the shifting emphases which feature in the present eclectic approach to policy, make it unlikely that the subtleties can find due reflection when quarterly data are employed.

SHORT- OR LONG-RUN DEMAND?

In the light of the foregoing comments one can ask, with considerable justification, whether we need a short-run demand-for-money function (Gordon, 1984). Once we reject a fully endogenous supply of money and give up the idea that quarterly observations of the money stock must necessarily trace out a demand-for-money function, the concept loses much of its appeal. What we want to know is whether the underlying demand curve is reasonably stable in the face of the mixture of supply shifts and induced responses, and this may be better revealed by long-run functions which are less confounded by the mixture of endogenous and exogenous responses which mark short-run behaviour.

The same point can be stated in somewhat different terms. Our examination of the actual conduct of monetary control revealed that central banks are not just concerned with the price stability and output goals emphasized in economic models, but also with the stability of the financial system, and have fashioned operating techniques which reflect this concern. These multiple objectives pursued with the one instrument of open market operations would seem likely to give rise to dilemmas for policy in terms of conflicting objectives – a point often stressed by monetarists. Some years ago, Niehans (1978) made the illuminating observation that the one instrument of market operations could be thought of as (at least) three if one switched from thinking in the time domain to considering the frequency domain, i.e. in terms of cycles of differing length. Much like Musgrave's (1959) different 'branches' of fiscal policy, the central bank is conceived here as having different departments, but in this case operating to offset disturbances of different periodicities. The price department watches over secular price movements, the output branch watches over cyclical disturbances which last over several quarters, while the liquidity branch looks after day-to-day or week-to-week financial flurries. Viewed in terms of these frequencies, it follows that the quarterly studies of the demand for money may fall between two stools. They are unable to serve as guides for the daily or weekly liquidity operations, nor can they tell us much about the longer-run stability of the demand for money, for which the studies of the long-run function seem more suited.

Before attention switched to the short-run demand for money, examinations of the demand for money typically used annual data over time periods stretching from the late nineteenth century to 1960. By comparing recent studies with them we may be able to ascertain whether these long-run functions have survived the recent experience.

Those studies in Table 1.3 by Graves and Batts and Dowling for the United Kingdom and Wenninger for the United States offer little encouragement on this point. Both of the UK studies report income elasticities which are well below those of earlier studies, and also lower interest rate elasticities. In the case of Graves, these result from the inclusion of variables to show the impact of the growth of urbanization and demographic shifts upon the long-run demand function. The impact of such 'institutional variables' upon the demand for money (velocity) are explored further in Bordo and Jonung (1987) and Capie and Wood (1986). Wenninger's (1988) study employs newly published quarterly data covering the period 1915–87. This data set enables him to compare the stability of the usual time series used in quarterly studies, 1950–73, with earlier and later periods. He finds that 'the stable demand for M1 over the 1950–73 period was a rather unique experience. Longer-term results reveal a more persistent pattern of instability in the demand for M1' (p 40). The study does, however, differ from other long-run studies by using quarterly rather than yearly data.

Two of the studies, one for the United Kingdom and one for the United States, are based directly on earlier empirical work. Artis and Lewis (1984) examine how far a demand-for-money function of the simplest form, namely Equation (1.20) with p^e and r_m left out, i.e.

$$M/Y = f(r) \qquad (1.20a)$$

can go in accounting for recent UK data. A function of this form was originally explored by Dow (1960) and Paish (1959; 1960) over the period 1920–57. The function was estimated for this period, and projected ahead from 1957. Observations through to 1983 (see Lewis, 1985) generally lay along the projected line except for a severe displacement during the years 1973–6 which the authors attribute to a supply shock which pushed demanders temporarily 'off' their demand curve. There was also evidence of a shift of the demand curve during the war years. Patterson (1987), using formal stability tests, found that the function did indeed shift during the war years and the years 1973–6.

One difficulty with the functional form employed by Artis and Lewis is the constraint of unity imposed upon the value of the income elasticity, although Patterson, in open estimates, confirms an income elasticity of unity and also Artis and Lewis's estimated interest elasticity, both of which conform with the estimates through to 1960 by Kavanagh and Walters (1966). Also, the definition of money employed (old M2, based on the deposits of the London clearing banks) was chosen to match in with the original studies, and has disappeared with the amalgamation for statistical purposes of the London clearing banks with their subsidiaries. Finally, in common with most other empirical work on the demand for money, the study is subject to the critique of the new monetary economics school levelled at the work of Friedman and Schwartz (see Hall, 1982). This school argues that conventional monetary relationships rely for their stability upon the continuance of current institutional norms and practices. It would query whether the apparent stability of the demand for money was not conditional on the continuity, *inter alia*, of the clearing banks as institutions.

In a parallel study for the United States, Lucas (1987) re-estimated Meltzer's (1963) equation, also through to 1957. When later data through to 1985 are added in open estimates, a single stable function for the whole period cannot be found. When, however, the income elasticity is constrained to unity, so producing a functional form similar to that of Artis and Lewis, data scatters show that the recent observations do seem to correlate with the prior sample.

Friedman and Schwartz (1982) also report stability of the demand-for-money function over the years 1874–1975, and for both the United States and the United Kingdom, although they find it necessary to add dummy variables for transitory deviations in the immediate post-war years and during the inter-war years.[18] We have also noted above Friedman's (1988) examination of the impact of stock market prices upon the demand for money, in which he suggested that the instability in recent years of the arguments of the demand for money, if not of the function itself, was due to price instability accompanying the transition to fiat money in 1971.

A characteristic of Friedman and Schwartz's research is the use of cycle-average data, i.e. observations converted into averages of business cycle phases, so as to eliminate short-term cyclical movements (when transactors can be 'off' their demand curves). Their research methods are criticized by Hendry and Ericsson (1983) as falling below the standards of best-practice econometric techniques. Phase averaging results in a loss of information and in combination with the *ad hoc* use made of dummy variables effectively prejudges what is a transitory departure from equilibrium and what is a major alteration to the underlying relationship. Thus Friedman and Schwartz are charged with failing to integrate a description of steady-state behaviour with a dynamic process of adjustment to equilibrium in the way that is a characteristic of the 'general to specific' model-selection methods of Hendry (1979) and Mizon (1977), which are widely employed in modern econometric work.

These econometric procedures are not themselves free from criticism (see Pagan, 1987; Darnell, 1988). It may be expecting too much of noisy, highly collinear data to determine both the disequilibrium adjustment process and the appropriate equilibrium model. This being the case, there is something to be said for starting from a precise theoretical model – in effect, working from the specific to the general. As we noted earlier, this is not usual in empirical studies of the demand for money. Hendry and Ericsson's critique is also blunted by the later analysis of Longbottom and Holly (1985) which re-estimated Friedman and Schwartz's model for the United Kingdom using annual rather than phase-average data and employed Hendry-style econometric procedures, yet reports virtually identical results. There are, however, some signs of instability in the 1970s and dummy variables are included for the war years. Hendry and Ericsson (1987) themselves, in revised estimates, establish a model which has parameter constancy over the entire period 1875–1970, but it also exhibits instability when extended to the troublesome 1971–5 period discussed earlier.[19]

These long-run results point to a greater underlying stability of the demand-for-money function than is evident from the short-run studies. That observation in itself does not say much, and it is probably too soon to seek to do so in view of the limited number of long-run studies which extend the data sample beyond 1975.

CONCLUDING REMARKS

It will come as no surprise to students of monetary economics that our survey confirms the breakdown of the standard demand-for-money function, as applied to short-run data, and finishes with a question mark over the stability of the long-run relationships. We have also been unable to establish definitively why the demand for money function seems to have exhibited instabilities over the last fifteen years.

What we have argued, and not just with the benefit of hindsight (see Artis and Lewis, 1974; Lewis, 1978), is that no one ought to have been surprised by the econometric record. The minimum requirement for a study of monetary phenomena is the definition of: the determinants of demand; the conditions affecting supply; and the processes by which demand and supply are equated. Observed instabilities become more understandable when we reflect on the jump made from theories of the demand for money to the simple demand functions used in empirical work, the disparity which exists between the approaches to money-stock determination and the actual procedures followed by central banks in the United States and United Kingdom (and other countries), and the variety of mechanisms which exist for reconciling demand and supply. Added to this we have the switch to floating exchange rates, unstable exchanges, deregulation, financial innovations, inflation and disinflation, and a chopping and changing of monetary policy regimes. Any one of these shocks seems capable of blowing the simple functional relationships off course.

Our discussion has focused on three explanations. One is that financial innovations and deregulation have shifted the demand-for-money function (and perhaps altered permanently the character of money itself). The second possibility is that the function is unchanged but that its arguments have altered in an unstable way due to the historically unprecedented inflation of the 1970s which accompanied the move to a fiat money standard, followed by disinflation. Finally, we suggest that instability may exist in the supply curve, again a consequence of the move to fiat money, with shifts independent of demand pushing transactors away from the aggregate demand curve.

Appropriate policy responses differ. If innovation and deregulation have set off an ongoing process of competition and change in financial markets, further unanticipated alterations to the short-run and long-run demand for money seem likely, ruling out the relationships as guides to policy. The second explanation carries no such implication. Once the economic environment has settled down and time is allowed for cash balances to adjust to the new position, then the original stable relationship should be re-established. The third explanation has no need at all for a short-run function. All that is required to guide policy is knowledge that the underlying long-run demand-for-money function has remained reasonably stable in the face of the supply shocks.

We can see no reason why all three explanations might not have contributed to the outcome, and, to the extent that a faster rate of growth of bank deposits is justified in the light of a more competitive and dynamic banking system, there is the further question of how that is to be achieved. The larger real monetary balances can be met by allowing money supply targets to overspill at more or less existing rates of inflation (as would seem to have occurred in the United Kingdom with sterling M3) or they can come about by disinflation at the targeted rates of growth of the monetary aggregates in nominal terms, as the larger real balances are generated by a lower rate of increase of prices.

To conclude, we return to the question posed in the introduction about the portents for future policy. While the stability of the demand-for-money function remains an open question, monetary authorities seem likely to follow open market dealing strategies which accommodate the possibility of unanticipated shifts occurring in the demand for money and thus continue with the new electicism.

NOTES

1. If *rr* refers to the reserve requirement which is applicable to demand deposits, then the multiplier (1.6) would be applied to an M1 definition of money. For broader definitions of money, *d* would need to be widened to include time and savings deposits and the required reserve ratio regarded as a weighted average of the reserve ratio requirements applicable to the various classes of deposits (see Burger, 1971, for a fuller account).
2. Kareken (1967) and Dewald and Lindsey (1972) call expressions such as Equation (1.7), where the money stock is related to exogenous variables, 'pseudo-supply functions'. This is in contrast to 'true money supply functions' which would reveal the quantity of money that the suppliers would be willing to supply at particular market rates. Such functions require an examination of bank portfolio behaviour, as in Brunner and Meltzer (1987).
3. If, however, banks respond to reserve discrepancies by changing the interest rates paid on deposits and charged for lending, so inducing responses in *d* and *e*, the quantitative effects on money may be small. The view thus presupposes that bank interest rates do not respond significantly to changes in bank portfolios (Niehans, 1978).
4. These markets are examined in Lewis and Davis (1987).
5. The finance motive is examined by Smith (1979).
6. An excellent account is contained in Cuthbertson (1985).
7. Goodfriend (1985) suggested a third interpretation for including lagged monetary variables in terms of measurement errors in interest rate and income variables.
8. The distinctions between the real and nominal adjustment models are analysed by Laidler (1982), Spencer (1985) and Merris (1987).
9. Recent examinations have been conducted by Judd and Scadding (1982), Gordon (1984), Thornton (1985) and Goldfeld (1986).
10. In recognition of this point, many US studies have employed the previous peak level of interest rates as a proxy for induced financial innovation.
11. This is a reflection of the failure to bring bank portfolio behaviour into the supply side, as observed in note 2. A number of writers have objected to the

idea of buffer-stock money on the grounds that any excess money would be used to repay outstanding loans, and this route is modelled by Davidson (1987). It presupposes a close interaction between bank deposit and bank loan markets. This is disputed by Brunner and Meltzer (1976).

12. The Carr–Darby approach creates econometric problems due to the appearance of monetary terms on both sides of the equation. See MacKinnon and Milbourne (1984).
13. There are, however, transitional problems, since the Fisher effect causes nominal rates of interest to rise, so bringing about a once-and-for-all reduction in the demand for money. In order that real balances fall, prices must temporarily grow faster than g_1.
14. For an excellent recent account, see Goodhart (1989, chapter 10).
15. The term 'safety valve' was coined in the useful survey of money market operations by Battelino and Macfarlane (1987).
16. This section has gained much from reading Melton (1985); Mugel (1985); Gilbert (1985); and Roth (1986).
17. Recent accounts are given by Allen (1984); Goodhart (1989); Llewellyn and Tew (1988).
18. Friedman and Schwartz's estimating equations produce semi-elasticities for the interest rate variable rather than elasticities, and so vary with the average value of the net interest rate. The interest elasticities reported in Table 1.3 are from the equation combining UK and US observations, using the average combined net interest rate; see Friedman and Schwartz (1982, p. 284). Their estimates for the income elasticities are constant elasticity estimates and are reported for the separate equations for each country.
19. The period 1970–5 is also identified as disturbing the relationship of money demand to prices and incomes by Lubrano *et al.* (1986).

REFERENCES

Akerlof, G.A. and Milbourne, R.D. (1980) 'The short run demand for money', *Economic Journal*, vol. 90, pp. 885–900.

Allen, W.A. (1984) 'Recent developments in monetary control in the United Kingdom' in L.H. Meyer (ed.), *Improving Money Stock Control*, Boston: Kluwer-Nyhoff Publishing.

Andersen, L.C. (1967) 'Three approaches to money stock determination', *Federal Reserve Bank of St Louis Review*, October, pp. 6–13.

Andersen, P.S. (1985) 'The stability of money demand functions: an alternative approach', BIS Economic Papers, Basle, no. 14, April.

Artis, M.J. and Lewis, M.K. (1974) 'The demand for money: stable or unstable?', *The Banker*, vol. 124, pp. 239–47.

Artis, M.J. and Lewis, M.K. (1976) 'The demand for money in the UK, 1963–1973', *Manchester School*, vol. 44, pp. 147–81.

Artis, M.J. and Lewis, M.K. (1981) *Monetary Control in the United Kingdom*, Oxford: Philip Allan.

Artis, M.J. and Lewis, M.K. (1984) 'How unstable is the demand for money in the United Kingdom?', *Economica*, vol. 51, pp. 473–6.

Atkinson, P. and Chouraqui, J.-C. (1987) 'The formulation of monetary policy: a reassessment in the light of recent experience', *Monetary Policy and Financial Systems No. 1*, OECD Working Paper no. 32.

Bank of England (1988) *Bank of England Operations in the Sterling Money Market*, October.
Batts, J. and Dowling, J.M. (1984) 'The stability of the demand-for-money function in the United Kingdom: 1880–1975', *Quarterly Review of Economics and Business*, vol. 24, no. 3, pp. 37–48.
Battelino, R. and Macfarlane, I.J. (1987) 'Open market operations: some international comparisons', Conference on Australian Monetary Policy Post Campbell, Melbourne, 7–8 August.
Baumol, W.J. (1952) The transactions demand for cash: an inventory theoretic approach, *Quarterly Journal of Economics*, vol. 66, pp. 545–56.
Bordo, M.D. and Jonung, L. (1987) *The Long-run Behaviour of the Velocity of Circulation*, Cambridge: Cambridge University Press.
Boughton, J.M. (1979) 'Demand for money in major OECD countries', *OECD Economic Outlook*, Occasional Studies, January.
Burger, A.E. (1971) *The Money Supply Process*, Belmont, CA: Wadsworth.
Bronfrenbrenner, M. and Mayer, T. (1960) 'Liquidity functions in the American Economy', *Econometrica*, October.
Brown, A.J. (1939) 'Interest, prices, and the demand schedule for idle money', *Oxford Economic Papers*, vol. 2, May, pp. 46–69. Reprinted in T. Wilson and P. Andrews (eds), *Oxford Studies in the Price Mechanism*, Oxford: Clarendon Press, 1951.
Brunner, K. (1973) 'A diagrammatic exposition of the money supply process', *Schweizerischen Zeitschrift für Volkswirtschaft und Statistik*, 4 December, pp. 481–533.
Brunner, K. (1987) 'Money supply' in John Eatwell (ed.), *New Palgrave Dictionary of Economics*, London: Macmillan.
Brunner, K. and Meltzer, A.H. (1976) 'An aggregative theory for a closed economy' in J.L. Stein (ed.), *Monetarism*, Amsterdam: North-Holland.
Brunner, K. and Meltzer, A.H. (1987) 'Money supply', Working Paper GPB 87–14, University of Rochester.
Cagan, P. (1965) 'Determination and Effects of Changes in the Stock of Money 1865–1960', National Bureau of Economic Research.
Cagan, P. and Schwartz, A. (1975) 'Has the growth of money substitutes hindered monetary policy?', *Journal of Money, Credit, and Banking*, vol. 7, May, pp. 137–60.
Capie, F. and Roderik-Bali (1986) 'The behaviour of money and its determinants in interwar Britain', City University Business School, Centre for Banking and International Finance, February.
Capie, F. and Wood, G.E. (1986) 'The long run behaviour of velocity in the UK', Centre for Banking and International Finance, Centre for the Study of Monetary History, City University, Discussion Paper no. 23, May.
Carr, J. and Darby, M.R. (1981) 'The role of money supply shocks in the short-run demand for money', *Journal of Monetary Economics*, vol. 8, pp. 183–99.
Chow, Gregory C. (1966) 'On the long-run and short-run demand for money', *Journal of Political Economy*, April, pp. 111–31.
Clower, R.W. (1967) 'A reconsideration of the microfoundations of monetary theory', *Western Economic Journal*, vol. 6, pp. 1–9.
Coghlan, R.T. (1979) 'A small monetary model of the UK economy', Bank of England Discussion Paper no. 3.
Cuthbertson, K. (1985) *The Demand and Supply of Money*, Oxford: Basil Blackwell.

Cuthbertson, K. and Taylor, M.P. (1987) 'Buffer-stock money: an appraisal', in C. Goodhart, D. Currie and D.T. Llewellyn (eds), *The Operation and Regulation of Financial Markets*, London: Macmillan.

Darnell, A. (1988) '"General to specific" modelling: a methodological perspective', Working Paper no. 90, Department of Economics, University of Durham.

Davidson, J. (1987) 'Disequilibrium money: some further results with a monetary model of the UK' in C. Goodhart, D. Currie and D.T. Llewellyn (eds), *The Operation and Regulation of Financial Markets*, London: Macmillan.

Davis, K.T. and Lewis, M.K. (1982) 'Can monetary policy work in a deregulated capital market?', *Australian Economic Review*, 1.

De Leeuw, F. (1965) 'The demand for Money-Speed of Adjustment, Interest Rates and Wealth', Staff Economic Studies, Board of Governors of the Federal Reserve System, Washington, DC.

Dewald, W.G. (1975) 'Banking and the economy', College of Administrative Science, Ohio State University.

Dewald, W.G. and Lindsey, D.E. (1972) 'A critique of standard money supply models', Report 7216, Division for Economic Research, Department of Economics, Ohio State University.

Dow, J.C.R. (1960) 'The economic effect of monetary policy 1945–57' in Committee on the Working of the Monetary System, *Principal Memoranda of Evidence*, vol. 3, London: HMSO, pp. 76–105.

Enzler, J., Johnson, L. and Paulus, J. (1976) 'Some problems of money demand', *Brookings Papers on Economic Activity*, 1.

Eshag, E. (1963) *From Marshall to Keynes. An Essay on the Monetary Theory of the Cambridge School*, Oxford: Basil Blackwell.

Feige, E.L. (1967) 'Expectations and adjustments in the monetary sector', *American Economic Review*, vol. 57, pp. 462–73.

Friedman, M. (1953) *Essays in Positive Economics*, Chicago: University of Chicago Press.

Friedman, M. (1956) 'The quantity theory of money: a restatement' in M. Friedman (ed.), *Studies in the Quantity Theory of Money*, Chicago: University of Chicago Press.

Friedman, M. (1959) 'The demand for money: some theoretical and empirical results', *Journal of Political Economy*, vol. 67, no. 4, pp. 327–51.

Friedman, M. (1969) *The Optimum Quantity of Money and Other Essays*, Chicago: Aldine.

Friedman, M. (1987) 'Money: Quantity theory', in John Eatwell (ed.), *New Palgrave Dictionary of Economics*, London: Macmillan.

Friedman, M. (1988) 'Money and the stock market', *Journal of Political Economy*, vol. 96, no. 2, pp. 221–45.

Friedman, M. and Schwartz, A. (1963) *A Monetary History of the United States*, Princeton, NJ: National Bureau of Economic Research.

Friedman, M. and Schwartz, A. (1970) *Monetary Statistics of the United States*, Princeton, NJ: National Bureau of Economic Research.

Friedman, M. and Schwartz, A. (1982) *Monetary Trends in the United States and the United Kingdom: Their Relation to Income, Prices and Interest Rates, 1867–1975*, Chicago: University of Chicago Press.

Gandolfi, A.E. and Lothian, J.R. (1976) 'The demand for money from the Great Depression to the present', *American Economic Review*, vol. 66, May, pp. 46–51.

Garcia, G. and Pak, S. (1979) 'Some clues in the case of the missing money',

American Economic Review, vol. 69, May, pp. 330–4.
Gilbert, R.A. (1985) 'Operating procedures for conducting monetary policy, *Federal Reserve Bank of St Louis Review*, vol. 67, no. 2.
Goldfeld, S.M. (1976) 'The case of the missing money', *Brookings Papers on Economic Activity*, no. 3, pp. 683–730.
Goldfeld, S.M. (1987) 'Demand for money: empirical studies' in John Eatwell (ed.), *New Palgrave Dictionary of Economics*, London: Macmillan.
Goodfriend, M. (1985) 'Reinterpreting money demand regressions', in K. Brunner and A.H. Meltzer (eds), *Understanding Monetary Regimes*, Carnegie-Rochester Conference Series on Public Policy, vol. 22, Amsterdam: North-Holland, pp. 207–42.
Goodfriend, M. (1987) *Monetary Policy in Practice*, Federal Reserve Bank of Richmond.
Goodhart, C.A.E. (1975) *Money Information and Uncertainty*, London: Macmillan.
Goodhart, C.A.E. (1979) 'Problems of monetary management: the UK experience' in A.S. Courakis (ed.), *Inflation, Depression and Economic Policy in the West: Lessons from the 1970s*, Mansell and Alexandrine Press.
Goodhart, C.A.E. (1984) *Monetary Theory and Practice*, London: Macmillan.
Goodhart, C.A.E. (1987) 'Monetary base', in John Eatwell (ed.), *New Palgrave Dictionary of Economics*, London: Macmillan.
Goodhart, C.A.E. (1989) *Money Information and Uncertainty*, 2nd edn, London: Macmillan.
Goodhart, C.A.E. and Crockett, A.D. (1970) 'The importance of money', *Bank of England Quarterly Bulletin*, June, pp. 159–98.
Gordon, R.J. (1984) 'The short-run demand for money: a reconsideration', *Journal of Money, Credit and Banking*, November.
Graves, P.E. (1980) 'The velocity of money: evidence for the UK, 1911–1966', *Economic Inquiry*, vol. XVIII, pp. 631–9.
Green, C. (1984) 'Preliminary results from a five-sector flow of funds model of the United Kingdom, 1972–77', *Economic Modelling*, July, pp. 304–26.
Grice, J. and Bennett, A. (1984) 'Wealth and the demand for £M3 in the United Kingdom 1963–1978', *Manchester School.*
Hacche, G.J. (1974) 'The demand for money in the United Kingdom: experience since 1971', *Bank of England Quarterly Bulletin*, September, pp. 284–305.
Hall, R.E. (1982) 'Monetary trends in the United States and the United Kingdom: a review from the perspective of new developments in monetary economics', *Journal of Economic Literature*, vol. XX, December, pp. 1552–6.
Hamburger, M.J. (1977) 'The demand for money in an open economy: Germany and the United Kingdom', *Journal of Monetary Economics*, vol. 3, pp. 25–40.
Heller, H.R. (1965) 'The demand for money: the evidence from the short-run data', *Quarterly Journal of Economics*, May.
Hendry, D.F. (1979), 'Predictive failure and econometric modelling in macroeconomics: the transactions demand for money', in Paul Ormerod (ed.), *Economic Modelling*, London: Heinemann, pp. 217–42.
Hendry, D.F. and Ericsson, N.R. (1983) 'Assertion without empirical basis: an econometric appraisal of "Monetary Trends in ... the United Kingdom" by Milton Friedman and Anna Schwartz' in *Monetary Trends in the United Kingdom*, Bank of England Panel of Academic Consultants, Paper no. 22, pp. 45–101 (with additional references).
Hendry, D.R. and Ericsson, N.R. (1987) 'Assertion without empirical basis: an

econometric appraisal of *Monetary Trends ... in the United Kingdom*, University of Oxford Applied Economics, Discussion Paper no. 25, March.
Jonson, P.D., Moses, E.R. and Wymer, C.R. (1977) 'A minimal model of the Australian economy', Reserve Bank of Australia, Research Discussion Paper no. 7601. Reprinted in W.E. Norton (ed.), *Conference in Applied Economic Research*, Sydney: Reserve Bank of Australia.
Jordan, J.L. (1969) 'Elements of money stock determination, *Federal Reserve Bank of St Louis Review*, October, pp. 10–19.
Judd, J.P. and Scadding, J.L. (1982) 'The search for a stable money demand function: a survey of the post-1973 literature', *Journal of Economic Literature*, vol. XX, no. 3, pp. 993–1023.
Kaldor, N. (1970) 'The new monetarism', *Lloyds Bank Review*, April.
Kareken, J. (1967) 'Commercial banks and the supply of money: a market determined rate', *Federal Reserve Bulletin*, vol. 53, pp. 1699–712.
Kavanagh, N.J. and Walters, A.A. (1966) 'The demand for money in the United Kingdom, 1877–1961', *Bulletin of the Oxford University Institute of Economics and Statistics*, vol. 28, pp. 93–116.
Keynes, J.M. (1930) *A Treatise on Money, Volume 1* London: Macmillan.
Keynes, J.M. (1936) *The General Theory of Employment, Interest and Money*, London: Macmillan.
Kent, R.J. (1985) 'The demand for the services of money', *Applied Economics*, no. 17, pp. 817–26.
Khan, M.S. (1974) 'The stability of the demand-for-money function in the United States, 1901–1965', *Journal of Political Economy*, November–December, pp. 1205–19.
Klein, B.J. (1977) 'The demand for quality-adjusted cash balances: price uncertainty in the U.S. demand for money function', *Journal of Political Economy*, vol. 85, August, pp. 691–715.
Knoester, A. (1984) 'Theoretical principles of the buffer stock mechanism, monetary quasi-equilibrium and its spillover effects', *Kredit und Kapital*, vol. 17, no. 2, pp. 243–60.
Laidler, D. (1966) 'Some evidence on the demand for money', *Journal of Political Economy*, February.
Laidler, D. (1971) 'The influence of money on economic activity: a survey of some current problems' in G. Clayton, J.C. Gilbert and R. Sedgwick (eds), *Monetary Theory and Policy in the 1970s*, London: Oxford University Press.
Laidler, D. (1982) *Monetarist Perspectives*, Oxford: Philip Allan.
Laidler, D. (1984) 'The buffer stock notion in monetary economics', Selected Papers from the RES/AUTE Annual Conference, vol. 94, pp. 17–34.
Laidler, D. and Bentley, B. (1983) 'A small macro-model of the post-war United States', *Manchester School*, vol. 51, pp. 317–400.
Laidler, D. and Parkin, J.M. (1970) 'The demand for money in the United Kingdom, 1955–67: preliminary estimates', *Manchester School*, vol. 38, pp. 187–208.
Latane, H.A. (1954) 'Cash balances and the interest rates: a pragmatic approach', *Review of Economics and Statistics*, November.
Laumas, G.S. and Mehra, Y.P. (1977) 'The Stability of the Demand for Money Function', *Journal of Finance*, vol. 23, no. 3, pp. 911–16.
Lewis, M.K. (1978) 'Interest rates and monetary velocity in Australia and the United States', *The Economic Record*, April, pp. 111–26.
Lewis, M.K. (1985) 'Money and the control of inflation in the UK', *Midland Bank*

Review, Summer, pp. 17–23.
Lewis, M.K. (1986) 'Financial services in the United States' in R.A. Carter, B. Chiplin and M.K. Lewis (eds), *Personal Financial Markets*, Oxford: Philip Allan.
Lewis, M.K. and Davis, K.T. (1987) *Domestic and International Banking*, Cambridge, Mass.: MIT Press.
Llewellyn, D. and Tew, B. (1988) 'The sterling money market and the determination of interest rates', *National Westminster Bank Quarterly Review*: May, pp. 25–37.
Longbottom, A. and Holly, S. (1985) 'Econometric methodology and monetarism: Professor Friedman and Professor Hendry on the Demand for money', Discussion Paper no. 131, London Business School.
Lubrano, M., Pierse, R.G. and Richard, J.-F. (1986) 'Stability of a UK money demand equation: a Bayesian approach to testing exogeneity', *Review of Economic Studies*, vol. 53, no. 4, pp. 603–34.
Lucas, R.E. (1987) 'Money demand in the United States: a quantitative review', paper given at Carnegie-Rochester Conference, November.
MacKinnon, J.G. and Milbourne, R.D. (1984) 'Monetary anticipations and the demand for money', *Journal of Monetary Economics*, vol. 13, pp. 263–74.
Markowitz, H. (1959) '*Portfolio Selection: Efficient Diversification of Investments*', Cowles Foundation, Yale University.
Meltzer, A.H. (1963) 'The demand for money: the evidence from the time series', *Journal of Political Economy*, June.
Merris, R.C. (1987) 'Testing stock-adjustment specifications and other restrictions on money demand equations', Research Department, Federal Reserve Bank of Chicago, February.
Meyer, L.H. (1976) 'Alternative definition of the money stock and the demand for money', *Federal Reserve Bank of New York Monthly Review*.
Miller, M.H. and Orr, D. (1966) 'A model of the demand for money by firms', *Quarterly Journal of Economics*, vol. 80, pp. 413–35.
Mizon, G.E. (1977) 'Model selection procedures' in M.J. Artis and A.R. Nobay (eds), *Studies in Modern Economic Analysis*, Oxford: Basil Blackwell, pp. 97–120.
Modigliani, F., Rasche, R. and Cooper, J. (1970) 'Central bank policy, the money supply and the short-term rate of interest', *Journal of Money, Credit and Banking*, May.
Mugel, R.L. (1985) 'Reserve borrowings and the money market', *Federal Reserve Bank of Cleveland, Economic Commentary*, 1 November.
Mundell, R.A. (1963) 'Capital mobility and stabilization policy under fixed and flexible exchange rates', *Canadian Journal of Economics and Political Science*, November.
Musgrave, R.A. (1959) *Theory of Public Finance*, Homewood, IL: Irwin.
Niehans, J. (1978) *The Theory of Money*, Baltimore, MD: Johns Hopkins University Press.
Pagan, A. (1987) 'Three econometric methodologies: a critical appraisal', *Journal of Economic Surveys*, vol. 1, no. 1, pp. 3–24.
Paish, F.W. (1959) 'Gilt-edged and the money supply', *The Banker*, vol. 109, January.
Paish, F.W. (1960) 'The future of British monetary policy' in Committee on the Working of the Monetary System, *Principal Memoranda of Evidence*, vol. 3, London: HMSO, pp. 182–8.

Patinkin, D. (1976) *Keynes' monetary thought. A study in its development*, Durham, NC: Duke University Press.

Patterson, K.D. (1987) 'The specification and stability of the demand for money in the United Kingdom', *Economica*, vol. 54, pp. 41–55.

Pierce, J.L. (1975) 'Interest rates and their prospect in the recovery', *Brookings Papers on Economic Activity*, 1.

Price, L.D.D. (1972) 'The demand for money in the United Kingdom: a further investigation' *Bank of England Quarterly Bulletin*, March.

Roth, H.L. (1986) 'Federal Reserve open market techniques', *Federal Reserve Bank of Kansas City, Economic Review*, March.

Selden, R.T. (1956) 'Monetary velocity in the United States' in M. Friedman (ed.), *Studies in the Quantity Theory of Money*, Chicago: University of Chicago Press.

Sims, G.E. and Takayama, A. (1985) 'On the demand for and supply of money: an empirical study', *Keio Economic Studies*, vol. 22, pp. 1–26.

Spencer, D.E. (1985) 'Money demand and the price level', *Review of Economics and Statistics*, vol. 67, pp. 490–6.

Smith, P.R. (1979) 'A reconsideration of Keynes' finance motive', *Economic Record*, September.

Steindl, F.G. (1973) 'Price expectations and interest rates', *Journal of Money, Credit and Banking*, November.

Thornton, D.L. (1985) 'Money demand dynamics: some new evidence', *Federal Reserve Bank of St Louis Review*', vol. 67, no. 3, March, pp. 14–23.

Tobin, J. (1947) 'Liquidity preference and monetary policy', *Review of Economics and Statistics*, vol. 29, pp. 124–31.

Tobin, J. (1956) 'The interest-elasticity of transactions demand for cash', *Review of Economics and Statistics*, vol. 38, pp. 241–7.

Tobin, J. (1958) 'Liquidity preference as behaviour towards risk', *Review of Economic Studies*, vol. 25, pp. 65–8.

Tobin, J. and Brainard, W.C. (1968) 'Pitfalls in financial model building', *American Economic Review*, May. Reprinted in J. Tobin, *Essays in Economics*, vol. 1, Chicago: Markham, 1971.

Tucker, D. (1966) 'Dynamic income adjustments to money supply changes', *American Economic Review*, vol. 56, pp. 433–49.

Wallich, H.C. (1984) 'Recent techniques of monetary policy', *Federal Reserve Bank of Kansas City, Economic Review*', May, pp. 21–30.

Weale, M. (1986) 'The structure of personal sector short-term asset holdings', *Manchester School*, June, pp. 141–61.

Wenninger, J. (1988) 'Money demand – some long-run properties', *Federal Reserve Bank of New York Quarterly Review*, vol. 13, no. 1, Spring, pp. 23–40.

2 · MONEY MARKET OPERATIONS OF THE BANK OF ENGLAND AND THE DETERMINATION OF INTEREST RATES

David T. Llewellyn

> ... when you come right down to it, the only effective instrument of monetary policy is the short-term rate itself.
>
> (Governor of the Bank of England, 1987)

This chapter focuses upon the Bank of England's (the Bank's) sterling money market operations in the conduct of monetary policy. The focus is upon the institutional mechanisms of monetary policy, and in the process an institutional view of the determination of interest rates is given.

There are many unique features of the UK institutional structure which, when combined, mean that the implementation and execution of monetary policy is a more complex process than in most, if not all, other countries. Some of these complexities derive from the central position of the Bank of England in the financial system, and the many roles it performs; it serves as the government's bank, the banks' bank, and it also manages the government's foreign exchange reserves and national debt. A major implication of this is that there are substantial injections and withdrawals of funds from the money markets in the normal course of business, and as these business transactions necessarily involve the Bank of England, and its relationship with banks and the central government, it cannot avoid being involved with substantial money market operations on a daily basis.

THE INSTITUTIONAL FRAMEWORK

In practice short-run monetary policy adjustments are made through Bank of England transactions in three key markets (money, bonds and foreign

---

I am grateful to Brian Tew, Paul Herrington and Subrata Ghatak for comments on an early draft of this chapter. The opinions expressed and any errors are my responsibility alone.

exchange). Two unique institutional features are particularly relevant to the way the Bank operates in these markets: the role of the operational deposits the clearing banks maintain at the Bank of England; and the pivotal position of the discount houses. In addition, the institutional mechanisms in the conduct of monetary policy derive partly from the many different roles performed by the Bank and in particular its role as banker to the central government and the clearing banks and discount houses. The central government maintains its own accounts at the Bank, and all banks are required to maintain cash-ratio deposits at the Bank. The Bank's monetary policy operations are conducted on the basis of a comparatively small balance sheet. The major transactions of the Bank are reflected in changes in the balance sheet of the Banking Department with bankers' deposits being of particular significance though observed *ex-post* changes will always be very small even though sometimes substantial *ex-ante* movements are the focus of the Bank's monetary policy operations.

Operational deposits

An important distinction is made between clearing banks and non-clearing banks. Non-clearing banks hold their own accounts for settlement purposes at clearing banks, while clearing banks maintain their working balances (known as *operational deposits* (ODs)) at the Bank of England. This means that the clearing banks have a pivotal position in *any* transaction that involves the Bank or central government.

In most countries banks are required to maintain deposits at the central bank, and in many countries the minimum amount of such deposits is fixed by reference to the total of each bank's liabilities. Under arrangements adopted in August 1981, all banks (clearing and non-clearing) are required to maintain cash-ratio deposits at the Bank equal to 0.5 per cent of eligible liabilities (0.4 per cent since 1986) but they perform no prudential or monetary policy role. Given that they receive no interest they are designed solely to generate income for the Bank to finance its own operating expenditure. In addition, clearing banks (the ultimate channel for payments as between banks and their customers, on the one hand, and the Bank and central government on the other) maintain additional amounts as ODs for the settlement of daily clearing balances and to meet withdrawals of bank notes; these are also included in bankers' deposits. No level is imposed by the Bank though each bank is required to declare its own target level and this is used by the Bank as the basis for its money market operations.

Operational deposits are the banks' means of net settlement in all transactions between themselves. Similarly, all transactions with the Bank and central government (either on their own account or by the banks' customers) are settled through ODs. In practice, while the banks' cash-ratio deposits necessarily rise in line with their total eligible liabilities, there is no trend in ODs. The demand for ODs is a function not of the size of the balance sheet but of expected net clearings which are not related in any systematic way to the volume of total deposits. The clearing banks always attempt to keep their ODs at a minimum, given that no interest is received on them, and if a bank has ODs in excess of its declared target level it will immediately seek to exchange them for an earning asset. Conversely, if they fall below the target level action is taken to replenish them.

The total of bankers' deposits changes only through transactions which involve either the banks (clearing and non-clearing) or their customers and one of three counterparties: the Bank of England, the central government, or the discount houses. As the Bank of England is the banker to the government, the clearing banks and the discount houses, it is necessarily involved on a day-to-day basis with the transactions that take place either between them or with the banks' customers. Given the size and daily volatility of central government transactions, there can be substantial net changes in ODs deriving from net payments to (receipts from) the central government.

The main instruments of monetary policy are transactions in financial markets by the Bank, and the effects of these are complex and depend upon who the counterparties are. Any transaction where the counterparty is a non-bank induces an equal change in both bank deposits and the banks' operational deposits. On the other hand, if the counterparty is a bank there is no direct effect upon the money supply but banks' operational deposits are affected. If, for instance, the Bank of England purchases commercial bills from a clearing bank the latter's operational deposits rise though this is reversed when the bills mature. All Bank transactions have a direct impact on ODs irrespective of who the counterparty is.

The discount market

Before considering the detailed operational procedures of the Bank of England reference needs to be made to the discount market. The eight discount houses that make the market are a unique feature of the British financial system and, despite its comparatively small size, the discount market plays a central role in the way the Bank conducts its monetary policy operations. The discount houses make secondary markets in a range of short-term financial instruments including Treasury and commercial bills. As market-makers in commercial bills they stand ready to buy and sell from the banks.

The discount houses stand between the Bank of England and the banks as far as monetary policy transactions are concerned. Their role in this derives from the Bank dealing almost exclusively with discount houses and always being prepared (at a price) to provide liquidity to the market via the purchase of bills or by direct loans secured by money market paper. This gives the discount houses a unique role in the way monetary policy transactions are conducted. By providing the link between the Bank and the clearing banks they are the channel for the Bank's money market transactions, whereas in other countries the central bank conducts its operations directly with banks. The discount houses have a pivotal position; clearing banks can adjust their liquidity position via transactions with the discount market, and the Bank provides support to the banking system via the discount houses. In their continuous daily operations (with discount houses, the Bank of England and the central government) banks gain and lose operational deposits which may be adjusted via transactions with the discount houses. The specific role of the discount houses in the Bank's money market operations is considered in detail on pages 73–5.

Supply and demand for operational deposits

In view of the pivotal role of bankers' deposits in the transactions of the Bank of England the factors determining their supply and demand are summarized. Demand has two components: cash-ratio deposits of all banks, and operational deposits of the clearing banks only. As the former must be maintained at 0.4 per cent of eligible liabilities the demand rises proportionately with the size of the balance sheet, though with a six-month lag, given that cash-ratio deposit requirements are calculated on a six-month basis.

The clearing banks' demand for ODs is small and related not to the absolute size of the balance sheet but to anticipated net clearings. Each clearing bank is required to set a target level and to declare this to the Bank of England, and there is only a comparatively small tolerance of deviations from this target; any amount above this level implies an unnecessary loss of earnings to the bank which means that it will always (on a daily basis) seek to switch from excess ODs into an earning asset perhaps via a transaction with a discount house or another bank. The Bank of England, on the other hand, will not tolerate a persistent shortfall below a bank's declared target level. While cash-ratio deposits have risen steadily, ODs have been remarkably stable, suggesting that the need for ODs is not related to the absolute size of the banks' balance sheets.

The volume of ODs is determined by the net flow of all financial transactions between the private sector (banks and non-banks), on the one hand, and the Bank or central government, on the other. Because the central government banks with the Bank of England, any financial flow from the private sector to the central government (e.g. through taxation payments or purchase of central government debt) or to the Bank of England (e.g. the Bank sells foreign currency) implies an automatic and equal reduction in operational deposits. This is true whether the transaction of the Bank of England is with a bank customer (banking with either a clearing bank or a non-clearing bank), a non-clearing bank, or a clearing bank.

The financial flows determining the volume of bankers' deposits can be categorized as follows:

1. Autonomous flows:
(a) central government borrowing requirement or debt repayment;
(b) foreign exchange market intervention;
(c) issue of notes and coin;
(d) Bank of England purchases of bonds with a year or less to maturity (the Bank regularly buys these bonds ahead of the date of maturity).

2. Policy-induced flows: sales of central government debt to the non-bank private sector.

3. Money market management flows:
(a) Bank of England loans to discount houses;
(b) Bank of England purchases of bills from discount houses;
(c) sale and repurchase transactions with banks and discount houses;
(d) foreign exchange 'swaps';
(e) Bank of England sales of Treasury bills to banks and discount houses.

4. Maturity flows: the reverse flows implied by the maturing of an asset under (3).

Autonomous flows are those (such as tax payments and government expenditure) which are neither specifically designed to affect the money supply, nor made as part of the Bank's management of domestic money markets. *Policy-induced flows* are those associated directly with attempts to restrain the growth of bank deposits held by the private sector. *Money market management flows* are those transactions undertaken by the Bank with either the discount houses or (unusually) the banks specifically in order to restore or lower operational deposits. Such transactions are associated with day-to-day management of the money markets and are closely related to the Bank's current interest rate policy. *Maturity flows* are the counterpart of money market management flows and are substantial on a daily basis, given the volume of management transactions and their short maturity.

It follows that through category (3) transactions the Bank has the over-

Table 2.1 Influences on bankers' deposits at the Bank of England (+ is a factor increasing bankers' deposits)

	Factors affecting market's cash position					Bank of England offsetting operations					
Month/ year	Central government borrowing requirement (+)	Net sales (–) of central government debt[a]	Increase (–) in currency in circulation	Other[b]	Total	Net increase (+) in Bank's commercial bills	Net increase (–) in Treasury bills in market	Securities acquired (+) under sale and repurchase agreements	Other[c]	Total	Net change in bankers' balances
3/81–5/81	+5.0		-5.1		-0.1	-0.4	+0.3	—	—	-0.1	-0.2
6/81–8/81	+4.9		-3.1		+1.8	—	-1.4	—	-0.2	-1.6	+0.1
9/81–11/81	—		-2.9		-2.9	+1.6	+1.0	—	+0.1	2.7	-0.1
12/81–2/82	-1.3		-2.1	—	-3.4	+2.9	+0.1	+0.4	—	+3.4	—
3/82–5/82	+1.1		-2.8		-1.7	+1.3	+0.2	—	+0.2	+1.7	—
6/82–8/82	+3.3	-3.2	-0.4	+0.1	-0.1	+0.4	-0.1	—	-0.2	+0.2	—
9/82–11/82	+2.9	-3.5	+0.1	—	-0.5	+1.5	-0.5	—	-0.4	+0.6	+0.1
12/82–2/83	+1.4	-1.6	-0.2	-0.9	-1.3	-0.3	+0.6	+0.9	—	+1.3	-0.1
3/83–5/83	+6.0	-2.5	-0.3	-0.2	+2.9	-1.6	-0.3	-0.9	-0.1	-2.9	—
6/83–8/83	+4.9	-3.6	-0.3	—	+1.1	-1.1	-0.3	+0.9	-0.7	-1.1	—
9/83–11/83	+2.3	-4.3	—	—	-2.0	+2.1	+0.3	—	-0.2	+2.1	+0.1

12/83–2/84	+0.3	-2.7	-0.1	-0.3	-2.8	+2.6	+0.1	—	+0.2	+2.8	+0.1
3/84–5/84	+4.3	-2.7	-0.3	-0.5	+0.3	-1.0	-0.1	—	+0.2	-0.9	-0.1
6/84–8/84	+3.1	-3.2	-0.4	-0.1	-0.5	+0.6	—	—	-0.2	+0.4	-0.1
9/84–11/84	+3.4	-4.3	—	+0.5	-0.3	+0.8	+0.2	—	—	+1.0	+0.2
12/84–2/85	-1.6	-3.1	—	—	-4.7	+1.5	-0.1	+3.2	+0.1	+4.6	-0.1
3/85–5/85	+3.6	-4.4	-0.3	+0.5	-0.5	+0.7	—	+0.2	-0.3	+0.7	+0.1
6/85–8/85	+3.8	-2.5	-0.4	+0.9	+1.8	-2.2	-0.2	+0.1	+0.4	-1.9	-0.1
9/85–11/85	+4.9	-2.4	+0.2	-0.3	+2.4	-0.4	—	-1.8	-0.1	-2.3	+0.1
12/85–2/86	-2.0	-0.2	-0.1	+0.4	-2.7	+2.1	+0.4	+0.8	-0.4	+2.6	-0.1
3/86–5/86	+6.8	-1.7	-0.4	+1.4	+6.1	-3.3	-0.3	-1.9	-0.4	-5.9	+0.2
6/86–8/86	+4.2	-5.1	-0.3	-0.1	-1.3	+1.1	—	—	+0.2	+1.3	-0.1
9/86–12/86	-1.1	-3.0	-1.0	+0.9	-4.2	+5.0	-0.4	—	-0.4	+4.2	-0.1
1/87–3/87	+1.3	+0.7	+1.0	+0.7	+3.7	-5.7	-0.4	+1.1	+1.4	-3.6	+0.1
4/87–6/87	+4.0	-2.2	-0.4	+4.4	+5.8	-2.3	-1.3	-1.1	-1.2	-5.9	-0.1
7/87–9/87	+0.4	-2.0	-0.3	+0.6	-1.3	+0.4	+0.9	—	-0.1	+1.2	-0.1
10/87–12/87	-1.6	-3.0	-1.4	+5.5	-0.3	+2.0	-1.4	—	-0.2	+0.4	+0.1

[a]Excluding Treasury bills
[b]Including change in foreign currency reserves
[c]Including loans to discount houses

whelming influence on the volume of bankers' deposits as in principle it can choose how, with whom, and by how much to transact. In the final analysis a Bank of England purchase of *any* asset from *any* sector generates an equal volume of bankers' deposits. But the Bank operates on a daily basis so as to supply its own estimate of the need for operational deposits. The Bank never refuses to meet the demand for bankers' deposits and in that sense the volume might be said to be 'demand-determined'. A summary of the influences on the volume of bankers' deposits is given in Table 2.1 in terms of the factors daily identified and published by the Bank of England. The factors are divided into what earlier were termed *autonomous* and *policy-induced*, on the one hand, and those associated specifically with the Bank's operations in the markets to influence the volume of operational deposits, on the other. Throughout the Table a plus sign represents a factor increasing the volume of bankers' deposits.

Two features emerge from the data in Table 2.1. First, there are large offsetting flows within the three categories. This is especially the case with respect to central government flows in that the effect on bankers' deposits of large borrowing requirements has almost invariably been offset by central government debt sales. The second observation is that while the *autonomous* and *policy* pressures may at times be substantial, they are always almost exactly offset by Bank of England market transactions. Thus while the sum of *policy* and *autonomous* transactions has been as high as £6 billion, the net change in bankers' deposits has never exceeded £0.2 billion in any quarter.

OPERATIONS OF THE BANK OF ENGLAND

Most of the Bank's money market transactions are conducted in eligible bills comprising Treasury bills, eligible local authority bills and eligible bank commercial bills. In practice the bulk of transactions are conducted against commercial bills as the volume of Treasury bills (historically the more important) held by the banks has declined to a low level (Bank of England, 1982a; 1982c). Between 1980 and 1986 the volume of Treasury bills held by banks was reduced from £2 billion to £0.5 billion.

Although the Bank always accommodates the need for bankers' deposits, the techniques it adopts have varied over time. The traditional approach was for the Bank to announce its official discount rate (the Bank Rate until 1972 and thereafter the official Minimum Lending Rate (MLR) until 1981) which was the rate at which it would provide funds to the discount houses either by direct loans or by rediscounting Treasury bills. Commercial banks in turn set their interest rates on the basis of the Bank's rate. The Bank would make its own rate effective (through issuing Treasury bills in excess of what was necessary to meet the central government's own financing requirement) by ensuring that the discount houses were always short of funds (Bank of England, 1963, 1983). This was always effective as the discount houses agreed to cover the whole of each week's Treasury bill issue. Thus the Bank would always aim to keep the market slightly short of funds on a daily basis so that it could maintain its control over interest rates via the terms on which it itself relieved the shortages that were deliberately created. In the period 1972–8 MLR was itself determined by a formula related to Treasury bill rates but this procedure was abandoned as the Bank wished to re-establish full control over MLR.

Under the old regime (and until 1981) the Bank operated in bill markets at rates which were known and predetermined and set for a week at a time. The market always knew the rate of interest at which the Bank would make assistance available. Interest rates were viewed as being unambiguously determined by the Bank.

The Conservative government elected in 1979 planned to give greater primacy to monetary policy in the management of the economy. It also judged that market mechanisms should play a greater role and that the Bank and government should have a less obtrusive role in the determination of interest rates. There was, as a result of this, considerable policy debate about the conduct of monetary policy and, in particular, about monetary base control which would imply setting a target for the monetary base and allowing interest rates to adjust to resultant market pressures (Bank of England, 1980). Several changes were planned to take effect in 1981 (Bank of England, 1983), though, in practice, the changes under the new regime have proved to be less significant than was intended:

1. The Bank would no longer quote prices at which it would deal in bills; it would respond to offers made by the discount houses but would not necessarily deal.
2. The practice of deliberately creating a permanent shortage in the money markets by the overissue of Treasury bills would cease.
3. The intention was that the Bank would intervene in the money markets so as to keep very short-term (up to seven days) interest rates within an unpublished band. Intervention was to be restricted predominantly to the very short end of the market (and then within the range of an unpublished band) leaving other interest rates to be determined by market pressures.
4. The formal weekly announcement of MLR was abandoned on 13 August 1981, though for some time previously it had been of symbolic significance only as the Bank had reduced its direct dealing via the discount office with the discount houses and had been charging other rates of interests.

5. The Bank would concentrate its support operations on transactions in bills rather than loans to the discount houses (this new procedure having been adopted in November 1980). Under the previous regime the Bank was at times prepared to lend on a continuous basis to the discount market as the houses could not meet their requirements in any other way.

The objective was for there to be an approximate balance in the markets on a daily basis, and to allow market forces to play a more dominant role in the determination of interest rates and to 'depoliticize' the process. At the same time more flexibility would be introduced into the Bank's market operations.

In fact the 'new regime' has not worked as originally envisaged. From the outset it was strained because, as a result of overfunding (itself due to the sale of gilts to moderate the growth of the money stock) and the continuous liquidity pressures associated with maturing bills held by the Bank, there has been a permanent shortage of funds and the market has been continuously seeking Bank of England assistance. In practice, the ending of the overissue of Treasury bills was a necessary but not sufficient condition to prevent the market having a permanent shortage of central bank money. The system has not operated as originally intended in three other ways:

1. The unpublished 'band' has always been very narrow, with the Bank setting a precise level of its intervention rates.
2. The Bank has not restricted its intervention to the very shortest end of the maturity spectrum of bills (band 1, i.e. 1–14 days' maturity; see below) and frequently intervenes in longer maturities.
3. The Bank frequently offers assistance directly to the discount houses via loans.

The main factor undermining the original intention has been the almost permanent daily shortages in the market. This has necessitated large-scale one-way intervention by the Bank. As the market has therefore needed almost permanent assistance from the Bank, the Bank's transactions have become an integral part of the 'market mechanism'. In practice, therefore, the new regime has not been fundamentally different from the traditional practice of the Bank's market operations.

Current practice

Soon after the markets open each day the Bank publishes the first forecast of the expansionary and contractionary factors expected during the day determining changes in the volume of operational deposits. The way the

Bank makes the forecast is described in Bank of England (1988). The Bank may revise its forecast during the day and, similarly, banks and discount houses will be making forecasts of their own daily position. Thus, the Bank knows whether the banks will be short of ODs in the absence of official intervention. The precise daily timetable of operations is given in Bank of England (1982a).

In most countries any aggregate shortage of the equivalent of ODs (e.g. Federal funds in the United States) is replenished by the central bank transacting directly with the banks with a shortage. The institutional mechanism is more complex in the United Kingdom because of the intermediate role of the discount houses. Any shortage of ODs relates to the position of clearing banks and the Bank of England is the ultimate source of ODs to the system. But as, in its money market operations, the Bank deals only with the discount houses, any shortage must somehow be passed to them. Thus two mechanisms and sets of transactions need to be considered: how the clearing banks respond to a shortage of ODs; and how the discount houses subsequently balance their own books, bearing in mind that they are not passive agents in the process but have their own portfolio and profits to consider.

The banks' reactions

If, as a result of the various pressures, a clearing bank is short of ODs, it has six basic options in rectifying this situation:

1. It can attempt to secure more customer deposits.
2. It can bid in the interbank market.
3. It can call in loans from the discount houses, though only before noon.
4. It can borrow from a discount house at any time.
5. It can sell bills to the discount houses.
6. It can conduct a transaction directly with the Bank of England, though this is rare and occurs only at the initiative of the Bank.

An individual clearing bank may gain ODs through transactions (1) and (2), though, as this causes an equal loss by another clearing bank (whether the funds secured are from a clearing or a non-clearing bank), this is not a mechanism for relieving an aggregate shortage. As the ultimate source of ODs is the Bank of England, and as, in its money market operations, the Bank deals only with discount houses, eventually an aggregate shortage of ODs must be reflected in clearing bank transactions with the discount houses – transactions (3), (4) and (5). This, in effect, passes the 'problem' to the discount houses.

A bank can withdraw call money (the bank gains ODs and loses call money assets) or sell assets (an exchange of bills for ODs), or borrow from a discount house. In practice, banks tend not to use the first option as there is now little genuine call money, with the majority of deposits with the discount houses being placed for fixed periods of three months but with an informal understanding that they may be called in need – 'callable fixtures'. In practice, calls are rarely made and cause considerable upset when they are because it involves breaking a term deposit. In general, withdrawal of deposits from the discount houses happens through the non-renewal of overnight or short fixed-term deposits rather than calling *per se*. In all cases the bank gains ODs (because the discount houses bank at the Bank of England) and either a loss of some other asset or a liability against a discount house.

The discount houses' response

Thus shortages will be passed to the discount houses with which the Bank transacts in its normal money market business. Discount houses receive assistance from the Bank in several ways. The first is through transactions in bills, with the houses usually being able to sell eligible bills to the Bank at noon, i.e. after banks have withdrawn or placed call money and undertaken transactions in bills with the discount houses. A second opportunity to transact in bills may be made available at 2 p.m. If a discount house becomes short after its 2 p.m. dealing in bills it can seek a direct loan ('late assistance') from the Bank at 2.45 p.m. Direct assistance from the Bank can also be sought at 3 p.m. or even later, but at a mild penal rate, and a discount house should not use this facility on a regular basis. There are in practice daily variations in the procedure. Thus, the discount houses have two basic options in a situation where they have to balance their own books because of transactions with clearing banks: offer bills to the Bank of England, or borrow from the Bank against the collateral of bills. If, for any reason, they wish to hold on to their holdings of bills (perhaps because of an expectation of a fall in interest rates) they will choose to borrow from the Bank, doing so at 2.45 pm. or later.

In practice, and given the size of daily shortages (partly because of the large volume of maturing bills held by the Bank) it is frequently the case that both types of transaction are undertaken. For instance, in the period from September 1986 to November 1988 a sample selection of months indicates that late assistance (i.e. direct borrowing by discount houses from the Bank) was given on 66 per cent of the Bank's trading days. It is possible, for instance, that, knowing the dealing rate at which the Bank transacts with them, the discount houses are not prepared to accept bills from the banks at the rates being offered; in which case the banks will bid for funds in the money markets (including from the discount houses) until interbank interest rates rise to a level that makes it profitable for the discount houses to contemplate borrowing from the Bank so as effectively to on-lend to the banks. Clearly, whether it is through loans or by purchase of bills, the discount houses will only accommodate the banks' requirements for ODs at a rate of interest which is above the rate of interest or discount rate at which the Bank of England will deal with them. Thus, in one way or another, interest rates adjust so as to ensure that the discount houses accommodate the banks' requirements. It is ultimately through (in practice very small) money market interest rate adjustments that the discount houses profitably accommodate the banks while balancing their own books through transactions with the Bank of England. Whatever the precise mechanism is, the discount houses effectively act as an intermediary between the Bank of England and the clearing banks and on occasion this may mean borrowing from the Bank in order to lend to the banks.

In order to relieve a shortage of funds (the normal position) the Bank usually invites the discount houses to offer eligible bills to the Bank for sale against same-day settlement. Usually, such sales are on an 'outright' basis though at times there may be sale and repurchase transactions (see below). Bills may be offered in four maturity bands (remaining, not original, maturity): band 1, 1–14 days; band 2, 15–33 days; band 3, 34–63 days; band 4, 64–91 days. The Bank decides at its discretion which offers to accept and normally buys paper only up to the estimated amount of the shortage of ODs.

While dealing in eligible bills via the discount market is the norm, there are other techniques in addition to direct loans to the discount houses. If cash is acutely short in the banking system, the Bank may purchase gilt-edged stock directly from commercial banks on a sale and repurchase basis. The future repurchase date may be chosen to coincide with an expected surplus in the market. Sale and repurchase transactions may also be made in bills when, because of interest rate expectations, the market is reluctant to sell bills outright. In the case when the market has a surplus the Bank, at its discretion, invites both the discount houses and the clearing banks to bid for Treasury bills so as to absorb the surplus. The Bank decides on the maturity of the Treasury bills it wishes to offer (usually short-term and often one-day) and invites bids for them.

THE LEVEL OF INTEREST RATES

Having outlined the institutional mechanisms and techniques of Bank of England operations in the money markets, we turn to an analysis of the determination of short-term interest rates within this framework. The focus is upon two central issues: the extent of the power of the Bank of England to influence the level of short-term interest rates; and the precise mechanism through which the power operates. Neither is uncontroversial.

Thus the Chancellor of the Exchequer in the 1988 Autumn Statement said: 'When I think [short-term interest rates] should go up they go up, and when I think they should come down they come down.' He later argued that this is done by the Bank of England through its operations in the money markets. On the other hand, the Bank of England has claimed: 'Our ability to determine interest rates is limited, though it is a powerful influence' (Bank of England, 1987).

Any central bank has a powerful potential influence on short-term interest rates because it is the monopoly supplier of bank reserves (Federal funds in the United States, ODs in the United Kingdom) through the transactions it conducts either with the banks or their customers. In the context of the United Kingdom the Bank can determine the precise volume of operational deposits through its market transactions in ways described earlier. The Bank's influence on short-term interest rates ultimately derives from this power although the precise mechanism is not as straightforward as it might at first appear.

The focus of interest rate determination is the volume of ODs and the terms upon which the Bank relieves any shortages through transactions with the discount houses. As already noted, the banks' demand (for target balances) is both very small and totally inelastic with respect to interest rates. On a daily basis there are massive money market flows involving the central government and Bank of England that impinge upon the volume of operational deposits. On the fact of it, therefore, a comparatively small deficiency of ODs could have a major impact on interest rates as banks bid in the markets to restore them to the target levels.

The Bank has two possible routes through which to influence interest rates: by aggressively determining the volume of ODs; and/or by determining the price at which it relieves shortages in the market. The former, if it were used, would be a version of monetary base control. In practice the Bank always ensures that, through its market transactions with the discount houses, the banks are provided with their target level of ODs. However, the Bank determines the terms of support by the price at which it is prepared to buy bills from the discount houses.

The two alternative routes (polar cases) are illustrated in Figure 2.1; we leave for the moment the crucial issue as to what rate of interest is measured on the vertical axis. The key issue is the nature of the supply curve as determined by the Bank of England. Under a strict monetary base control regime the central bank would operate on the banks' *total* deposits at the central bank, the demand for which is a derived demand determined by the banks' overall balance sheet position. The banks' elasticity of demand for reserves would be derived from the interest sensitivity of the banks' total balance sheet position. In this regime the central bank supplies its chosen level of central bank money and interest rates adjust to any

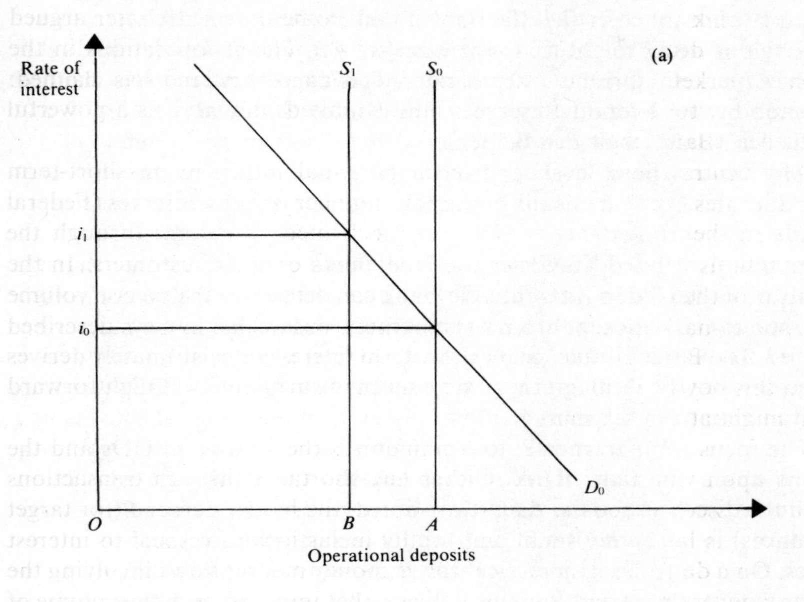
(a)
Rate of interest
S_1
S_0
i_1
i_0
D_0
O
B
A
Operational deposits

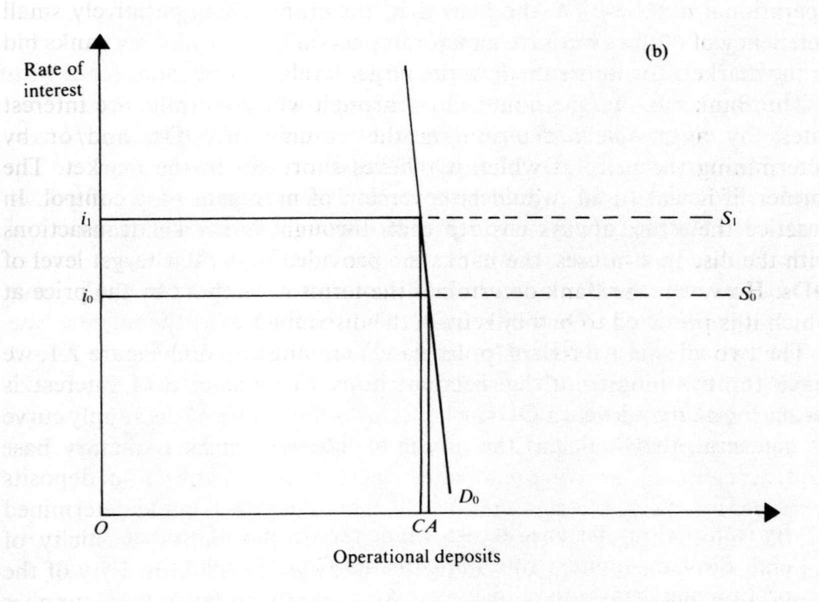
(b)
Rate of interest
i_1
S_1
i_0
S_0
D_0
O
C
A
Operational deposits

Figure 2.1

excess supply or demand (Llewellyn, 1985). If, for instance, initial equilibrium in Figure 2.1(a) were at i_0 with the volume of operational deposits determined at *OA*, the Bank could engineer a rise in interest rates to i_1 by operating to reduce the volume by *AB*. The excess demand (*BA*) induces the desired rise in interest rates. This approximates to the method adopted by the Federal Reserve in the United States between 1979 and 1982. The same result can be achieved by a shift in an infinitely elastic supply curve whose level is determined exogenously by the Bank of England and set at its dealing rate (i.e. the rate at which it is willing to relieve any shortages).

If, as in the United Kingdom, the Bank operates on ODs rather than the total of bankers' deposits, the relevant demand curve will be completely inelastic as ODs are kept to a basic minimum and the banks' demand is not related to the size of the balance sheet. An infinitely elastic supply curve indicates that the Bank is prepared to supply any amount of ODs (through its transactions in bill markets) but only at its chosen interest rate. Thus a shift in Figure 2.1(b) from S_0 to S_1 achieves the same rise in interest rates. If there is a shortage of *AC* (either because the Bank has deliberately created it, or because the daily flow of funds produces a net flow to the Bank of England) the Bank can shift its dealing rate to i_1 and its supply curve from S_0 to S_1. In practice, the Bank only purchases bills up to an amount that is necessary to relieve the market shortage on a daily basis; in terms of Figure 2.1(b), this means that the supply curve is not perfectly elastic at all volumes but becomes vertical at *OA*.

Figure 2.1 is for illustrative purposes only and must be interpreted with caution as, unlike in the United States and other countries, there is no explicit or observable market in ODs and hence no corresponding interest rate. The volume of ODs changes because of any transactions which involve financial flows to either the central government or the Bank of England. Thus the supply curve represents an amalgam of a wide variety of transactions. In practice, however, the Bank of England always ensures through its own operations with the discount houses that the banks have the small volume of ODs they require. Thus in Figure 2.1 the interest rate on the vertical axis is the Bank of England's dealing rate on bills; the rate at which it buys bills from the discount houses to ensure that the banks obtain their target level of ODs.

In general, the Bank has the power to influence market rates in four ways:

1. By transactions designed to determine the volume of bankers' deposits and allowing interest rate adjustments to act directly as the equilibrating mechanism to adjust any excess supply or demand.
2. By setting an administered interest rate (e.g. its dealing rate) and

relieving any shortgage (whether deliberately created or as a result of money market flows) in full at its own dealing rate, and relying upon arbitrage transactions to influence other interest rates.
3. By moral suasion directed at banks, perhaps through a signal (such as a change in an administered interest rate).
4. By operating on market expectations of future interest rates.

In practice the difference is between mechanisms, such as (1), which induce changes in interest rates directly in a 'market-mechanistic' way (i.e. directly in response to excess supply or demand), and those which rely more upon indirect influences though possibly based upon actual or threatened transactions. Thus, the differences between (2), (3) and (4) are of degree rather than fundamental. The power of moral suasion derives ultimately from the banks' and market operators' knowledge that the Bank can, through a comparatively small volume of money market transactions at the margin, determine the volume of ODs and that by initially creating a surplus or deficiency it can then choose the terms under which this is absorbed or relieved. Thus the power of moral suasion derives from the power of the Bank in markets and hence (2) and (3) merge. The fourth mechanism may also be a variant of the other two in that, if the market accepts that the Bank has power, and interprets its actions as a view about what the Bank believes the future course of interest rates should be, then again the Bank is powerful. In this case the Bank may have an influence on maturities longer than the very short-term.

The Bank has never sought to operate variants of monetary base control, preferring instead always to make available whatever level of ODs is necessary to meet the banks' target (Llewellyn and Tew, 1988). Thus route (1) is not in practice followed. The actual method is a complex amalgam of the others. Little has changed over the decades with respect to the basic *modus operandi* of the Bank's operations; it is, as it has always been, by ensuring that the market is short, and hence has to deal with the Bank on its own chosen terms. The precise institutional mechanisms have, however, changed. Historically, the Bank made its rate effective by overissuing Treasury bills thereby creating a shortage which it relieved on its own terms. Since 1981 the Bank has accumulated substantial holdings of commercial bills either in the Issue or Banking departments. The origin of this was a policy of overfunding whereby the government would issue public sector debt in excess of its own borrowing requirement so as to offset the money supply effect of substantial bank lending. In order to relieve the money market pressure on interest rates due to the resultant loss of ODs, the Bank of England purchased substantial volumes of bills from the market during the period 1981–5. The amount held by the Bank in

1988 was £7 billion out of an outstanding total of £21 billion. The amount of the Bank's holdings maturing each day is approximately £300 million and this in itself is a drain on ODs. The 'bill mountain' means that the Bank does not have to aggressively create shortages in the market as the constant daily flow of maturing bills achieves the same effect of enabling the Bank to relieve shortages on its own terms.

The Bank is in a particularly powerful position because it is the monopoly supplier of ODs but can also set the price of its accommodation. As with any monopolist this is possible only because the demand curve is completely inelastic. Thus, in Figure 2.1(b) initial equilibrium is at *OA* and i_0. The Bank induces an initial shortage of *AC*, but restores it through an equal amount of bill purchases, now at a rate i_1 with the new supply curve S_1.

The spectrum of interest rates

The analysis has been considerably simplified by assuming an unspecified single interest rate. Although money market interest rates move closely in line (Figure 2.2), they are not identical and a different analysis is required for each, although, given the high degree of substitutability and the power of arbitrage in efficient markets, the determination of any one would have an influence on all others. Interests rates can be linked through four mechanisms: arbitrage; potential arbitrage (i.e. the setting of one rate automatically induces a change in another as price-setters recognize and anticipate the potential volume of arbitrage transactions); expectations, such as when a shift in, say, the dealing rate, causes expectations to change across the spectrum of interest rates; and moral suasion.

Arbitrage is a powerful mechanism in the London money market as many of the instruments are substitutable for both borrowers and lenders, and banks are substantial holders of commercial bills as well as substantial transactors in the interbank market. In February 1988, of a total of £21.5 billion of bills outstanding, 76 per cent were held by the Bank of England, and 24 per cent by the banks and discount houses. Several arbitrage channels will ensure that the different money market rates do not diverge substantially. Thus, banks would not lend in the interbank market if they are able to secure a higher rate on commercial bills. Similarly, large borrowing customers can switch between bill financing and bank loans based on interbank rates (see Bank of England, 1982b; Hall, 1983). Some borrowers also have the choice between borrowing priced on the basis of Base Rate or interbank rates. In practice, market rates fluctuate around the dealing rate (Figure 2.2) but within limits set by arbitrage and expectations of future movements in short-term rates.

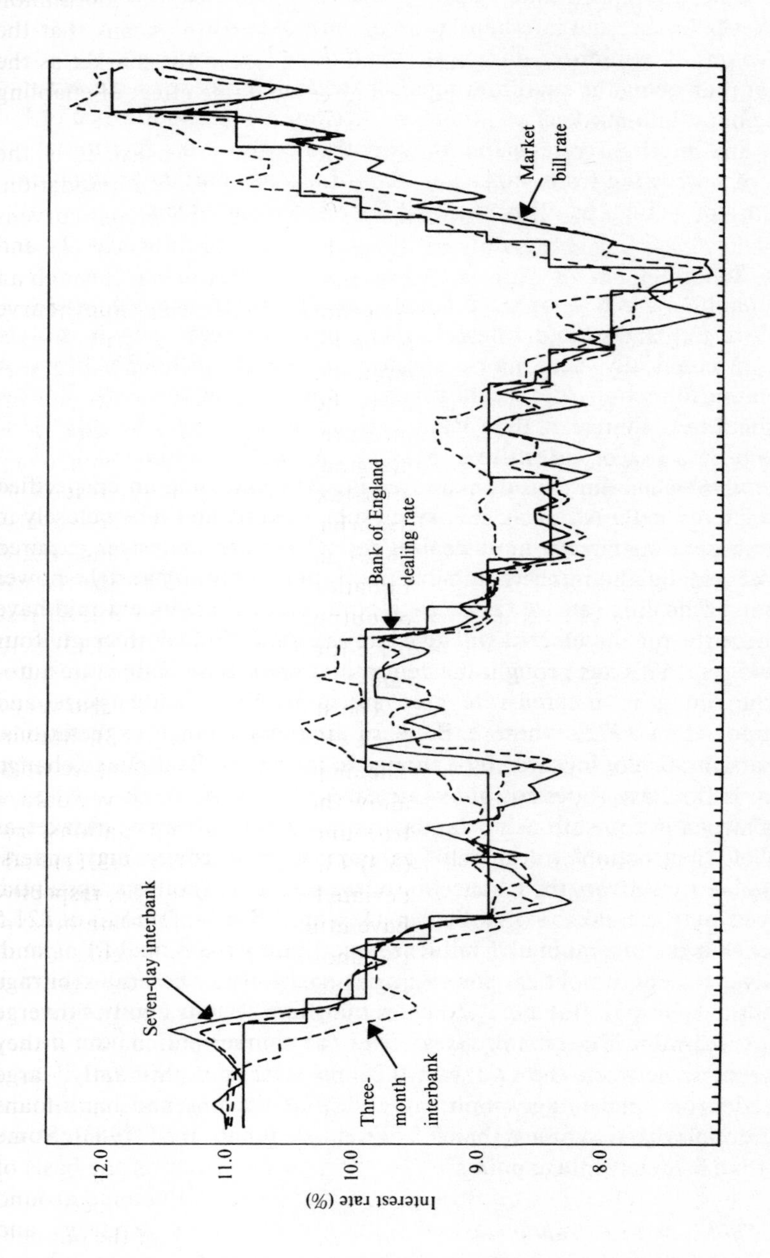

Figure 2.2 UK short-term interest rates

Five sets of short-term interest rates in particular need to be explained: Base Rate; the Bank's band 1 dealing rate; the dealing rate on other bands; market bill rates; and interbank rates of various maturities. This amounts to two sets of administered interest rates (in that they are set autonomously rather than being the equilibrating mechanism in response to excess supply or demand in a market) and three market rates. The significance of Base Rate and interbank rates is that they are the bench-marks determining the cost of borrowing from banks and the former has particular significance because of its high public profile and announcement effects.

Base Rate

The banks' Base Rate is maintained at a level 0.125 per cent above the Bank of England's band 1 dealing rate and in this way one administered rate mechanically determines another. However, although the overwhelming direction of causation runs from a signal from the Bank of England to a change in Base Rate, this is not invariably the case. There have been a few occasions (e.g. May and July 1984, January, April and June 1985) when Barclays Bank moved its Base Rate first, possibly against the wish of the Bank of England which subsequently and reluctantly made a corresponding change in its dealing rate. The norm, however, is for the Bank formally and publicly to move first in one of two ways: by changing its band 1 dealing rate; or, as on each occasion in 1988, by announcing in advance the rate at which it will give late assistance to the discount houses at 2.45 p.m. This has brought the determination of Base Rate almost back to the old administered-rate mechanism of Bank Rate (which was abandoned in 1972) where a Bank of England change in Bank Rate was automatically followed by a change in the banks' Base Rate. Thus the norm is for Base Rates to follow a clear signal of the Bank of England. This mechanistic relationship can be interpreted in two ways: either as an implicit 'instruction' (ultimately, as implied by the statement quoted earlier, deriving from the Chancellor of the Exchequer) or as a signal to be obeyed by the banks (as implied in Dow and Saville, 1988, when they argue that the central bank's influence over Base Rate is analogous to the 'elusive concept of political power'); or alternatively by banks anticipating potential arbitrage. Table 2.2 indicates that Base Rate is highly correlated with three-month interbank rates. Over the sample period, the average differential between the two was 0.22 percentage points and it never exceeded one percentage point; over 90% of the observations indicate differentials equal to or less than 0.5 percentage points and 70% equal to or less than 0.25 percentage points.

The Bank's band 1 dealing rate

This is an administered rate and can, for most purposes, be taken as

Table 2.2 Interest rate differentials (percentage points)

	Dealing rate and band 1 market rate (1)	Dealing rate and 7-day interbank rate (2)	Market bill rate and 7-day interbank rate (3)	7-day and 3-month interbank rate (4)	Dealing rate and 3-month interbank rate (5)	Base rate and 3-month interbank rate (6)
(1) *7 January – 20 May 1987*						
Average	0.16	0.23	0.11	0.34	0.25	0.30
Maximum	0.38	0.75	0.38	1.25	0.82	0.94
Observed differentials						
⩽0.5 percentage points	100%	85%	100%	80%	95%	80%
⩽0.25 percentage points	90%	80%	95%	60%	80%	55%
(2) *27 April – 21 September 1988*						
Average	0.40	0.59	0.36	0.98	0.33	0.21
Maximum	1.25	1.63	1.00	1.75	0.75	0.63
Observed differentials						
⩽0.5 percentage points	72%	41%	77%	18%	86%	95%
⩽0.25 percentage points	45%	18%	50%	9%	45%	73%
(3) *7 January 1987 – 21 September 1988*						
Average	0.22	0.34	0.20	0.55	0.28	0.22
Maximum	1.25	1.63	1.00	1.75	1.37	0.94
Observed differentials						
⩽0.5 percentage points	90%	73%	93%	58%	90%	93%
⩽0.25 percentage points	71%	59%	74%	34%	57%	70%

[a]Signs of differentials are ignored when calculating averages.

exogenous. On the face of it, it might be argued that if this rate acts as an anchor and is the dominant influence on all others then the Bank is decisive in the determination of short-term interest rates. However, this conclusion cannot be accepted without further investigation, as three issues need to be addressed. First, is the Bank a totally free agent in the setting of this rate? Second, if it does influence other rates, which of the various mechanisms described above (arbitrage, etc.) is the correct explanation? Third, how precise and stable is the relationship with other interest rates?

Other dealing rates

The Bank gives assistance by buying bills from the discount houses in any of the four maturity bands. In most cases this is done on the basis of a slightly declining *discount* curve. Thus the discount rate on band 4 bills may be up to 0.25 percentage points below band 1 bills. Arithmetically, this implies a flat *yield* curve and this is the norm in the Bank's transactions. Nevertheless, there have been periods (e.g. from December 1982 to March 1983, and from May 1987 to August 1988) when the discount rates were the same in all four bands, implying a rising yield curve. These were periods when the Bank initially allowed interest rates to fall because of exchange rate pressure on sterling, though on domestic grounds it judged that a fall in interest rates was inappropriate. A rising yield curve was viewed as a signal to this effect by the Bank, which felt that any decline would be temporary. In the second period Base Rates were lowered from 9.5 per cent in April 1987 to 7.5 per cent in May 1988. The flat yield curve was reinstated in August 1988 after interest rates had risen to 12 per cent, which the Bank considered more appropriate on domestic grounds.

Market bill rates

As the banks and the Bank of England are dominant holders of bills, and the Bank conducts its money market transactions in this instrument, it is unlikely that the market rate on short-term bills could deviate substantially from the Bank's dealing rate. Table 2.2 indicates that, over the sample period from January 1987 to September 1988, the market rate on band 1 bills differed from the Bank's dealing rate on average by 0.22 percentage points, though it fluctuated around this figure and, for one week in September 1988, widened to as much as 1.25 percentage points. However, of the ninety weekly observations in Table 2.2, in only six did the market rate diverge from the dealing rate by more than 0.5 percentage points. Thus, the Bank's chosen dealing rate is reflected in one of the money market rates. In May 1988 the Bank bought £8.6 billion in bank bills (about £400 million per weekday), and in June purchased £3.5 billion. This suggests that over 50 per cent of the bills accepted are at some stage bought by the Bank. Table 2.3 indicates that the Bank's daily operations in the

Table 2.3 Bank of England money market operations, 1987 (£ million)[a]

	Bills	Late assistance	Total	Sale and repurchase agreements
January	8.1	1.6	9.7	3.7
February	8.3	1.5	9.8	2.4
March	7.8	3.2	11.0	4.0
	– 0.1			
April	9.7	1.2	10.9	0.9
	– 0.1			
May	5.8	1.7	7.5	0.7
	– 0.4			
June	9.6	1.9	11.5	—
July	11.7	2.2	13.9	0.7
August	5.2	1.9	7.1	—
	– 0.2			
September	4.2	2.0	6.2	—
	– 0.4			
October	5.3	2.8	8.1	2.3
	– 0.1			
November	6.6	3.6	10.2	3.9
December	10.3	3.0	13.3	3.1

[a]Sum of daily volumes: minus figures are sales of Treasury bills to absorb market surpluses.

money markets (predominantly in bills) are substantial and hence that it is not feasible to imagine that the Bank's dealing rate would not be closely reflected in the interest rate on bills in the market; this is clearly reflected in Figure 2.2.

Interbank rates

Arbitrage normally ensures that interbank rates also reflect movements in the Bank's dealing rate. In practice, the longer the maturity of interbank rates the less precise is the relationship with the Bank's dealing rate as the role of expectations about future movements in interest rates becomes more significant, and therefore bills and interbank transactions become less substitutable. In practice, for instance, in the period from January 1987 to September 1988, the three-month interbank rate fluctuated around the dealing rate within a margin of about ± 1.5 per cent, and tended to be lower than the Bank's intervention rate when interest rates were expected to fall and *vice versa*. However, over the sample period, although the differential between the Bank's dealing rate and the three-month interbank rate widened to as much as 1.75 percentage points, of the ninety observations in the sample period, seventy-eight ranged from –0.5 to +0.5 percentage points, and fifty ranged from –0.25 to +0.25 percentage points.

Case study: 1987 and 1988

The structure of short-term interest rates is summarized in Figure 2.2 and Table 2.2 for a sample period from January 1987 to September 1988 – a total of ninety Wednesday observations. The five rates considered are the Bank of England's band 1 bill dealing rate; the market rate on band 1 bills; seven-day and three-month interbank rates; and the banks' Base Rate. The comparison of levels and differentials is not strictly accurate in that the dealing rate and the market rate for bills are quoted on a discount basis while others are on an interest-yield basis. The latter is higher than the former by an amount that depends upon the maturity of the instrument. When yields are around 10% the yield calculation exceeds the discount calculation by about 0.25 percentage points.

Figure 2.2 shows a powerful trend parallel movement of short interest rates; the Base Rate is not shown but is invariably above the dealing rate by 0.125 percentage points. However, it also indicates that, except for the impact on Base Rate, the Bank's influence on market interest rates (market bill rates or interbank rates) through the setting of its dealing rate is far from precise or stable. Market rates are not rigidly determined by the Bank of England but fluctuate around the Bank's dealing rate. It cannot be said that the Bank in any way 'fixes' the whole spectrum of short-term interest rates, though, while variable, the correlation between the dealing rate and other rates is high.

The period is summarized in Table 2.2 with respect to calculated interest rate differentials which ignore the sign; thus the average of two differentials +0.5 and –0.5 is shown as 0.5 and not zero. As there is a presumption that differentials might be wider and more volatile when rates are moving frequently and sharply two sub-periods (one where the trend of interest rates was sharply downwards and the other when interest rates were on a strong rising trend) have been highlighted. Taking the period as a whole the closest relationship appears to be between market bill rates and the seven-day interbank rate (column 3); over 90% of the observations were of a differential equal to or less than 0.5 percentage points and 74% with a differential equal to or less than 0.25 percentage points. Thus arbitrage between these instruments is likely to be high. Similarly, there is a close relationship between the Bank's dealing rate and the market rate on short-term bills (column 1).

Given the role of expectations, it might be expected that the Bank's dealing rate might not be highly correlated with the three-month interbank rate. In fact for the period as a whole (although it was not typical in that all four dealing rates were always the same) 90% of the observations indicated a differential of 0.5 percentage points or less and 57% of 0.25 percentage points or less (column 5).

An apparent paradox

A central proposition in the analysis has been that ODs are the centrepiece of the determination of short-term interest rates. On the face of it, it might appear curious that a wide range of money market and bank interest rates are driven, if not explicitly determined, by Bank of England transactions with banks (via the discount houses) which are a small proportion of the volume of total transactions in the money market and the banks' total business and balance sheet. It might appear to be a case of the 'tail wagging the dog'! This scepticism is adopted by Dow and Saville who, for instance, argue that the amount of bankers' deposits needed by the banks is so small that the costs that the central bank can impose on them by raising its dealing rate 'are in fact trivial' (Dow and Saville, 1988, p. 132). This also seems to be based upon the view that the Bank is only one of many transactors and hence has no particular influence.

There is no simple, clear-cut explanation for this apparent paradox because in truth the determination of short-term interest rates is a complex and varying mixture of four pressures: moral suasion and custom; market mechanisms related to supply and demand pressures for instruments and facilities (such as accommodation from the Bank of England); arbitrage transactions involving the whole range of instruments and borrowing options; and expectations which can be powerfully influenced by the Bank of England's policy and potential power in the markets.

The contention made in this chapter is, however, that the Bank of England does exercise a powerful influence on short-term interest rates, and that this is associated with the transactions (sometimes, but not always, small in volume) it conducts in order to relieve shortages of ODs and on its own terms. In the regime of Bank Rate it was universally accepted that, as a question of custom, the banks adjusted their Base Rate automatically in line with Bank Rate. If such a custom is universally and invariably accepted there need be no actual transactions to bring about the Bank's influence on interest rates. In a regime where one administered interest rate of the Bank (Bank Rate or a dealing rate) unambiguously determines another set by the banks (Base Rate) arbitrage can be relied upon to induce a corresponding adjustment of all other market rates, although the relationship might not be as precise as between the two administered rates. In this case custom and moral suasion is the unambiguous route and no market transactions need be brought into the analysis. It might be a curious mechanism but nevertheless an accurate description. Indeed, in this model the question to ask is not how interest rates are determined, for they are determined by fiat, but why the banks should respond in this way. One justification is that the banks knew that, in the final analysis, the Bank of England could impose its will through enforced transactions. Indeed, under the Bank Rate regime it was the policy of the Bank always to make Bank Rate effective by forcing the market into the Bank. There was, therefore, a market mechanism to reinforce the power of custom and moral suasion.

This leaves to be resolved the question whether it is custom and moral suasion, or the influence of the transactions, that gives the Bank power over short-term interest rates. If it is the latter the paradox noted at the outset remains. Under the current regime there is no Bank Rate but the Bank does have a dealing rate in bills and it is through this mechanism that the Bank exerts its undoubted influence. Thus the question is why a change in the Bank's dealing rate should influence other interest rates – market rates and Base Rate. There are still influences deriving from custom and moral suasion and the influence on expectations. However, both are in practice reinforced by the acknowledged power of the Bank ultimately to force its will through transactions. Indeed, this potential reinforcement may be a necessary and sufficient condition for the custom and moral suasion route and the influence of expectations to operate.

So it is necessary to argue that the Bank's transactions (actual or potential) are a necessary and sufficient condition for it to influence short-term interest rates. The 'market route' influence is twofold. First, the administered rate is a dealing rate on bills the market volume of which is substantial and held almost entirely either by the Bank, banks or discount houses. Thus, a change in the Bank's dealing rate will immediately and necessarily be reflected in market bill rates as otherwise the same homogeneous product would be traded in an ultimately non-segmented market at two prices. This means that a change in the Bank's dealing rate is immediately and necessarily reflected in interest rates on an important segment of money market instruments. In other words, the market route derives not so much because of the volume of the Bank's transactions but because they are conducted in instruments that constitute a significant part of the money market, and most especially because they are extensively traded by the banks and discount houses.

The second route derives from this. If one money market rate (that on bills) is determined then arbitrage (either by banks or their customers) will influence all other market interest rates. In a well-developed, active and efficient set of markets, where arbitrage transactions can be substantial, it is necessary to explain only one interest rate for all to be determined, albeit with varying degrees of precision.

The Dow and Saville conclusion is inappropriate, for their scepticism is based on the volume of transactions and the small amount of ODs rather than on the instrument through which the Bank conducts its money market operations. The conclusion, therefore, is that the paradox noted at the outset is more apparent than real. The Bank of England has undoubted power over the level of short-term interest rates.

Limits to the Bank's power

A central theme has been that the Bank has a powerful influence on the level of short-term interest rates in four ways: it has the actual or potential power to determine the volume of banks' operational deposits; it relieves market shortages at its chosen interest rate on bills (its dealing rate); its own action can have a powerful effect upon market expectations; and arbitrage generalizes the impact of changes in the dealing rate to all other money market rates. However, the Bank's influence is in practice constrained and a distinction must be made between the Bank's technical capacity and the costs of it using its potential.

There is a high, though not perfect, correlation between the Bank's dealing rates and other short-term interest rates (Figure 2.2). In itself this does not demonstrate that the Bank has a decisive influence on interest rates as the Bank, rather than setting its own dealing rates at its own chosen level, may passively adjust them to autonomous movements in market rates. The central theme of this chapter is that the Bank has the technical capacity to determine short-term interest rates, ultimately through operations that determine the volume of ODs and the terms on which relief is given. However, whether it chooses to do so against sceptical market expectations is a different issue, for a 'confrontation' is likely to cause considerable market disruption and volatility, and the costs of imposing its will might be viewed by the Bank as too great. Such a conflict is likely to have major implications for interest rates, money market flows, monetary aggregates, the exchange rate and the position of key institutions in the money markets.

Thus the Bank could judge that the side-effects of executing its technical capacity are too great. Similarly, if the Bank were to attempt to set interest rates at a level substantially out of line with what the market felt to be appropriate there would also eventually emerge more general economic consequences that would be judged undesirable. There is a constant interplay between the views of the market and the Bank's view and operations, and the outcome varies dependent upon the strength of convictions of each. The Bank of England (1987) has put it this way:

> The extent of our influence should not be exaggerated. The financial markets are themselves an immensely powerful influence which we can never afford to ignore ... If we sought to impose a level of rates against strong market opposition, we are liable to be forced to change our stance. This could result from pressures at other points on the money market yield curve beyond the point at which we were ourselves operating, or in the foreign exchange or gilt-edged or equity markets, any or all of which could have effects on the wider economy that were inconsistent with our policy aims at the time.

At any one time the market has a general view about the appropriate level of interest rates but within a band. Within that band, the Bank can set its dealing rate (and hence expect to influence market rates) exogenously and the market follows because it has no firm view about the precise level within the band. However, in circumstances of firmly held market views (perhaps determined by the expected inflation rate or pressure on the exchange rate) while the Bank might have the technical capacity to determine very short-term rates (by aggressive action on the supply of ODs) it could in practice do so only at what would prove to be unacceptable costs resulting from the market's response and transactions.

CONCLUSIONS

The central conclusions with respect to interest rates may be summarised as follows:

1. The Bank of England has a powerful influence on the level of very short-term interest rates.
2. This influence ultimately derives from its actual or potential money market operations which determine the volume of banks' operational deposits in the context of an inelastic demand; the Bank's influence is substantial even though the operating base is small. However, in practice, and given the daily shortages, the Bank influences interest rates not by inducing permanent shortage of ODs, but through the terms on which it makes them available (i.e. its dealing rate).
3. It is a fiction to assert (though it may at times be convenient to argue) that short-term interest rates are set 'by the market' independently of the Bank's influence.
4. The Bank's influence is not total and market rates can and do diverge (sometimes significantly) from the Bank's dealing rate.
5. The link with money market interest rates more generally is through arbitrage, moral suasion, and expectations.
6. While the Bank has the technical capacity to determine short-term interest rates it may be constrained in imposing its will, and its power diminishes as the maturity lengthens.

There is a substantial academic tradition which emphasizes the role of 'money' in the determination of interest rates. At its crudest, movements in 'the' rate of interest are viewed as the equilibrating mechanism between the supply and demand for money; the rate of interest moves until the supply of money is willingly held. The approach adopted here is quite different in two major respects. First, it is banks' operational deposits (rather than the money supply) that is the centrepiece of the analysis. Second, given the institutional arrangements, the operations of the Bank of England have a powerful effect because they are the ultimate determinant of the volume of operational deposits.

REFERENCES

Bank of England (1963) 'The management of money day by day', *Quarterly Bulletin*, March.

Bank of England (1980) 'Methods of monetary control', *Quarterly Bulletin*, December.

Bank of England (1982a) 'The role of the Bank of England in the money market', *Quarterly Bulletin*, March.

Bank of England, (1982b) 'The supplementary special deposits scheme', *Quarterly Bulletin*, March.

Bank of England (1982c) 'Bills of exchange: current issues in historical perspective', *Quarterly Bulletin*, December.

Bank of England (1983) 'The Bank's operational procedures for meeting monetary objectives', *Quarterly Bulletin*, June.

Bank of England (1987) 'The instruments of monetary policy', *Quarterly Bulletin*, August.

Bank of England (1988) 'Bank of England operations in the sterling money market', *Quarterly Bulletin*, October.

Dow, J.C.R. and Saville, I. (1988) *A Critique of Monetary Theory and British Experience*, Oxford: Clarendon Press.

Hall, M.J.B. (1983) *Monetary Policy since 1971*, London: Macmillan.

Llewellyn, D.T. (ed.) (1985) *Framework of UK Monetary Policy*, London: Heinemann, Chapter 2.

Llewellyn, D.T. and Tew, J.H.B. (1988) 'The sterling money market and the determination of interest rates', *National Westminster Bank Review*, May.

3 · REAL INTEREST RATES AND THE ROLE OF EXPECTATIONS

Kajal Lahiri and Mark Zaporowski

Irving Fisher (1930) hypothesized that the anticipated rate of inflation should be fully reflected in the nominal interest rate, leaving the real rate unaffected. It is now generally recognized that *ex-ante* real interest rates have varied considerably over time. In order to examine the behaviour of the *ex-ante* real rate, it is necessary to ascertain the market's perception of the future rate of inflation. Current research has utilized two alternative approaches to model anticipated inflation. The first approach imposes the rational expectations hypothesis (REH) in order to identify the *ex-ante* real rate. Under REH, the *ex-ante* real rate is simply the *ex-post* real rate less a random inflation forecast error. Mishkin (1981) and Fama and Gibbons (1984) describe how the *ex-ante* real rate can be estimated by using the *ex-post* real rate as its observable proxy. The expected inflation rate is then obtained by subtracting the estimated *ex-ante* real rate from the nominal rate. The second approach involves the use of survey data to represent the rate of expected inflation in the market. Here, the emphasis is on quantifying the impact of anticipated inflation, fiscal and monetary policies and other macroeconomic variables on the real rate in the context of a reduced-form interest rate equation explicitly derived from a structural macroeconomic model. Recent studies which have utilized the survey data approach include Peek and Wilcox (1983), Wilcox (1983), Makin and Tanzi (1984), Peek (1982), Melvin (1982) and Levi and Makin (1979). Each of these studies has used Livingston's survey data directly as an unbiased measure of true inflation expectations.[1] Lahiri and Zaporowski (1987) suggest a more flexible approach to the use of this survey data set where one does not necessarily treat the survey data as an unbiased proxy of the true rate of anticipated inflation.

The estimated *ex-ante* real rates obtained from the survey data approach are quite different from the same obtained by using REH. A simple

Partial financial support was provided by the National Science Foundation under grant SES-8208900 at SUNY-Albany and the Canisius College School of Business.

comparison of reported real rates in Carlson (1977) or Makin and Tanzi (1984) with those in Mishkin (1981) or Antoncic (1986) will make this point clear. As we will illustrate, the mean of the after-tax *ex-ante* real rate over the period 1952–79 using twelve-month Treasury bill rates as the nominal rate and the Livingston data is 0.263 (with standard deviation 1.49) whereas with the REH model it is –1.05 (with standard deviation 2.34). The mean of the one-year-ahead inflation forecasts from the Livingston survey over the same period is 2.71 (standard deviation 2.61) whereas the mean inflation forecasts implied by the rationally expected real rates is 3.93 (with standard deviation 3.38).

In this chapter, we will examine the two aforementioned approaches to modelling real interest rates. We will outline the nature of the differences in the estimated after-tax real rates and inflation expectations implied by the alternative approaches. We accomplish this by estimating the two models in a more general econometric framework in which the survey data need not be treated as an unbiased or fully calibrated measure of true inflation expectations, and in which the after-tax *ex-ante* real rate is not modelled strictly as a random-walk process.[2] Apart from the twelve-month-ahead predictions of inflation from the Livingston survey, we also use the one-year-ahead predictions based upon the Survey Research Center (SRC) data (cf. Maddala *et al.*, 1983), and a three-month-ahead prediction of inflation rates based on the American Statistical Association–National Bureau of Economic Research (ASA–NBER) *Business Outlook* surveys (cf. Zarnowitz, 1979).

Wilcox (1983), Tanzi (1980) and Levi and Makin (1979) have shown that once additional variables such as GNP gap, supply shocks, liquidity and exogenous real demand are introduced in the Fisher equation, the coefficient of the inflation expectations variable becomes very close to unity. We will show that the Fisher coefficient is approximately 0.25, even in this extended framework, where the nominal rate is adjusted for changes in the marginal tax rate on interest income. The result is similar to Summers's (1983) recent estimate of the Fisher coefficient. We estimate a lower Fisher coefficient partly due to the fact that, of the three expectations surveys, only the ASA–NBER data yielded unbiased or fully calibrated estimates of the true expectations. As a result, our estimated *ex-ante* real rate series is quite different from those implied by the above studies. We will show that the more flexible use of survey data greatly reduces the differences between the estimated real interest (and expected inflation) rate series implied by the two approaches.

The chapter is organized as follows. In the next section, we will briefly describe the two alternative approaches to estimating *ex-ante* real rates. This is followed by a presentation of our empirical results. The final section offers some concluding remarks.

TWO APPROACHES TO MODELLING REAL RATES

The rational expectation model

The after-tax nominal rate of interest for a one-period bond can be decomposed as:

$$(1-\tau_t)R_t = (1-\tau_t)i_t + \pi_t^e \tag{3.1}$$
$$= i_t^* + \pi_t^e \tag{3.1a}$$

where R_t is the nominal return for holding the bond over period t; π_t^e is the expected inflation rate formed at time t-1 over period t; i_t^* is the expected after-tax real rate; i_t is the expected before-tax real rate over the same time period, formed at point t-1; and τ_t is the marginal tax rate on interest income.

The expected inflation rate, π_t^e, is obtained as the mathematical expectation of the inflation rate π_t, conditional on the information set I_{t-1}, available at the time t-1. That is:

$$E(\pi_t - \pi_t^e \mid I_{t-1}) = 0 \tag{3.2}$$

where $E(\ )$ is the expectation operator. One of the implications of Equation (3.2) is that:

$$\pi_t = \pi_t^e + \epsilon_t \tag{3.3}$$

where ϵ_t is a random, serially uncorrelated forecast error associated with the REH. It has a zero expectation and finite variance $\sigma_{\epsilon t}^2$. In our empirical estimation, we allow ϵ_t to be conditionally heteroskedastic.

We define the *ex-post* real interest rate, r_t, as:

$$R_t - \pi_t = r_t = i_t - \epsilon_t \tag{3.4}$$

and the *ex-post* after-tax real interest rate, r_t^*, as

$$(1-\tau_t)R_t - \pi_t = r_t^* = i_t^* - \epsilon_t \tag{3.4a}$$

The following model is used to describe the temporal behaviour of the after-tax *ex-ante* real rate:[3]

$$i_t = \alpha + \phi i_{t-1} + w_t \tag{3.5}$$

where w_t is the random error term with expected value $E(w_t) = 0$ and variance $V(w_t) = \sigma^2{}_{wt}$. In the present context, the absolute value of w_t is expected to be very small (see Mishkin, 1981). Combining Equations (3.3), (3.4a) and (3.5), we obtain the following equation in terms of observables:

$$r_t^* = \alpha + \phi r_{t-1}^* + U_t \tag{3.6}$$

where

$$U_t = w_t - \epsilon_t + \phi\epsilon_{t-1} \tag{3.7}$$

such that the covariance of U_t and U_{t-1} $C(U_t, U_{t-1}) = \phi\sigma^2_{\epsilon_t}$.

Due to REH, ϵ_t will be serially uncorrelated, with $E(\epsilon_t w_{t-s}) = 0$, for all $s > 0$. Note that Equation (3.6) generalizes the simple random-walk model of Fama and Gibbons (1984).

Equation (3.6) cannot be estimated consistently by ordinary least squares since U_t is expected to be correlated with r^*_{t-1}. However, r^*_{t-i} $(i = 2, 3, \ldots)$ can be used as valid instruments for r^*_{t-1}. Since the error process U_t in Equation (3.7) has a first-order moving average representation, $U_t = V_t - \theta V_{t-1}$, the conventional instrumental variable procedure will not only yield inefficient slope estimates in Equation (3.6) but also inconsistent standard errors of estimates. Also, note that the instruments, though predetermined, are not strictly exogenous. Efficient estimation techniques in the context of similar models have recently been developed by Cumby *et al.* (1983), Hayashi and Sims (1983), and Hansen (1982). In this chapter, we will implement the two-step two-stage least squares (2S2SLS) procedure due to Cumby *et al.* (1983) which has the advantage of permitting the errors to be conditionally heteroskedastic. Thus, we should be able to obtain asymptotically efficient parameter estimates.

In order to estimate Equations (3.6) and (3.7), we need data for the marginal tax rate on interest income, τ_t. We have followed Peek (1982) in constructing a series for τ_t from data contained in annual editions of *Statistics of Income, Individual Income Tax Returns*. This tax rate is calculated as a weighted average of marginal personal income tax rates for each adjusted gross income class. The weights for each class are computed by taking the percentage of interest income received by that class in relation to the interest income received by all adjusted gross income classes. The resulting annual series has been smoothed using a three-year moving average centred on the current period. This procedure yields second- and fourth-quarter estimates of τ_t. These estimates are then interpolated to yield corresponding third- and first-quarter estimates respectively.

The IS-LM-aggregate supply model

The following structural model provides an alternative framework for examining the behaviour of real interest rates. For the sake of comparison, we use the exact structural model of Peek and Wilcox (1983; 1984). The model consists of Equations (3.8)–(3.10) and (3.13) in the following:

$$Y_t - Y^N_t = a_0 - a_1 i^*_t + a_2 Z_t + a_3(X_t - Y^N_t) + a_4(M_t - P_t - Y^N_t) - a_5 SS_t - a_6 FB_t + u_{1t} \tag{3.8}$$

$$R_t(1-\tau_t) = b_0 + b_1(Y_t - Y_t^N) - b_2 FB_t - b_3(M_t - P_t - Y_t^N) + u_{2t} \tag{3.9}$$

$$P_t = c_0 + P_t^e + c_1(Y_t - Y_t^N) + u_{3t} \tag{3.10}$$

$$\bar{\pi}_t^e = d_0 + d_1 \pi_t^e + u_{4t} \tag{3.11}$$

$$P_t^e = \sum_{i=1}^{7} w_i P_{t-1} + \sum_{i=1}^{5} l_i M_{t-1} + f_1(X_t - Y_t^N) + f_2 Z_t + f_3 SS_t + f_4 FB_t + f_5(M_t - Y_t^N) + f_6 T_t + u_{5t} \tag{3.12}$$

$$i_t^* = R_t(1-\tau_t) - \pi_t^e \tag{3.13}$$

where Y is the log of actual real GNP; Y^N is the log of potential real GNP; Z is the percentage change in actual real GNP lagged one period; X is exogenous real demand; M is the log of the nominal money supply (M1); P is the log of the actual price level; SS is the supply shock proxy; FB is domestic bonds held by foreigners; P^e is the log of the expected price level; π^e is the true unobservable rate of expected inflation; $\bar{\pi}^e$ is the survey measure of expected inflation; R is the nominal interest rate; τ is the marginal tax rate on interest income; T is a time trend; and i^* is the *ex-ante* after-tax real rate of interest. The u_{it} ($i = 1, \ldots, 5$) represent random disturbances. All parameters are assumed to be positive. Equations (3.8)–(3.10) are the IS, LM and aggregate supply functions, respectively. Equation (3.10) embodies the natural rate hypothesis in that the deviation of output from its natural level results in systematic errors in aggregate price forecasts. Equation (3.13) defines the *ex-ante* after-tax real interest rate.

The structural model is also very similar in spirit to those examined by Peek (1982), Wilcox (1983), Melvin (1982) and Levi and Makin (1979). The major difference is that we treat price expectations endogenously and allow the expectations survey data, $\bar{\pi}_t^e$, to deviate systematically from the true unobservable expectations, π_t^e. Therefore, we augment Equations (3.8)–(3.10) and (3.13) by (3.11) and (3.12) where d_0 and d_1 are allowed to deviate from zero and one, respectively. The previously mentioned studies have utilized the survey data on expected inflation, $\bar{\pi}_t^e$, directly to replace the unobservable π_t^e, forcing $d_0 = 0$ and $d_1 = 1$. This procedure has the limitation of ignoring the possibility of bias in the survey measures of expected inflation although such bias has been illustrated in more recent literature by Pearce (1979), Brown and Maital (1981), Figlewski and Wachtel (1981) and Lahiri (1981). Our more flexible procedure treats π_t^e as well as $(Y_t - Y_t^N)$, $R_t(1-\tau_t)$ and P_t endogenously. Peek (1982) and Peek and Wilcox (1984) have established the role of taxes in the present context.

Following Wilcox (1983), we have included a variable (SS) to depict the role of aggregate supply shocks in the determination of interest rates. SS is measured as the ratio of the implicit price deflator for imports to the GNP deflator, multiplied by the effective exchange rate, in order to remove variation in the import price deflator due to exchange rate variations. The variable purporting to capture movement in the level of exogenous demand, X, is defined as the log of the sum of real Federal government defence expenditures and real exports, less the log of potential GNP. We utilize the potential GNP series developed by Rasche and Tatom (1977) since it explicitly considers both labour and energy usage and avoids the upward bias associated with those potential output measures that fail to account for energy developments.

We also include an investment accelerator term (Z) and a foreign bond holdings variable (FB) in our model specification. FB is measured as the ratio of foreign holdings of US government securities to the sum of foreign and private domestic holdings of US government securities. These quarterly series were provided by the Flow of Funds section of the Board of Governors of the Federal Reserve System (see Peek and Wilcox, 1983, for the rationale on including these variables).

Equations (3.8)–(3.10) and (3.13) can be combined to yield the following pseudo-reduced-form equation for the deviation of real GNP from its natural level:

$$(Y_t - Y_t^N) = A_0 + A_1 \pi_t^e + A_2(M_t - Y_t^N - P_t^e) + A_3(X_t - Y_t^N) + A_4 Z_t + A_5 SS_t + A_6 FB_t + u_{6t} \quad (3.14)$$

where u_{6t} is a composite random disturbance. Substituting Equations (3.14) and (3.10) into (3.9) yields the following pseudo-reduced-form equation for the after-tax nominal rate:

$$R_t(1 - \tau_t) = B_0 + B_1 \pi_t^e + B_2 (M_t - Y_t^N - P_t^e) + B_3(X_t - Y_t^N) + B_4 Z_t + B_5 SS_t + B_6 FB_t + u_{7t} \quad (3.15)$$

where u_{7t} is a composite random disturbance. Since π_t^e and P_t^e are unobservables, it is not possible to estimate Equations (3.14) and (3.15) directly. Rearranging Equation (3.11) as:

$$\pi_t^e = -(d_0/d_1) + (1/d_1)\bar{\pi}_t^e - (1/d_1)u_{4t} \quad (3.16)$$

and using the approximation $\pi_t^e = P_t^e - P_{t-2}$, for the Livingston data which are biannual,[4] we obtain the following expression for the log of the expected price level:

$$P_t^e = -(d_0/d_1) + (1/d_1)\bar{P}_t^e + [(d_1 - 1)/d_1]P_{t-2} - (1/d_1)\, u_{4t} \quad (3.17)$$

where $\bar{P}_t^e$ represents the log of the aggregate price level expected by Livingston survey respondents. Substituting Equation (3.17) into Equations (3.14) and (3.15) yields the following estimable pseudo-reduced-form relations:

$$(Y_t - Y_t^N) = \{A_0 + [d_0(A_2 - A_1)]/d_1\} + A_2(M_t - Y_t^N) + [(A_1 - A_2)/d_1]\, P_t^e - \{[A_1 + A_2(d_1 - 1)]/d_1\}\, P_{t-2} + A_3(X_t - Y_t^N) + A_4 Z_t + A_5 SS_t + A_6 FB_t + u_{8t} \quad (3.18)$$

$$R_t(1 - \tau_t) = \{B_0 + [d_0(B_2 - B_1)]/d_1\} + B_2(M_t - Y_t^N) + [(B_1 - B_2)/d_1]\, P_t^e - \{[B_1 + B_2(d_1 - 1)]/d_1\} P_{t-2} + B_3(X_t - Y_t^N) + B_4 Z_t + B_5 SS_t + B_6 FB_t + u_{9t} \quad (3.19)$$

where u_{8t} and u_{9t} represent composite random disturbances. Substituting Equation (3.17) into Equations (3.10) and (3.12) yields the following estimable aggregate supply function and an estimable expectations formulation equation:

$$P_t = [c_0 - (d_0/d_1)] + (1/d_1)P_t^e + [(d_1 - 1)/d_1]P_{t-2} + c_1(Y_t - Y_t^N) + u_{10,t} \quad (3.20)$$

$$P_t^e = d_0 + (1 - d_1 + d_1 w_1)P_{t-2} + d_1 \sum_{i=1}^{7} w_i P_{t-1} + d_1 \sum_{i=1}^{5} l_i M_{t-i} + d_1 f_1(X_t - Y_t^N) + d_1 f_2 Z_t + d_1 f_3 SS_t + d_1 f_4 FB_t + d_1 f_5(M_t - Y_t^N) + d_1 f_6 T_t + u_{11,t} \quad (3.21)$$

where the $u_{10,t}$ and $u_{11,t}$ are composite random disturbances.

Equations (3.18)–(3.21) can be estimated by the non-linear, three-stage, least-squares procedure to obtain estimates of the 36 parameters $A_0, \ldots, A_6, B_0, \ldots, B_6, c_0, c_1, d_0, d_1, w_1, \ldots, w_7, l_1, \ldots, l_5, f_1, \ldots, f_6$.

EMPIRICAL RESULTS

Before examining the empirical results, let us briefly describe the three series of survey data on inflation expectations which are utilized in this chapter.

Livingston's data

The Livingston survey, carried out in June and December of each year by the *Philadelphia Inquirer*, asks a group of approximately fifty business and academic economists for their six- and twelve-month-ahead forecasts of the Consumer Price Index (CPI). These forecasts have been extensively used in recent years and are currently available from the Federal Reserve Bank of Philadelphia. We use six- (1959–79) and twelve-month (1952–79) Treasury bill rates to match the six- and twelve-month-ahead Livingston surveys, following Levi and Makin (1979).

SRC data

The Survey Research Center (SRC) of the University of Michigan has been collecting price expectations data from a random sample of US households every quarter since 1948. Since the second quarter of 1966 the SRC has asked two price expectations questions in its surveys: a qualitative or directional question (whether 'prices will go up, prices will remain the same, or prices will go down'), and a quantitative follow-up question (only for those who reply 'prices will go up'). The follow-up question asks for point estimates of the inflation rate expected over the next twelve months. Thus, the quantitative responses cannot be considered as unconditional point estimates of expected future inflation (see Fishe and Lahiri, 1981), since those who feel prices will remain the same or decline are omitted from consideration. Using a maximum likelihood method, Maddala *et al.* (1983) have generated a quarterly inflation expectations series that utilizes the entire sample of those surveyed, including both those who feel prices will rise and those who feel they will stay the same or fall. We use twelve-month Treasury bill rates to match these forecasts over the period from the second quarter of 1968 to the second quarter of 1977.

ASA–NBER data

Each quarter since the last quarter of 1968, the ASA–NBER *Business Outlook* survey has presented single- and multi-period forecasts of the Implicit Price Deflator for GNP (IPD). The survey is a compilation of the forecasts of approximately sixty professional economists. This survey is somewhat unique in that, in addition to point forecasts, respondents are asked to specify probabilities that various rates of change in IPD will occur in the future.[5] For present purposes, we will utilize the three-month-ahead predictors of the IPD, which contrasts with the previously mentioned surveys that forecast CPI. This allows us to examine how well the broader IPD measure of inflation works in the context of the Fisher equation. Since these surveys are collected in the middle month of each quarter, we use three-month Treasury bill yields corresponding to secondary market monthly averages in the middle month of each quarter. We will now proceed to analyse the empirical results with reference to the two alternative models.

The REH model

We estimate Equations (3.6) and (3.7) over the period 1953–79 using quarterly data on three-month Treasury bill rates and inflation rates based upon the seasonally unadjusted CPI. We truncate the sample in the last quarter of 1979 due to the structural instability introduced into the model as a result of the new operating procedures of the Federal Reserve after that quarter.[6] The two-step two-stage least square (2S2SLS) estimate of the model which allowed for conditional heteroskedasticity was:[7]

$$r_t^* = 0.938 r_{t-1}^* + V_t - 0.544 V_{t-1} \tag{3.22}$$

$$R^2 = 0.37 \qquad \rho_1 = -0.42 \qquad \text{SEE} = 2.28$$

The standard error of ϕ was estimated to be 0.039. Except for the first-order autocorrelation coefficient (ρ_1), all other higher-order autocorrelations in the residuals were statistically insignificant (i.e. within $\pm 2/\sqrt{T}$).[8] We used r_{t-i} ($i = 2, 3, \ldots, 7$) as the instruments. Following Phillips (1987), we calculated the usual t-statistic as $(0.938-1)/0.039 = -1.614$ which is compared to a 10% left-tail critical value of -1.61 from Table 8.5.2 in Fuller (1976, p. 373). Thus, we conclude that the autoregressive parameter is not statistically different from one at the 10% level of significance, supporting the random-walk hypothesis (see Antoncic, 1986; Fama and Gibbons, 1984; and Garbade and Wachtel, 1978).

For purposes of comparison, we utilize the twelve-month-ahead predictions of the Livingston survey data in calculating i_t^* and estimate Equation (3.5) using quarterly data on twelve-month Treasury bill yields. Because the holding period is now longer than the observation interval, the data set is overlapping and hence one expects U_t to be a third-order moving average (MA(3)). The 2S2SLS estimate of the model allowing for conditional heteroskedasticity over 1953–79 is:[9]

$$i_t^* = 0.922 i_{t-1}^* + V_t + 0.294 V_{t-1} + 0.164 V_{t-2} + 0.232 V_{t-3} \tag{3.23}$$

$$R^2 = 0.91 \qquad \text{SEE} = 0.71$$

The standard error of ϕ was 0.048.[10] To test the unit root hypothesis, Phillips's (1987, p. 287) Z_t-statistic was calculated to be -1.932. Since the innovations are well represented by a third-order moving average, the lag truncation number was chosen to be 3. This Z_t-value permits rejection of the null hypothesis at the 10% level, but not at the 5% level of significance. It may be noted that this test remains valid even when the innovations are heterogeneously distributed, as they are in this case. The high R^2-value and the presence of an MA(3) error process are precisely what one would expect due to the use of overlapping data (cf. Huizinga and Mishkin, 1984). The autocorrelation function of the residuals (ACF) was (0.27 0.16 0.22 0.02 0.10 −0.02 −0.05 −0.03). Even though this ACF may be consistent with a moving-average representation for U_t of order 3 or less, there is some evidence (Lahiri *et al.*, 1985) which suggests that innovations in the real rate process are serially uncorrelated. It may be noted that the smaller moving-average error terms in Equation (3.23) relative to those

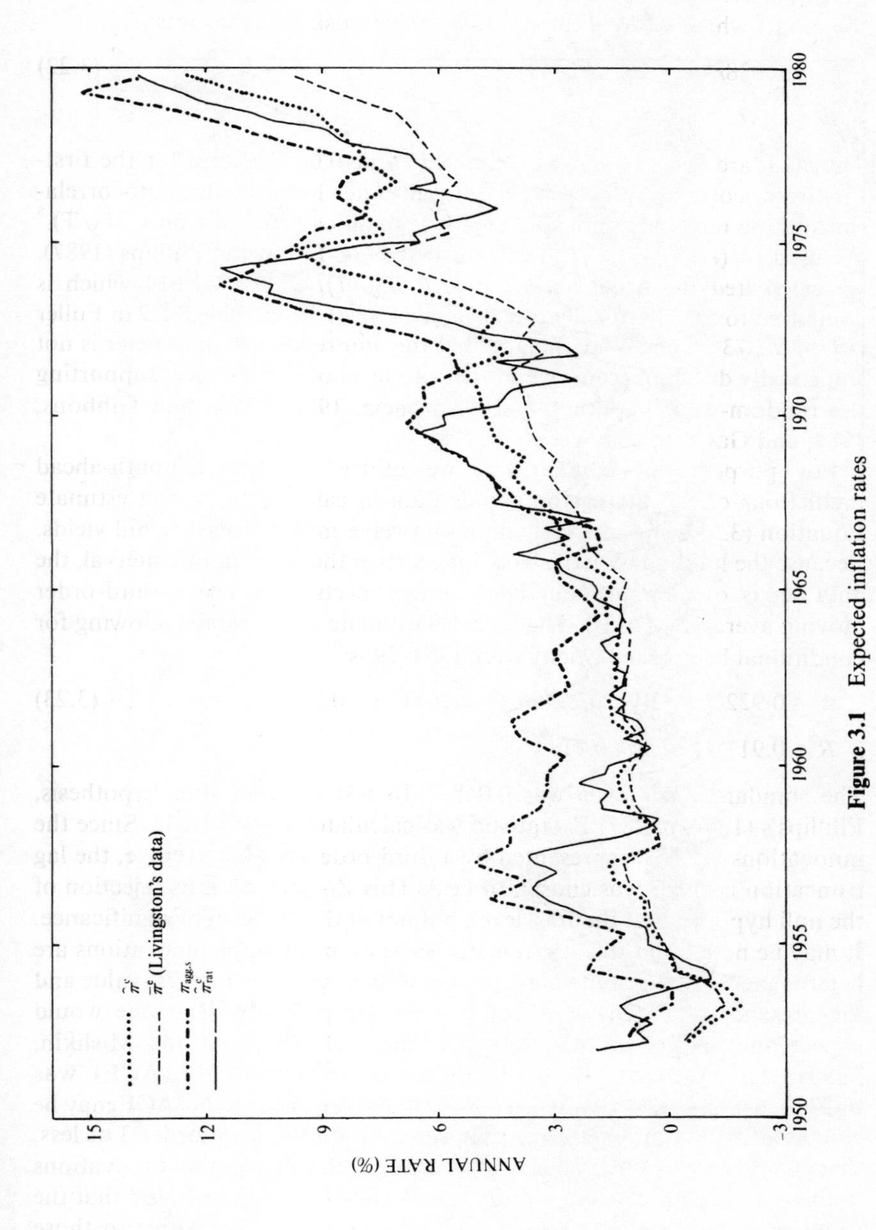

Figure 3.1 Expected inflation rates

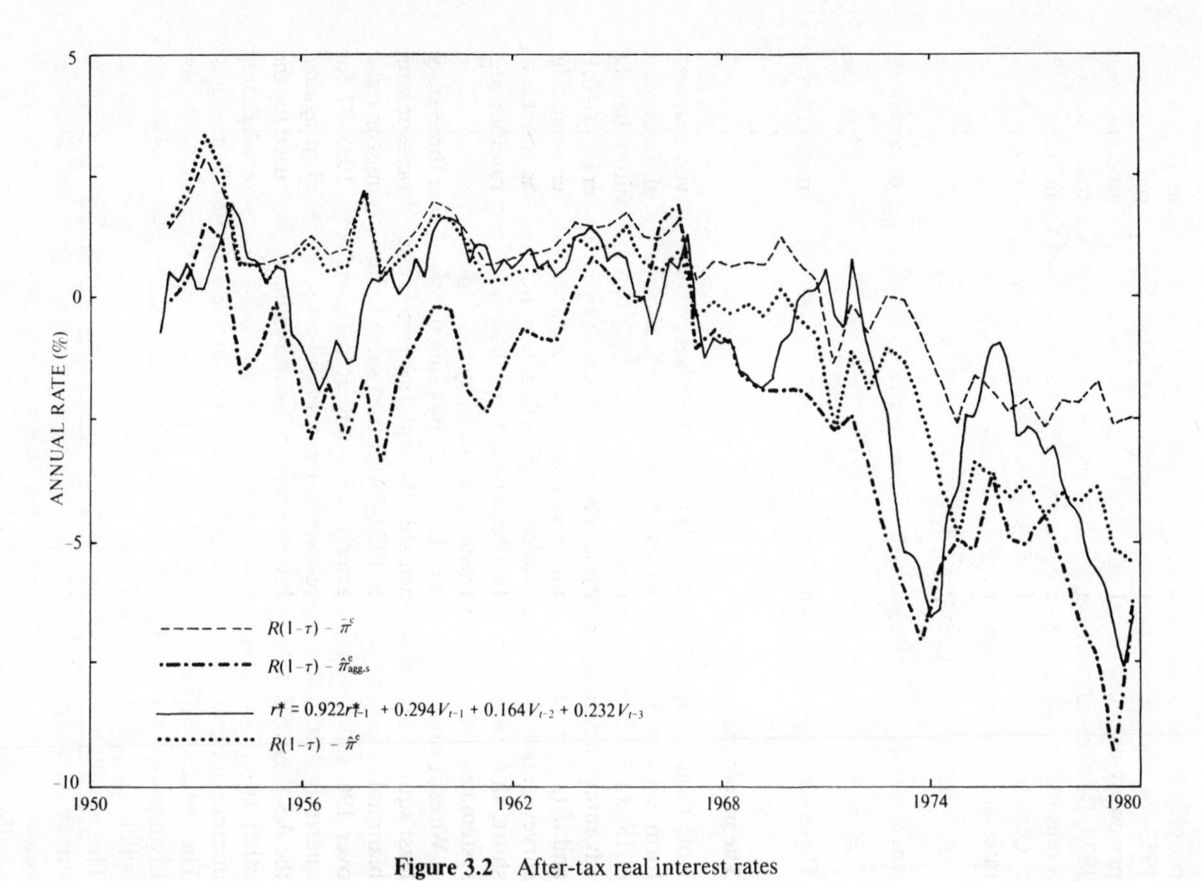

Figure 3.2 After-tax real interest rates

found in Huizinga and Mishkin (1984) and Brown and Maital (1981) are due to the presence of a lagged endogenous variable. In obtaining 2S2SLS estimates, i^*_{t-i} (i = 4, 5, ..., 10) were used as instruments. To check if ϕ can roughly be taken as a fixed parameter, we first estimated the model over 1953–74, and then calculated ϕ recursively by updating the original sample period by one additional observation at a time up to the last quarter of 1979. By examining these ϕ-values we concluded that the assumption was a reasonable one (see also Antoncic, 1986 and Kinal and Lahiri, 1988).

Quarterly estimates of one-year-ahead *ex-ante* after-tax real interest rates are then estimated as:

$$\hat{i}^*_t = 0.922 i^*_{t-1} + 0.294 V_{t-1} + 0.164 V_{t-2} + 0.232 V_{t-3} \quad (3.24)$$

where $V_t = i^*_t - \hat{i}^*_t$. The corresponding inflation forecasts are obtained as:

$$\hat{\pi}^e_t = R_t(1-\tau_t) - \hat{i}^*_t \quad (3.25)$$

These series are plotted in Figures 3.1 and 3.2 as $\hat{r}^*$ and $\hat{\pi}^e_{rat}$, respectively.

The macro model

Note that Equations (3.18–(3.21) constitute our partially solved reduced-form equations for the structure (3.8)–(3.13). Estimation of Equations (3.18)–(3.21), imposing the non-linear constraints across equations, has the advantage of enabling estimation of the structural parameters C_i (i=0,1) and d_j (j=0,1). Direct estimates of (d_0, d_1) will indicate whether or not the survey data is biased in relation to π^e_t which is implied by the model. In short, this procedure is flexible enough to allow for both random and systematic errors in the measurement of π^e_t by $\bar{\pi}^e_t$.

We estimated Equations (3.18)–(3.21) by using the non-linear three-stage least squares algorithm available through the Time Series Processor with biannual observations over 1952–79 for the twelve-month Livingston data, over 1968–80 for the quarterly ASA–NBER data and over 1968–77 for quarterly SRC data. Three-month Treasury bill rates are matched against the ASA–NBER data and twelve-month Treasury bill rates are used for the other two. The estimates are reported in Table 3.1. An overwhelming number of parameters are statistically significant and have justifiable signs. The reduced-form Fisher coefficient, B_1, is estimated to be 0.456, for the Livingston data, 0.28 for the ASA–NBER data and 0.33 for the SRC data, which are all significantly less than its often hypothesized value of one. This result is very similar to that of Summers (1983). The Livingston survey data are found to be biased in relation to π^e_t, since the estimated value of d_1 is 0.769. This is less than unity even at the 10 per cent level of significance. d_0 is estimated to be –0.488 with a t-statistic of only 1.39. Similar results are obtained for the SRC data. By viewing Equation (3.12),

Table 3.1 Non-linear three-stage least squares estimates of Equations (3.18)–(3.21)

Parameters	Livingston data* 12-month bills (1952–79)	ASA–NBER data** 3-month bills (1968–80)	SRC data** 12-month bills (1968–77)
d_0	−0.4882	−0.3065	−0.0855
	(1.39)	(0.25)	(0.08)
d_1	0.7692[a]	0.9764[a]	0.6905[a]
	(18.42)	(9.00)	(9.77)
B_0	0.3394	−0.8260[b]	−0.0289
	(1.42)	(2.22)	(0.05)
B_1	0.4562[a]	0.2800[b]	0.3316[a]
	(4.80)	(2.02)	(5.04)
B_2	0.0054	−0.0210	−0.0120
	(0.43)	(1.10)	(0.47)
B_3	0.0159	0.9279[a]	0.0273
	(1.42)	(4.50)	(1.05)
B_4	0.0615[a]	−0.0098	−0.0091
	(2.79)	(0.40)	(0.46)
B_5	−0.0274[a]	−0.0326[a]	−0.0153
	(4.41)	(2.42)	(1.05)
B_6	- 0.0588[a]	0.0002	−0.0795[a]
	(3.60)	(0.01)	(2.92)
A_0	1.0934[b]	−0.2385	0.8513
	(1.93)	(0.40)	(0.83)
A_1	0.7612[b]	−0.4118	−0.6245[a]
	(2.01)	(1.53)	(3.44)
A_2	0.0745	0.1763[a]	−0.0108
	(1.48)	(4.62)	(0.15)
A_3	0.0931[b]	1.9705[a]	0.4187[a]
	(2.04)	(4.75)	(5.72)
A_4	0.5051[a]	0.1234[a]	0.0203
	(5.59)	(2.53)	(0.37)
A_5	−0.0642[a]	0.0218	−0.0324
	(2.55)	(0.82)	(0.78)
A_6	−0.0309	0.3232[a]	0.4539[a]
	(0.47)	(3.86)	(5.95)
c_0	0.6520	−0.0735	−0.1226
	(1.43)	(0.23)	(0.08)
c_1	0.4580[a]	0.0937[a]	0.7624[a]
	(5.80)	(3.03)	(7.59)
w_1	1.3186[a]	1.2570[a]	0.0325
	(13.89)	(15.74)	(0.11)
w_2	- 0.0874	−0.2078[b]	−0.5618
	(0.65)	(1.80)	(1.62)
w_3	−0.3177[a]	−0.0165	1.1318[a]
	(2.56)	(0.14)	(3.40)
w_4	−0.0136	0.0529	1.7931[a]
	(0.12)	(0.46)	(4.77)
w_5	−0.0569	−0.3301[a]	−0.0337
	(0.52)	(2.81)	(0.11)
w_6	−0.0895	0.2628[b]	−0.9542[a]
	(0.84)	(2.34)	(2.65)
w_7	0.1879[a]	−0.1081	−0.2650
	(2.91)	(1.64)	(1.02)

Table 3.1 *continued*

l_1	-0.2044[b]	-0.0562	-0.0556
	(1.79)	(1.22)	(0.31)
l_2	0.0492	0.1297[a]	0.0704
	(0.42)	(2.70)	(0.36)
l_3	0.0171	0.0075	0.1582
	(0.15)	(0.16)	(0.68)
l_4	0.1125	-0.0181	-0.3736
	(0.99)	(0.34)	(1.29)
l_5	0.0251	0.0077	0.0347
	(0.34)	(0.16)	(0.13)
f_1	-0.0039	0.0877	0.0184
	(0.23)	(0.72)	(0.33)
f_2	0.0264	0.0147	0.0041
	(0.61)	(1.62)	(0.09)
f_3	-0.0181	0.0071	-0.0344
	(1.40)	(1.65)	(0.099)
f_4	-0.0394[b]	-0.0282	0.0745
	(1.75)	(0.82)	(0.68)
f_5	0.2274[a]	-0.0204	-0.2331
	(2.79)	(0.78)	(1.45)
f_6	0.0024[b]	0.0007	0.0021
	(2.22)	(0.69)	(0.47)

Equation	R^2	SEE	DW	R^2	SEE	DW	R^2	SEE	DW
	0.48	0.0288	0.99	0.58	0.0239	1.02	0.76	0.0648	1.59
	0.92	0.0067	1.73	0.81	0.0114	2.20	0.66	0.0248	1.67
	0.99	0.0214	0.82	0.99	0.0072	1.55	0.99	0.0696	1.45
	0.99	0.0057	1.30	0.99	0.0030	1.87	0.99	0.0231	2.27

*Biannual data beginning April and October
**Quarterly data
[a] Significant at the 1% level
[b] Significant at the 5% level

The numbers in parentheses are t-ratios, SEE is the standard error of estimate and DW is the Durbin–Watson statistic.

we find that the use of Livingston's or the SRC survey as unbiased measures of expectations (i.e. $d_1=1$), would unduly inflate the estimated Fisher coefficient. It is interesting to note that the ASA–NBER data exhibit no such underestimation. c_1 is significantly positive in each case, supporting the existence of the short-run Phillips curve phenomenon, which is a very important feature in Keynesian macro models. Note that the c_1 coefficient using ASA–NBER data is significantly smaller than that using the other two series. This is because ASA–NBER data are more informationally efficient than the other surveys.[11]

We can now estimate the *ex-ante* real after-tax rate of interest using the expected inflation rate generated from within the model as $R(1-\tau) + (d_0/d_1)$

$- (1/d_1)\bar{\pi}^e$, and compare it with the real rate estimated conventionally as $R(1-\pi) - \bar{\pi}^e$, where the Livingston data are used directly as an unbiased proxy for π^e. An important aspect of the after-tax real interest rates obtained from our model is that they are considerably lower than those implied by such studies as Carlson (1975, 1977), Melvin (1982), Wilcox (1983), Makin and Tanzi (1984) and others who have used the Livingston data directly as a measure of π_t^e. One major problem with some of these studies is that to obtain i_t^* from Equation (3.13), one does not necessarily have to use the survey measure, $\bar{\pi}_t^e$, for π_t^e, but can also use Equation (3.10) to get:

$$P_t^e = P_t - \hat{c}_0 - \hat{c}_1 (Y_t - Y_t^N) \tag{3.26}$$

and hence π_t^e. Therefore, the model can generate two quite different series for the real rate. In Figure 3.1, we have plotted the survey data ($\bar{\pi}^e$), the π^e series obtained from Equation (3.10), $\pi^e_{agg.s}$ and the π^e series we calculated from Equation (3.16), π^e.[12] The corresponding real rates are plotted in Figure 3.2. These figures illustrate the often large differences between each of the measures of π_t^e. The main advantage of the π^e_{rat} series generated by our procedure is that it is consistent with the entire structural model.[13] Therefore, the *ex-ante* real after-tax interest rate series we estimate is consistent with our structure in the sense that it is generated from an internally consistent model.

The means and variances of the estimated real interest rates and inflation forecasts come from four sources: Livingston's survey data ($\bar{\pi}^e$); an appropriately calibrated Livingston's series ($\hat{\pi}^e$); π^e obtained from the aggregate supply equation ($\pi^e_{agg.s}$); and those implied by the autoregressive real rate model (π^e_{rat}). These are given in Table 3.2. It is clear from Table 3.2 and also from Figures 3.1 and 3.2 that Livingston's measure and the aggregate supply equation yield very different estimates of π^e and the

Table 3.2 Means and variances of alternative estimates of after-tax expected real interest and inflation rates, 1952–79[a]

Source	Expected inflation rates Mean	Variance	After-tax mean rate variance	Ex-ante real
$\bar{\pi}^e$ (Livingston data)	2.71	6.83	0.263	2.23
$\bar{\pi}^e=(-d_0/d_1)+(1/d_1)\bar{\pi}^e$	4.15	11.55	-1.183	4.99
$\hat{\pi}^e_{agg.s}$	5.26	12.89	-2.28	6.44
$\hat{\pi}^e_{rat}$	3.93	11.44	-1.05	5.51

[a]Calculations are based on biannual observations (T=56), except for those in the last column, which are based on quarterly observations (T=112).

Table 3.3 Tests for unbiasedness of inflation forecasts[a]

Coefficients	Livingston's data (π^e)	$\hat{\pi}^e=(-d_0/d_1)+(1/d_1)\pi^e$	π^e from random-walk real rate model
a	0.782[b] (0.285)	0.194 (0.190)	0.091 (0.160)
b	1.20[c] (0.075)	0.929 (0.058)	0.994 (0.019)
R^2	0.82	0.82	0.96
DW	0.70	0.70	1.45

[a]Regressions are of the form $Y_t=a+bX_t+U_t$, where Y_t is actual inflation rate, X_t is estimated price forecast and U_t is random disturbance term. Standard errors are in parentheses. DW is the Durbin–Watson statistic.
[b]Significantly different from zero at the 5% significance level.
[c]Significantly different from one at the 5% significance level.

after-tax *ex-ante* real rate i^*. The mean of π^e derived from Equation (3.10) is 5.26 whereas the same from the Livingston series is only 2.71. This result also indicates that the mean of the after-tax real rate implied by Equation (3.10) is –2.28 as against 0.263 implied by π_t^e. However, the means and variances of π^e and i^* estimated by the autoregressive model and the calibrated Livingston measure are very similar. The tests for unbiasedness of the estimated price forecasts are presented in Table 3.3. Whereas the Livingston series significantly underestimates the actual inflation rate, our adjusted series, $\hat{\pi}^e$, shows no such underestimation. The Durbin–Watson statistics indicate significant autocorrelation in the residuals. This, by itself, is not inconsistent with rationality because our forecast span is longer than the observation period (cf. Brown and Maital, 1981). The root mean square prediction errors of inflation (RMSPE) over 1952–79 for the Livingston data and our adjusted series ($\hat{\pi}^e$) were calculated to be 2.046 and 1.557, respectively. The RMSPE for the rationally expected inflation forecasts implied by our estimated real rate model is estimated to be only 0.692. Thus, the RMSPE of the appropriately calibrated Livingston series is nearly 25 per cent less than the original data while the RMSPE of the Livingston series is nearly three times that of the rationally expected inflation forecasts. Pearce (1979), Brown and Maital (1981), Figlewiski and Wachtel (1981), Lahiri (1981) and others, have also rejected the rationality hypothesis for the Livingston forecasts. Struth (1984) has demonstrated that the Livingston forecasts are considerably less accurate than forecasts generated with a simple Kalman filter using past price information only. The relative efficiency of inflation forecasts based on interest rate models was first demonstrated by Fama and Gibbons (1984). Lahiri and Zaporowski (1987) have suggested a more flexible way of using survey data in the context of macroeconomic models, which considerably reduces the downward bias of the surveys in relation to subsequently observed inflation and consequently improves real rate forecasts.

CONCLUSION

We have compared the estimated after-tax *ex-ante* real interest rates and the inflation forecasts implied by two alternative real rate models: the rational expectations model in which the real rate is assumed to have an autoregressive structure (cf. Fama and Gibbons, 1984); and the use of survey data directly as a measure of expected inflation. The latter approach has been used in a large number of recent studies. We estimated the first model using the two-step two-stage least-squares estimator due to Cumby *et al.* (1983), and compared the estimated real interest and expected inflation rates against those obtained from the second approach. We find that the forecasts of inflation and the real rate from the two approaches vary considerably. A number of studies have shown that the Livingston data typically underestimate the true market expectations, so that these data should be used in empirical work with considerable caution (cf. Mishkin, 1981). We found that the RMSPE of inflation implied by the Livingston data is almost three times that of the rational expectations model. The expected inflation series resulting from the rationally expected real rate model supports the hypothesis of unbiasedness. However, the original Livingston data do not support the unbiasedness property. Since the Livingston series typically underestimates the true market expectations, the use of this data set to compute real interest rates will tend to overestimate actual *ex-ante* real interest rates.

We have estimated the macro model of Peek and Wilcox (1983) in a manner whereby the survey data, which proxies for expected inflation, need not be taken as an unbiased measure of the true expectations underlying the structural model. Using three separate series of survey data, we find that the Livingston and SRC data systematically underestimated the true expectations by nearly 25 per cent while the ASA–NBER series was found to be unbiased. The use of either Livingston's or the SRC data directly to represent the unobservable inflation expectation is incompatible with other 'indicators' of the same latent variable implied by the structural model. This does not imply that these data should not be used, however. Rather, we have suggested a more flexible approach which calibrates the survey data, yielding estimates of the *ex-ante* real rate which are very similar to those obtained via the rational expectations approach.

NOTES

1. Demery and Duck (1978) used the survey data approach in the context of British, and Volker (1982) in the context of Australian interest rate models.
2. Huizinga and Mishkin (1985) and Litterman and Weiss (1985) have found evidence in favour of an autoregressive process for the *ex-ante* real rate with autoregression coefficients significantly less than one.
3. Yun (1984) has recently established the role of taxes in this class of models.
4. The approximation becomes $\pi_t^e = P_t^e - P_{t-1}$ for the ASA–NBER data (quarterly data with quarterly forecasts) and $\pi_t^e = P_t^e - P_{t-4}$ for the SRC data (quarterly data with annual forecasts).
5. For further explanation of the data, and how the information it contains can be used in empirical estimation see Zarnowitz and Lambros (1987) and Lahiri *et al.* (1988).
6. Evidence on the structural instability produced in models of this type when the sample is extended beyond 1979 is given in Lahiri *et al.* (1985) and Kinal and Lahiri (1988).
7. It should be noted that the constant term in Equation (3.6) dropped from the model. α was estimated to be –0.091 with a standard error of 0.191, indicating statistical insignificance. Since we are primarily interested in the resulting estimates of the *ex-ante* after-tax real rate from Equation (3.6) and how this series compares over time to the estimated *ex-ante* after-tax real rate directly from Equation (3.5) using the Livingston data on inflation expectations, we have estimated the model omitting α.
8. Note that this test does not consider the fact that we have a lagged endogenous variable as one of the regressors. A proper test for the significance of the jth autocorrelation can be conducted by estimating Equations (3.6) and (3.7) as before with U_{t-j} as an additional regressor and testing for its significance. This procedure also indicated that all lagged autocorrelations except ρ_1 are statistically insignificant. We are grateful to Adrian Pagan for suggesting the approach (see Pagan, 1984).
9. 2S2SLS estimates in Equations (3.22) and (3.23) were obtained without assuming that errors are conditionally homoskedastic (cf. White, 1980; Nicholls and Pagan, 1983). White's test resoundingly rejected homoskedasticity in all our experiments. We should point out that higher-order autoregressive terms were found to be insignificant.
10. The constant term in Equation (3.5) was dropped and the model reestimated since α was not statistically different from zero at even the 25% level.
11. To keep the size of this chapter within a reasonable limit, in what follows, we shall restrict our discussion to Livingston's data only.
12. Since d_0 was statistically insignificant, we did not include this term while adjusting the Livingston data.
13. The pseudo-reduced-form equations (3.18)–(3.21) contain 36 restricted estimable parameters with four restrictions. We tested the validity of these overidentifying restrictions by using the F-test (cf. Theil, 1971, p. 314). The F-value was calculated to be 0.289. Since the critical F-value with (4, 188) degrees of freedom is 1.35 at the 25% level of significance, we accept the restrictions quite comfortably.

REFERENCES

Antoncic, M. (1986) 'High and volatile real interest rates: where does the Fed fit in?', *Journal of Money, Credit, and Banking*, vol. 18, February, pp. 18–27.

Brown, B.W. and Maital, S. (1981) 'What do economists know? An empirical study of experts' expectations', *Econometrica*, vol. 49, March, pp. 491–504.

Carlson, J.A. (1975) 'Are price expectations normally distributed?', *Journal of the American Statistical Association*, vol. 70, December, pp. 749–54.

Carlson, J.A. (1977) 'Short term interest rates as predictors of inflation: comment', *American Economic Review*, vol. 67, June, pp. 469–75.

Cumby, R.E., Huizinga, J. and Obstfeld, M. (1983) 'Two step two stage least squares estimation in models with rational expectations', *Journal of Econometrics*, vol. 21, pp. 333–55.

Darby, M.R. (1975) 'The financial and tax effects of monetary policy on interest rates', *Economic Inquiry*, vol. 13, June, pp. 266–76.

Demery, D. and Duck, N.W. (1978) 'The behavior of nominal interest rates in the United Kingdom, 1961–73', *Economica*, vol. 45, pp. 23–37.

Fama, E.F. and Gibbons, M.R. (1984) 'A comparison of inflation forecasts', *Journal of Monetary Economics*, vol. 13, May, pp. 327–48.

Feldstein, M. (1976) 'Inflation, income taxes and the rate of interest: a theoretical analysis', *American Economic Review*, vol. 66, December, pp. 809–20.

Figlewski, S. and Wachtel, P. (1981) 'The formation of inflationary expectations', *Review of Economics and Statistics*, vol. 63, February, pp. 1–10.

Fishe, R.P.H. and Lahiri, K. (1981) 'On the estimation of inflationary expectations from qualitative responses', *Journal of Econometrics*, vol. 16, pp. 89–102.

Fisher, I. (1930) *The Theory of Interest*, New York: Macmillan.

Fuller, W.A. (1976) *Introduction to Statistical Time Series*, New York: John Wiley.

Garbade, K. and Wachtel, P. (1978) 'Time variation in the relationship between inflation and interest rates', *Journal of Monetary Economics*, vol. 4, November, pp. 755–65.

Hansen, L.P. (1982) 'Large sample properties of generalized method of moments estimators', *Econometrica*, vol. 50, July, pp. 1029–54.

Hayashi, F. and Sims, C.A. (1983) 'Nearly efficient estimation of time series models with predetermined but not exogenous instruments', *Econometrica*, vol. 51, May, pp. 783–98.

Huizinga, J. and Mishkin, F.S. (1984) 'Inflation and real interest rates on assets with different risk characteristics', *Journal of Finance*, vol. 39, July, pp. 699–714.

Huizinga, J. and Mishkin, F.S. (1985) 'Monetary policy regime shifts and the unusual behavior of real interest rates', NBER Working Paper no. 1679, August.

Kinal, T. and Lahiri, K. (1988) 'A model for *ex ante* real interest rates and derived inflation forecasts', *Journal of the American Statistical Association*, vol. 83, pp. 665–73.

Lahiri, K. (1981) *The Econometrics of Inflationary Expectations*, Amsterdam: North-Holland.

Lahiri, K., Kinal, T. and Zaporowski, M. (1985) 'A model for *ex ante* real interest rates', *The Proceedings of the American Statistical Association*, Business and Economic Statistics Section, pp. 98–102.

Lahiri, K. and Zaporowski, M. (1987) 'On more flexible use of survey data on expectations in macroeconomic models', *Journal of Business and Economic Statistics*, vol. 5, January, pp. 69–76.

Lahiri, K. and Zaporowski, M. (1988) 'A comparison of alternative real rate estimates', *Oxford Bulletin of Economics and Statistics*, vol. 50, August, pp. 303–12.

Lahiri, K., Teigland, C. and Zaporowski, M. (1988) 'Interest rates and the subjective probability distribution of inflation forecasts', *Journal of Money, Credit, and Banking*, vol. 20, May, pp. 233–48.

Levi, M. and Makin, J.H. (1979) 'Fisher, Phillips, Friedman and the measured impact of inflation on interest', *Journal of Finance*, vol. 34, March, pp. 35–52.

Litterman, R.B. and Weiss, L. (1985) 'Money, real interest rates, and output: A reinterpretation of post-war U.S. data', *Econometrica*, vol. 53, pp. 129–56.

Maddala, G.S., Fishe, R.P.H. and Lahiri, K. (1983) 'A time series analysis of popular price expectations data', in A. Zellner (ed.), *Time Series Analysis of Economic Data*, Washington, DC: Bureau of Census, pp. 278–86.

Makin, J.H. and Tanzi, V. (1984) 'The level and volatility of interest rates in the United States: the roles of expected inflation, real rates and taxes' in V. Tanzi (ed.), *Taxation, Inflation and Interest Rates*, Washington, DC: International Monetary Fund, pp. 110–42.

Melvin, M. (1982) 'Expected inflation, taxation and interest rates: the delusion of fiscal illusion', *American Economic Review*, vol. 72, September, pp. 841–5.

Mishkin, F.S. (1981) 'The real interest rate: an empirical investigation' in K. Brunner and L. Meltzer (eds), 'Costs and consequences of inflation', *Carnegie-Rochester Conference Series on Public Policy*, pp. 151–200.

Nicholls, D.F. and Pagan, A.R. (1983) 'Heteroskedasticity in models with lagged dependent variables', *Econometrica*, vol. 51, July, pp. 1233–41.

Pagan, A.R. (1984) 'Model evaluation by variable addition', in D.F. Hendry and K.F. Wallis (eds), *Econometrics and Quantitative Economics*, Oxford: Basil Blackwell.

Pearce, D.K. (1979) 'Comparing survey and rational measures of expected inflation', *Journal of Money, Credit, and Banking*, vol. 11, November, pp. 447–56.

Peek, J. (1982) 'Interest rates, income taxes and anticipated inflation', *American Economic Review*, vol. 72, December, pp. 980–91.

Peek, J. and Wilcox, J. (1983) 'The postwar stability of the Fisher effect', *Journal of Finance*, vol. 38, September, pp. 1111–24.

Peek, J. and Wilcox, J. (1984) 'The degree of fiscal illusion in interest rates: some direct estimates', *American Economic Review*, vol. 74, December, pp. 1061–6.

Phillips, P.C.B. (1987) 'Time series regression with a unit root', *Econometrica*, vol. 55, March, pp. 227–301.

Rasche, R. and Tatom, J.A. (1977) 'Energy resources and potential GNP', *Federal Reserve Bank of St Louis Review*, vol. 59, pp. 10–24.

Struth, F.K. (1984) 'Modelling expectations formation with parameter adaptive filters: an empirical application to the Livingston forecasts', *Oxford Bulletin of Economics and Statistics*, vol. 46, August, pp. 211–39.

Summers, L.H. (1983) 'The non-adjustment of nominal interest rates: a study of the Fisher effect' in J. Tobin (ed.), *Macroeconomics, Prices and Quantities*, Washington, DC: Brookings Institution, pp. 201–44.

Tanzi, V. (1980) 'Inflationary expectations, economic activity, taxes and interest rates', *American Economic Review*, vol. 70, pp. 12–21.

Theil, H. (1971) *Principles of Econometrics*. New York: Wiley.

Volker, P.A. (1982) 'Expectations of inflation and short-term interest rates in Australia, 1968 (1)–1979 (2)', The Australian National University Center for Economic Policy Research, Discussion Paper no. 41, January.

White, H. (1980) 'A heteroskedasticity-consistent covariance matrix estimator and a direct test for heteroskedasticity', *Econometrica*, vol. 48, May, pp. 817–38.

Wilcox, J. (1983) 'Why real interest rates were so low in the 1970's'. *American Economic Review*, vol. 73, March, pp. 44–54.

Yun, Y.S. (1984) 'The effects of inflation and income taxes on interest rates: some new evidence', *Journal of Financial and Quantitative Analysis*, vol. 19, December, pp. 425–48.

Zarnowitz, V. (1979) 'An analysis of annual and multiperiod quarterly forecasts of aggregate income, output and the price level', *Journal of Business*, vol. 52, pp. 1–33.

Zarnowitz, V. and Lambros, L. (1987) 'Consensus and uncertainty in economic prediction', *Journal of Political Economy*, vol. 95, June, pp. 591–621.

4 · PUBLIC SECTOR DEFICITS AND THE MONEY SUPPLY

P.M. Jackson

> There is no necessary relation between the size of the Public Sector Borrowing Requirement and monetary growth ... the size of the PSBR does affect the level of interest rates. However, for given monetary growth, the major effect on interest rates is exerted by the real PSBR not the nominal PSBR.
>
> Friedman (1980, pp. 56–7)

> The Government is quite correct to believe that in practice the rate of growth of the money supply depends upon the PSBR.
>
> Beenstock and Minford (1980)

INTRODUCTION

The nature of the money supply process is of central importance to macroeconomic theory and policy. Whether or not it is exogenously or endogenously determined is an issue which has been hotly disputed, as, too, is the role of the public sector in its determination; this is clear from the different views expressed in the introductory quotations by two groups who come from the monetarist school, broadly defined.

Elementary textbooks have set down a well-established relationship between the monetary base and general monetary aggregates (i.e. mainly bank deposits). This translation is made through the money multiplier. Determination of the money base and the factors influencing the size of the multiplier are the interesting empirical questions. A mechanical approach to the determination of the money stock ignores the complexity of the money supply 'process'. For example, it washes out the analysis of the role played by financial institutions. This omission is of importance, especially if financial institutions are modelled as profit maximizers whose portfolio decisions (balancing risks and returns) will themselves impinge at various points of the money supply process. Monetarists assume a stable demand for money and regard the government as having direct control over the

Table 4.1 General government budget deficits (% of nominal GNP or GDP)

	1985	1986	1987
USA	3.3	3.5	2.4
Japan	0.8	0.9	0.9
West Germany	1.1	1.2	1.5
France	2.6	2.9	2.7
UK	2.7	2.9	2.7
Italy	14.0	12.6	12.6
Canada	6.6	5.4	4.9

Source: OECD, *Economic Outlook*, June 1987. Data are on a standardized system of national accounts basis, except for the UK and USA, where national data are used.

monetary base of the system so that the money stock is exogenously determined by the monetary authorities. If, on the other hand, the bank deposit multiplier is variable or if the monetary base is changed in response to aggregate real demand then the money supply is clearly endogenous.[1]

In recent years old fears that monetized public sector deficits will eventually cause inflation have been rekindled. The German hyperinflation of the Weimar government resulted, in part, from central bank monetization of government deficits whose origins were to be found in the First World War. An erosion of the tax base following the war, coupled with reparations expenditures, accumulated war expenditures, and rising interest and debt repayments on the existing public sector debt all made for a very unstable situation. In 1920–1 public sector debt was 65 per cent of spending. A similar tale is told about the Austrian inflation of the 1920s. After the First World War the Austro-Hungarian empire was split up, with most of the public debt and the bureaucracy which had run the empire ending up in Austria. In 1919 the public deficit was 50 per cent of spending, but this had increased to over 80 per cent in 1923. In both Germany and Austria most of the deficit was financed from credit creation.

It was with fears of this kind in mind that some governments in the industrialized world introduced stringent financial policies in the early 1980s. The stagflation of the 1970s had caused public sector deficits to rise and, along with them, an increased anxiety that large deficits could not be sustained in the long run without causing severe imbalances in the world economy and a threat to the financial stability of the banking system of the Western world (see Table 4.1). These severe financial policies of balancing public sector budgets overrode the Keynesian automatic stabilizers and contributed to the world-wide recession in the early 1980s. The exception, however, was the supply-side policy of the United States. The Reagan administration cut taxes but maintained an upward growth in defence and aerospace spending without corresponding reductions in civilian welfare spending programmes. Escalating US deficits (government and trade deficits) promoted anxiety and fears in financial markets not only in the United States but also in other financial centres around the world.

In comparison the Thatcher government had, since 1979, aimed to cut the public sector deficit. A central tenet of the Medium Term Financial Strategy was the firm 'belief' that in order to stabilize the broad money supply (sterling M3) and interest rates the government had to cut back on its own borrowing requirement. Targeting the public sector borrowing requirement (PSBR) became a prime policy objective irrespective of the state of the real economy (output and employment).

The question addressed in this chapter is, what logical or empirical basis is there to the fears and beliefs that public sector deficits will result in an expansion of the money supply and hence, financial instability and inflation? When the literature is reviewed it is found that no simple unambiguous set of relationships exists. A number of theories exist. These can be classified for the purpose of this chapter as:

1. Monetization approaches:
   (a) direct monetization;
   (b) the monetary base approach;
   (c) the unpleasant monetarist arithmetic approach of the Minnesota School.
2. Public sector deficits, interest rates, and the money supply.

Each of these theories is explained and assessed in turn, and the chapter concludes with an examination of the available empirical evidence.

MONETIZATION APPROACHES

Direct monetization

Monetization refers to the process through which an increase in government debt results in an increase in the money stock. This happens when the debt is purchased by the banking system – either by the central bank or the commercial banks. If government debt is taken into the portfolios of the commercial banks then their reserve assets are increased, unless offset by other transactions. This allows the commercial banks to expand their lending to the private sector and so the money supply, by definition, expands. If the central bank wishes the commercial banks to purchase government debt then it provides the banking system with the necessary cash reserves to do so. The central bank, therefore, increases its liabilities and hence the money stock expands.

The story told above, which is the common textbook presentation of monetization, is, however, too mechanistic and simplistic. It washes out the complex realities of real banking systems, especially their portfolio management: see Chapter 2 in this volume. Once these complexities are taken on board it soon becomes apparent that there is nothing inevitable about the link between an expansion in government debt and money stock. In order to understand the nature of the relationship it is useful to begin with some elementary balance sheet and flow-of-funds accounting relationships.

The monetary base approach

Monetary economics textbooks set down the relationship between the monetary base of the banking system and the money supply.[2] This is summarized as follows. By definition,

$$M^s = C_p + D \quad (4.1)$$

$$B = X_p + X_B \quad (4.2)$$

where M^s is the money supply; C_p is cash held by the non-bank private sector; D is the deposits of the banking system; B is high-powered money or the monetary base (i.e. cash and bankers' balances at the central bank); X_p is the money base held by the non-bank private sector; and X_B is the money base held by the banking sector.

Rearranging Equations (4.1) and (4.2) produces the basic relationship:

$$M^s = \frac{\left(1 + \frac{C_p}{D}\right)}{\left(\frac{X_p}{D} + \frac{X_B}{D}\right)} B \quad (4.3)$$

This can be written more simply as

$$M^s = mB \quad (4.4)$$

where m is defined as the money multiplier.

From Equation (4.4) it is readily seen that the money stock (supply) depends, mechanically, upon cash to deposit ratios and reserve asset to deposit ratios as contained in the money multiplier expression. If these ratios are predictable or stable then the multiplier is predictable also and the monetary authorities could effect control of the money stock by influencing the money base B.

What is the relationship between the high-powered money base of the system and the public sector deficit? To answer this question a set of flow-of-funds accounting identities is examined.

Flow-of-funds accounting

The naive Keynesian textbook approach to fiscal policy ignored one of the most fundamental questions – how the fiscal policy is to be financed. The way in which a fiscal policy is financed, especially the financing of deficits, will have important consequences for the efficiency of that policy. It was not, however, until the late 1960s that economists considered the government budget constraint seriously (see Christ, 1968; Silber, 1970; and Blinder and Solow, 1973; 1974).

An increase in government spending can be financed out of an increase in tax revenues; an issue of government debt (bonds) to the non-bank private sector; or an expansion in the money stock. Let us ignore tax finance and concentrate upon deficit finance, either bond or money financing. The accounting identity for the financing of the public sector deficit is:

$$PSD \equiv OMO + NMD - MAT + ECF + \Delta B \tag{4.5}$$

where PSD is the public sector deficit; OMO is operations in marketable debt, i.e. sale of bonds (gilts), Treasury bills, etc. to the non-bank private sector; NMD is non-marketable debt, i.e. post office deposits, national savings, etc.; MAT is the use of funds to pay off maturing debt; ECF is finance obtained or acquired to accommodate external flows; and ΔB is the *increase* in public sectors' monetary liabilities, i.e. an increase in high powered money. Equation (4.5) can be rearranged as

$$\Delta B \equiv PSD - OMO - NMD + MAT - ECF \tag{4.6}$$

It is clear that combining the identity of Equation (4.6) with Equation (4.4) will give an expression of changes in the broadly defined money stock (M^s) as a function of changes in the monetary base (ΔB) which originates with the public sector deficit. Moreover, the change in M^s is a multiple (m) of those changes.

A simple relationship which lies behind the monetization of the public sector deficit has been established. To the extent that the deficit is not covered by the sale of debt (OMO) or non-debt items (NMD) – in both cases for the non-bank private sector – then it will be financed through an expansion of the money supply. All of this is true by definition, as the accounting identities show.

The degree of monetization of public sector deficits varies from country to country, depending upon the precise nature of the financial institutional arrangements. In developing countries which have no access to financial markets, financing public sector deficits through the banking system is inevitable. For developed countries it depends upon the relationship between the monetary and the fiscal authorities. For example, in West Germany and the United States the central bank is not responsible for the way in which the public sector deficit is financed. Government, in the view of these central banks, is just like any other bank customer. They are interested in the *total* of bank lending not its composition. In the United States the Federal Reserve Bank does not see itself as obliged to help the government finance its debt. There is, therefore, a problem of co-ordinating monetary and fiscal policies (see Blinder, 1983). It also means that the chairman of the Federal Reserve is more powerful than the governor of the Bank of England. Equally, the government is not obliged to manage its debt to help monetary policy. This situation can be compared with that in the United Kingdom, where the Bank of England stands ready to provide residual finance for the budget deficit if required to do so. It does this by supplying whatever cash reserves are required by the financial system (i.e. commercial banks and discount houses) to purchase the debt. The discount houses cover the Treasury bill tender on the assumption that the Bank of England will provide the cash.[3] In the United States it is, in fact, illegal for the Federal Reserve Bank to purchase government debt directly from the government.

Mid-way between the US and the UK systems are those of Australia and Japan, where the commercial banks are captive markets for government debt. The central bank sets ratios so that the commercial banks will hold a minimum amount of debt. A system similar to this is often used during wartime.

A government can run a large deficit without fear of inflationary consequences the more developed is its financial system (financial markets) and the more prepared are individuals and financial institutions to hold that debt (see McKinnon, 1973). Again, this is seen from the accounting identities. With a well-developed financial system *OMO* and *NMD* will be high (provided the non-bank private sector demands the government debt) thereby taking pressure off the money supply. In the United Kingdom there is a strong demand for government debt from the insurance and pension funds which use gilts for matching their portfolios (i.e. ensuring that the term structure of assets matches the term structure of liabilities). This means that the government can often sell its debt without increasing interest rates (see Bain, 1982a; 1982b). Non-market debt (e.g. national savings) is purchased mainly by the personal sector. Such debt tends to be interest-elastic. Also, debt sales have been secured as much by financial innovation, such as the introduction of index-linked bonds, as by changes in interest rates.

The above discussion shows that the more sophisticated and developed is a country's financial system the less likely it is that public sector deficits will be monetized. Furthermore, the institutional structure of the financial system, the rules and regulations surrounding financial transactions and the relationships between the central bank and the commercial banks together circumscribe the extent to which monetization of government debt will occur.

There is, however, another set of important constraints upon the money creation process which is set in train by the monetization of government debt through the banking system. This is usually ignored by simple textbook treatments. Returning attention to Equation (4.4) and the flow-of-funds accounting identity, it is clear that if the public sector's financial deficit is financed through the banking sector's acquisition of public debt then the high-powered money base (*B*) is expanded and the broad based money supply (*M*) by a multiple thereof. This treatment, however, begs a number of questions. In particular, it ignores the question of how the commercial banks manage their portfolios. The question of the extent to which commercial banks are able to create credit is captured in the 'new view' due to Tobin (1963) and Gurley and Shaw (1960).

The identities considered above simply give a description of balance sheet equalities which must by definition hold true in the long run. The high-powered money base is, in this approach, taken as exogenously given. This is in essence the 'old view' and that which underlies much modern monetarist thinking. In the 'new view', however, the money base is endogenous since it responds to changes within the model, in particular interest rate differentials. This portfolio adjustment approach takes into account the asset preferences of the general public and the liability management of the financial system.

One of the major groups of actors in the credit expansion process is, of course, the commercial banks. It is now common practice to regard a bank just like any other commercial firm. Following Baltensperger (1972), a bank is thought of as a profit-maximizing entity operating within a specific market setting (oligopoly) and has a particular risk-preference schedule (e.g. risk aversion). Different specifications of the model over these dimensions will generate different asset demand and supply functions (see Cuthbertson, 1986). Bank expansion of credit will only take place if, at the margin, it is profitable. The relevant question to ask within the 'new view' is under what conditions the commercial banks will be prepared to take public sector debt into their portfolios. If the banks are obliged by law to take up the debt then the question is of no interest. On the other hand, if profit-maximizing banks are free to decide then the question contains much that is of interest: in particular, it is necessary to examine in greater detail than hitherto the behaviour of portfolio decision-makers with respect to liability management of the commercial banks. If the demand for credit is price-elastic and if the supply of credit is price-elastic then the expansion of credit, even under penal conditions created by the central bank, must be profitable for the commercial banks. Whether or not a bank deposit multiplier process exists depends crucially upon the portfolio decisions of profit-maximizing banks facing different risks. The multiplier process, for example, will be truncated if the banks, for whatever reason, decide to hold reserve assets above the legal minimum (and vice versa).

Commercial banks purchase government debt and convert it into the output of the banking system – that is, deposits. A proft-maximizing bank will purchase government debt if it holds expectations that interest rates will fall. In that case it anticipates a rise in the price of bonds and the prospects of making capital gains. This kind of argument, within the context of portfolio management is, of course, relative. Much depends upon the performance of gilts relative to other assets. Furthermore, the management of a portfolio is not just driven by the objective of profit (short- or long-run). There is also the question of how much risk is acceptable within the portfolio. Banks might purchase government debt when they wish to reduce their overall exposure to risk.

While it is overstating the case to suggest, as Buchanan and Wagner (1978) have done, that economists do not have an adequate theory of the money supply process, nevertheless, the actual process is undoubtedly much more complex than the simple theory supposes. This also means that while there is a simple accounting relationship between public sector borrowing and the money stock, in practice, the exact nature of the relationship is likely to be more complex, depending upon the portfolio decisions of the different agents within the financial system.[4]

The discussion outlined above has demonstrated that monetization of public sector debt is not inevitable in the short run. There is no necessary one-to-one relationship between government deficits and the money stock; just as there is no one-to-one relationship between private sector deficits and the money stock. In economies with well-developed capital markets government deficits need not be financed through the banking system. Instead, under the right set of circumstances (i.e. spot interest rates relative to expected future rates) the private sector will stand willing and waiting to take up marketable government debt into its portfolios. In a flow-of-funds framework a deficit must, by definition, be matched *ex post* by a surplus elsewhere. This point is developed later in this chapter when the link between public sector deficits and interest rates is analysed. In the meantime, it is argued that in the long run there are important constraints placed upon the government to finance its deficit through interest-bearing nominal debt. When these limits are reached, recourse to bank borrowing is inevitable and the deficit is, therefore, monetized. These points are now considered in the next section.

The unpleasant monetarist arithmetic approach

The long-run constraints placed upon the ability of the government to sell marketable debt have been brought out clearly in an article by Sargent and Wallace (1981) entitled 'Some unpleasant monetarist arithmetic'[5] and can be referred to as the Minnesota School of debt monetization. This is within the general framework of the 'new classical' macroeconomics.

Sargent and Wallace demonstrated that a permanently higher government deficit must eventually be accommodated by an increase in the monetary base. In other words, monetary policy cannot be manipulated independently (exogenously) when the growth path of government expenditures and the tax structure are both fixed. The choice which faces the central bank is not whether to monetize a public sector deficit but when – now or later. This result follows from the government budget constraint (see Appendix 4A) plus an upper bound on the *real* per capita stock of interest-bearing public sector debt held by the private sector.

In the long run, according to unpleasant monetarist arithmetic, the growth in the money stock is governed by the fiscal deficit. Thus, while inflation is prima facie a monetary phenomenon, inflation is, in fact, in the long run according to this model, a fiscal phenomenon. The Sargent and Wallace analysis is a dynamic extension of the stationary state that was explored by Blinder and Solow (1973; 1974); Tobin and Buiter (1980); and Steindl (1974).

What are the elements of the Sargent and Wallace approach? First, there is a limit to the growth of interest-bearing nominal government debt, relative to nominal income. This is referred to as the *transversality* condition on debt growth. Suppose that, for political or any other reasons, the current-period government is not prepared to increase taxes in order to finance the additional public spending. Issuing interest-bearing debt implies that future-period governments will face higher debt charges that will result in higher tax rates or larger future deficits. This does not produce a stable long-run equilibrium, especially if individuals fully anticipate this (i.e. the Barro–Ricardo equivalence theorem) and respond by increasing current-period savings. The response of future governments to this state of affairs will be to monetize the debt. In order to prevent the government debt to income ratio rising faster than its limit, to secure a long-run equilibrium path for the economy, the government must monetize some of its debt. 'Current excess debt growth will be financed, at least in part, by future money growth, although current money growth may not be affected' (Protopapadakis and Siegel, 1987, p. 35). Clearly then, debt policy will affect monetary policy.

Second, there is the 'time inconsistency problem'. This problem refers to the set of incentives which policy-makers face when solving a dynamic game.[6] Nominal fixed-interest government debt gives the authorities an incentive to produce unanticipated inflation and, thereby, to reduce the real value of the debt and the real value of future tax liabilities. To do this there is strong attraction either to monetize the debt directly or to expand the money supply through some other route. The problem is to generate the optimal amount of 'surprise' inflation and this, in turn, raises the question of how much of the debt should be monetized. Again, however, a link between deficit financing and an expansion of the money supply in the long run is established.

It is instructive to compare the unpleasant monetarist arithmetic of the Minnesota School with the results of the modern Barro–Ricardo equivalence theorem. In a strict Ricardian regime government deficits have no effect upon the price path because government deficits are assumed to be temporary and are expected to be offset against future taxation (or government surpluses). This is stated formally as

$$B(t) = E_t \sum_{j=0}^{\infty} R^{-1}_{tj} \, [T(t+j+1) - G(t+j+1)] \quad \text{for all t}$$

where

$$R_{tj} = \prod_{i=0}^{j} [1 + r(t+i)]$$

i.e. the real value of interest-bearing government debt B at time t equals the present value of prospective government surpluses; R^{-1} is the rate of discount; T is future taxes; and G is government spending.

Under these conditions the government acts like a private firm. A firm borrows by offering a claim on future revenue streams. The government in a Ricardian regime is assumed to do the same – it finances its current deficit by promising to run surpluses in the future. In a Ricardian world agents perceive bond sales as deferred monetization.

Too much should not be made of the distinction between the Ricardian approach of Barro and the Minnesota approach of Sargent and Wallace. Both are elements of the new classical macroeconomics and arrive at the same result, albeit via different routes. Current debt must be paid off by future taxes. Sargent and Wallace limit the increase in future 'fiscal' taxes and concentrate upon monetary (inflation) taxes. The Barro–Ricardo view ignores monetary taxes and concentrates on fiscal taxes.[7]

Two issues raised above are theoretical possibilities. Whether or not they are empirically relevant will depend upon whether the economy is close to the critical value of its debt to income ratio. The definition of this critical value is not a trivial exercise and no known attempts have been pursued to establish such a value for any economy. Deciding upon whether or not a Ricardian or Minnesota world exists in practice centres upon two considerations. If bonds are continuously issued then taxes will never need to be collected to pay back the debt. On the other hand, if bonds are not net wealth to the private sector then the size of the bond stock should be irrelevant. There is no reliable empirical evidence to decide which view is correct.

GOVERNMENT DEFICITS, INTEREST RATES AND THE MONEY SUPPLY

This section examines in detail the relationship between government deficits and interest rates. Some attention was given to this earlier in the context of debt monetization. The arguments are quite straightforward but the underlying logic is somewhat ambiguous. If the non-bank private sector is to be encouraged through an appropriate set of economic incentives to take public sector debt into its portfolios then interest rates must rise. Unless the non-bank private sector does accept the debt then the government will be forced to finance its deficit through bank borrowing and the money supply will expand. Increases in the rate of interest, however, also increase the probability of the government losing control over the money supply if its objective is to achieve money supply control at politically acceptable (relatively low) rates of interest and if it is only prepared to use the single instrument of interest rates.

Simple statements linking changes in the public sector's borrowing to changes in interest rates ignore the complexity of the financial flows that might produce such a result. There is nothing inevitable about the relationship. Furthermore, there are many different ways of generating the relationship, some more plausible than others.

Within the flow-of-funds framework it is recognized that by definition a deficit, such as the public sector deficit, must be matched against a surplus elsewhere in the system, *ex post*. Public sector deficits cause incomes in the economy to rise. This is the message of the Keynesian multiplier analysis. A reduction in taxation causing an increase in the deficit (for a given level of public spending) will increase personal disposable income as, too, will an increase in public spending on infrastructure items (for a given tax yield). These income increases will increase the level of savings (surpluses) which can be used to finance the government deficit. The deficit generates its own surplus and is self-financing. Also, an increase in business savings (retained earnings or profits) will reduce the corporate sector's demand for capital finance. Thus, if while the public sector deficit increases the corporate sector's deficit falls and the personal sector's deficit falls, then the total demand for finance will not rise. The result is that interest rates need not rise.

Public sector deficits do not automatically cause interest rates to rise. By the same logic, large public sector deficits need not cause large increases in interest rates. The observed relationship between public sector deficits

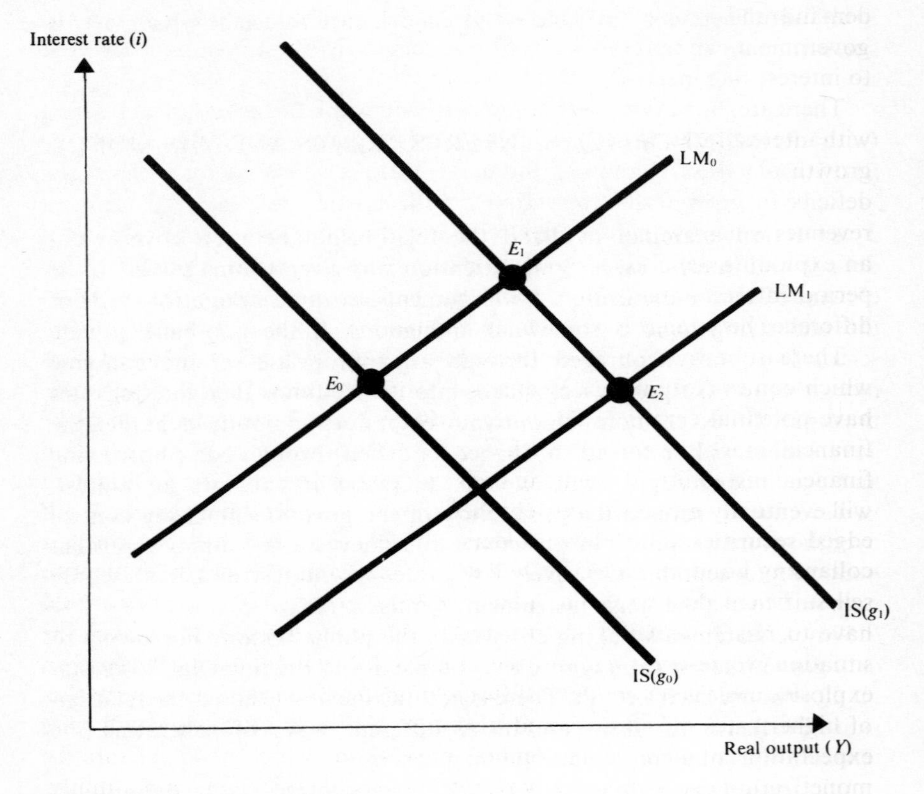

Figure 4.1

(indeed any sector's deficit) and the rate of interest is the resultant of complex financial flows which are conditional upon the state of the economy and its institutional structure.

Another route is via the notion of 'transactions crowding out'. If the money supply is fixed an increase in real disposable incomes caused by the deficit will cause interest rates to rise because the transactions demand for money will have increased. This is illustrated in Figure 4.1 by a movement from E_0 to E_1. But was this caused by the deficit or by a failure on the part of the authorities to increase the money supply?

Finally, in terms of portfolio adjustment, it is not necessary to use interest rates to make government debt sufficiently attractive to the non-bank private sector. The public sector, through financial innovations, can vary the nature of its debt instruments to match investors' asset preferences. Also, if, as Bain (1982a; 1982b) pointed out, we start from a position of disequilibrium in the sense that there is a mismatch in the demand and supply of assets prior to the government deficit, then the government can tailor its debt instruments to fill the gap without recourse to interest rate increases.

There are, however, other arguments which link the government's deficit with interest rates. When the interest rate on government debt exceeds the growth of Gross National Product (GNP) then interest rates can cause deficits to grow faster than GNP. With existing tax rates government revenues will grow in line with GNP but will not rise fast enough to prevent an exploding deficit. This growth path is unstable since in the next time period interest rates will rise and the process is repeated.[8] There is no difference between this problem and that of transversality outlined above.[9]

There is, however, a link between public sector deficits and interest rates which comes close to the Minnesota School's approach and which does have potential empirical relevance. A large government deficit can make financial markets nervous. Such nervousness, however mild, can result in financial instability. If agents in such markets believe that the government will eventually monetize the debt then they will expect falling prices of gilt edged securities. Thus debt holders will fear that they will end up in a collapsing bond market. This will make it difficult for the government to sell sufficient debt to the non-bank private sector. To do so they would have to raise interest rates to make the debt attractive. This makes the situation worse and increases the likelihood of monetization because an explosive cycle is set up. Fear of future monetization raises the expectation of higher rates of inflation and, through the Fisher effect, this will raise expectations of increases in nominal interest rates which feed back into the monetization decision, thereby reinforcing the original fears and amplifying the cycle. Because of these fears of an explosive cycle agents in the bond market will demand a higher nominal rate on long bonds – higher than is justified by the current inflation.

The increase in nominal interest rates has further knock-on effects which almost make the fears and expectations self-fulfilling and reinforcing. An increase in nominal interest rates raises the cost of working capital faced by the private sector firms. This will promote bankruptcies and crisis borrowing from the banking sector which will show up as an expansion in bank lending to the private sector and hence as increase in the broad based money supply. Furthermore, the rise in nominal interest rates *relative* to those in the rest of the world will cause an appreciation in the exchange rate. The volume of exports will fall and that of imports will rise as international competitiveness changes (assuming no productivity improvements) and this will again promote bankruptcies, crisis borrowing and an expansion in bank lending to the private sector and hence an increase in the money supply. Thus, a large public sector deficit is, a priori, generally associated with a rapid growth in the money supply. In this case, however, the effect is indirect through changes in interest rates.

The appropriate empirical question to ask of this theory is what the link is between the government deficit and interest rates. This is not an easy question to answer since different monetary policy regimes can mask the effects. Consider, for example, a case in which monetary policy is easy and fiscal policy is relaxed. If an increase in public spending and/or a reduction in taxation is accompanied by an accommodating monetary policy then obviously the link between the deficit and the change in interest rates will not be observed. But there will be a correlation between the change in the deficit and an expansion in the money supply – but did the deficit *cause* the money supply increase? Surely this is the outcome of a policy choice since the authorities could have allowed interest rates to rise.

There is an associated argument which focuses on the authorities' loss of ability to control the money supply in the face of deficits which force up interest rates. In the United Kingdom, where interest rates, rather than the monetary base, are used to control the money stock, this argument could be important. If public sector deficits do cause interest rates to rise and if, for reasons given above, the money supply also rises then there comes a point in time when interest rates are so high that the monetary authorities would find it impossible to raise them further. At that point they lose control over the money supply. This thinking lies at the heart of recent UK Treasury policy.

> To control the money supply the government would have to induce the private sector to hold an ever increasing proportion of wealth in non-monetary forms. This implies that interest rates would be continuously raised. Thus, in the long run fiscal policy cannot be varied independently of the money supply (Treasury and Civil Service Committee, 1980, para. 33).

> If the Treasury model is a plausible description of the economy the implication is that in order to pursue stability in £M3 and interest rates, the authorities may have to stabilize their own borrowing requirement and not the economy. If the authorities counteract the automatic stabilizers, then the economy will tend to become more unstable. A spontaneous fall in private domestic demand may result in calls for cuts in government spending (or in the increases in taxes) in order to prevent the rising PSBR from pushing the money supply figures off course. The experience of 1980 seems to represent such a case. However, this has not always been the pattern in previous cycles (Treasury and Civil Service Committee, 1981, para. 6.25).

Finally, to complete this argument, return to the basic credit multiplier identity, Equation (4.3). It was shown earlier that the items in parentheses formed the basis of the money multiplier which was assumed to be stable over time. However, is the money multiplier stable? Are these items invariant to changes taking place within the economy? In particular, how do they respond to changes in interest rates? If the money multiplier does vary with changes in the economy then the money supply is exogenously determined in part even if the monetary base (B) is under the direct control of the monetary authorities.

During the 1980s in the United Kingdom the money multiplier grew rapidly. This, it could be argued, was due to a massive reduction in the currency ratio X_B/D as interest rates rose, thereby increasing the opportunity cost of holding cash balances. The counterpart to the expansion in the money multiplier has been a rapid increase in bank lending and monetary growth. This line of reasoning once again provides a potential link between public sector deficits and expansions in the money supply to the extent that the deficits promote an increase in interest rates.

SUMMARY OF THE THEORETICAL LINKS BETWEEN DEFICITS AND THE MONEY SUPPLY

The discussion so far has explored at length a number of routes through which an *increase* in public sector deficits might be associated with an *increase* in the money stock. While a set of theoretical linkages have been established there is nothing inevitable or unambiguous about the relationships in practice, as a number of authors have made clear:

> the links between the public sector borrowing requirement and the rate of money creation are far from mechanical or automatic. They depend, not only upon the sources of variation in that borrowing requirement but also crucially upon the institutional framework of the financial system (Laidler, 1981, p. 176).

> It would be wrong to assume from the identity relationship that a given increase in the PSBR would produce an increase of the same size in £M3, or that there is any close relationship, year by year, between them. Different public expenditure and tax measures, which have the same effect on the PSBR, can have very different effects on real demand and hence on private sector savings and investment and monetary conditions (Middleton, 1981, p. 97).

> The financial effects of fiscal policy also depend upon how the authorities seek to finance the PSBR (Middleton, 1981, p. 98).

Clearly, then, the precise link between changes in public sector deficits and changes in the money supply depends upon a host of factors which will include institutional detail and the nature of the financing decision. To unscramble these influences and to establish the net effect of public sector deficits on the money supply requires detailed empirical analysis.

DOES MONETIZATION MATTER?

This question can be answered on a number of levels. First, does the monetization of public sector deficits enhance fiscal policy compared to pure bond financing? Second, does monetization of deficits have an impact upon inflation? These are two possible approaches to answering the question 'does monetization matter?' Doubtless there are others.

It has already been seen in Figure 4.1 that, unless the money supply is increased, the full impact of a public sector deficit on income and employment will be dissipated through interest rate increases caused by transactions crowding out. Monetization of part of the deficit is, therefore, important if fiscal policy is to be successful and, furthermore, if adverse supply-side effects are not to be established because of high interest rates. That is, to move the economy from E_0 to E_2 without causing *real* interest rates to rise. Monetization of deficits has potential benefits as well as costs and the policy-maker needs to balance these risks.

Whether or not the monetization of deficits matters also depends upon what is happening elsewhere in the economy, in particular the growth of real incomes. Suppose the economy is growing at 5 per cent per annum in real terms. Then the transactions demand for money will grow at approximately 5 per cent per annum also. This simple arithmetic suggests that the monetary base could grow at 5 per cent per annum without causing inflationary pressures to build up in the economy. Thus, provided that the monetized public sector does not expand the monetary base faster than the real growth of the economy, there is no worry about monetization of the debt. When, then, is monetization a potential problem? A problem might arise if fiscal decisions cause the government debt to increase at a rate faster than the rate of growth of real output. But whether this will result in inflation or a rise in interest rates will depend upon whether or not there exists excess demand for government debt. If individuals are willing to take up the additional debt into their portfolios then this will take pressure off financial and money markets – there will be no need for the authorities to expand the monetary base, nor will interest rates need to increase.

In summary, therefore, an increase in government debt, *per se*, will not necessarily result in macroeconomic pressures. The impact of government debt on other macroeconomic variables depends crucially upon the rate of growth of real output and the state of demand for financial assets by the private non-bank sector.

EMPIRICAL EVIDENCE

Seigniorage is the process of creating external fiat which provides government with a source of revenue. In terms of the government budget constraint the government finances extra public spending by rolling the printing press and increasing the money stock. This direct link between public sector deficits and the money stock has dominated much of the discussion of Latin American inflations as well as those of less-developed countries. King and Plosser (1985) have shown that for this class of economy, in which the tax base (as a source of government revenues) and taxable capacity are small, and which does not have access to domestic or international capital markets, seigniorage has been an important source of revenue to governments.

What has been the experience of developed economies? For the United States over the period 1953–82 seigniorage was about 0.55 per cent of GNP. Historically seigniorage revenue in the United Kingdom has been insignificant.[10]

Another way of finding out how important government borrowing has been for changes in the money stock is to examine the data produced by flow-of-funds statements. The national income accounting identities relating public sector borrowing to the money stock were reviewed earlier. It was demonstrated that there is no a priori simple one-to-one relationship between the PSBR and sterling M3. If one of the other components of the identity changed at the same time as the PSBR then this would weaken any observed empirical relationship between the PSBR and sterling M3. This is of significance to econometric models which, using reduced forms and aggregate data, tend to ignore the flows which lie behind the stocks that are used as data.

Table 4.2 sets out the simple correlations between sterling M3 and its asset counterparts, while Table 4.3 presents the variance and coefficient of variation. Both tables cover the period 1975–85. They show that while the relationship between the PSBR and sterling M3 has dominated policy thinking and policy formation, the outturn of sterling M3 has been dominated by bank lending to the private non-bank sector. This was in large measure caused by crisis borrowing by firms during 1979–83 to avoid bankruptcy. It was also a rational response by borrowers who did not wish

Table 4.2 Correlations between sterling M3 and asset counterparts, 1975–85

	1	2	3	4	5	6
1. Sterling M3	1.00					
2. PSBR	0.54	1.00				
3. Debt sales (G_p)	–0.24	0.10	1.00			
4. Bank lending (GL_g)	–0.57	0.10	0.61	1.00		
5. Externals (*Ext*)	–0.26	–0.26	0.12	–2.20	1.00	
6. Net non-deposit liabilities	–0.26	–0.17	–0.20	–0.63	–0.11	1.00

Source: Goodhart (1984).

Table 4.3 Variance and coefficient of variation of sterling M3 and its asset counterparts

	Variance	Coefficient of variation
Sterling M3	10×10^5	55
PSBR	25×10^5	71
Debt sales	94×10^4	- 36
Bank lending	32×10^5	45
Externals	60×10^4	–214
Net non-deposit	20×10^4	–142

Source: Goodhart (1984).

to borrow long-term when the current rate of inflation was high (and hence current nominal rates of interest were high) and their expectations were for the rate of inflation to fall. Therefore, they borrowed short-term from the banks.

Any observed statistical relationship between public sector deficits and the money stock will be influenced by the government's debt management policy. If the authorities actively seek, as part of their macroeconomic/ monetary management policy, to minimize the amount of debt that is monetized then to the extent that they are successful the relationship between observed changes in government debt and the money stock will be weakened. The analysis of time-series data is, therefore, not invariant to the policy regime in force and changes in these policy regimes must be taken into account. It was stressed earlier that the banks would only take public sector debt into their portfolios if it was profitable for them to do so (or if they were compelled by law). Debt management policy influences the terms of trade under which it is profitable for commercial banks to purchase government debt.

The Bank of England could, as in 1980–1, rely upon moral suasion and request banks not to purchase gilts and government bonds and bills. This was not particularly successful. Profit-maximizing commercial banks can obtain gilts by roundabout routes. For example, a domestic bank can obtain gilts by lending to its non-domestic subsidiaries who purchase them on its behalf.

Public sector debt can be made attractive to the non-bank private sector, in particular the pension fund and life assurance companies. If the Bank of England issues maturities which are longer than those preferred by the banks, say three years, then there is a greater probability that this debt will be taken up into the portfolios of the non-bank financial institutions since its term to maturity more closely satisfies their asset preferences. Another strategy is to issue low-coupon bonds which are in high demand by those in the non-bank private sector who pay high marginal rates of tax.

Index-linked savings certificates ('granny bonds') were introduced in the United Kingdom in 1975 and index-linked gilts in March 1981. For the first year the index linked gilts were restricted to pension funds, life assurance companies and friendly societies. Their availability was extended to the personal sector in 1982. Despite these various devices the commercial banks can always obtain gilts from a variety of sources in the secondary markets when it is profitable to do so.

The Bank of England can also purchase, in the open market, short-dated gilts which are attractive to the banks, thereby causing a shortage of such gilts in the commercial banks' portfolios. Finally, the government can create incentives to encourage those parts of the public sector, such as local authorities and the nationalized industries which borrow directly from the open market, to do so in such a way that reduces their bank borrowing. For example, in 1982, UK local authorities were able to borrow at a variable interest rate from the Public Works Loans Board. Until then the Public Works Loans Board interest rate was fixed, which meant that when the rate of inflation was high local authority portfolio managers were encouraged to borrow short-term from the banks, thereby contributing to an expansion of the money supply (see *Bank of England Quarterly Bulletin*, 1983).

A recent feature of UK public debt management has been a return to overfunding. This refers to a situation in which the Bank of England sells more debt than is required to cover the deficit. If the debt is sold to the non-bank private sector then the money supply (sterling M3) will fall – see the accounting identity set out above. A policy of overfunding destroys any simple empirical relationship that might exist between the public sector deficit and changes in the money stock. Moreover, if the public sector debt is sold to overseas investors and the sterling required to make the purchase is obtained from the UK non-bank sector, then a fall in UK sterling bank deposits will be recorded and the money supply will fall.

The degree of overfunding of the UK deficit is shown in Table 4.4. Overfunding can cause a shortage of liquidity in the banking sector. To alleviate this, and to take pressure off short-term interest rates, the Bank of England used the excess funding to purchase commercial bills and thereby pump liquidity back into the economy. This has resulted in the accumulation of a 'bill mountain', which is a resource that can be run down in the future. The purchase of commercial bills, which this policy requires, implies that the monetary authorities are determining short-term interest rates and overriding market forces.

The above discussion indicates that any simple statistical association between public sector borrowing and the money stock will hide the complex flows that give rise to the series. Furthermore, if the public sector deficit is caused by a slump in aggregate demand then this will be reflected

Table 4.4 Overfunding of the UK public sector deficit

	Public sector borrowing requirement £ billion (1982 prices)	Overfunding (–)
1952–54	+ 4.9	+3.7
1955–59	+ 3.7	–0.4
1960–65	+ 4.8	–
1966–70	+ 4.4	+ 1.7
1971–75	+10.8	+ 3.2
1976–80	+15.7	+ 3.4
1981–84	+10.9	– 1.7
1980–81	+15.3	+ 2.5
1981–82	+ 9.5	– 3.9
1982–83	+ 9.2	– 1.5
1983–84	+ 9.6	– 3.6

Source: *Bank of England Quarterly Bulletin*, December 1984, Table 2, p. 490.

in an increase in bank borrowing by the private sector. Crisis borrowing to stave off bankruptcy is a feature of the early stages of any down-turn. To attribute the increase in the money supply, caused by private sector bank borrowing, to the rise in public sector borrowing is to confuse causality and the associated movements of two separable time series. Simple correlations between public sector borrowing and the money stock will pick up something – but the question is, what?

ECONOMETRIC STUDIES

A number of empirical studies have sought to establish an econometric relationship between public sector deficits and the money stock. Niskanen (1978, p. 601), using time-series data for the United States and adjusting for the monetary policy regime in force, found that, 'in any given year, the federal deficit does not appear to have any significant effect upon the rate of change in the money supply . . . This suggests a more complex theory of the supply of money is necessary'. Barro (1977; 1978) and Barro and Rush (1980), using annual and quarterly data for the United States over the period 1941–76, like Niskanen, could find no positive significant relationship. These results were, however, challenged by Hamburger and Zwick (1981), who used a modified definition of Federal debt and found that US public sector deficits did have a positive and significant impact on the money supply.

An important study is that carried out by Allen and Smith (1983). They were critical of the Niskanen, Barro, and Hamburger–Zwick studies.

Rather than using the current-period public sector deficit they used the change in public sector debt. They also used the monetary base rather than the money stock. Allen and Smith (1983) found in their study a positive and significant impact of the real trend value of the change in the stock of government debt upon the growth of the monetary base.

An examination of government deficits and the money stock in seven industrialized economies was conducted by Protopapadakis and Siegel (1984). They found that an increase in public debt was associated with a modest increase in the monetary base and M1 in the United States. For France and the United Kingdom the growth in debt was associated with a decrease in the monetary base; in West Germany, Japan and Switzerland the growth in public sector debt was associated with a decrease in both the money base and M1. They concluded that they could not find a simple overall relationship between debt growth and money base growth and that, at the very best, there was only a weak relationship between debt growth and M1 growth (for the United States, United Kingdom and Italy, where the debt to income ratio is high). In their cross-national study, Dornbusch and Fischer (1981) could only find a significant positive relationship between budget deficits and money growth in three countries – Guatemala, Israel and Norway. Thornton (1984), Joines (1985) and King and Plosser (1985) could find no evidence to support the thesis that public sector deficits were monetized.

Using UK data, Parkin (1975) found a positive link between the public sector deficit and the money supply, as did Akhtar and Wilford (1979). These results were criticized by Cobham (1980) and Kearney and MacDonald (1985), who could find no single systematic relationship between public sector borrowing, the money supply and interest rates. Others have used macro-forecasting model simulations to search for a relationship. Budd and Burns (1979) used the London Business School model and found no relationship, whereas Middleton *et al.* (1981) concluded that 'if the Treasury model is a plausible description of the economy, the implication is that in order to pursue stability in Sterling M3 and in interest rates the authorities may have to stabilize their own borrowing and not the economy'.

While the econometric evidence is clearly in dispute the balance tips in favour of those studies which conclude that to the extent that a positive relationship between public sector deficits and the money supply does exist, then it is at best weak. To understand the nature of the relationship it is necessary to look behind the aggregate data and to consider the flows and policy regimes that give rise to them.

PUBLIC SECTOR DEFICITS AND INTEREST RATES

In the earlier theoretical discussion one route by which a public sector deficit might influence the money supply was through the impact of the deficit on interest rates. Thus, the empirical question is whether increases in public sector deficits cause interest rates to rise. Kearney and MacDonald (1985) could find no relationship for the United Kingdom. Evans (1985) and Plosser (1982) found no relationship for the United States. While Feldstein (1981) did find a relationship in the United States between public deficits and interest rates, his data base has been challenged by Leimer and Lesnoy (1982) and Seater and Mariano (1985).[11]

CONCLUSIONS

What, then, is the relationship between public sector deficits and the money stock? The studies which have been reviewed demonstrate that any answer to this question must be highly qualified because it all depends upon the place and time to which the study refers. In some economies for some time periods public sector deficits are monetized and play a significant role in determining the money stock. However, the consistent message which is dominant in the majority of studies is that while large public sector deficits do have the *potential* to increase the money stock, this is seldom realized, primarily because of the debt management policies of governments.

It is, therefore, difficult to find an objective basis for many of the strongly held popular beliefs about the impact of public sector deficits on the money supply and hence ultimately upon inflation.[12] Many of the issues are no better understood today than they were two hundred years ago. If there is no predictive content to current-period public sector deficits then neo-classical models predicated upon rational expectations will find no link between deficits, the money supply, interest rates and inflation.

Does this mean that we need better theory to constrain further empirical work in this area? The answer is probably no. Until now theory has been used to generate any conclusion imaginable. What is needed is better empirical work to constrain the theorising (see Blinder, 1985) and that means empirical studies which pay more attention to the institutional features of the economy which is being studied.

APPENDIX 4A: THE GOVERNMENT BUDGET CONSTRAINT[13]

The government's dynamic budget constraint links debt accumulation to the level of debt, interest rates, and the non-interest budget surplus:

$$B_{t+1} = (B_t - V_t)(1 + i_t) \tag{4A.1}$$

where B_t is nominal debt at the beginning of period t: i_t is the nominal rate of interest from t to $(t+1)$; and V_t is the market value of the debt. Equation (4A.1) can be written as

$$B_t = V_t + [1/(1+i_t)]\, B_{t+1} \tag{4A.2}$$

Starting from time zero and solving recursively forward in time gives:

$$B_0 = S_0 + \left(\frac{1}{1 + i_0} V_1 \ldots \frac{1}{(1+i_0)\ldots(1+i_{t-1})} V_t\right) + \frac{1}{(1+i_0)\ldots(1+i_{t-1})} B_{t+1} \tag{4A.3}$$

where S_t is the nominal primary surplus.

The intertemporal budget constraint is then obtained by using a transversality condition, that nominal debt does not grow faster than the nominal rate of interest for ever. That is to say, at least some of the debt service must be earned through non-interest surpluses rather than entirely borrowed. It follows, therefore, that:

$$\lim_{t\to\infty} ([1+i_0]\ldots[1+i_t])^{-1} B_{t-1} = 0 \tag{4A.4}$$

Equation (4A.4) does not imply that debt is ever repaid or even remains constant.

Combining Equations (4A.3) and (4A.4) gives:

$$B_0 = \sum_{t=0}^{\infty} R_t V_t \tag{4A.5}$$

where $R_t = ([1 + i_0]\ldots[1+i_t])^{-1}$. Equation (4A.5) is the government budget constraint which states that the present value of debt service must equal the value of debt outstanding.

Now define

$$Y_{t+1} = (1 + y_t)(1 + p_t)\, Y_t$$

where Y_t is nominal GNP at period t; y_t is the growth rate of output; and p_t is inflation. Dividing both sides of Equation (4A.2) by Y_t gives:

$$b_t = v_t + [\,(1+y_t)(1+p_t) / (1+i_t)\,]\, b_{t-1}$$

where b_t is the debt to GNP ratio and v_t the surplus to GNP ratio.

Repeating the process as before gives:

$$b_0 = \Sigma\ \gamma_t^t\ v_t \qquad (4A.6)$$

where

$$\gamma_t{}' \equiv \left[\frac{(1+y_0)\,(1+p_0)}{(1+i_0)} \cdots \frac{(1+y_{t-1})\,(1+p_{t-1})}{(1+i_{t-1})} \right]$$

Equation (4A.6) is another way of looking at the budget constraint of Equation (4A.5), focusing instead on the debt income ratio and the non-interest surplus as a fraction of GNP.

If v is constant then:

$$b_0 = [\ \Sigma\ \gamma^{\,t}\,]\ v\ = \frac{1}{1-\gamma}\ v$$

i.e.

$$v = (1-\gamma)\ b_0 = \left(\frac{r-y}{1+r} \right) b_0$$

where r is the average, or long-term, real interest rate.

From the government budget constraint we know that money plus debt creation, in real per capita terms, equals the non-interest deficit plus debt service:

$$\frac{\dot{M}}{NP} + \frac{\dot{B}}{NP} = v + ib \qquad (4A.7)$$

$$\frac{\dot{B}}{NP} = (n+p)\ b \qquad (4A.8)$$

where N and n are, respectively, the population and its growth rate, and $\dot{X}=\mathrm{d}X/\mathrm{d}t$. Equation (4A.8) gives the condition for constant per capita real debt. Combining Equations (4A.7) and (4A.8) gives the growth rate of money, u, as an increasing function of the stock of debt. This is implicitly defined as:

$$um = v + (r-n)b \qquad (4A.9)$$

From equation (4A.9) it follows that a policy leading to increased debt accumulation must ultimately lead to more inflation, assuming that the demand for money is less than unit-elastic with respect to the interest rate.

NOTES

1. This is part of a long-running debate between Keynesians and monetarists (see Kaldor, 1970; Tobin, 1970). The essence of the Keynesian argument is that in

order to finance their real expenditure plans (demand) individuals will demand more credit; profit-maximizing financial institutions, especially banks, will respond to this incentive and expand bank lending to the private sector, thereby increasing the money supply. If rising interests do not discourage borrowing then the lender of the last resort facility allows bank reserves to increase in direct response to the increased demand for credit (see Minsky, 1982; and Chick, 1983).

2. For an excellent presentation of the derivation of this relationship see Cuthbertson (1986).
3. See *Bank of England Quarterly Bulletin*, December 1984, p. 487. While this argument is of theoretical significance, covering the tender during the 1980s has been largely irrelevant, especially since in the United Kingdom the government has in recent years been overfunding the deficit.
4. In this chapter I have set out the process of credit creation in broad theoretical terms. The empirical relevance of such theories is, of course, heavily bounded by institutional features of real banking systems. Again, see Llewellyn's chapter in this volume, which outlines the features of the UK banking system.
5. This approach has not gone undisputed: see Buiter (1985); Darby (1984); McCallum (1984); Protopapadakis and Siegel (1987).
6. See Barro and Gordon (1983a; 1983b). The time-inconsistency problem was treated as 'seigniorage' in an earlier literature: see King and Plosser (1984).
7. I am grateful to an unknown referee who helped me clarify this point on an earlier draft.
8. If the government runs a big deficit then fighting inflation with tight monetary policy will result in high interest rates which in turn will result in the monetization of government deficits and the engineering of an inflation tax. Thus a tight monetary policy will eventually lead to inflation. This is the Sargent and Wallace unpleasant arithmetic result.
9. Darby (1984) found that for the United States the real discount rate was less than the real growth rate. McCallum (1984) advances a similar argument. However, Miller and Sargent (1984) replied to these criticisms that in the long run the large deficits would force up interest rates and reverse this. McCallum (1984) has also pointed out that the optimization carried out in the original Sargent and Wallace paper was not the only possibility. Using infinite-lived individuals with money entering their utility functions, McCallum showed that optimization rules out the interest rate exceeding the growth rate. Burbidge (1984) produced similar results.
10. See King and Plosser (1985); Buiter (1985); Kaldor (1980). Seigniorage seems to have been more important in Italy.
11. See also Tanzi (1985) and Seater (1985).
12. Walters (1985, p. 152), one of the architects of the post-1979 UK macroeconomic strategy, has argued that any relationship between the PSBR and sterling M3 is likely to be a *long-run* one: 'there is no close correlation year to year in the growth of Sterling M3 and the PSBR ... But it was correctly thought that a *persistently* high PSBR would be bound to be reflected ultimately in a high rate of growth in Sterling M3 and, therefore, into the rate of inflation'.
13. See Blanchard *et al.* (1985).

REFERENCES

Akhtar, M.A. and Wilford, D.S. (1979) 'The influence of the United Kingdom's public sector deficit on its money stock, 1963–1979', *Bulletin of Economic Research*.

Allen, S.D. and Smith, M.D. (1983) 'Government borrowing and monetary accommodation', *Journal of Monetary Economics*, vol. 12, pp. 605–16.

Alt, J.E. (1985) 'It may be a good way to run an oil company but . . . oil and the political economy of Thatcherism', mimeo: Washington University, St Louis, MO.

Bain, A.D. (1982a) *Bank Lending, Monetary Control and Funding Policy*, Paper no. 19, presented to the Bank of England's Panel of Academic Consultants.

Bain, A.D. (1982b) 'Finance in the mixed economy', in Lord Roll (ed.), *The Mixed Economy*, London: Macmillan.

Baltensperger, E. (1972) 'Economics of scale, firm size and concentration in banking', *Journal of Money, Credit and Banking*, vol. 4.

Bank of England Quarterly Bulletin (1983) 'Monetary effects of the financing of local authorities', December, p. 76.

Barro, R.J. (1974) 'Are government bonds net wealth', *Journal of Political Economy*, vol. 82, November–December.

Barro, R.J. (1977) 'Unanticipated money growth and unemployment in the United States', *American Economic Review*, vol. 67, March.

Barro, R.J. (1978) 'Unanticipated money, output and the price level', *Journal of Political Economy*, vol. 68, August.

Barro, R.J. (1978) 'Comments from an unreconstructed Ricardian', *Journal of Monetary Economics*.

Barro, R.J. and Gordon, D.B. (1983a) 'Rules, discretion, and reputation in a model of monetary policy', *Journal of Monetary Economics*, vol. 12, pp. 101–21.

Barro, R.J. and Gordon, D.B. (1983b) 'A positive theory of monetary policy in a natural rate model', *Journal of Political Economy*, vol. 91, pp. 589–610.

Barro, R.J. and Rush, M. (1980) 'Unanticipated money and economic activity', in S. Fischer (ed.), *Rational Expectations and Economic Policy*, Chicago: University of Chicago Press.

Beenstock, M. and Minford, P. (1980) Evidence presented to the Treasury and Civil Service Committee, *Memoranda on Monetary Policy*, London: HMSO.

Blanchard, O., Dornbush, R. and Buiter, W. (1985) *Public Debt and Fiscal Responsibility*, Centre for European Public Policy Studies, Paper no. 22.

Blinder, A.S. (1983) 'On the monetization of deficits' in L.H. Meyer (ed.), *The Economic Consequences of Government Deficits*, Boston: Kluwer-Nijhoff Publishing.

Blinder, A.S. (1985) 'Comments on Dwyer's paper', *Journal of Money, Credit and Banking*, vol. 17, no. 4.

Blinder, A.S. and Solow, R.M. (1973) 'Does Fiscal Policy Matter?', *Journal of Public Economics*, November.

Blinder, A.S. and Solow, R.M. (1974) 'Analytical foundations of fiscal policy', in A.S. Blinder *et al.*, *The Economics of Public Finance*, Washington, DC: Brookings Institution.

Buchanan, J.M. and Wagner, R. (1978) 'Dialogues concerning fiscal religion', *Journal of Monetary Economics*, August.

Budd, A. and Burns, T. (1979) 'Should the PSBR be cut next year?', *Economic*

Outlook, vol. 3, August.
Buiter, W.H. (1985) 'A guide to public sector deficits', *Economic Policy*, vol. 1, no. 1.
Burbidge, J.B. (1984) 'Government debt: reply', *American Economic Review*, September, pp. 766–7.
Chick, V. (1983) *Macroeconomics After Keynes: A Reconsideration of the General Theory*, Oxford: Philip Allan.
Christ, C. (1968) 'A simple macroeconomic model with a government budget restraint', *Journal of Political Economy*, January.
Chrystal, A. (1984) 'Dutch disease or monetarist medicine? The British economy under Mrs Thatcher', *Federal Reserve Bank of St Louis Review*, vol. 66, no. 5.
Cobham, D. (1980) 'Comment on Akhtar and Willett', *Bulletin of Economic Research*, November.
Cobham, D. (1985) 'Macro policy under Thatcher, Healey and Mitterrand: assessment and comparison', mimeo: University of St Andrews.
Cuthbertson, K. (1986) 'Techniques of monetary control in the UK', *Journal of Economic Studies*, vol. 11, no. 4, pp. 46–68.
Darby, M.R. (1984) 'Some pleasant monetarist arithmetic', Federal Reserve Bank of Minneapolis, *Quarterly Review*, Spring.
Dornbusch, R. and Fischer, S. (1981) 'Budget deficits and inflation' in J. Flanders and A. Razin (eds), *Development in an Inflationary World*, London: Academic Press.
Dwyer, G.P. (1985) 'Federal deficits, interest rates and monetary policy', *Journal of Money, Credit and Banking*, vol. 17, no. 4.
Evans, P. (1985) 'Do large deficits produce high interest rates?', *American Economic Review*, March.
Feldstein, M.S. (1981) 'Government deficits and aggregate demand', *Journal of Monetary Economics*, vol. 9.
Feldstein, M.S. (1982) 'Government deficits and aggregate demand', *Journal of Monetary Economics*, vol. 10.
Feldstein, M.S. (1984) 'Can an increased budget deficit be contractionary?', NBER Discussion Paper.
Friedman, M. (1980) Evidence presented to the Treasury and Civil Service Committee, *Memoranda on Monetary Policy*, London: HMSO.
Gale, D. (1982) *Money in Equilibrium*, Cambridge: Cambridge University Press.
Gale, D. (1983) *Money in Disequilibrium*, Cambridge: Cambridge University Press.
Goodhart, C.A.E. (1984) *Monetary Theory and Practice – The U.K. Experience*, London: Macmillan.
Gordon, R.J. (1980) 'Comment' (on Barro and Rush) in S. Fischer (ed.), *Rational Expectations and Economic Policy* Chicago: University of Chicago Press.
Gurley, J.G. and Shaw, E.S. (1960) *Money in a Theory of Finance*, Washington, DC: Brookings Institution.
Hamburger, M.J. and Zwick, B. (1981) 'Deficits, money and inflation', *Journal of Monetary Economics*, January.
Jackson, P.M. (1985) 'Perspectives on practical monetarism' in P.M. Jackson (ed.), *Implementing Government Policy Initiatives: The Thatcher Administration 1979/83*, London: Royal Institute of Public Administration.
Joines, D.H. (1985) 'Deficits and money growth in the United States 1972/83', *Journal of Monetary Economics*, vol. 16.
Kaldor, M. (1980) Evidence presented to the Treasury and Civil Service

Committee, *Memoranda on Monetary Policy*, London: HMSO.
Kearney, C. and MacDonald, R. (1985) 'Public sector borrowing, the money supply and interest rates', *Oxford Bulletin of Economics and Statistics*, vol. 47, no. 3.
King, R.G. and Plosser, C.I. (1984) 'Money, deficits and inflation', mimeo: University of Rochester, July.
King, R.G. and Plosser, C.I. (1985) 'Money deficits and inflation' in K. Brunner and A.H. Meltzer (eds), *Understanding Monetary Regimes*, Carnegie-Rochester Conference Series on Public Policy, vol. 22, Amsterdam: North Holland.
Laidler, D. (1976) 'Inflation in Britain: a monetarist perspective', *American Economic Review*, vol. 66, no. 4.
Laidler, D. (1981) 'Comments on the paper by P.E. Middleton, C.J. Mowl, J.C. Odling-Smee and C.J. Riley' in B. Griffiths and G.E. Wood (eds), *Monetary Targets* London: Macmillan.
Leimer, D.R. and Lesnoy, S.D. (1982) 'Social security and private saving: new time series evidence', *Journal of Political Economy*, vol. 90.
McCallum, B. (1984) 'Are bond financed deficits inflationary? A Ricardian analysis', *Journal of Political Economy*, vol. 92, February, pp. 123–35.
McKinnon, R.I. (1973) *Money and Capital in Economic Development*, Washington, DC: Brookings Institution.
Meyer, S.A. (1982) 'Margaret Thatcher's economic experiment: are there lessons for the Reagan administration?', *Federal Reserve Bank of Philadelphia Business Review*, May–June.
Middleton, P.E. (1981) 'The relationship between monetary and fiscal policy', in M.J. Artis and M.H. Miller *Essays in Fiscal and Monetary Policy*, Oxford: Oxford University Press.
Middleton, P.E., Mowl, C.J., Odling-Smee, J.C. and Riley, C.J. (1981) 'Monetary targets and the public sector borrowing requirement' in B. Griffiths and G.E. Wood (eds), *Monetary Targets*, London: Macmillan.
Miller, P.R. and Sargent, T.J. (1984) 'A reply to Darby', *Federal Reserve Bank of Minneapolis Quarterly Review*, Spring, pp. 21–6.
Minsky, H.P. (1982) *Inflation, Recession and Economic Policy*, Brighton: Wheatsheaf.
Mishkin, F.S. (1982) 'Does anticipated aggregate demand policy matter? Further econometric results', *American Economic Review*, vol. 72, September.
Niehaus, J. (1978) *The Theory of Money*, Baltimore, MD: Johns Hopkins University Press.
Niskanen, W.A. (1978) 'Deficits, government spending and inflation: what is the evidence?', *Journal of Monetary Economics*, vol. 4.
Parkin, M. (1975) 'Where is Britain's inflation going?', *Lloyds Bank Review*, July.
Parkin, M. (1984) 'The United Kingdom: political economy and macroeconomics: a comment on the Walters papers', Carnegie-Rochester Conference Series on Public Policy, vol. 21, Amsterdam: North Holland.
Plosser, G.I. (1982) 'Government financing decisions and asset returns', *Journal of Monetary Economics*, May.
Protopapadakis, A.A. and Siegel, J.J. (1984) 'Government debt, the money supply and inflation: theory and evidence for seven industralised countries', Federal Reserve Bank of Philadelphia Working Paper 84(4), August.
Protopapadakis, A.A. and Siegel, J.J. (1987) 'Are money growth and inflation related to government deficits? Evidence from ten industralised economies', *Journal of International Money and Finance*, vol. 6, pp. 31–48.

Sargent, T.J. and Wallace, N. (1981) 'Some unpleasant monetarist arithmetic', *Federal Reserve Bank of Minneapolis, Quarterly Review*, vol. 5, Fall.
Seater, J.J. (1985) 'Does government debt matter?', *Journal of Monetary Economics*, vol. 16, no. 1.
Seater, J.J. and Mariano, R.S. (1985) 'New tests of the life cycle and tax discounting hypotheses', *Journal of Monetary Economics*, vol. 15.
Silber, W. (1970) 'Fiscal policy in IS–LM analysis: a correction', *Journal of Money, Credit and Banking*, November.
Small, D.H. (1979) 'Unanticipated money growth and unemployment in the United States: comment', *American Economic Review*, vol. 69, December.
Steindl, F.G. (1974) 'Money and income: the view from the government budget restraint', *Journal of Finance*, vol. 29, September, pp. 1143–8.
Tanzi, V. (1985) 'Fiscal deficits and interest rates in the United States: an empirical analysis, 1960–84', *IMF Staff Papers*, December.
Thornton, D.L. (1984) 'Monetizing the debt', *Federal Reserve Bank of St Louis, Quarterly Review*, December.
Tobin, J. (1963) 'Commercial banks as creators of money', in D. Carson (ed.), *Banking and Monetary Studies*, Homewood, IL: Irwin.
Tobin, J. (1970) 'Money and income: *post hoc ergo propter hoc*?' *Quarterly Journal of Economics*, vol. 84, May.
Tobin, J. (1980a) *Asset Accumulation and Economic Acitivty*, Oxford: Basil Blackwell.
Tobin, J. (1980b) 'Government deficits and capital accumulation', in D. Currie and H. Peters, *Contemporary Economic Analysis*, vol. 2, London: Croom Helm.
Tobin, J. (1982) 'Money and finance in the macroeconomic process', *Journal of Money, Credit, and Banking*, May.
Tobin, J. and Buiter, W.H. (1980) 'Fiscal and monetary policies, capital formation and economic activity' in G.M. von Furstenberg (ed.), *The Government and Capital Formation*, Cambridge, MA: Ballinger.
Treasury and Civil Service Committee (1980), *Memoranda on Monetary Policy*, London: HMSO.
Treasury and Civil Service Committee (1981), *Memoranda on Monetary Policy*, London: HMSO.
Walters, A.A. (1984) 'The United Kingdom: political economy and macroeconomics', Carnegie-Rochester Conference Series on Public Policy, vol. 21, Amsterdam: North Holland.
Walters, A.A. (1985) 'Deficits in the United Kingdom', in P. Cagan (ed.), *Essays in Contemporary Economic Problems, 1985: The Economy in Deficit*, American Enterprise Institute.
Weintraub, R. (1980) 'Comment' (on Barro and Rush) in S. Fischer (ed.), *Rational Expectations and Economic Policy*, Chicago: University of Chicago Press.
Whiteley, P.F. (1985) 'Evaluating the monetarist experiment in Britain', paper presented to the PSA Annual Meeting, University of Manchester.

5 · THE INTERNATIONAL TRANSMISSION OF INFLATION

George Zis

INTRODUCTION

In the second half of the 1960s inflation emerged as a major policy problem in all industrial economies. The world-wide character of inflation was one of the phenomena which economists seeking to isolate the principal determinants of rising prices had to explain.[1] In the intense debate on the causes of inflation, the relative adequacy of the competing theories was largely judged on the basis of the assumed channels via which price rises are transmitted across countries. However, analyses of the transmission of inflation did not only serve as an argument in the attempts to discriminate among the competing hypotheses of the main determinants of the rate of inflation. They also featured prominently in the studies of the deepening crisis of the Bretton Woods international monetary system. But while economists sharply disagreed on the causes of inflation, the late 1960s witnessed a growing consensus in favour of exchange rate flexibility. This development largely reflected a belief that under a system of flexible exchange rates individual economies would be less exposed to, if not totally insulated from inflationary pressures emanating from the rest of the world. Given, then, that economists agreed on the insulation properties of exchange rate flexibility and, by implication, therefore, accepted that the transmission of inflation is affected by the exchange rate regime, one may express surprise at how sharply they diverged in their diagnoses of the causes of inflation. However, the intellectual climate of the 1960s and early 1970s was hardly conducive in generating consistency in economists' views on the determinants of the inflation rate and on the properties of alternative exchange rate regimes. Analyses of macroeconomic phenomena, such as inflation, usually rested on the 'closed economy' assumption. For most macroeconomists inflation and the gradual disintegration of the IMF international monetary system were two distinct problems, only very loosely connected. Solutions to either problem were not perceived to be of much pertinence to the other. Indeed, as will be argued later, even analyses of the causes of inflation by economists who explicitly recognized the implications of openness were profoundly influenced by the closed economy assumption when prescribing exchange rate flexibility as a means of insulating countries from external inflationary pressures. Be that as it may, the consensus among economists regarding the insulation properties of flexible exchange rates provides a useful basis for organizing the discussion of the mechanisms by which inflation is transmitted across countries. That is, economists' views on the international transmission of inflation will first be discussed in relation to the Bretton Woods system and then as presented for the post-1973 'system' of flexible exchange rates.

What were the international features of inflation in the period up to 1973 which the competing theories of inflation had to explain? In the seven year period 1953–9 the average annual rate of inflation for all industrial countries was 1.8 per cent. This rose to 2.2 per cent for the quinquennium 1960–4, after which inflation continually accelerated in all industrial countries. For the period 1965–70 the average rate at which prices increased was 4.0 per cent per annum, climbing to 7.7 per cent in 1973. In addition to the time trends of national inflation rates, there was a second feature of the pre-1973 experience which attracted the attention of economists. Pattison (1976), for example, presented statistical evidence revealing a high degree of convergence among countries' rates of inflation during the period 1956–72. Pattison's evidence was all the more impressive because it showed that even after rates of price increases started to accelerate during the second half of the 1960s, there was no change in their degree of convergence as measured by their standard deviation. Therefore, the competing theories of inflation had to explain, first, the simultaneous acceleration of national inflation rates, and, second, their convergence. Attempts to account for these two phenomena involved, of course, considerations of the channels via which inflation can potentially be transmitted across countries.

The next two sections outline, first, the principal schools of thought on the causes of inflation and, then, the mechanisms of transmission associated with them. These will be followed by a discussion of the main arguments for flexible exchange rates and an evaluation of the experience with exchange rate flexibility after 1973. The discussion will provide a basis for an assessment of the implications of recent developments in the theory of the demand for money for the transmission of monetary disturbances across countries, for anti-inflation policy and for the case for flexible exchange rates. The final section contains some conclusions.

COMPETING THEORIES OF THE CAUSES OF INFLATION

By the end of the 1960s economists had advanced a variety of diagnoses of the causes of world inflation which provided the bases for various policy prescriptions. However, the debate was essentially between two schools of thought. The fundamental distinction between these was, as Johnson (1972a, p. 9) observed, whether world inflation was to be perceived 'as a series or collection of individual national problems, essentially sociological in origin, [or] as an international monetary problem'. This characterization of the debate on the causes of inflation is, perhaps, an oversimplification as within each camp there existed sharply divergent, and often incompatible, views, while a third group of economists adopted an eclectic stance arguing that inflation is the outcome of both sociological and international monetary forces.[2] Be that as it may, Johnson's summary description of the alternate hypotheses is useful as it highlights the reasons why economists could not agree on the most appropriate policies for the control of inflation.

Johnson (1972a; 1972b; 1973) and Laidler and Nobay (1976) traced the emergence of the sociological view of inflation to the intellectual influence of Keynes (1936). A somewhat uncritical adoption of Keynes's assumptions resulted in economists developing their analyses of macro-economic phenomena as if economies were closed. A country's rate of inflation was perceived as the outcome of essentially domestic forces. That there could exist systematic interactions among countries' rates of inflation was a proposition that received hardly any attention. Bronfenbrenner and Holzman (1965), in their major survey of inflation theory, entirely ignored the international aspects of inflation. The second feature of Keynes (1936) which influenced analyses of the determinants of inflation in the 1950s and 1960s was the treatment of the money wage rate as an exogenous variable. Prices were, therefore, seen as determined by a mark-up on money wages. This perception of price determination resulted in what Laidler and Nobay (1976) described as a 'curious phenomenon' whereby although price inflation was the problem under investigation economists concentrated their attempts on explaining wage inflation. This practice involved a line of thought which implied that understanding the determinants of wage inflation was sufficient for the understanding of price inflation. Further, this practice implied that the control of money wage rate changes would automatically ensure the control of the rate of inflation. But Keynes's treatment of the money wage rate as an exogenous variable had another, equally significant, consequence. Any conceivable hypothesis regarding money wage determination was, in principle, consistent with the Keynesian doctrine. In brief, there were as many 'Keynesian' theories of inflation as hypotheses regarding money wage determination with all, however, sharing the perception of inflation as an essentially national problem.

Prior to the acceleration of inflation in the second half of the 1960s the distinction between cost-push and demand-pull inflation dominated the debate on the causes of rising prices. In the presence of unemployment, other things equal, an increase in aggregate expenditure would lead to a rise in real output. If, alternatively, the economy were fully employed, then an increase in aggregate expenditure would result in wages being pulled up and, therefore, in price rises.

Proponents of the cost-push explanation maintained that trade unions could push wages up, *independently* of the state of demand in the labour market, by exploiting their 'monopoly' power. In response to such wage increases employers were assumed to raise prices in order to maintain their profit margins. Thus trade union militancy was diagnosed as the principal source of inflationary pressures in the economy. The policy implication of this diagnosis was that trade union power should be curbed, or at least, that governments should impose limits to wage increases. The advocacy of statutory or voluntary incomes policies firmly rested on the cost-push explanation of inflation.

The plausibility of the cost-push hypothesis was not seriously undermined by the impressive statistical evidence presented by Phillips (1958) indicating an inverse relationship between money wage inflation and the level of unemployment. Lipsey (1960), when attempting to provide a theoretical rationale for this evidence, argued that the Phillips curve was neutral between the demand-pull and cost-push hypotheses. Trade union militancy could alter the trade-off between wage inflation and unemployment. Thus, though the Phillips curve implied that fiscal and, perhaps, monetary policies could play a role in the control of inflation, it was not incompatible with the proposition that incomes policies could permanently improve the trade-off between the rate of change of money wage rates and the level of unemployment. The Phillips curve was, of course, fully consistent with the prevailing Keynesian intellectual environment. Price inflation was to be explained by developments in the domestic labour market, though Phillips himself was careful to note the potential influence of fluctuations in import prices.

Developments in the second half of the 1960s sharply contradicted existing beliefs regarding the principal causes of inflation. In contrast to expectations based on the Phillips curve, inflation and unemployment rose simultaneously. There was a upsurge in industrial unrest, especially in the public sector of the economy. Conventional indices of trade union militancy could not explain the acceleration of price inflation. Thus economists such as Bach (1973) and Jones (1973) argued that what was being observed was a 'new' type of inflation reflecting social tensions and conflicts. Harrod (1972), for example, argued that the inflation and the students' unrest of the late 1960s stemmed from closely interrelated causes, both phenomena reflecting society's more permissive attitudes. Marris (1972) maintained that trade unions had ceased to fear unemployment and, consequently, had become more militant. Their aggressiveness was prompted by 'frustrations' arising from low rates of growth. Balogh (1970) suggested that income inequalities and conspicuous consumption had provoked trade unions to demand large wage increases which employers willingly conceded because they could raise their prices. Hicks (1974) was also among the economists who regarded the post-1965 inflation as a 'new' phenomenon largely sociological in character. He identified two stages in the development of inflation. During the first, rates of change of prices moved broadly in line with the predictions of the Phillips curve. However, even in this phase, unlike past experience, wages increased in sectors which were not experiencing boom conditions. Wages rose 'not because of labour scarcity but because of *unfairness* (Hicks, 1974, p. 71).

In the second stage 'social' pressures for wage increases became dominant. Hicks (1974, p. 71) felt that it was 'no longer the case that the main force that is raising wages is labour scarcity'. Consistent with the emerging view that the observed inflation was 'new', Bispham (1972) drew attention to the NIESR abandoning its attempts to forecast wages on the basis of indicators of pressures of demand, of past prices, or of previous rises in real income.

The sociological view of the causes of inflation was consistent with the Keynesian tradition of treating the money wage level as an exogenous variable and of ignoring the implications of economies being open. However, the sociological explanation contrasted with the cost-push hypothesis in one important respect. Economists adhering to the latter theory did accept that their hypotheses could be subjected to empirical testing. But this was not the case with those economists who viewed inflation as a sociological phenomenon. If post-1965 inflation was 'new' then past episodes of persistently rising prices could shed no light on current experience. Further, it was suggested, the sociological character of inflation necessarily implied that there could not exist predictable and systematic relationships between the relevant variables, even if these could be adequately proxied. Thus the acceptance or rejection of the sociological explanation of inflation could not rest on empirical evidence and, instead, became a matter of faith.[3] In terms of policy, the sociological school of thought argued, the 'problem' facing each national government was to formulate incomes and prices policies which were appropriate to each particular economy given that the nature of social tensions leading to inflationary pressures differed among countries.

The alternative to the hypothesis that world inflation in the late 1960s was the sum of independent national sociological problems was the view that inflation was an international phenomenon to be explained by developments at the world rather than the country level. Mundell (1971; 1972) and Johnson (1972a; 1972b; 1973) provided the early statements of this view. The perception of inflation as an international problem rested, first, on the judgement that inflation is a monetary phenomenon and, second, on an assessment of the implications of the Bretton Woods system of essentially fixed exchange rates for national price levels to move independently of each other. It was argued that fixed exchange rates result in countries being linked with each other in a way similar to that in which regions within an economy are linked through the use of a common currency. The monetary theory of inflation in a closed economy can then be applied to the world economy, the components of which are the individual national economies. That is, the rate of growth of the world money supply determines the world rate of inflation which individual countries have to accept. If inflation is an international monetary problem, the policy prescription that followed was that for inflation to be controlled it was necessary and sufficient that the rate of growth of the world money supply was kept in line with the rate of growth of the world demand for money. This policy implication raised fundamental questions regarding the nature of the Bretton Woods international monetary system and, especially, in relation to the role of the United States in international monetary relations. Further, the diagnosis of inflation as an international monetary problem implied that the capacity of individual countries to influence the world rate of inflation and, therefore, their own rate of inflation, directly depended on their size or, more specifically, on the ratio of their money supply to the world money supply. The higher the ratio, the greater would be the impact of a country's monetary policy on the world rate of inflation. Now, this proposition focused attention on US monetary policy. It was argued that given the size of the United States relative to the world economy, the US money supply growth rate would play a significant role in determining the world rate of inflation. This was especially the case because of the reserve currency status of the dollar. First, the United States was largely free of balance of payments constraints when formulating its monetary policy. Second, Genberg and Swobada (1977) argued that because the dollar was a reserve currency the impact on the world money supply growth rate of an increase in the domestic credit expansion in the United States would be greater than that of an equivalent increase in the domestic credit expansion in, say, France.

For the perception of inflation as an international problem the rapid growth of the Eurodollar market since the early 1960s had a number of implications. If Eurodollars could legitimately be counted as part of the world money supply, then the spectacular growth in their volume could be perceived as an independent source of inflationary pressures. Economists focusing on the world money supply growth rate did not adopt a common approach to the treatment of the Eurodollars. Parkin *et al.* (1975) and McKinnon (1984), for example, utilized world money supply aggregates which did not include Eurocurrencies. In doing so, it is arguable that their analyses of world money supply trends during the era of the Bretton Woods system are somewhat incomplete. But, as Sweeney and Willett (1977) have argued, it is not legitimate to add Eurocurrencies to the aggregate of national money supplies on a one-to-one basis. Such a procedure, by exaggerating world money supply growth rates, would yield misleading results. However, the size of the Eurodollar market, though it raised important questions relating to the measurement of the world money supply, was not particularly significant for the diagnosis of inflation as an international monetary problem.

The principal implication of the rapid growth of the Eurodollar market was that capital became increasingly mobile and the various exchange controls increasingly ineffective. Therefore, in terms of the Fleming–Mundell model, the short run, during which countries could enjoy a degree of monetary autonomy, was continuously reduced in chronological terms during the 1960s. That is, whatever the inflationary pressures emanating from the Eurodollar market may have been, the main effect of the growth of the market was to increase the speed by which inflationary impulses were transmitted across countries.

As is well established, for inflation to be a monetary phenomenon in a closed economy, with its control necessitating the control of the money supply growth rate, it is necessary that the demand for money function be stable. Under fixed exchange rates, it was argued, the world economy could be treated as a closed economy. Thus, for inflation to be an international monetary problem it required that there existed a stable world demand-for-money function. Gray *et al.* (1976) presented statistical evidence suggesting the existence of such a stable function. Miller (1976) challenged the interpretation of their findings and argued that if countries' demand-for-money functions were stable, then their aggregate, the world demand-for-money function, would also be stable. However, Duck and Zis (1978) showed that Miller's criticism would be valid only if countries' demand-for-money functions were identical. Duck and Zis assumed that the demand-for-money functions in countries A and B are of the form:

$$M^d_A = K_A \bar{Y}_A P_A \qquad (5.1)$$

$$M^d_B = K_B \bar{Y}_B P_B \qquad (5.2)$$

where Y denotes full-employment income and P the price level. If no relationship between P_A and P_B is postulated, then the concept of a world price level, P_w, has no economic meaning. However, for illustrative purposes they defined P_w as the weighted average of P_A and P_B:

$$P_w = \frac{P_A \bar{Y}_A + P_B \bar{Y}_B}{\bar{Y}_A + \bar{Y}_B} \tag{5.3}$$

which can be rewritten as

$$P_w = dP_A + (1-d)P_B \tag{5.4}$$

The implication of assuming no systematic relationship between P_A and P_B is that no unique combination of P_A and P_B is associated with any particular level of P_w.

The world demand for money, M_w^d, is given by

$$M_w^d = K_A \bar{Y}_A P_A + K_B \bar{Y}_B P_B \tag{5.5}$$

and the world money supply by

$$M_w^s = M_A^s + M_B^s \tag{5.6}$$

Equilibrium requires that

$$M_w^s = M_w^d \tag{5.7}$$

Duck and Zis then proceeded to assume that country A increases and country B decreases its money supply in such a way that M_w^s and P_w remain unchanged. If

$$\Delta M_w^s = \Delta M_A + \Delta M_B = 0 \tag{5.8}$$

it follows that

$$K_A \bar{Y}_A \Delta P_A = K_B \bar{Y}_B \Delta P_B \tag{5.9}$$

while

$$\Delta P_w = d\Delta P_A + (1-d)\Delta P_B = 0 \tag{5.10}$$

implies that

$$d\Delta P_A = -(1-d)\Delta P_B \tag{5.11}$$

Dividing Equation (5.11) by Equation (5.9) and rearranging yields

$$\frac{d}{1-d} = \frac{K_A \bar{Y}_A}{K_B \bar{Y}_B} \tag{5.12}$$

Using Equation (5.4), this implies that

$$\frac{\bar{Y}_A}{\bar{Y}_B} = \frac{K_A \bar{Y}_A}{K_B \bar{Y}_B} \tag{5.13}$$

Therefore, Duck and Zis were able to demonstrate that for $\Delta M_w^s = \Delta P_w = 0$, it is necessary that

$$K_A = K_B \tag{5.14}$$

which would be the case only if A and B had identical demand-for-money functions. The existing empirical literature on national demand for money functions did not support the proposition that they were identical. Thus Duck and Zis concluded that the empirical findings of Gray *et al.* (1976) were not the outcome of simply aggregating stable national demand-for-money functions.

Statistical evidence in support of the diagnosis that inflation was an international monetary problem was also presented by Genberg and Swoboda (1977), Duck *et al.* (1976) and Meiselman (1975), while studies of individual economies, explicitly allowing for the implications of openness, in Brunner and Meltzer (1978), Parkin and Zis (1976a) and Laidler (1976) strongly suggested the superiority of the international monetary approach over the sociological view when analysing the determinants of a country's inflation rate.[4] However, there existed sufficient ambiguities that no consensus emerged and in the attempt to discriminate between the competing theories, their respective treatments of the international aspects of inflation attracted increasing attention.

TRANSMISSION CHANNELS

The simultaneous acceleration of national inflation rates in the second half of the 1960s was inevitably a source of difficulties for 'Keynesian' analyses which sought to explain rising prices in terms of predominantly domestic forces. Thus a variety of judgements were advanced when considering the international character of inflation. OECD (1970) attributed the 'generalised nature of price increases' to the 'unusual coincidence' of a number of the major countries simultaneously experiencing high levels of excess aggregate demand. Consistent with the view that the simultaneous acceleration of national inflation rates was largely the outcome of an 'unusual coincidence', the OECD (1970, p. 7) appeared to be somewhat puzzled by the observation that there had been 'noticeably more synchronization in [countries'] price movements than in demand conditions'. Similarly Dicks-Mireaux (1971, p. 179) introduced his study of external influences on the UK rate of inflation by describing the world-wide increase in inflation rates as 'an extraordinary accident'. After considering channels via which the United Kingdom could have been importing inflationary pressures, Dicks-Mireaux (1971, p. 184) concluded against this line of investigation and in favour of looking 'to factors closer at home not all of which, perhaps, are economic'. Turvey (1971), after maintaining that the observed price behaviour was 'new' in character and accepting the breakdown of the established wage equations in nearly all the major economies, goes on to argue that discussions of transmission mechanisms are irrelevant since the identification of such mechanisms alone does not justify the perception of inflation as a world-wide phenomenon. This line of reasoning provides the basis for Turvey (1971, p. 200) to suggest that economists will not be able to explain the collapse of the Phillips curve after 1967 until they 'become multi-disciplinary'. Such arguments allowed economists to persist in prescribing policies as if the source of each country's inflation rate were to be located domestically, though OECD (1973) recommended that governments should attempt to co-ordinate their incomes policies which were seen as potentially the most effective anti-inflation policy instrument.

If inflation were a national sociological problem and, therefore, world inflation a collection of such national problems, then the observed simultaneous acceleration of national rates of inflation gave rise to the question why social tensions in all major countries appeared to become more severe at the same time. Was it a coincidence or was there some systematic force at work? Merigo (1972, p. 321) suggested that though the impact of monetary forces was ambiguous what was known was

> that in a certain number of European countries at the same time – and perhaps for the same reasons which are either common from a sociological point of view, *or transmitted because there are demonstration effects among countries after all* – there were wage explosions which have something to do with ... sociology ..., and which surely we do not understand, because if we did, we would have predicted them. (emphasis added)

The implied hypothesis, therefore, was that, for example, changes in trade union militancy were transmitted through a demonstration effect across countries and, consequently, simultaneous wage explosions resulted in countries' rates of inflation accelerating at the same time. It is arguable that if this hypothesis were true, then we should expect measures of social conflict to be correlated across countries. Strike activity is potentially a measure of social conflict. Laidler (1976) presented statistical evidence indicating that the correlations in strike activity in five major countries were more frequently negative than positive. However, it can be objected that Laidler's tests were not appropriate for the demonstration effect hypothesis. If the post-1965 inflation was a 'new' phenomenon and essentially sociological in origin, regression analysis could shed no light on the new type of relationships that were emerging. But suppose that inflation were 'new' and of the character suggested by the sociological school of thought. Suppose, further, that a demonstration effect was in fact operating so that social militancy was being transmitted across countries. Adopting these assumptions could provide some basis for an explanation of the simultaneous acceleration of national inflation rates. It could not explain why these rates of inflation continued to be very similar even after they began to increase. That is, economists adhering to the sociological view of inflation had no explanation of the convergence of inflation rates during the Bretton Woods system of fixed exchange rates. It was this inability of the sociological explanation of inflation to account for the international aspects of inflation which eventually resulted in its fading out as a credible theory of the determinants of price changes.

The perception of inflation as an international monetary problem, on the other hand, rested on the assertion that arbitrage would equate prices in countries A and B, assuming that the exchange rate between their respective currencies were unity. If, further, we were to suppose that all goods were traded, that the terms of trade were constant and that each good had a constant weight in each country's price index, then it would necessarily follow that the two countries' inflation rates would be equalized. However, as Swoboda (1977) observes, it is not necessary to assume that all goods are traded. Provided that the relative price of traded and non-traded goods is constant, it is still the case that national rates of inflation will tend to be equalized in the longer run. Swoboda (1977) also draws attention to the fact that for rates of inflation to be equalized it is not necessary that the price for any given good is the same across countries. So long as the equilibrium price differential is constant, then countries' inflation rates will of necessity tend to be the same. In brief, arbitrage ensures that under fixed exchange rates national inflation rates will converge.

The presence of arbitrage, though sufficient for inflation rates to converge does not, by itself, imply that inflation under fixed exchange rates is an international monetary problem. Such a perception also requires that there exists a *world* demand-for-money function, as conventionally defined, which is stable. If such a function did exist, then the world money supply growth rate relative to the rate of growth of the world demand for money would determine the world rate of inflation which would prevail in all countries. But in studies such as Johnson (1972a) and Mundell (1971) the additional assumption that national demand-for-money functions were stable was made. This assumption, though empirically well founded, is not necessary, as Duck and Zis (1978) showed, for inflation to be an international monetary phenomenon. The implication of postulating stable national demand-for-money functions is that for any given world money supply there exists a unique distribution of this world money stock which is consistent with general equilibrium in the individual economies and the world economy. Mundell (1971) and Swoboda (1977), among others, were, therefore, able to demonstrate how an increase in the world money supply, induced by the authorities of some country, will result in balance of payments disequilibria which will persist until the equilibrium distribution of the world money stock is restored. This proposition can be demonstrated with the aid of Figure 5.1. Assume, for the sake of simplicity, that absolute purchasing power parity holds and that the exchange rate between the respective currencies of countries A and B is equal to unity. The purchasing power parity assumption implies that the concept of a world price level does have an economic meaning while this assumption, combined with that of the exchange rate being equal to unity, results in the equalization of price levels in A and B. The world price level, P_w, is measured on the vertical axis and the world nominal money supply on the horizontal. Again for simplicity assume full employment. $O_A A$ *and* $O_B B$ portray the relationship between the price level and the quantity of money balances demanded. They are drawn from the origin so as to reflect the homogeneity postulate. Let the world money supply be $O_A O_B$. Monetary equilibrium requires that the price level be P'_w. Country A will hold $O_A G$ of money balances and country B will demand $O_B G$ of money balances. If the price level was different from P'_w, then monetary equilibrium would not exist. Suppose now that country B expands its money supply by $O_B O^*_B$. It follows that the world money supply is now equal to $O_A O^*_B$. At price P'_w there will emerge a world excess supply of money equal to GK which, of course, is equal to $O_B O^*_B$. At P'_w monetary equilibrium in A is maintained but in B there exists an excess supply of money equal to GK. Given the full-employment assumption, the price level will rise to P''_w to eliminate the excess supply of money. The new equilibrium is defined by the point of intersection between $O_A A$ and $O^*_B B$.

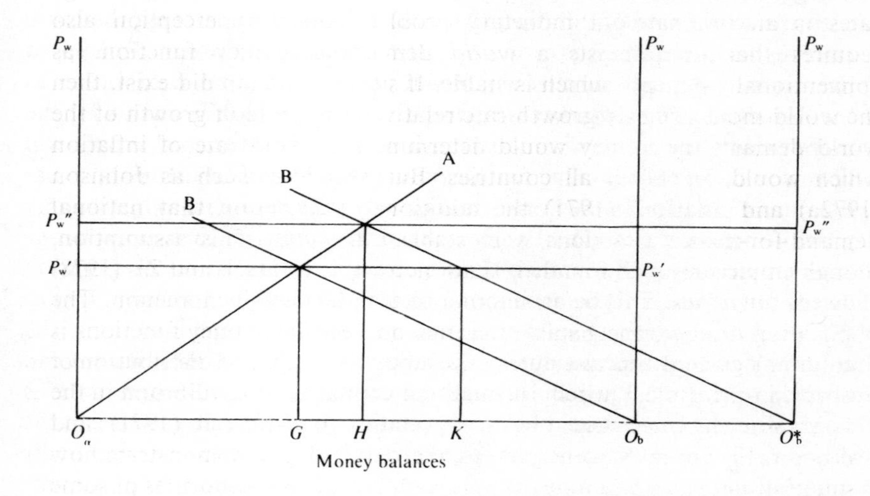

Figure 5.1 (*Source*: Swoboda 1977, p. 19)

The money supply in country A increases by GH. Country B's excess money balances are eliminated partly by the increase in the price level and partly through a balance of payments deficit amounting to GH. That is, country A 'imports' the additional money balances required by the new equilibrium via a balance of payments surplus. The increase in price from P'_w to P''_w eliminates excess nominal money balances equal to HK. A's reserves will have increased by GH while B will have sustained exchange reserve losses of an equal amount. Therefore, the increase of the world money supply, $O_B O_B^*$, has led to the price level rising from P'_W to P'_W. Because of the homogeneity postulate the proportionate increase in the price level equals the proportionate increase in the world money supply. That is, $P'_w P''_w / O_A P'_W = O_B O_B^* / O_A O_B$. It follows that when equilibrium is restored the money holdings in A and B will have increased by the same proportion as the price rise, i.e.

$$P'_w P''_w / O_A P'_w = GH / O_A G = HK / O_B G = O_B O_B^* / O_A O_B.$$

With monetary equilibrium restored in both countries, the balance of payments disequilibrium is eliminated. Only the distribution of the world money supply implied by H is consistent with general equilibrium.

The perception of inflation under fixed exchange rates as an international monetary problem is compatible with a variety of mechanisms of transmission of inflationary impulses between countries. However, proponents of this view emphasized a particular channel of transmission. Suppose inflation in the rest of the world increases. Domestic firms which operate in world rather than domestic markets immediately raise their prices. The domestic rate of inflation rises in line with the world rate of inflation. An excess demand for money, therefore emerges in the domestic economy. The domestic economy develops a balance of payments surplus which will persist until stock equilibrium in the domestic money market is restored. The more mobile capital is, the more rapidly the equilibrium distribution of the world money supply will be restored. The noteworthy feature of this sequence of adjustments is that the rate of inflation in the domestic economy rises before its money supply growth rate increases. That is, changes in the country's foreign exchange reserves accommodate rather than cause the transmission of inflation across countries. This transmission channel, labelled by Laidler (1976) as the 'price transfer mechanism', carries no necessary implications for the country's current account during the adjustment process. Adjustment can occur, in principle, entirely through the capital account. Second, there is no reason why there should be an expectation to observe an increase in the domestic economy's aggregate excess demand prior to the rise in its inflation rate.

In contrast, the traditional price specie flow mechanism postulates a sequence of adjustments which involves the domestic economy's money supply growth rate increasing prior to the rise in the domestic rate of inflation. Thus, an increase, in, say, the US money supply growth rate results in the US rate of inflation rising above the world rate. The United States develops a balance of payments deficit with its current account, at least, deteriorating. Countries in the rest of the world experience balance of payments surpluses and, therefore, increases in their money supplies. The latter lead to rises in countries' aggregate excess demands which in turn result in inflation rates increasing. In other words, variations in a country's inflation rate can ultimately be traced to variations in its monetary expansion which may be caused by developments in its balance of payments.

Both the price transfer and the price specie flow mechanism are consistent with the hypothesis that inflation under fixed exchange rates is an international monetary phenomenon. Such a perception of inflation does not require that only one of the mechanisms be operational. It is possible to argue that both may simultaneously be acting as the channels via which inflationary impulses are transmitted across countries. If that were the case we would not expect to observe systematic relationships between monetary variations and changes in excess aggregate demand or between the former and variations in the inflation rate when the subject of study is the individual economy. Only at the world level would we need to observe variations in monetary expansion to precede changes in the world excess aggregate demand and in the world rate of inflation. Therefore, the observation that a country's rate of inflation changes before or after its money supply growth rate is altered has no diagnostic value in determining the nature of inflation unless the country under study is large relative to the world economy. In terms of the post-1965 experience only the United States was sufficiently large to affect the world money supply growth rate and, therefore, the world rate of inflation. Sims (1972) presented statistical evidence suggesting that the US experience was consistent with monetarist hypotheses. But when Williams *et al.* (1976) applied the Sims test of causality to UK data, their findings were rather mixed. The difference in the results of the two studies can in principle be explained in terms of the relative size of the two countries, with only the Sims study being pertinent for the diagnosis of inflation as a monetary phenomenon.[5] Be that as it may, when Genberg and Swoboda (1977) applied the Sims test of causality to *world* data their findings supported the hypothesis that inflation under the Bretton Woods system was an international monetary problem.

It follows, therefore, that statistical tests of the relative significance of the price transfer and price specie flow mechanisms provide no basis for accepting or rejecting the treatment of inflation as a world monetary problem. Cross and Laidler (1976) and Laidler (1976) concluded that their empirical findings suggested the predominance of the price transfer mechanism but statistical evidence against this judgement was identified by Cassese and Lothian (1983). Kravis and Lipsey (1977) presented statistical analyses indicating that manufactured goods' markets are highly integrated but, also, that national price levels are not as closely linked as assumed by those subscribing to the perfect arbitrage hypothesis.

Economists subscribing to the view that inflation was an international monetary problem, therefore, had no difficulty in explaining either the convergence of inflation rates up to 1973 or the simultaneous acceleration of national rates of inflation after 1965. But national inflation rates were not identically the same. Differences could be observed. If the international monetary theory of inflation were to be complete, it had to explain these differences, as Laidler and Nobay (1976) observed. This was accomplished by employing the distinction between traded and non-traded goods.[6] Assume that the world rate of inflation increases. Via the price transfer mechanism the rate of inflation of the traded goods prices instantaneously rises in the domestic economy to the world rate. However, because of the existence of non-traded goods the domestic rate of inflation does not rise by the full amount of the increase in the world rate of inflation. The relative price of non-traded goods, therefore, declines and demand switches towards these goods. This demand shift will lead to the rate of inflation of the non-traded goods prices rising. Sumner and Zis (1982) showed that for general equilibrium to be restored the rate of inflation of non-traded goods prices must first rise above the world rate of inflation and then fall back to it. Now, throughout the period during which the domestic rate of inflation adjusts to the new world rate, the two will differ. The differences in national inflation rates during the era of the Bretton Woods system were sufficiently small to be explainable by the presence of non-traded goods.

In brief, the theory of inflation as an international monetary phenomenon was more complete and empirically better founded than the sociological explanation of inflation. However, a number of economists who adopted either an eclectic view or a 'Keynesian' economic explanation of inflation suggested a variety of channels of transmission which placed less emphasis on the role of money. One such channel focuses on the effects of the foreign trade multiplier. Thus an expansion of foreign demand for domestic goods leads via the multiplier to domestic prices, output and incomes increasing. The 'Keynesian' nature of this mechanism derives from the assumption that monetary authorities can indefinitely sterilize balance of payments disequilibria and from defining monetary equilibrium in flow rather than stock terms. Branson (1975; 1977) employed the foreign trade multiplier in providing a 'Keynesian' theory of the convergence of national inflation rates under fixed exchange rates. He postulated a price Phillips curve whereby domestic output determines the domestic rate of inflation. The latter, relative to the world rate of inflation, determines the country's trade balance which, in turn, via the multiplier, determines domestic output. In equilibrium the domestic rate of inflation is equal to the world rate of inflation and domestic output is at a level consistent with trade balance equilibrium. Suppose next that the domestic rate of inflation and output are below their equilibrium values. The associated trade balance surplus will pull both via the foreign trade multiplier up towards their equilibrium values. Thus inflation rates will tend to converge.[7] The emphasis in this theory is on changes in relative prices inducing variations in aggregate demand, via the foreign trade multiplier, which determine the domestic rate of inflation and output. However, there is no explanation of the world rate of inflation towards which the domestic rate will tend. Branson defines the former simply as the 'average' of all national rates of inflation. Second, Branson refrains from considering the role of expectations in the determination of price inflation. But as Sumner and Zis (1982) showed, it is possible to utilize an expectations-argumented Phillips curve framework of analysis to demonstrate the international monetary character of inflation under fixed exchange rates.

Import prices have also been discussed as transmitters of inflation across countries. It is usually assumed that countries specialize in the production of their exports but produce none of the goods which are imported. Further, it is postulated that countries consume both the exports which they produce and imports. Now if the distinction between imports and exports is to be preferred to that between traded and non-traded goods, as Swoboda (1977) has argued, it is necessary to assume that each country has monopoly power over the good it exports and is a price-taker for its imports. If these conditions were to prevail, then the terms of trade could change, and it would be appropriate to use the imports and exports distinction. However, in a world in which such conditions did prevail, it is not easy to see how countries could import inflation through import prices for any length of time. It is certainly not possible, without additional assumptions, to derive the prediction that import prices will transmit the necessary impulses for the convergence of national inflation rates.

Another transmission mechanism involves capital flows. Swoboda (1977) has argued that analyses of imported inflation which focus on capital flows have tended to suffer from two deficiencies. First, they neglected to identify the determinants of the capital flows; and second, they appeared to ignore the implication that for an individual economy to be importing inflation via capital flows it must be the case that the rest of the world is also inflating. If that were not so, then capital flows would be reversed.

The above discussion is sufficient to show that economists advanced a variety of analyses of how inflation can be transmitted across countries.[8] Though they debated the relative merits of each mechanism, there was general agreement that fixity of exchange rates does facilitate the spreading of inflation across countries. In the spring of 1973 the failure of the major economies to reform the Bretton Woods system finally resulted in the collapse of the system and the world was forced to accept a 'system' of flexible exchange rates.

FLEXIBLE EXCHANGE RATES

The principal statements of the case for flexible exchange rates prior to 1973 are to be found in Friedman (1953), Meade (1955), Sohmen (1969) and Johnson (1969). Friedman (1953, p. 200) argued that exchange rate flexibility would ensure the

> interdependence among countries through trade with a maximum of internal monetary independence; [flexible exchange rates] are a means of permitting each country to seek for monetary stability according to its own lights, without either imposing its mistakes on its neighbours or having their mistakes imposed on it.

The advantages of policy autonomy which a system of flexible exchange rates would yield were forcefully argued by Johnson (1969, p. 199):

> The fundamental argument for flexible exchange rates is that they would allow countries autonomy with respect to their use of monetary, fiscal and other policy instruments, consistent with maintenance of whatever degree of freedom in international transactions they chose to allow their citizens, by automatically ensuring the preservation of external equilibrium.

It followed, therefore, that (p. 210):

> Flexible rates would allow each country to pursue the mixture of unemployment and price trend objectives it prefers, consistently with international equilibrium, equilibrium being secured by appreciation of the currencies of 'price stability' countries relative to the currencies of 'full employment' countries.

That is, a system of flexible exchange rates would provide an environment in which the differences in countries' preferences with respect to their desired rates of inflation could be accommodated. Johnson (1969, p. 210) contrasted this with the prevailing conditions which had generated international tensions as follows:

> Under the present fixed exchange-rate system, ... nations are pitched against each other in a battle over the rate of inflation that is to prevail in the world economy, since the fixed rate system diffuses that rate of inflation to all the countries involved in it.

The academics' disenchantment with the Bretton Woods system was shared by policy-makers. Emminger (1973), for example, argued that fixity of exchange rates and US policies had undermined West Germany's attempts to control its rate of inflation. Greater exchange rate flexibility was seen as the principal solution to the problem of imported inflation. But exchange rate flexibility had become increasingly attractive even for governments that were attaching a greater priority to full employment than to the control of inflation. Thus Barber (1972), when introducing as Chancellor of the Exchequer the highly expansionary budget of 1972 maintained that

> it is neither necessary nor desirable to distort economies to an unacceptable extent in order to maintain unrealistic exchange rates ... I do not believe that there is any need for this country ... to be frustrated on this score in its determination to sustain sound economic growth and to reduce unemployment.

In June of that year sterling was allowed to float.

Exchange rates have not behaved since 1973 as predicted by advocates of exchange rate flexibility.[9] Exchange rate changes have been large and unpredictable. These changes have not systematically offset inflation rate differentials. Thus real exchange rate changes have been large and unpredictable. Disillusion with exchange rate flexibility significantly contributed to the establishment of the European Monetary System in 1979 while the 1985 Plaza and 1987 Louvre agreements suggest that even the United States and the United Kingdom, though not yet prepared to negotiate on an international monetary system, are now less convinced of the alleged advantages of flexible exchange rates.

It is no longer maintained that exchange rate flexibility can insulate an economy from external disturbances. Swoboda (1983), for example, presented empirical evidence indicating that the level of synchronization of the movements in real economic activity and of monetary variables in the six major industrial countries has been at least as high since 1973 as it was during the Bretton Woods system era. Studies such as those by Mussa (1979), Saidi (1980) and Dornbusch (1983) have demonstrated that a wide variety of assumptions is consistent with the theory of economic interdependence under flexible exchange rates. Frenkel and Mussa (1981) identified commodity market, capital market and monetary linkages as the principal manifestations of national economies' interdependence. These linkages were, of course, also present prior to 1973. However, what has now come to be better appreciated is that the exchange rate regime cannot affect the existence of channels of transmission of disturbances across countries. What it does influence is the nature of the processes by which a country imports external disturbances. Somewhat paradoxically, the insulation properties of flexible exchange rates can ultimately be traced to economists' practice of developing their analyses on the basis of what McKinnon (1981) termed the 'insular economy'. McKinnon (1981) argued that though the insular economy was open, its links with the rest of the world rested on three assumptions. First, only a small fraction of its GNP was assumed to be associated with foreign trade and, therefore, exchange rate changes could have negligible effects on its price level. Second, it was supposed either that there was no integrated international capital market or that exchange controls were effective in restricting private capital movements so that capital flows could not finance current account disequilibria. Third, the insular economy could sterilize balance of payments disequilibria and, consequently, determine its own money supply growth rate independently of the rest of the world. Now, the insular economy may have been typical of the 1940s and, perhaps, even of the 1950s. But from the mid-1960s it was entirely inadequate as a basis for economic analysis and policy prescription. The last quarter of a century has witnessed the rapid internationalization of capital markets while goods markets became increasingly integrated, especially as production processes have taken on an international character. The assumption of no or limited financial and commodity arbitrage has long ceased to be 'useful' or 'convenient'. But, as McKinnon (1981) observes, macroeconomics, whether of the 'Keynesian' or the 'monetarist' variety, has been very slow to adjust.

The failure of exchange rate flexibility to generate the insulation of economies can be largely attributed to capital becoming increasingly mobile since the mid-1960s. Capital account transactions now overwhelm current account transactions in foreign exchange markets. The conventional model of exchange rate determination which assumed that the price of currency in terms of other currencies is basically determined by the demands for and supplies of currencies associated with countries' imports and exports has ceased to be of any empirical relevance. Thus the exchange rate has come to be regarded as an asset price and, as such, its changes are viewed as mainly the result of changes in expectations about future policies and events.[10] This perception of the exchange rate, with its emphasis on the role of expectations, is consistent with the volatility and unpredictability of exchange rates experienced since 1973. When combined with the observation that countries' price levels are 'sticky', for whatever reason, then the treatment of exchange rates as asset prices implies that changes in expectations will result in large and unpredictable changes in real exchange rates. Thus exchange rate changes, rather than insulating the individual economy, provide the channel through which external disturbances can be imported.

It is still, however, the case that exchange rate flexibility is said to have the relative merit of allowing countries to determine their desired long-run rate of inflation. For example, Dornbusch (1983, p. 4) has maintained that

> what flexible exchange rates are still credited with is an ability to isolate a country from the world inflation *trend*, while it is recognised that they cannot isolate a country from either the effects of policies that initiate a *change in trend* or from any other disturbances. (emphasis in original)

Now whether this is a compelling argument for flexible exchange rates is debatable. But, more significantly, the rationale for this prediction has increasingly been challenged in the literature on currency substitution.

CURRENCY SUBSTITUTION

The conventional monetarist policy prescription in favour of a monetary rule rests on two conditions. First, the demand-for-money function must be stable. Second, exchange rates need be market determined without monetary authorities intervening in the foreign exchange markets. If exchange rates are flexible countries can control the rate of growth of their respective money supplies. The rate, then, of a country's monetary expansion combines with the stable demand-for-money function to determine the domestic rate of inflation. Thus, the individual economy can determine its own long-run rate of inflation, though in the short run other forces may temporarily exert some influence on the rate of change of prices.

The above line of reasoning derives from a framework which essentially treats economies as if they are closed. Though it recognizes the implications for a country's money supply growth rate of persistent balance of payments disequilibria, it ignores the implications of openness for the demand-for-money specification. It is usually assumed that the domestic demand for money depends on domestic variables. This Friedmanite specification of the demand-for-money function presupposed that, say, UK residents hold only sterling balances. Therefore, the demand for money in the United Kingdom is identical to the demand for sterling. Thus if the latter is stable then it is assumed that the former is also stable. The assumption that UK residents hold only sterling balances, residents in France hold only French francs, and so on, has come under increasing challenge in the currency substitution literature.[11] For example, Miles (1978a) has described it as 'quite dubious'. He argued that one of the consequences of the world economy becoming more integrated is the emergence of strong incentives for multinational corporations, national firms and even individuals to diversify the currency composition of their cash balances. This composition may alter even if the demand for money remains unchanged. But if economic agents hold portfolios of currencies, the composition of which they may alter by substituting between currencies, then it is possible to distinguish between a country's demand for money and the demand for its currency. There follows from this distinction an important implication. Since it is no longer valid to identify a country's demand for money with the demand for its currency, instability of the latter is perfectly compatible with stability of the former. It is, therefore, arguable that problems encountered during the last decade in empirical studies of the demand for money are, at least, partly due to the phenomenon of currency substitution.[12]

Diversified currency portfolios transmit inflationary pressures even under flexible exchange rates. Suppose that dollars are held by economic agents in countries other than the United States and that the latter increases once and for all the supply of dollars. Conventional monetarism would predict an equiproportionate rise in the US price level and devaluation of the dollar. However, as Miles (1978b) shows, if dollars are held outside the United States, then the US price level will rise proportionately less than the increase in the supply of dollars, while countries in the rest of the world will also experience increases in their price level. That is, national inflation rates will at least be partially determined by foreign money supply growth rates. Thus national money supply growth rates will not be systematically correlated with domestic rates of inflation. This was one of the findings presented by McKinnon (1982). He also showed that there exists a correlation between the world money supply growth rate and the world rate of inflation.

McKinnon (1982) and Boyer and Kingston (1987), in their analyses of currency substitution, drew attention to the possibility of negative transmission of inflation. Suppose that the foreign country's money supply growth rate increases inducing a shift in economic agents' preferences towards the domestic currency. The impact effect of the reduction in the demand for the foreign currency is to raise the foreign rate of inflation above what it would otherwise be while the increase in the demand for the domestic currency reduces the domestic rate of inflation.

The currency substitution hypothesis has yet to be refined and incorporated in macroeconomic theory. The empirical literature has not yielded unambiguous results regarding the quantitative importance of the phenomenon but its presence can hardly be disputed. Currency substitution would appear to deprive the case for flexible exchange rates of any rationale and reinforce the policy message of other strands of analysis that in an integrated world economy individual countries have no alternative but to co-ordinate their macroeconomic policies. The suggestion that shifts in the demand for money could be accommodated by a country's monetary authorities, advanced, for example, by Frenkel (1983), is an inadequate response to the proposition that currency substitution results in the individual economy losing all control over its rate of inflation even though exchange rate flexibility allows it to control the rate of growth of the supply of its currency. Flexible exchange rates can provide no policy autonomy which if pursued could be to the advantage of either the individual economy or the world economy.

CONCLUSIONS

The debate on the causes of inflation in the 1960s and 1970s, though it did not yield a consensus among economists, did pave the way towards a greater awareness of the implications of economies being open. The proponents of the view that inflation under the Bretton Woods system was an international monetary problem may, perhaps, have exaggerated their case. Commodity arbitrage may not be as perfect as they hypothesized. However, their insistence that the analysis of inflation had to rest on the explicit recognition that economies are interdependent forced the study of the channels through which inflationary impulses are transmitted across countries. This, in turn, encouraged the analysis of how disturbances, in general, are diffused around the world, and stimulated the investigation of the nature of balance of payments disequilibria. The focus on the integration of the world economy provided the basis for the developments in the theory of exchange rate determination and specially in the asset theory of exchange rates.

The sociological theory of inflation was discredited, at least partly, because of its inability to provide an adequate explanation of the international aspects of inflation. But with that view of inflation, the 'usefulness' of the closed economy assumption was also discredited. However, the development of open economy macroeconomics is yet to be completed. The currency substitution literature has exposed at least one area in macroeconomics where progress has been disappointingly slow.

The study of the transmission of inflation inevitably revealed the importance of the size of a country. That the United States could transmit inflationary impulses throughout the world is a reflection of its dominance of the world economy. Again, that US policies have been perceived to be of crucial importance for developments in the rest of the world after 1973 indicates that flexible exchange rates cannot insulate a small open economy from disturbances originating in a large country. But, significantly, the 1980s have demonstrated that even a country of the size of the United States cannot pursue policies independently of the rest of the world without eventually running into serious economic difficulties. Channels of transmission run in both directions and even a large country cannot impose policy regimes. The analysis of these channels of transmission, whether exchange rates are flexible or fixed, strongly suggests that countries, large and small, have little choice but to co-ordinate their macroeconomic policies. The history of the European Monetary System provides ample proof of the benefits that can be derived from the co-ordination of national economic policies. It remains to be seen how long it will take the United States and the United Kingdom to learn this lesson.

NOTES

1. For a fuller discussion of the phenomena which competing theories of inflation had to explain, see Zis (1976).
2. Lindbeck (1980) has provided the most complete statement of the eclectics's position on the determinants of inflation. See also Haberler (1976).
3. Purdy and Zis (1974a) argued that the cost-push hypothesis could also not be empirically refuted. Statistical evidence contradicting the hypothesis could always be dismissed as reflecting the inadequacy of the employed proxy for trade union militancy. For empirical studies relevant to the cost-push hypothesis, see Hines (1964); Godfrey (1971); Taylor (1972); Pencavel (1970); Ashenfelter *et al.* (1972); Ashenfelter and Johnson (1969); Johnston and Timbrell (1973); Purdy and Zis (1974b); Ward and Zis (1974); Nordhaus (1972); and Perry (1975).
4. For an excellent exposition of the theory of inflation as an international monetary problem and a synthesis of the relevant empirical literature, see Parkin (1977).
5. Putnam and Wilford (1978) reconciled the two sets of findings by drawing attention to the implications of the dollar being a reserve currency.
6. The distinction is very similar to that between the 'sheltered' and the 'exposed' sectors of an economy which featured prominently in the Nordic model of inflation. This model, however, though it could explain the transmission of inflation, could not explain its origins. See Aukrust (1977) and Paunio and Halttunen (1976).
7. This process of adjustment towards equilibrium specified by Branson is incorrect. Given the role of relative prices, the domestic rate of inflation must rise above the world rate and then fall back to it for general equilibrium to be restored. See Sumner and Zis (1982).
8. For a comprehensive survey of the literature on the international transmission of inflation, see Salant (1977).
9. For assessments of the performance of exchange rate flexibility, see Artus and Young (1979); IMF (1984); and Obstfeld (1985).
10. Developments in the theory of exchange rate determination are surveyed by Frenkel and Mussa (1985). For a review of the empirical literature, see Levich (1985).
11. Among the principal studies on currency substitution are those by Miles (1978a; 1978b); McKinnon (1982); Girton and Roper (1981); Boyer (1978); Boyer and Kingston (1987); Daniel (1985); Calvo and Rodriguez (1977); and Melvin (1985).
12. For a survey of the literature on the demand for money, see Laidler (1985).

REFERENCES

Artus, J.R. and Young, G.H. (1979) 'Fixed and flexible exchange rates: a renewal of the debate', *IMF Staff Papers.*

Ashenfelter, O.C. and Johnson, G.E. (1969) 'Bargaining theory, trade unions and industrial strike activity', *American Economic Review.*

Ashenfelter, O.C., Johnson, G.E. and Pencavel, J.H. (1972) 'Trade unions and the rate of change of money wage rates in United States manufacturing industry', *Review of Economic Studies.*

Aukrust, O. (1977) 'Inflation in the open economy: a Norwegian model', in L.B. Krause and W.S. Salant (eds), *Worldwide Inflation: Theory and Recent Experience*, Washington DC: Brookings Institution.

Bach, G.L. (1973) *The New Inflation: Causes, Effects, Cures*, Englewood Cliffs, NJ: Prentice Hall.

Balogh, T. (1970) *Labour and Inflation*, Fabian Tract 403, London: Fabian Society.

Barber, A. (1972) 'Budget statement', *Hansard*, vol. 833, col. 1354, London: HMSO.

Bispham, G.A. (1972) 'The current inflation and short-term forecasting', in M. Parkin and M. Sumner (eds), *Incomes Policies and Inflation*, Manchester: Manchester University Press.

Boyer, R.S. (1978) 'Currency mobility and balance of payments adjustment' in B.H. Putman and D.S. Wilford (eds), *The Monetary Approach to International Adjustment*, New York: Praeger.

Boyer, R.S. and Kingston, G.H. (1987) 'Currency substitution under finance constraints', *Journal of International Money and Finance.*

Branson, W.H. (1975) 'Monetarist and Keynesian models of the transmission of inflation', *American Economic Review.*

Branson, W.H. (1977) 'A "Keynesian" approach to worldwide inflation', in L.B. Krause and W.S. Salant (eds), *Worldwide Inflation: Theory and Recent Experience*, Washington, DC: Brookings Institution.

Bronfenbrenner, M. and Holzman, F.D. (1965) 'A survey of inflation theory', in *Surveys of Economic Theory*, Volume I, London: Macmillan.

Brunner, K. and Meltzer, A.H. (eds) (1978) *The Problem of Inflation*, Carnegie-Rochester Conference Series on Public Policy, vol. 8, Amsterdam: North-Holland.

Calvo, G.H. and Rodriguez, C.H. (1977) 'A model of exchange rate determination under currency substitution and rational expectations', *Journal of Political Economy.*

Cassese, A. and Lothian, J.R. (1983) 'The timing of monetary and price changes and the international transmission of inflation', in M.R. Darby and J.R. Lothian (eds), *The International Transmission of Inflation*, Chicago: Chicago University Press.

Claassen, E. and Salin, P. (eds) (1972) *Stabilisation Policies in Interdependent Economies*, Amsterdam: North-Holland.

Cross, R. and Laidler, D. (1976) 'Inflation, excess demand and expectations in fixed exchange rate open economies: some preliminary empirical results', in M. Parkin and G. Zis (eds), *Inflation in the World Economy*, Manchester: Manchester University Press.

Daniel, B.C. (1985) 'Monetary dynamics and exchange rate dynamics under currency substitution', *Journal of International Economics*.

Darby, M.R. and Lothian, J.R. (eds) (1983) *The International Transmission of Inflation*, Chicago: Chicago University Press.

Dicks-Mireaux, L. (1971) 'External influences and inflation in the United Kingdom', in H.G. Johnson and A.R. Nobay (eds), *The Current Inflation*, London: Macmillan.

Dornbusch, R. (1983) 'Flexible exchange rates and interdependence', in A.W. Hooke (ed.), *Exchange Rate Regimes and Policy Interdependence*, Washington DC: IMF.

Duck, N., Parkin, M., Rose, D. and Zis, G. (1976) 'The determination of the rate of change of wages and prices in the fixed exchange rate world economy, 1956–71' in M. Parkin and G. Zis (eds), *Inflation in the World Economy*, Manchester: Manchester University Press.

Duck, N. and Zis, G. (1978) 'World inflation, the demand for money and fixed exchange rates', *Scottish Journal of Political Economy*.

Emminger, O. (1973) *Inflation and the International Monetary System*, Basle: Per Jacobson Foundation.

Frenkel, J.A. (1983) 'Turbulence in the foreign exchange markets and macro-economic policies', in D. Bigman and T. Taya (eds), *Exchange Rate and Trade Instability: Causes, Consequences, and Remedies*, Cambridge, MA: Ballinger.

Frenkel, J.A. and Mussa, M.L. (1981) 'Monetary and fiscal policies in an open economy', *American Economic Review*.

Frenkel, J.A. and Mussa, M.L. (1985) 'Asset markets, exchange rates and the balance of payments' in R.W. Jones and P.B. Kenen (eds), *Handbook of International Economics*, Amsterdam: North-Holland.

Friedman, M. (1953) 'The case for flexible exchange rates', in M. Friedman, *Essays in Positive Economics*, Chicago: Chicago University Press.

Genberg, H. and Swoboda, A.K. (1977) 'Causes and origins of the current world-wide inflation' in E. Lundberg (ed.), *Inflation Theory and Anti-inflation Policy*, London: Macmillan.

Girton, L. and Roper, D. (1981) 'Theory and implications of currency substitution, *Journal of Money, Credit, and Banking*.

Godfrey, L. (1971) 'The Phillips curve: incomes policy and trade union effects' in H.G. Johnson and A.R. Nobay (eds), *The Current Inflation*, London: Macmillan

Gray, M.R., Ward, R. and Zis, G. (1976) 'The world demand for money function: some preliminary results in M. Parkin and G. Zis (eds), *Inflation in the World Economy*, Manchester: Manchester University Press.

Haberler, G. (1976) 'Some currently suggested explanations and cures for inflation' in K. Brunner and A.H. Meltzer (eds), *Institutional Arrangements and the Inflation Problem*, Carnegie-Rochester Conference Series on Public Policy, vol. 3, Amsterdam: North-Holland.

Harrod, R. (1972) 'The issues: five views', in R. Hinshaw, *Inflation as a Global Problem*, London: Johns Hopkins University Press.

Hicks, J. (1974) *The Crisis in Keynesian Economics*, Oxford: Basil Blackwell.

Hines, A.G. (1964) 'Trade unions and wage inflation in the United Kingdom', *Review of Economic Studies*.

Hinshaw, R. (1972) *Inflation as a Global Problem*, London: Johns Hopkins University Press.

Hooke, A.W. (ed.) (1983) *Exchange Rate Regimes and Policy Interdependence*,

Washington, DC: IMF.
IMF (1984) 'The exchange rate system: lessons of the past and options for the future', Occasional Paper no. 30.
Johnson, H.G. (1969) *The Case for Flexible Exchange Rates*, Hobart Papers 46, The Institute of Economic Affairs, London.
Johnson, H.G. (1972a) *Inflation and the Monetarist Controversy*, Amsterdam: North-Holland.
Johnson, H.G. (1972b) 'Inflation: a "monetarist" view in H.G. Johnson, *Further Essays in Monetary Economics*, London: Allen & Unwin.
Johnson, H.G. (1973) 'Secular inflation and the international monetary system', *Journal of Money, Credit, and Banking*.
Johnson, H.G. and Nobay, A.R. (eds) (1971) *The Current Inflation*, London: Macmillan.
Johnston, J. and Timbrell, M. (1973) 'Empirical tests of a bargaining theory of wage determination', *Manchester School*.
Jones, A. (1973) *The New Inflation: The Politics of Prices and Incomes*, Harmondsworth: Penguin.
Jones, R.W. and Kenen, P.B. (eds) (1985) *Handbook of International Economics*, Amsterdam: North-Holland.
Keynes, J.M. (1936) *The General Theory of Employment, Interest and Money*, London: Macmillan.
Krause, L.B. and Salant, W.S. (eds) (1977) *Worldwide Inflation: Theory and Recent Experience*, Washington, DC: Brookings Institution.
Kravis, I.B. and Lipsey, R.E. (1977) 'Export prices and the transmission of inflation', *American Economic Review*.
Laidler, D. (1976) 'Inflation: alternative explanations and policies, tests on data drawn from six countries' in K. Brunner and A.H. Meltzer (eds), *Institutions, Policies and Economic Performance*, Carnegie-Rochester Conference Series on Public Policy, vol. 4, Amsterdam: North-Holland.
Laidler, D. (1985) *The Demand for Money: Theory, Evidence and Problems*, 3rd edn, New York: Harper and Row.
Laidler, D. and Nobay, A.R. (1976) 'International aspects of inflation: a survey' in E. Claassen and P. Salin (eds), *Recent Issues in International Monetary Economics*, Amsterdam: North-Holland.
Laidler, D. and Purdy, D. (eds) (1974) *Inflation and Labour Markets*, Manchester: Manchester University Press.
Levich, R.M. (1985) 'Empirical studies of exchange rates: price behaviour, rate determination and market efficiency', in R.W. Jones and P.B. Kenen (eds), *Handbook of International Economics*, Amsterdam: North-Holland.
Lindbeck, A. (1980) *Inflation: Global, International and National Aspects*, Leuven: Leuven University Press.
Lipsey, R.G. (1960) 'The relation between unemployment and the rate of change of money rates in the United Kingdom, 1862–1957', *Economica*.
McKinnon, R.I. (1981) 'The exchange rate and macroeconomic policy: changing postwar perceptions, *Journal of Economic Literature*.
McKinnon, R.I. (1982) 'Currency substitution and instability in the world dollar standard', *American Economic Review*.
McKinnon, R.I. (1984) *An International Standard for Monetary Stabilisation*, Washington, DC: Institute for International Economics.
Marris, S. (1972) 'World inflation: panel discussion' in E. Claassen, and P. Salin (eds), *Stabilisation Policies in Interdependent Economies*, Amsterdam:

North-Holland.
Meade, J. (1955) 'The case for variable exchange rates', *Three Banks Review*.
Meiselman, D.I. (1975) 'Worldwide inflation: a monetarist view' in D.I. Meiselman and A.B. Laffer (eds), *The Phenomenon of Worldwide Inflation*, Washington, DC: American Enterprise Institute for Public Policy Research.
Melvin, M. (1985) 'Currency substitution and Western European Monetary unification', *Economica*.
Merigo, E. (1972) 'Panel discussion' in E. Claassen and P. Salin (eds), *Stabilisation Policies in Interdependent Economies*, Amsterdam: North-Holland.
Miller, M.H. (1976) 'A comment' in M. Parkin and G. Zis (eds), *Inflation in the World Economy*, Manchester: Manchester University Press.
Miles, M.A. (1978a) 'Currency substitution, flexible exchange rates, and monetary independence', *American Economic Review*.
Miles, M.A. (1978b) 'Currency substitution: perspective, implications and empirical evidence', in B.H. Putnam and D.S. Wilford (eds), *The Monetary Approach to International Adjustment*, New York, Praeger.
Mundell, R.A. (1971) *Monetary Theory: Inflation, Interest, and Growth in the World Economy*, Pacific Palisades, CA: Goodyear.
Mundell, R.A. (1972) 'The issues: five views' in R. Hinshaw, *Inflation as a Global Problem*, London: Johns Hopkins University Press.
Mussa, M.L. (1979) 'Macroeconomic interdependence and the exchange rate regime' in R. Dornbusch and J.A. Frenkel (eds), *International Economic Policy*, London: Johns Hopkins University Press.
Nordhaus, W.D. (1972) 'The worldwide wage explosion', *Brookings Papers on Economic Activity*, no. 2.
Obstfeld, M. (1985) 'Floating exchange rates: experience and prospects', *Brookings Papers on Economic Activity*, no. 2.
OECD (1970) *Inflation: The Present Problem*, Paris: OECD.
OECD (1973) *Economic Outlook (July)*, Paris, OECD.
Parkin, M. (1977) 'A "monetarist" analysis of the generation and transmission of world inflation", *American Economic Review*.
Parkin, M., Richards, I. and Zis, G. (1975) 'The determination and control of the world money supply under fixed exchange rates, 1961–1971', *Manchester School*.
Parkin, M. and Zis, G. (1976a) *Inflation in Open Economies*, Manchester: Manchester University Press.
Parkin, M. and Zis, G. (eds) (1976b) *Inflation in the World Economy*, Manchester: Manchester University Press.
Pattison, J.C. (1976) 'The international transmission of inflation' in M. Parkin and G. Zis (eds), *Inflation in the World Economy*, Manchester: Manchester University Press.
Paunio, J.J. and H. Halttunen (1976) 'The "Nordic" approach to inflation: interpretation and comments' in M. Parkin and G. Zis (eds), *Inflation in the World Economy*, Manchester: Manchester University Press.
Pencavel, J.H. (1970) 'An investigation into industrial strike activity', *Economica*.
Perry, G. (1975) 'Determinants of wage inflation around the world', *Brookings Papers on Economic Activity*, no. 2.
Phillips, A.W. (1958) 'The relationship between unemployment and the rate of change of money wage rates in the United Kingdom, 1861–1957', *Economica*.
Purdy, D. and Zis, G. (1974a) 'Trade unions and wage inflation in the UK: a reappraisal', in D. Laidler and D. Purdy (eds), *Inflation and Labour Markets*,

Manchester: Manchester University Press.
Purdy, D. and Zis, G. (1974b) 'On the concept and measurement of trade union militancy' in D. Laidler and D. Purdy (eds), *Inflation and Labour Markets*, Manchester: Manchester University Press.
Putnam, B.H. and Wilford, D.S. (eds) (1978) *The Monetary Approach to International Adjustment*, New York: Praeger.
Putnam, B.H. and Wilford, D.S. (1978) 'Money, income and causality in the United States and the United Kingdom', in B.H. Putnam and D.S. Wilford (eds), *The Monetary Approach to International Adjustment*, New York: Praeger.
Saidi, N.H. (1980) 'Fluctuating exchange rates and the international transmission of economic disturbances', *Journal of Money, Credit, and Banking*.
Salant, W.S. (1977) 'International transmission of inflation', in L.B. Krause and W.S. Salant (eds), *Worldwide Inflation: Theory and Recent Experience*, Washington, DC: Brookings Institution.
Sims, C.A. (1972) 'Money, income and causality', *American Economic Review*.
Sohmen, E. (1969) *Flexible Exchange Rates*, revised edn, Chicago: Chicago University Press.
Sumner, M.T. and Zis, G. (1982) 'On the relative bias of flexible exchange rates' in M. Sumner and G. Zis (eds), *European Monetary Union: Progress and Prospects*, London: Macmillan.
Sweeney, R.J. and Willet, T.D. (1977) 'Eurodollars, petrodollars, and world liquidity and inflation', in K. Brunner and A.H. Meltzer (eds), *Stabilisation of the Domestic and International Economy*, Carnegie-Rochester Conference Series on Public Policy, vol. 5, Amsterdam: North-Holland.
Swoboda, A.K. (1977) 'Monetary approaches to worldwide inflation', in L.B. Krause and W.S. Salant (eds), *Worldwide Inflation: Theory and Recent Experiences*, Washington, DC: Brookings Institution.
Swoboda, A.K. (1983) 'Exchange rate regimes and European–US policy interdependence' in A.W. Hooke (ed), *Exchange Rate Regimes and Policy Interdependence*, Washington, DC: IMF.
Taylor, J. (1972) 'Incomes policy, the structure of unemployment and the Phillips curve: the United Kingdom experience, 1953–70' in M. Parkin and M. Sumner (eds), *Incomes Policy and Inflation*, Manchester: Manchester University Press.
Turvey, R. (1971) 'Some features of incomes policy, and comments on the current inflation' in H.G. Johnson and A.R. Nobay (eds), *The Current Inflation*, London: Macmillan.
Ward, R. and Zis, G. (1974) 'Trade union militancy as an explanation of inflation: an international comparison', *The Manchester School*.
Williams, D., Goodhart, C.A.E. and Gowland, D.H. (1976) 'Money, income and causality: the UK experience', *American Economic Review*.
Zis, G. (1976) 'Inflation: an international monetary problem or a national social phenomenon?', in M. Parkin and G. Zis (eds), *Inflation in the World Economy*, Manchester: Manchester University Press.

6 · A CRITIQUE OF MONETARY THEORIES OF THE BALANCE OF PAYMENTS: NIHIL EX NIHILO

M.L. Burstein

THEORIES OF MONEY AND THE BALANCE OF PAYMENTS

In monetary theories of the balance of payments (MTBOP) in fixed foreign exchange rate regimes, 'excessive' domestic credit expansion engenders direct absorption effects that drain monetary reserves, braking money supply. The stable dynamic process also entails direct capital outflow: excess *j*-dollars are converted into specie and reserve currencies which are tendered for *i*-dollars. Influxes of specie and reserve currencies will stimulate foreign economies if their authorities do not sterilize reserve inflows.

In floating rate regimes, under MTBOP, monetary balances are rapidly adjusted by exchange rate changes. If wages and prices are sticky, 'excessive' monetary expansion in the *j*th economy first leads to a *more positive* current account of its balance of payments, followed by faster inflation, leading to current-account deterioration – which may *overshoot* before the current account stabilizes.

The controlling mechanism revolves around narrowly defined monetary assets: excess demand for (supply of) non-monetary assets, unaccompanied by disequilibrium in markets for monetary assets, is not to affect the current account.

MTBOP were quite fully developed by Ricardo (see Perlman, 1986). And the bullionist version of MTBOP is shown below to be easily transformed into a quite formal dynamic system.

Montiel (1984) points out that MTBOP can be made truistic; but we finesse this peril by constructing a scheme whose results are surely operationally distinguishable from those yielded by Keynesian and other approaches.

Perlman (1986, p. 745) says that Ricardo, 'the hard-line bullionist, argued that a necessary and sufficient condition for a balance of trade deficit was a redundant currency. With convertibility this would lead to an outflow of gold; with convertibility ... to a change in the exchange rate'.

This is an unmitigated version of MTBOP. Indeed Thornton and Malthus properly pointed out that Ricardo went too far: 'they also believed that such a deficit could occur because of changes in the real sector of the economy' (Perlman, 1986, pp. 745–6). We go further than Malthus and Thornton; we shall show that balance-of-payments disturbances may have non-monetary financial sources; and that portfolios everywhere may be rejiggered without any flows, real or financial, across frontiers.

Perlman's (1986, pp. 759–61) Appendices A and B are intriguing. His Appendix A shows that Thornton (1802) anticipated modern macroeconomic theory – in particular our coverage on pages 185–7 below on fiscal theories of the balance of payments. Perlman's (1986, p. 761) discussion of the problem of Appendix B-2, 'A bad harvest', brings out a tenuous line of argument that may prop up Ricardo:

> Ricardo was willing to concede to Malthus that a bad harvest will have an income effect on the demand for money and therefore will affect gold flows under convertibility or the price level and the exchange rate under inconvertability ... For Ricardo ... the effects of a bad harvest ... would be ... [like those] of a change in the quantity of money.

According to Montiel (1984, p. 685):

> The monetary approach is not itself a structural model, but rather a framework of analysis that is compatible with diverse macroeconomic models, which in turn may each possess quite different implications for the effects of stabilization policies on the balance of payments and on other macroeconomic variables.

He goes on to assume that an economy's central bank is its only financial institution. Then

$$F + D = M$$

where 'F is the domestic currency value of the bank's net foreign assets, D ... domestic credit extended by the bank and M ... its ... monetary liabilities (Montiel, 1984, p. 685). Since current-account deficits must be financed,

$$BOP = \dot{F} = \dot{M} - \dot{D} \tag{6.1}$$

where $\dot{F} = \mathrm{d}F/\mathrm{d}t$, and $\dot{M}$ and $\dot{D}$ are similarly defined. If the 'money market' is in continuous equilibrium, and P and L represent the domestic price level and real demand for money, then

$$\dot{M} = \mathrm{d}(PL)/\mathrm{d}t \tag{6.2}$$

Substituting into Equation (6.1):

$$BOP = \dot{F} = \mathrm{d}(PL/\mathrm{d}t - D) \tag{6.3}$$

The balance of payments of an economy in a fixed foreign exchange rate regime, is equal to the difference between the rate of growth of money-demand and domestic-credit expansion. Thus, if domestic credit-expansion growth exceeds money-demand growth, the balance of payments must deteriorate. (And note that, for $d(PL)/dt = 0$, so that $\dot{M}$ is zero, foreign assets must fall one-to-one with domestic credit expansion.)

Montiel (1984, p. 686) calls Equation (6.3) 'the fundamental equation of the monetary approach'. And he goes on to assert, and then to demonstrate, that

> the monetary approach merely describes the effects of stabilization policies on the balance of payments in terms of effects on the flow demand for money, on the flow supply of domestic-source money, or on both; the monetary approach does not, however, commit one to any particular view about the effects of such policies on the balance of payments.

(It would have been better if Montiel had characterized the 'fundamental equation' this way rather than MTBOP itself.)

Confirming Montiel's assertion about the implications of Equation (6.3), consider a crude hyper-Keynesian system's temporary equilibrium properties. Its balance of payments is determined by Equations (6.4) and (6.5):

$$\bar{y} = [1/(1-\beta_1)]\,[x^0 + G^0 + I(r^0)] \tag{6.4}$$

$$BOP = x^0 - \beta_2\bar{y} \tag{6.5}$$

where x is exports; β_1 is the propensity to consume home goods; β_2 is the propensity to import; G is government expenditure; and $I(r^0)$ determines investment.

As for money,

$$\bar{M} = L(r^0, \bar{y}) \tag{6.6}$$

The domestic price level is given throughout; and the domestic *numéraire* controls throughout.

The foreign-finance requirement (positive or negative), denoted as $\dot{F}$, is given by:

$$\dot{F} = X^0 - \beta_2\bar{y} \tag{6.7}$$

Continuous monetary equilibrium requires that $\dot{M} = 0$, since demand for money is constant. Therefore, when the current account is in deficit, Montiel's bank must expand its credit at the rate $\beta_2\bar{y} - x^0$. Fresh credits are used to buy foreign assets from the central bank – to finance imports. So,

$$BOP = \dot{F} - (-\dot{D}) \tag{6.8}$$

A hyper-Keynesian scheme strictly obeys a truistic fundamental

MTBOP equation. (Think of a Fisherine quantity theory of money in which V in $MV=PT$ is a slack variable.)

Ricardo's version of MTBOP, and that of Johnson (1972), are not empty. Nor is the following scheme empty:

$$z_j = z_j\,(\bar{\chi}_j - \chi_j) \tag{6.9}$$

where z_j is the current account of the jth BOP; χ_j is the proportion of globally available specie held in the jth economy; and $\bar{\chi}_j$ is the equilibrium value of that proportion (see Burstein, 1986, chapter 11). Contact with the 'fundamental' Equation (6.3) is regained in an obvious way.

Finally, it is possible to retain the principal properties of a non-empty MTBOP without requiring continuous equilibrium of the 'money market'. (Equations (5.10)–(5.15) tacitly adopt the 'law of one price'.)

$$z_j = \phi\;(L_j^* - M_j) \tag{6.10}$$

$$D^*_j = \psi\,(l_j - l^*_j) \tag{6.11}$$

where L_j^* is stipulated demand for money in the jth economy; $l = F/M$ = the bank's desired liquidity ratio; and, l^* is the bank's desired liquidity ratio. The scheme reduces to

$$\dot{F} = \dot{F}\,(F, M) \tag{6.12}$$

$$\dot{M} = \dot{M}\;(F, M) \tag{6.13}$$

Of course, Equations (6.12) and (6.13) comprise a canonical form. And study of the stability of the system proceeds along exceptionally well-defined lines. Setting $\dot{F} = \dot{M} = 0$ in Equations (6.12) and (6.13), we obtain the rest point $(\bar{F}, \bar{M})$. Approximating the system linearly in the neighbourhood of its rest point, and defining variables υ and μ as deviations from $\bar{F}$ and $\bar{M}$

$$\dot{\upsilon} = a_{11}\upsilon + a_{12}\mu \tag{6.14}$$

$$\dot{\mu} = a_{21}\upsilon + a_{22}\mu \tag{6.15}$$

stability properties, relative to the transformed origin $(\bar{F}, \bar{M}) = (0,0)$, are determined by the eigenvalues of the quadratic characteristic equation in well-known ways (see Arrowsmith and Place, 1982). Economic intuition suggests that, especially since the scheme avoids autonomous speculative processes, phase portraits will exhibit stable foci or attracting spirals.

The current account of the balance of payments supplies the underlying motive power. When the rest point is achieved, when $(F, M) = (\bar{F}, \bar{M})$, the current-account engine (cf. Equation (6.10)) shuts itself off.

The scheme represented by Equations (6.10)–(6.15) appears to represent the Ricardian scheme quite adequately; and is likely to be strongly identifiable. Its implications are observationally highly distinguishable from those of, say, Keynesian models. The scheme carries the weight of serious MTBOP analysis, and is indeed the target of the salvoes that follow.

The preferred theory in innovated economies

The preferred theory pivots on generalized portfolio analysis; and introduces *quasi-banking*. An agent prepared to be a quasi-banker warps his portfolio, for a fee, to accommodate others' plans to revise their portfolios. In innovated foreign exchange regimes, shifts in asset preferences, or exogenous changes in monetary-base growth, lead to countervailing switches in balance sheets of financial intermediaries, including quasi-bankers. In floating rate regimes, changes in base-money supplies or asset preferences lead to changes in exchange rates as well as to balance-sheet switches. The following material establishes the equivalence of disequilibrium in monetary and other financial markets while eliding intricacies posed by floating rate regimes.

Monetary disequilibrium

In the preferred theory, excess supply of *j*-dollar-denominated monetary assets causes their relative yields to rise (and excess demand causes monetary yields to fall). And excess supply of *j*-dollar-denominated monetary assets causes balance sheets to be rejiggered so that supplies of such assets fall.

Even in a *closed* system, more rapid expansion of the reserve base need not lead to expansion of narrowly-defined monetary stocks. True, broadly-defined liquid asset measures will be affected. But analysis of the consequences lies outside the domain of *monetary* theories of the balance of payments.

Elements of an innovated open analysis include the following. If monetary, or monetized, *j*-dollar assets are in excess supply, traders' spreads (implying fees) on sales of *j*-dollar obligations will shrink. And substantial quantities of *j*-dollar-denominated assets (which may call for delivery of equivalent *i*-dollar sums) will *disappear*: e.g. options entitling holders to payments in *j*-dollars will run off without being replaced (or will be closed out prematurely). And *i*-dollar holdings ($i \neq j$) will spring up as dealers take advantage of profitable writing opportunities.[1] The following transaction is revealing; for one thing, it does not entail deals in underlying stocks. Holders of options to put assets for *j*-dollars will trade them in to dealers, taking back options to put assets for *i*-dollars.

Non-monetary disequilibrium in real asset markets

MTBOP adherents deny that excess demand for Southwold land

significantly affects the British balance of payments. So do we. MTBOP and the preferred theory are in agreement on the point. But there is an important difference: in the preferred theory, monetary and non-monetary asset-market vibrations are *equivalent*. Equilibrium will be restored, following excess demand for land in the *j*th economy, by higher relative prices of land – just as, in the preferred theory, relative decreases in yields of monetary assets accommodate excess demand for money (land is interestingly, if erratically, analysed by Keynes, 1936, chapter 17).

Reproducible assets require stock–flow analysis. At impact, equilibrium is restored by higher source prices.

Impact effects, just discussed, engender higher values of Tobin's *q*; flow equilibrium requires increased production of new sources – points encompassed by a strictly closed analysis.

In the preferred theory, vibrations of preferences for financial assets provoke corresponding adjustments in supplies – or virtual supplies; cf. changes in textures of options positions. This proves to have profound implications for both open and closed macroeconomic analysis.

A sketch of a mathematical model

Before introducing our mathematical model, we set out a number of important concepts from Markov chain theory which will be needed later:

1. A stochastic matrix is a square matrix with row sums of unity.
2. A row vector is called a probability vector if it consists of non-negative components summing to unity.
3. The probability vector ($\mathbf{t}$) is a fixed point of the transformation $\mathbf{tP}$; i.e. $\mathbf{t} = \mathbf{tP}$. $\mathbf{P}$ is a transition matrix; $\mathbf{t}$ is an absorbing state.
4. The stochastic matrix $\mathbf{P}$ is regular if all its elements are positive. Any regular matrix is *ergodic*.
5. If $\mathbf{P}$ is a regular stochastic matrix, $\mathbf{P}^n \rightarrow \mathbf{T}$ as $n \rightarrow \infty$.
6. Each row of $\mathbf{T}$ is the same probability vector $\mathbf{t}$. If $\mathbf{p}$ is any probability vector, $\mathbf{pP}^n \rightarrow \mathbf{t}$ and $\mathbf{t}$ is the unique fixed point probability vector of $\mathbf{P}$.

In our model, the stochastic matrix is designated $(\mathbf{a}_{ij})$. The element $\mathbf{a}_{ij}$ describes the proportion of real liquid-asset holdings of the *i*th economy devoted to *j*-dollar-denominated (or guaranteed) claims. Consider the particular matrix $(\mathbf{a}_{ij})^*$, satisfying global portfolio preferences. In our model, an arbitrary initial stochastic matrix $(\mathbf{a}_{ij})^{**}$ maps into $(\mathbf{a}_{ij})^*$ once $(\mathbf{a}_{ij})^*$ is obtained, it transists into itself.

Actions of monetary authorities may displace an initial equilibrium state. But the dynamic process, including quasi-banking, generates a Modigliani–Miller-like effect so that, in another language, the system's phase portrait displays a stable node or attracting spiral. For example, quasi-bankers warp their portfolios *à la* Modigliani–Miller writers of virtual corporate securities or conventional bankers. They buy and sell options and engage in forward transactions, etc., enabling portfolio managers to attain virtually desired positions; for instance, acquisition of a put option can make one's dollar asset virtually a sterling one. Quasi-bankers respond elastically to small changes in spreads (between buying and selling prices), but the process can break down, as it does when bubbles form.

It follows that monetary displacements are typically absorbed within the financial system; the circuits of 'energy transmission' bypass the current account and, indeed, the real economy generally.

Speculation

Paraphrasing Keynes (1936, p. 158), Townsend (1978, p. 482) wrote: 'The activity of forecasting the choice of others is called speculation, while [that] of forecasting the yield of assets over their whole life is called enterprise.' As for speculation and the real effects of foreign exchange rate fluctuation, if a fall in the *j*-dollar is expected to persist – if expectations are elastic – own rates of *j*-dollar-denominated assets must increase relative to those of *i*-dollar assets: cf. interest-rate-parity formulæ. If wages and prices are sticky, real interest rates will increase – with familiar contractionary effects. In the real world, wages and prices erratically lag speculatively-impelled exchange rate movements. Think of a gold standard under which the parities are on random walks!

Speculation worked in favour of the US dollar in 1983–5, partially offsetting effects on real US interest rates of massive public sector borrowing requirements.

Choice of currency

It is not obvious on an abstract plane that a borrower resident in the *j*th economy should issue *j*-dollar securities. In a frictionless economy in which choice of measure is open in all transactions, contracts would be written in a variety of measures, independently of what currencies are used to discharge debts. (The *res* is choice of *measure*, not currency; cf. Burstein, 1986, chapter 2.) Events in *j*-dollar currency markets of such an economy do not map into its real action.

Innovated responses to asset-preference shifts

In the preferred analysis, an increase in liquidity preference among the agents of the *j*th economy – putatively holding *j*-dollar claims – is accommodated by small increases in spreads obtainable by agents (anywhere) prepared to sell liquid *j*-dollar-denominated claims for illiquid ones. The settlement medium is immaterial.

The market's responses may defy conventional analysis: put options may be written on *i*-dollar assets held by agents of the *j*th economy, perhaps monetizing their assets in a *j*-dollar measure. Or *i*-economy agents may purchase calls on *j*-dollar assets, simultaneously buying put options entitling them to convert *j*-dollar profits, or, if they stand for delivery, proceeds of sales of acquired securities, into *i*-dollars on stated terms. Speculators easily absorb resulting pressure. (See McKinnon, 1979, on the adequacy of the 'supply of speculation'.)

In a small open economy, in which agents hold mostly foreign currency, changes in liquidity preference are accommodated by switches within $\mathbf{x}_{ij}$, a vector of *i*-dollar assets held by '*j*' agents ($i = 1, 2, \ldots, j-1, j+1, \ldots$).

Innovated money supply theory[2]

Orthodox paradigms, linking central bank sales and purchases of securities to money growth, postulate a rigid regulatory structure: banks – *the* regulated industry of the theory – always gain from gratuitous increases in deposit liability: changes in 'high-powered money' systematically influence money supply. In unregulated environments in which interest is flexibly paid on all bank balances, central banks can effectively manipulate money supply only by manoeuvring their posted lending and borrowing rates.[3] This follows from convexity properties of the equilibrium of a competitive firm: the representative bank cannot profitably expand its deposit-liability above its equilibrium value.

If the public are to be induced to hold relatively more monetary balances, yields on monetary assets must increase relative to market; spreads enjoyed by banks must narrow. If banks are to accept narrower spreads, they must earn more on deposits lodged with the central bank. So money supply is influenced, however weakly, by central bank lending and borrowing rates more than by decisions on the volume of central bank assets (liabilities).

Principal arguments

The pith of the essay contains two clusters. The 'supply of money' cannot be precisely defined under modern, innovated conditions. Nor is the linkage between central bank purchases and sales of securities and changes in balance sheets of financial institutions well-defined. The first cluster suffices to block MTBOP: the *money* of MTBOP cannot be operationally defined. The second cluster also leads towards generalized portfolio theory. Disequilibrium in *any* asset market may, or may not, activate disturbances affecting current accounts of balances of payments. The consequences are as follows:

1. Absorption is rejected.
2. Forces affecting demand cannot be separated from those affecting supply – importantly because quasi-banking finds many agents monetizing assets. Theorems like the Modigliani–Miller theorem lie close to the surface.
3. Perhaps the single most important market response to shifts in asset preferences is in spreads between agents' borrowing and lending rates. Say that the state of expectations concerning foreign exchange rates (where the 'state' encompasses the distribution of expectations of means, variances, etc., among agents) is given. And assume that currency preferences shift so that the public wants to increase its (perhaps virtual) dollar exposure and reduce its exposure to sterling. Options writers must shorten their net dollar positions to accommodate the public.

As we have set up the problem, competitive writers will require larger risk premiums, so that buy–sell options spreads will widen. But, if writers' expectations of foreign exchange rates are firmly planted, exchange rates may be little affected by the switch in asset preferences. In no case can the problem be properly defined in terms of excess supplies of or demand for 'currencies': one can increase one's dollar exposure by purchasing a put option entitling one to put a stock for a quantity of sterling equivalent to x dollars on that day; or one can sell a call option, entitling the buyer to call away one's dollar stock for a quantity of dollars equal to y pounds sterling on the call day – if one wants to lock in a profit obtained by betting on a rising dollar.

ABSORPTION AND MONETARY THEORIES OF THE BALANCE OF PAYMENTS

After describing, and rejecting, the absorption-based facet of MTBOP, we turn to a more subtle, and proper, Keynesian approach to the channels of influence of asset-market events on real economic action.

As for absorption, according to Friedman and Schwartz (1982, p. 28),

> Another strand of the classical analysis has ... been revived under the title 'the monetary theory of the balance of payments'. This theory is logically equivalent to the specie-flow mechanism except that it makes different assumptions about adjustment speeds of the several variables ... If the quantity of money in a country is 'too low', domestic nominal demand will not be adequate to absorb domestic output. Export of the surplus will produce a balance of payments surplus for that country, which will raise the quantity of money. Specie flows are still the adjustment mechanism but they are produced not by discrepancies in prices but by differences between demand for output in nominal terms and the supply of output at world prices.

Critique of absorption

Keynes (1936, p. 167) acknowledges that 'money' must be defined quite arbitrarily:

> We can draw the line between 'money' and debts at whatever point is most convenient for handling a particular problem ... It is often convenient in practice to include in *money* even such instruments as e.g. treasury bills. As a rule, I shall assume that money is co-extensive with bank deposits.

Whatever it is, the quantity of money is to determine the real rate of interest: 'the quantity of money is the other factor, which, in conjunction with liquidity preference, determines the actual rate of interest in given circumstances' (Keynes, 1936, pp. 167–8). Few can now swallow this proposition whole. But its descendants, along with those of Wicksell's natural-rate analysis (also confusing real with nominal magnitudes), survive. A reduced-form inequality of the IS–LM scheme supplies an example (where H is 'base money'): $\partial r / \partial H < 0$. Whatever money is, it powerfully influences the real rate of interest!

If competitively-determined interest is paid on money (whatever it is), excess supply of money does not imply falling interest rates (real or nominal). Then monetary disequilibrium must map directly into displacements of goods markets if indeed goods markets are to be affected. Friedman and Schwartz suggest this is the case, but (*pace* Friedman and Schwartz) perhaps MTBOP also entails direct capital-account effects (see Frenkel and Johnson, 1976, pp. 28–9). Keep in mind that excess demand for narrowly-defined money may imply nothing more than excess supply of time deposits and/or excess supply of debentures, etc. For MTBOP to explain absorption, 'money' must be defined so broadly that it is congruent with *financial assets*. MTBOP theorists typically sidestep this point, excluding non-monetary financial assets from the universe of discourse.

Influence of asset-market events on real economic action

The cost of capital to a company is determined by the price of its shares relative to its 'true' earnings potential. And the share price is sensitive to autonomous speculative processes capable of producing bubbles or implosions. Share-price movements obviously influence real costs of capital – and real action.

As for the supply of shares, three points must be considered:

1. The supply of shares is functionally related to *demand*. Demand vibrations affect new issue.
2. Forward and futures transactions, together with options writing, lead

to effective changes in supply independently of the actions of the firm's board, a counterpart to a central bank.

3. If the supply of stock (of the *underlying commodity*) increases, the equilibrium share price would plausibly fall. But, just as in monetary models, quasi-issue may be negatively correlated with the supply of underlying stock.

Consider two corollaries to the third point. First, when the analysis if projected into MTBOP space, *j*-dollar securities may be issued by the *i*th authority or agent: in MTBOP space what matters are qualities of balance sheets – positive and negative positions will be taken across the whole spectrum of 'issue', so that the balance sheet of each agent displays a hodgepodge of 'denominations'. Second, an increase in an underlying stock makes it easier to sustain short positions; for one thing, dangers of delivery squeezes are mitigated.

The Wicksell connection[4]

It is convenient to begin with closed systems. The traverse from the *Treatise* to the *General Theory* importantly concerned a transformation of Keynes's view of the natural rate of interest: 'I am no longer of the opinion that the concept of a 'natural' rate of interest ... has anything very useful or significant to contribute... It is merely the rate of interest which will preserve the status quo' (Keynes, 1936, p. 243). In particular, where $\bar{r}$ associates with 'full employment', $r > \bar{r}$ becomes an equilibrium rate of interest if output falls appropriately. Indeed what makes the *General Theory* general is that output is a dependent variable.

Reaching farther back into the *General Theory*, 'the' rate of interest can be plausibly perceived to be determined by speculative forces – where, again, speculation concerns others' opinions rather than intrinsic values. So Dennis Robertson was right: Keynes's is a bootstrap theory of the rate of interest. To summarize: 'The rate of interest generated by the bourse is transformed into a natural rate of interest by an appropriate decrease in output ... [r]eal markets may respond, more or less passively, to changes in data generated by financial markets.' (Burstein, 1986, p. 154)

If asset-market events influence, let alone dominate, foreign exchange rate fluctuation, an economy with floating rates may imitate one whose wages and prices must ceaselessly chase after equilibrium levels determined by the antics of a Mad Hatter who jerks the parities about. Successful adaptation of open economies to asset-market events in a regime of clean floating may require infeasible wage–price flexibility.

The Wicksell connection and its extensions supply a *raison d'être* for agitation of current accounts of balances of payments by asset-market events. But *money* is not in the picture.

MONETARY INNOVATIONS AND MONEY-SUPPLY THEORY

The innovations

Denationalization

The representative agent contracts for liabilities in various measures, and arranges for cover, like agents with short commodity positions. The underlying stock includes government bonds as well as central bank liabilities; and there is a tenuous connection with delivery-squeeze peril. In the upshot, the *j*th monetary authority cannot exercise control over the volume of *j*-dollar denominated liquid assets (liabilities).

The *j*th banks' assets and liabilities will be written up in any number of monies of account. True, *j*-dollar obligations of *j*-banks may be preferred: *j*-banks are apt to have privileged access to the *j*th central bank. Still Barclay's Bank can obtain overdraft facilities from Chase (perhaps as part of a swap) so that Barclays can surely meet on sight US dollar demands. It need not hold quick US dollar assets, although it may choose to purchase federal funds.

Banks are portfolio managers who hold and issue claims defined in a variety of measures. The supply of money in the *j*th economy cannot properly be defined in terms of liquid liabilities of *j*-institutions expressed in *j*-dollars.

Interest on money

All financial assets are stipulated flexibly to yield interest in competitive markets – noting that transactions costs and convenience-yield factors may cause the *r*th asset's nominal yield to be nil in equilibrium.

'Interest on money' may confuse operators of the IS–LM scheme. If the model is defined in *r*–*y* space, so that there is *an* interest rate (and a baby model), 'interest on money' erases the substitution effect of a change in the interest rate: the LM curve becomes vertical: equilibrium income becomes determined by the quantity of money so that the intrinsic monetary theory of the real rate of interest behind IS–LM modelling is transformed into a monetary theory of real income, paired with a fiscally-based (IS) theory of the real rate of interest. If, instead of *r*, we consider a vector, **r**, the nightmare promptly dissipates: substitution effects are regained: LM shocks or shifts become largely absorbed by changes in spreads, a line of argument that is pitched up and intensified if the real cost of capital is an invariant (see Friedman, 1974; Burstein, 1986, chapter 3).

Competing currencies

Currency competition is pervasive. And along lines explained by Burstein

(1986, chapter 2), competition is more between metrics than currencies. Debts expressed in the *i*th metric can be discharged by *j*-dollar tenders. Again it is difficult to assign a role to monetary authorities as currency managers: liquid holdings in the *j*th economy cannot be assigned an exclusive *j*-dollar metric.

Central bank borrowing and lending[5]

Central banks pay interest on their liabilities and, of course, charge interest on their loans. If the deposit rate is increased, banks will plan to contract their advances in order to increase their deposits at the central bank: equilibrium bank-deposit levels will fall.

Less obviously, in the innovated monetary economy, manipulation of the central bank's deposit and lending rates replaces open-market operations as the principal mechanism of monetary policy (see below).

Quasi-banking

Banking functions are distributed over a continuous field, rather than clustering at nodes. Quasi-banks, like the banks of orthodox theory, distort their balance sheets in order to supply liquidity services – for a fee.

Options markets illustrate quasi-banking: B can monetize A's assets (in any measure) by selling A a put option. The upshot is important in at least two ways. First, money supply becomes ill-defined even in closed economies. Second, in an innovated open economy, agents' operations cannot properly be classified by 'economy of origin'. For one thing, options and futures contracts need not be settled in any one currency; a *j*-dollar option may be settled in *i*-dollars.

In one application of the quasi-banking model, there is to be a basic shift in currency preferences against the *j*-dollar. Two scenarios may be considered. In the orthodox scenario, specialists are forced to take in stock (*j*-dollars). So they will lower the price (in an *i*-dollar metric) they are prepared to pay for *j*-dollars. They will also widen their buy–sell spreads for *j*-dollars. In the innovated scenario, the effective supply of highly liquid *j*-dollar assets responds to demand. It is true that, in general, operators will go 'longer' on *j*-dollar account and 'shorter' on *i*-dollar account only if their spreads on *j*-dollar transactions widen – a conventional outcome of a once-over shift in market preferences against the *j*-dollar when subjective risk-distributions are stationary; i.e. when bubbles can be excluded.

When demand shifts towards the *i*-dollar, *j*-dollar options will be converted into *i*-dollar ones, with some adjustment of spreads. And an increase in the supply of 'conventional' *j*-dollars induces contraction of *j*-dollar options writing, just as a contraction of *j*-dollar supply stimulates quasi-issue.

Exchange rates in the preferred theory

In fixed-rate regimes, monetary disequilibria are corrected by counterbalancing shifts in the portfolios of market-makers, including quasi-bankers. But, in the preferred theory, the circuits conducting monetary-policy impulses are insulated from the real economy.

In floating rate regimes, *real* balances of monetary, and other, assets are adjusted by exchange rate movements as well as by shifts in portfolios of financial intermediaries.[6] In the short run, asset-market events, propelling exchange rates, may displace terms of trade from equilibrium values: wage–price inertia may be substantial. To the extent that short-run elasticities of substitution between elements of options writers' portfolios, for example, are small, exchange-rate adjustment will predominate. But in non-speculative markets driven by rationally-formed expectations, rapid convergence on equilibrium terms of trade is assured for the usual reasons.

As for *speculation*, large persistent *bubbles* may form, rational expectations or not (see Burmeister, 1980, esp. chapter 7). Then portfolio malleability promotes substantial, persistent departures of rates from equilibrium (rest point) values: for example, supplies of *j*-dollar call options dry up if the *j*-dollar is expected to climb. Huge bubbles in the US dollar in the 1980s supply an illustration.

Finally, note that in the preferred theory, actions of the *j*th central bank will not correlate well with price movements in a *j*-dollar measure; and that the analysis concerns financial markets generally, not just markets for claims arbitrarily designated as *money*.

Innovated debt discharge procedures

The theory must accommodate giro-type clearing, leading to monetary theory without money (see White, 1984; Burstein, 1986, chapter 1). In orthodox theory, following history, debts are cleared one at a time; in ancient times, coins crossed palms to extinguish debt. In innovated theory, one's balance 'against the house' continuously reflects transactions generating credits and debits to one's account in the context of a clearing process that continuously scans all activity.

Impose discontinuity on a giro operation for expository convenience. Say that a stroboscope pulses every x seconds, illuminating a data screen. If, over an x-second interval in phase with the stroboscope, a trader registers $10 million in credits and debits, her position 'against the house' will show no change. Traders will not be constrained by monetary balances (which indeed will not exist!); but instead by overdraft limits.[7] Not that unused overdraft facility properly defines a trader's cumulative deficit potential: she can generate credits from other traders by hypothecating assets.

Recapitulation: Erasure of the bank–non-bank distinction
In MTBOP literature, non-banking financial institutions are often ignored. But a proper theory of an innovated economy readily abstracts from banking institutions! Once regulatory obstructions are cleared away, it becomes improper to perceive 'issuers' of short-term liquid liabilities as expanding and contracting their balance sheets in discrete steps, responding to discontinuous official stimuli. The quasi-banks of the theory continuously expand and contract in profit-seeking response to stimuli received from the market. As a result, money supply, however defined, evolves in a closed-loop system.

Revised money supply theory

Under modern, innovated conditions, a critical variable for money demand is the yield on monetary claims *relative* to yields of other assets. And note Friedman's (1974, p. 40) remark:

> [i]t seems entirely satisfactory to take the anticipated real interest rate ... as fixed for the demand for money. There the real interest rate is at best a supporting actor. Inflation and deflation surely are centre stage ... The situation is altogether different for saving and investment.

Two important inferences follow at once. First, if a larger quantity of real cash balances, however defined, is to be absorbed by the public, the relative yield of 'cash' must increase. But such an adjustment of the yield curve will have minuscule effect on the real cost of capital. So an egregious consequence of IS–LM is quashed: the real cost of capital in equilibrium is not sensitive to monetary factors. Second, over an important range, the supply of money is perfectly elastic, relative to a spread. This follows from pure competition. Over this range, the supply of money is determined by *demand* – at least until new artillery (cf. manipulation of the central bank's deposit rate) is hauled up to the front.

Assume that the central bank's deposit rate is rigid and that fully informed agents form expectations rationally in an innovated economy. Then the central bank can accomplish open-market purchases only by offering a higher yield on deposits.[8]

The story is not over. Agents will demand more money only if its relative yield increases. And an enhanced central bank deposit rate will induce higher member-bank deposit rates; competition among banks assures this. As a result, money demand rises to meet supply in ways IS–LM cannot explain.

Whatever else is true, the innovated money-supply process does not intersect monetary theories of the balance of payments; and absorption paradigms fail.

APPLICATIONS

Fiscal theory of the balance of payments

Equation (6.16) identity describes any open economy:

$$j - x = (i+g) - (s+\tau) \quad (6.16)$$

where j is the proportion borne by imports to net national product (NNP); x is the proportion borne by exports to NNP; i is the proportion borne by investment expenditures to NNP; g is the proportion borne by government purchases to NNP; s is the proportion borne by savings to NNP; and τ is the proportion borne by tax revenues to NNP; We also observe that $(i+g)$ is the finance requirement of agents, public and private (tacitly, companies pay out all profits); and that $(s+\tau)$ = available domestic finance. Further,

$$c+i+g+x+-j = 1 \quad (6.17)$$

Interpolation

If the economy is in a Keynesian state, so that aggregate supply is perfectly elastic, an increase in public spending is self-financing. And an increase in the current account deficit of a fully-employed economy, subsequent to a higher public sector borrowing requirement, does not exert contractionary pressure: it merely permits a demand/supply gap to be filled in.

Analysis of a fully-employed economy is typically closed up by Equation (6.18), requiring 'foreign exchange market' equilibrium:

$$\phi = j - x \quad (6.18)$$

Ex post, capital inflow (ϕ) equals the current-account deficit. Equation (6.18) can be treated trivially: a current-account deficit must be financed. Or it can be infused with content – as Equations (6.19) and (6.20), functionally-active forms of Equations (6.16) and (6.18) make clear.

$$j(r,\xi) - x(r,\xi) = i(r, \xi) + g^0 - s(r,\xi) + \tau^0 \quad (6.19)$$

$$\phi(r,\xi) = j(\cdot) - x(\cdot) \quad (6.20)$$

Equations (6.19) and (6.20) are in the unknowns (r,ξ). Traditionally, the right-hand side of Equation (6.20) defines excess supply of our currency generated by a current-account deficit. Foreign exchange equilibrium appears to require that foreigners demand, on net, an equal volume of our securities, measured, *and issued*, in our money of account – where ξ measures terms of trade. If the aggregate finance requirement $[(i+g) - (s+\tau)]$ changes, Equation (6.16) requires that ϕ change accordingly.

In the preferred theory, the scenario does not require foreign exchange rate or interest rate adjustment; nor is anything monetary entailed. Nor is there an intrinsic connection between current-account positions and currency prices. For example, agents of the *r*th economy, including its government, may finance a current-account deficit by selling securities denominated in *s*-dollars, or guaranteed in *s*-dollar value. Indeed Mexico, Brazil and other countries have issued great quantities of US-dollar-denominated debt. Capital inflow does not require foreign willingness to acquire assets denominated in US dollars. True, these countries must be willing to extend credit to the United States; but that can be accomplished by their acceptance of US IOUs in their, or any other, measure.

Enlarging the phase space of the analysis
If the analysis if dynamized, state variables include balance sheet values. A flow-equilibrium entailing a current-account deficit and capital inflow may imply a deteriorating collective balance sheet: global claims against the *j*th economy may be increasing unsustainably rapidly.

Properties of stock–flow ('long-run') equilibrium
The rate at which an economy's foreign debt is increasing – if interest payments are financed by fresh borrowing – is given by $rD + U$, where D is foreign debt and U fresh borrowing beyond interest requirements. And the relative rate of increase is $r + U/D$, or $r + u/\delta$, where $u = U/y$ and $\delta = D/y$.

In a moving stock–flow equilibrium, real foreign debt per unit of output, foreign debt per unit of domestic wealth, etc., are constant. So, where the intrinsic real growth rate is ρ^0,

$$\rho^0 = r + u/\delta \tag{6.21}$$

Specifying that the interest rate, as well as the real-growth rate, is parametric, and rearranging terms,

$$u = \delta(\rho^0 - r^0) \tag{6.22}$$

As for δ, really δ_j, an element of the vector system

$$\dot{\delta} = \dot{\delta}(\delta), \tag{6.23}$$

go on to solve for a rest point of that system,

$$0 = \dot{\delta}(\delta) \tag{6.24}$$

The solution of Equation (6.24), $\bar{\delta}$, is a function of global asset preferences. Substituting the solution value of δ_j, $\bar{\delta}_j$, into Equation (6.22), we discover the equilibrium value of capital inflow per unit of output. We are able to solve for $\bar{u}$ directly. And interest payments per unit of output are $r^0\bar{\delta}_j$. It remains only to solve for the terms of trade that will be consistent with a current-account deficit per unit of output equal to the required capital inflow per unit of output.

The secular rate of expansion of the *j*th economy's money stock affects the evolution of its exchange rate but is neutral against its equilibrium current-account position – as classical theory says it should be.

Seigniorage in the extended argument

An economy able to deploy its currency as a vehicle, and to earn seigniorage profits in other ways, operates a more benign calculus. The United States is an example. But seigniorage potential is exhausted at the point at which demand for seigniorage services is unit elastic.

Concluding remarks

1. As for the deficit in the budget of the US government and the dollar exchange rate, let global preferences shift towards dollar-denominated financial assets. Textbooks say that capital inflow into the United States will increase; and that the current account will deteriorate – to an extent mitigated by depressing effects of the appreciated dollar on aggregate demand. As for interest rates, increased demand for dollar assets encourages lower interest rates in New York. To the extent that the US public sector borrowing requirement simultaneously increases, the dollar's appreciation is mitigated and pressures towards *lower* New York interest rates are indeed reduced. Our scenario differs from the textbook one in that ours does not require that capital inflow into the *j*th economy take *j*-dollar shape; finance ministers choose currency packages the way corporate treasurers choose theirs. In our scenario, the dollar rate(s) and the US PSBR are disconnected.
2. In innovated modelling, effects of changes in public sector borrowing requirements or in financial asset expansion may be invariant against choice of exchange rate regime. To repeat, a current account deficit of the *j*th economy may be denominated in *i*-dollars. If it persists, it may strain the creditworthiness of the *j*th economy, but, if financed by *i*-dollar-denominated issue, its effects will not spill over into foreign exchange markets.
3. In innovated modelling, the position of the *j*th economy is like that of the *j*th private agent in a giro scheme. (One way to pay for what one buys is to sell seigniorage services.) As the International Monetary Fund drill displays so prominently, overextended debtors, public or private, must generate net credits on the giro. The canonical problem belongs to the theory of finance, and does not have substantial 'monetary' content.

Monetary applications

This subsection further develops our discussion of monetary innovations and money-supply theory (pages 181–4) in order to complete preparations for study of the specific 'events' displayed in the next subsection (pages 189–91).

Denationalization of money
Sophisticated trading nexuses in open economies project the practices of Einaudi's (1952) medieval fairs onto a plane featuring inconvertible paper money. In an open monetary economy, modelled along lines suggested by Klein (1974) and Hayek (1976), various *i*-dollar claims will freely circulate, along with *j*-dollar ones, in the *j*th economy. Metrics will be freely elected.

Heyek (1976) shows that governments, jealous of seigniorage profits, systematically obstruct spontaneous evolution of monetary practices, an evolution entailing denationalization of money, in order to preserve predominant demand for *j*-dollar instruments in the *j*th economy.

In the economy of the preferred theory, one may borrow *x* French francs in French 'currency' and inject the proceeds directly into the UK economy. The loan may be repayable in a variety of currencies. Convex combinations of *n* basic vectors are admissable; *n* currencies discharge debt cast up in any number of metrical combinations. A debt in the *j*-dollar metric need not be discharged by a *j*-dollar tender. Nor need 'metrical vectors' constructed in the *j*th economy include the *j*-dollar.

Denationalization of money and monetary measurements
Conventional measurements of the stock of *j*-dollars are deceiving. Holders of *j*-dollars may have *i*-dollar guarantees; they may have bought put options. So *j*-dollar holdings may contribute to strategies keyed on 'the *i*-dollar'. In the limit, *j*-dollar holdings of '*j*' residents may be open-valued on a *j*-dollar scale and fixed in *i*-dollar value.

Speculative and other private sector intervention in the money supply process
Consider a situation in which supply is not equal to demand for *j*-dollars. Let us say that the supply of money – treasury currency and selected bank liabilities – is less than demand. Now let us insert quasi-banking. A small increase in spreads induces options writers to supply elastically enlarged stocks of monetized *j*-dollar assets, i.e. to write options virtually monetizing stocks in a *j*-dollar metric.

Relative to deterministic data shifts, options writers would not be resisting speculative pressures. Agents forming their expectations rationally would recognize that there had been a *once-over* preference shift. Professional options writers would demand higher spreads because their portfolios had become distended; *not* because of perceived increased vulnerability to speculative attack.

In the innovated model, virtual money supply is endogenous in open and closed systems.

It should be remarked here that speculative *bubbles* require a different script (see Townsend, 1978; Burmeister, 1980). But such autonomous processes also contradict MTBOP: they feed themselves; they are not fed by monetary authorities.

Speculative support of exchange rates and endogeneity of money supply

Speculators, defending exchange rates, become quasi-monetary authorities, adjusting global stocks of money (monetized) assets to demands.

Salant (1983) demonstrates the limits of such strategies. Speculators' balance sheets may ultimately break down as their obligations to deliver *i*-dollar paper grow relative to deliverable stocks. Still, at least two factors mitigate these qualms. First, available stocks are typically massive – encompassing stocks of government debt, for example. Second, a commitment to guarantee the *i*-dollar value of a stock need not be dischargeable by an '*i*-dollar substance'.

Application of the analysis

If the rise (to September 1985) in the US dollar were based on fundamentals such as secularly lower US inflation, requiring continuous appreciation in order to sustain purchasing power parity, or higher interest rates in New York, attracting uncovered capital transfers, then the (US/UK/French/West German/Japanese) consortium would surely have been futile. But it is plausible that dollar appreciation had been the result of an autonomous (self-sustaining) speculative process. Then market belief that the consortium's swap agreements would hold up could have been sufficient to make the market adapt its exchange rate expectations, *cum* portfolio preferences, to the consortium's targets. Resulting current-account effects – and the dollar did come down – could not be ascribed to the endogenous variables (M_i) . . . Alas, there is a fly in the ointment: the consortium appeared unable to influence what appears to have become a self-sustaining *fall* in the dollar in late 1985–6; it may have been irrelevant all the while.

Portfolio-management impulses and balance of payments

Disturbances or Switches

Four events are considered. In no case is the proper analysis monetary; in each case a pseudo-monetary analysis is illuminating. The four events are:

net global excess demand for *j*-dollar denominated assets; global excess demand for liquidity that is neutral against *j*-dollar (*i*-dollar) preferences; global excess demand for real assets, accompanied by excess supply of liquid assets; a legitimate real-balance effect setting off disturbances.[9]

Shifts in j*-dollar-asset preferences.* Assume that *real* assets sited in the *j*th economy become more preferred. Their relative prices will increase. But, even in floating-rate regimes, the *j*-dollar need not rise. Thus asset-preference shifts need not lead to net capital flows; assets may simply be swapped; in principle, *no* transaction is required. Or, *i*-economy agents, purchasing *j*-economy assets 'for *j*-dollars', may issue *j*-dollar-denominated paper – unless *j*-economy sellers are indifferent between '*i*-dollars' and '*j*-dollars'.

Once an asset is purchased, the buyer can 'metricize' it to his taste. The spectrum of hedging options encompasses myriad convex combinations of 'currencies'. The classic sequence – asset-preference shift→exchange rate movement→current-account change→*financement* of capital flows – is a special case. Finally, a temporary increase in demand for *j*-dollar finance for asset purchases will be readily accommodated by currency traders who will block substantial *i*-dollar depreciation: they know that, at most, once the traverse is crossed (and the asset switches completed), tiny changes in exchange rates will accommodate global asset portfolios to the minuscule relative magnitudes involved.

The following remarks supply guidelines for a purely financial analysis. There are many ways in which agents around the world, can write *j*-dollar-denominated, or -based, claims. Small changes in spreads induce shifts in virtual supplies, countering official actions; and shifts in 'currency preferences' are accommodated by quasi-banking operations. Again distinguish risks implicit in increased *j*-dollar exposure in a stochastically stationary environment from those entailed by elastic expectations in models able to generate bubbles (and their collapses). The former case is amenable to our theory. The latter poses disorderly possibilities – weakening the case for flexible exchange rates; and not buttressing Humpty Dumpty, MTBOP.

Global excess demand for liquidity. Neutral changes in liquidity preference, o'er the world, lie outside the domain of monetary theories of balances of payments. Only differentiated financial disequilibria affect trade-flows between economies. Indeed, in the preferred theory, increased liquidity preference will be largely absorbed by quasi-bank 'rewriting'.

Global excess demand for real assets. This case obviously lies outside the domain of *monetary* theories of balances of payments. But it is not remote from general portfolio theory: corporate treasurers will want to issue more shares and retire debt, for example. 'Financial space' must be studied to determine how revised portfolios should be remetricized.

Legitimate real balance effects. Actions of central banks, merely entailing asset/liability switches, cannot be expected to generate real balance effects (as for the Pesek–Saving fallacy, see Goodhart, 1975; and Burstein, 1986, chapter 9).

Current account surpluses (deficits) may inject excess liquidity into (drain liquidity from) an economy, but they do not engender wealth effects *à la* Haberler and Pigou. The real balance effects embedded in MTBOP are quite improper. (Stimulus from a trade surplus *à la* Keynesian multiplier is another matter; but Humpty Dumpty is not succoured.)

The following passages from Burstein (1986) may illuminate the real-balance-effect perplex.

> The *burden of the money supply* makes more sense than positive real-balance effects: why do so many who accept Barro's arguments about public debt insist that heaps of soiled paper should be perceived as collective wealth? Model consistency *does* require that Agent χ_1 take into account the strategies of Agents $\chi_2, \ldots, \chi_n$ for deployment of their liquid claims. In a crude counterpart to the proper model, χ_1 may find that the goods smörgasbord has been picked clean by the time she is ready to choose from it; she may end up with a fistfull of worthless currency (p. 126)

> The thrust of the Leontieff parable, permitting a coin to purchase the national output, leads to the possibility of chaos in a monetary economy. Each agent, able to exercise immense buying power, can wipe the table clean. In the absence of a 'balance of terror', panic buying would be endemic. Hyperinflation may alternate with hyperdeflation (pp. 129–30)

Pseudo-monetary theories of the balance of payments

If 'money' is defined very broadly, a theory based on it cannot be properly called 'monetary'. Crudely, if everything is money, nothing is money. Supply of and demand for a narrowly-defined monetary aggregate is less 'stable' than that for a more broadly-defined one. The demand for pork is not only more elastic than that for meat. It vibrates more: it is affected by shifts in meat preference.

So liquid-asset supplies exhibit forced as well as intrinsic oscillations. Switches in asset preferences trigger offsetting supply changes; the process imitates the Modigliani–Miller one. Whatever money supply is, it evolves in a closed-loop process.

SUMMARY

The asset subset, M, has no special importance for current-account fluctuations. All that survives of MTBOP are traces of a pseudo-monetary theory based on a broad spectrum of assets.

Even these trace quantities are suspect. The 'supply side' of the analysis is amorphous. Portfolio switches can be induced by small, even tiny, changes in spreads: elasticities of substitution are high. As a result, energy released by asset-preference shifts and central bank strategies is mostly absorbed within the global financial sector – without escaping into 'real economies'.

Under modern, innovated conditions, the 'supply of money' cannot be precisely, or operationally, defined.

Disequilibrium in *any* asset market may affect current accounts of balances of payments, but need not do so. We have studied three aspects of the upshot: absorption is rejected; forces affecting demand cannot be disentangled from those affecting supply; and in a regime of quasi-banking, currency-preference shocks are absorbed by (perhaps very small) changes in writers' spreads.

MTBOP entail absorption paradigms, but these break down for at least two reasons: first 'money' has become an evanascent idea; and second, real balance effects, never robust, are inadmissible in innovated modelling.

There are a number of valid channels of influence of asset-market shifts or shocks on the real economy. First, autonomous speculative processes may induce foreign exchange rate vibrations – leading to correlated vibration of terms of trade. The proper Keynesian upshot is on all fours with Leijonhufvud's *Wicksell connection*. Second, net global excess demand (supply) for *j*-dollar-denominated assets also transmits to the terms of trade to some degree over some inverval in most cases. Third, vibrations in real asset preferences (between economies) may communicate to the current account of the balance of payments, primarily through terms-of-trade effects.

MTBOP are committed to primitive money-supply processes excluding options-writing and other quasi-banking activity, along with demand for *i*-dollar-denominated assets in the *j*th economy. Our theory of innovated economies is based on free-market processes which swamp out official-sector monetary actions and freely cross national borders. And these processes often have unobservable effects: cf. the UK purchaser of a put option monetizing a real asset in a US dollar measure. The bulk of this chapter concerns a number of innovations that so break down the fibre of nationalized money that MTBOP cannot get off the ground: what are MTBOP *sans* money!

A number of innovations were then explored:

1. *Denationalization of monetary and quasi-monetary issue*. The representative agent of our theory arranges for cover of his exposure to

a variety of foreign-exchange-rate-rooted risks like an agent with a short commodity position; and assets and liabilities of financial institutions are written up in any number of accounting units. The supply of money in an economy cannot be properly defined in terms of liquid liabilities of its institutions, expressed in its dollar.

2. *Interest on money*. Excess supply of money no longer implies downward pressure on interest rates.
3. *Central bank lending and borrowing*. When central banks pay interest on their liabilities, manipulation of their lending and borrowing rates replaces open-market operations as the principal mechanism of monetary policy.
4. *Quasi-banking*. In regimes of quasi-banking, central banks merely make ripples on surfaces of lakes comprised of underlying stocks that include government debt.[10] Quantities of monetary, or monetized, assets evolve from spontaneous free-market transactions. Thus B can monetize A's asset (in any measure) by selling him a put option. In the innovated economy, monetary disequilibrium is corrected by changes in writers' portfolios. The adjustment process develops within the financial sector without impinging upon balances of payments.
5. *Innovated debt-discharge procedures*. Traders cease to be constrained by monetary balances; an indispensable underpinning for MTBOP is withdrawn.

A number of applications of the theory were then developed. First, fiscal perturbations were studied in isolation. Then some monetary ones were looked at, the most important being 'portfolio-management impulses'.

In examining fiscal perturbation, we saw that, if an economy's public-sector borrowing requirement increases, its current account may deteriorate – certainly if it is fully employed. Borrowings may be denominated in foreign measures: the *j*th economy can finance a current-account deficit by selling securities redeemable or guaranteed in *i*-dollars. Interest rates and currency prices need not be affected; nor need 'money markets' be disturbed.

In studying portfolio-management impulses, we saw that greater preference for assets sited in the *j*th economy may lead to capital inflow. But 'metricization' is open: hedging opportunities encompass myriad convex combinations of 'currencies'; *i*-economy agents purchasing *j*-economy assets may issue *j*-dollar-denominated paper that need not be redeemable in *j*-dollars; the paper may call for payment of the number of *i*-dollars that will, on maturity, purchase *x* *j*-dollars. There are many ways in which agents everywhere can write *j*-dollar-denominated, or -based, claims.

NOTES

1. A side-effect finds financial dealers (including banks) planning to sell *j*-dollar assets ('backing' *j*-dollar obligations) and place the proceeds in *i*-dollar assets. Volumes of resulting transactions will be minuscule relative to magnitudes of global stocks.
2. See Tobin (1963).
3. Analysis of Bank Rate is typically confused, importantly because the influential Wicksellian model is misspecified (see Wicksell, 1936). Thus Hicks (1946, p. 253) correctly points out that 'Wicksell's price-system consists of a perfectly determinate core – the relative prices of commodities and the rate of interest – floating on a perfectly indeterminate æther of money values.' And that 'It is a rather unfortunate thing that Wicksell and his immediate followers remained so long under the delusion that the possibility of discrepancy between the *money rate* and the *natural rate* was the keystone of his theory.'

   In 1988 I showed that, when Wicksell's model is properly interpreted, as it was by Ricardo(!), the rate of growth of *nominal* money supply is a function of the disparity between the administered Bank Rate and the natural rate – where both rates are 'real'. And I show that the Bank's decision on real Bank Rate leads to a well-defined equilibrium quantity of real cash balances; the lower is to be real Bank Rate, the less is the quantity of real cash balances in equilibrium. If Wicksell's bank displays money illusion, the resulting dynamic process will be unstable.
4. See Leijonhufvud (1981), discussed by Burstein (1986, chapter 10).
5. See Tobin (1982).
6. Neutrality cannot be preserved. If monetary issue in the *j*th economy increases, exchange-rate and wage–price adjustments can preserve the *i*-dollar value of *j*-dollar monetary balances, together with their real purchasing power in a *j*-dollar measure. But this implies depreciation of the real value of non-monetary assets in *i*-dollar and other measures.
7. In the simplest case, the house does not give credit to members; then the algebraic sum of positions against the house is nil; then debit positions are recorded by the house, but not 'supplied' by the house.
8. If monetary liabilities of banks temporarily exceed the quantity they wish to supply, banks will seek to retire the excess by making attractive one-off swap offers . . . Of course, total bank mediation can be sustained by substitution of non-monetary for monetary liabilities on bank balance sheets so that banks are more *comme les autres* . . . Finally, banks able to obtain market-sensitive yields on deposits with the central bank may exhibit weak preference for (or against) open-market investments – the alternative being open-market investment or deposit with the central bank.
9. An example of such a real-balance-based sequence may concern sixteenth-century Spain subsequent to American precious-metal finds. Examples are quite rare: changes in observed quantities of narrowly-defined money typically merely reflect asset-preference changes. And expansion of broadly-defined monetary magnitudes entails nothing more than double-entry bookkeeping.
10. I am indebted to Lester Telser in this connection.

BIBLIOGRAPHY

This chapter is more a critique than a survey of monetary theories of balances of payments, and the bibliography below includes references that may not have been consulted in the body of the chapter.

Aghevil, B.B. *et al.* (1971) *The Monetary Approach to the Balance of Payments*, Washington, DC: IMF.

Arrowsmith, D.K. and Place, C.M. (1982) *Ordinary Differential Equations*, London: Chapman and Hall.

Bilson, J.F. (1979) 'Recent developments in monetary models of foreign exchange rate determination', *IMF Staff Papers*, 26.

Blejer, M.I. and Leiderman, L. (1981) 'A monetary approach to the crawling peg system: theory and evidence', *Journal of Political Economy*, vol. 89.

Buiter, W.H. and Miller, M. (1981) 'Monetary policy and international competitiveness: the problems of adjustment' in W.A. Eltis and P.J.H. Sinclair (eds), *The Money Supply and the Exchange Rate*, Oxford: Clarendon Press.

Burmeister, E. (1980) *Capital Theory and Dynamics*, New York: Cambridge University Press.

Burstein, M.L. (1986) *Modern Monetary Theory,* London: Macmillan.

Burstein, M.L. (1988) 'Knut Wicksell and the closure of his system: critique and reconstruction of the Cumulative Process', in his *Studies in Banking Theory, Monetary History and Vertical Control*, London, Macmillan.

Corden, W.M. (1977) *Inflation, Exchange Rates and the World Economy*, Chicago: University of Chicago Press.

Dornbusch, R. (1975) 'A portfolio balance model of the open economy', *Journal of Monetary Economics*, vol. 1.

Einaudi, L. (1952) 'The theory of imaginary money' in L. Einaudi, *Enterprise and Secular Change*, Homewood, IL: Irwin (reprint).

Eltis, W.A. and Sinclair, P.J.N. (eds) (1981) *The Money Supply and the Exchange Rate*, Oxford: Clarendon Press.

Frenkel, J.A. (1976) 'A monetary approach to the exchange rate', *Scandinavian Journal of Economics*, vol. 2.

Frenkel, J.A. and Johnson, H.G. (eds) (1976) *The Monetary Approach to the Balance of Payments*, London: Allen & Unwin.

Frenkel, J.A. and Johnson, H.G. (1978) *The Economics of Exchange Rates: Selected Studies*, Reading, MA: Addison-Wesley.

Frenkel, J.A. and Rodriguez, C.A. (1975) 'Portfolio equilibrium and the balance of payments', *American Economic Review*, vol. 65.

Friedman, M. (1974) 'A theoretical framework for monetary analysis' in R.J. Gordon (ed.), *Milton Friedman's Monetary Framework*, Chicago: University of Chicago Press.

Friedman, M. (1986) 'The resource cost of irredeemable paper money', *Journal of Political Economy*, vol. 94.

Friedman, M. and Schwartz, A.J. (1982) *Monetary Trends in the United States and the United Kingdom*, Chicago: University of Chicago Press.

Friedman, M. and Schwartz, A.J. (1986) 'Has government any role in money?', *Journal of Monetary Economics*, vol. 17.

Goodhart, C.A.E. (1975) *Money, Information and Uncertainty*, London: Macmillan.

Hahn, F. (1977) 'The monetary approach to balance of payments', *Journal of International Economics*, vol. 7, pp. 231–500.
Hayek, F.A. von (1976) *Denationalization of Money*, London: Institute of Economic Affairs.
Hicks, J.R. (1946) *Value and Capital*, 2nd edn., Oxford: Clarendon Press.
Johnson, H.G. (1972a) *Further Essays in Monetary Theory*, London: Allen & Unwin.
Johnson, H.G. (1972b) 'The monetary approach to balance-of-payments theory', *Journal of Financial and Quantitative Analysis*, vol. 7.
Johnson, H.G. (1977) 'The monetary approach to the balance of payments: a non-technical guide', *Journal of International Economics*, vol. 7.
Keynes, J.M. (1930) *A Treatise on Money*, 2 vols, London: Macmillan.
Keynes, J.M. (1936) *The General Theory of Employment, Interest and Money*, London: Macmillan.
Klein, B. (1974) 'The competitive supply of money', *Journal of Money, Credit, and Banking*, vol. 6.
Kouri, P. and Porter, M.G. (1974) 'International capital flows and portfolio equilibrium', *Journal of Political Economy*, vol. 82.
Kreinen, M.E. and Officer, L.H. (1978) *The Monetary Approach to the Balance of Payments: A Survey*, Princeton Studies in International Finance no. 43, Princeton, NJ: Princeton University Press.
Krueger, A.O. (1983) *Exchange Rate Determination*, New York: Cambridge University Press.
Leijonhufvud, A. (1968) *On Keynesian Economics and the Economics of Keynes*, New York: Oxford University Press.
Leijonhufvud, A. (1981) *Information and Coordination*, New York: Oxford University Press.
McKinnon, R.I. (1979) *Money in International Exchange: The Convertible Currency System*, New York: Oxford University Press.
Montiel, P. (1984) 'Credit and fiscal policies in a "global monetarist" model of the balance of payments', *IMF Staff Papers*, no. 31.
Montiel, P. (1985) 'A monetary analysis of a small open economy with a Keynesian structure', *IMF Staff Papers*, no. 32.
Mussa, M. (1976a) 'Tariffs and the balance of payments: a monetary approach' in J.A. Frenkel and H.G. Johnson (eds), *The Monetary Approach to the Balance of Payments*, London: Allen & Unwin.
Mussa, M. (1976b) 'The exchange rate, the balance of payments and monetary and fiscal policy under a regime of controlled floating', *Scandinavian Journal of Economics*, vol. 2.
Perlman, M. (1986) 'The bullionist controversy revisited', *Journal of Political Economy*, vol. 94.
Rodriguez, C.A. (1976) 'Money and wealth in an open economy income-expenditure model' in J.A. Frenkel and H.G. Johnson (eds), *The Monetary Approach to the Balance of Payments*, London: Allen & Unwin.
Salant, S.W. (1983) 'The vulnerability of price stabilization schemes to speculative attack', *Journal of Political Economy*, vol. 91.
Telser, L.G. (1981) 'Why there are organized futures markets', *Journal of Law and Economics*, vol. 24.
Telser, L.G. (1986) 'Futures and actual markets: how they are related', *Journal of Business*, vol. 59.
Thornton, H. (1802) *An Enquiry into the Nature and Effects of the Paper Credit of*

Great Britain, London: Hatchard.
Tobin, J. (1963) 'Commercial banks as creators of "money"' in D. Carson (ed.), *Banking and Monetary Studies*, Homewood, IL: Irwin.
Tobin, J. (1982) 'Financial structure and monetary rules', *Tagung Geld, Banken und Versicherungen*, 2 (Universität Karlsruhe).
Townsend, R.M. (1978) 'Market expectations, rational expectations and Bayesian analysis', *International Economic Review*, vol. 19.
Wallace, N. (1979) 'Why markets in foreign exchange are different from other markets', *Federal Reserve Bank of Minneapolis Quarterly Review*, vol. 3.
White, L.H. (1984) 'Competitive payments systems and the unit of account', *American Economic Review*, vol. 74.
Whitman, M. von Neumann (1975) 'Global monetarism and the monetary approach to the balance of payments', *Brookings Papers on Economic Activity*, no. 3.
Wicksell, K. (1936) *Interest and Prices*, London: Macmillan.

7 · A FRAMEWORK FOR THE ANALYSIS OF TWO-TIER EXCHANGE MARKETS WITH INCOMPLETE SEGMENTATION

Jagdeep S. Bhandari and Bernard Decaluwe

INTRODUCTION

'Article VIII, Section 3, of the [International Monetary] Fund's Articles of Agreement prohibits a member from engaging in . . . any discriminatory currency arrangements or multiple currency practices without approval of the Fund . . .' (*Annual Report on Exchange Arrangements and Exchange Restrictions*, IMF, 1982). Under the par-value system, exchange rates outside the permitted 1 per cent margins or a spread of more than 2 per cent, were considered to give rise to multiple currency practices. The approval of the Second Amendment to the IMF Articles in 1978 (which removed the obligation of members to maintain margins around parity), necessitated a redefinition of multiple currency practices. Despite its continuing unfavourable attitude toward such arrangements, however (especially for current account transactions), the IMF reports that '42 members maintained multiple currency practices at the end of March 1982', of which nine members did so without its approval. The *Annual Report* of 1982 goes on to state that 'Seventeen members introduced at least one new multiple currency practice during the period January 1981–March 1982, generally in the form of a *dual* exchange market system, including 5 members that gave official recognition to parallel exchange markets already in existence' (emphasis added).[1]

Of the forty-two countries reported to be engaging in some form of multiple currency practices, at least seventeen can be identified as maintaining *widespread* legal dual exchange markets as at the end of 1982 (the rest employ parallel markets for only limited categories of transactions). These are Belgium and Luxembourg; Chile; Costa Rica; Dominican Republic; Ecuador; Egypt; El Salvador; Jamaica; Mexico; Nicaragua; Paraguay; Romania; Sierra Leone; Sudan; Syria; Uganda; and Venezuela. Dual exchange markets are also reported to have existed for some part of 1981–2 in Argentina; Bolivia; Columbia; and Mauritius. In addition, the French and Italian experiences with two-tier regimes in the early 1970s are well documented.[2]

It is clear, therefore, that there has been a wide variety of experience with officially sanctioned dual exchange markets. Despite the fact that the BLEU (Belgo-Luxembourg Economic Union) has continuously operated such a system since 1957, economic analyses of two-tier systems did not begin until the early 1970s. The last decade, however, has witnessed several attempts to address two principal questions – the efficacy of monetary and fiscal policies under such regimes and the insulation properties of the latter. Fleming (1971), Barattieri and Ragazzi (1971), Salin (1971), Decaluwe (1974), Swoboda (1974), Argy and Porter (1972), Decaluwe and Steinherr (1976), Cumby (1981), and Kiguel (1982) fall in the first category; while Dornbusch (1976), Flood (1978), Fleming (1974), Marion (1981) and Flood and Marion (1982a; 1982b) are more concerned with the formation of expectations and the insulation properties of such systems. Discussion of actual experiences with two-tier systems (such as those in France, Italy and the BLEU) can be found in Talent (1970), Abraham and Martin (1970), Abraham (1974), Decaluwe (1975) and Lanyi (1975).[3]

A curious feature of all of the above-mentioned theoretical analyses is the universal assumption that dual exchange markets can be and are, effectively segmented with no inter-market 'leakage'. Such an assumption, while analytically convenient, is patently false for two complementary reasons. First, illegal cross-operations between the financial and commercial exchange markets are widespread. Evidence on the existence of illegal transactions can be found by comparing export and import invoices which fail to match. This point has been noted before by Lanyi (1975) in the context of France, Italy and the BLEU.[4] In fact, the existence of illegal transactions through an expanding 'parallel market' may have been the principal catalyst in the demise of the dual rate systems in both France and Italy. According to a 1974 statement by the Banca d'Italia itself, by the time the system was abolished, the financial exchange market 'had lost all practical significance'. Second, and more importantly, a certain amount of leakage is *officially sanctioned* in every country that engages in dual exchange rate practices (either currently or in the past, such as France and Italy). Thus, several important categories of current account transactions are (were) officially assigned to the financial exchange market.

Tables 7.1 and 7.2 provide a summary picture of the nature of dual market arrangements and of legally sanctioned 'leakage' in various countries (including France and Italy for the early 1970s). It is immediately clear that certain types of invisible current-account transactions are settled in the financial market in every country mentioned in Tables 7.1 and 7.2 (in

Table 7.1 The nature of multiple exchange market arrangements, various countries

Dual market system (31 December 1981)	Free exchange market[a]	Exchange controls	Merchandise trade	Invisibles	Private transfers	Private capital	Average premium as of 31 December 1981 (%)
Ecuador	Controlled via intervention	Yes	O	O–F	F	O–F	31
Dominican Republic	Yes	Yes	O–F	O–F	O	O–F	29–30
Egypt	Yes	Yes	—	See notes	—	—	18
El Salvador	Yes	Yes	O–F	O–F	F	O–F	40
Paraguay	Yes	Yes	O	F	F	F	27–34
Sudan	Yes	Yes	O–F	F	—	O–F	70–132
Syria	Yes	Yes	O–F	O–F	F	F	No data
Costa Rica	Yes	No	O–F	F	F	F	80, 6.41
Nicaragua	Yes	Yes	O–F	O–F	O–F	O–F	No data (spread controlled)

[a]The official exchange rate is pegged to the US$.
O: official; F: free; O–F: depending on nature of transaction.
Source: Constructed by the authors from *Exchange Arrangements and Exchange Restrictions*, IMF, country pages, various years.

three countries, *all* invisibles are transacted in parallel markets). More importantly, Table 7.1 reveals that, with the exception of Ecuador and Paraguay, certain merchandise trade items (both exports and imports) must also be settled at the financial exchange rate(s). In most instances, this is effected by requiring that *specified proportions* of export receipts be surrendered at the financial exchange rate (for example, Sudan, Syria, Costa Rica) or that only certain categories of imports (deemed to be 'priority' imports) may be financed via the commercial exchange market (Egypt, Dominican Republic, El Salvador, Sudan).

An important and relevant question to ask, therefore, relates to the operation of a dual exchange market system, given incomplete segmentation. In particular, what are the properties of a regime characterized by inter-market transactions, with respect to dynamic stability, domestic economic policy and to externally-occurring disturbances, etc.? And how does the degree of leakage – determined (at least in part) by administrative fiat, as noted above – impinge upon these properties? What are the implications of variations in the 'penalty cost' attributed to illegal trade transactions? These questions have not been asked, much less answered, in the previous literature.

This chapter is intended to fill these lacunae in the literature. Specifically, we construct a simple stochastic equilibrium model of the open economy operating under a dual exchange market regime.[5] While there are at least two varieties of two-tier system, the regime we analyse involves a pegged commercial (official) rate and a floating financial (parallel) rate. With the exception of Italy, which employed a two-tier float for a brief period in 1974, this is, in fact, the type of regime that is currently in operation in all the countries listed in Table 7.1, in addition to the BLEU

Table 7.2 The nature of multiple exchange market arrangements, France, Belgium–Luxembourg and Italy

	France 1971–73		Belgium–Luxembourg 1953–71		Dec. 1981		Italy 1973–74
	In	Out	In	Out	In	Out	
Merchandise trade	O	O	O	Option	O	O	O
Invisibles	O–F	O–F	O–F	O–F	O–F	O–F	O–F
Private transfers	F	F	Option	F	F	F	F
Public sector current-account transactions	O	O	O–F	O–F	O–F	O–F	O

O: official; F: free; O–F: depending on nature of transaction; Option: transaction can be settled in either market.
Source: As Table 7.1.

(the commercial rate in the latter is managed within narrow limits as prescribed by the 'Snake' arrangement). Exchange markets in our framework are not completely segmented and a proportion of commercial trade transactions are settled in the financial market, on account of both legally-sanctioned 'leakage' and fraudulent transactions, in accordance with the stylized facts noted above.[6]

While a complete statement of our results would occupy considerable space, the following summary observations are in order here. In the absence of inter-market transactions or leakage, a floating financial exchange rate ensures that no net accumulation/decumulation of foreign assets can occur and the intrinsic dynamics of the economy are governed solely by reserve accumulation/decumulation. With cross-operations, however, changes in the stock of domestically-held foreign assests do occur since the floating financial rate ensures that the capital account *plus* leakage is now zero.

Thus, the dynamics of such an economy are capable of exhibiting richer patterns of adjustment, being guided by changes in *both* reserve stocks and foreign asset stocks. One of the costs of incomplete segmentation in the present framework appears to be the fact that increasing leakage is associated with a greater degree of 'persistence' in adjustment of certain key macrovariables in the economy. However, there is a sense in which leakage can be of potential benefit to the economy. Specifically, the vulnerability of the domestic economy (measured by almost every criterion) to external *unanticipated* nominal dusturbances is inversely related to the degree of leakage (for external *anticipated* disturbances such an unqualified statement is not possible). In addition, incomplete exchange market segmentation has the effect of imparting 'effectiveness' to domestic credit policy, where there is none without leakage. Thus, to the extent that the degree of leakage is a policy-controlled parameter, the authorities face a potential trade-off between the dynamic costs of leakage and its potential impact benefits.

We also investigate the dynamic and static implications of perturbations in certain other key parameters. An increasing parameter in this regard is the penalty cost incurred by engaging in illegal trade transactions. Increasing values of the (policy-determined) penalty cost are also seen to define a policy dilemma in the sense that the dynamic path of the economy exhibits greater 'persistence', while, at the same time, domestic credit policy is more effective and the economy better insulated from external inflation, for comparable degrees of leakage. A higher interest rate semi-elasticity of money demand (which may result from a lower interest rate per period) also implies a greater degree of 'persistence' in dynamic adjustment. But there are no compensatory impact benefits in this case and the efficacy of domestic credit policy is seen to be impaired to the extent that this parameter is larger. There are other results of interest and these are stated in the text.

The rest of the chapter is organized as follows. In the next two sections we specify the analytical framework and the technique for deriving the ultimate rational expectations solution to the model (some further details are provided in Appendix 7A). This is followed by an analysis of the nature of dynamic adjustment in the model, and an investigation of the one-period and long-run effects of various structural disturbances. We examine the sensitivity of both the dynamic and static properties of the model with respect to the degree of leakage, as well as various other structural parameters of interest. The chapter ends with a statement of our principal findings.

ANALYTICAL FRAMEWORK

The hypothetical world of this model consists of an open economy operating under a system of dual exchange rates with a pegged commercial exchange rate and a freely floating financial exchange rate. Domestic output is limited to a single final commodity which is perfectly substitutable (on the demand side) with foreign output. The domestic economy is small in all international markets; specifically, the foreign currency price of output as well as the foreign interest rate are regarded as exogenously given parameters. Goods are perishable so that domestic residents must allocate their wealth between the available financial assets. These are domestically issued money and a one-period riskless internationally-issued security.[7] There is no 'currency substitution', no physical capital accumulation and no transactions of transport costs.

We assume that the use of the Lucas supply function is no longer contentious. Thus, domestic output supply is governed by[8]

$$y_t = \bar{y} + b\,(p_t - E_{t-1},\, p_t) \tag{7.1}$$

where y_t is the logarithm of the current level of output; $\bar{y}$ the logarithm of the level of 'trend' output; and p_t the logarithm of the domestic price level. The operator E is an expectations operator and the subscript indicates the period in which this expectation is formed (based upon information available at that time). Such a supply function can be derived on the basis of profit maximization on the part of a firm, assuming that wages are tied to the expected price level. More elaborate supply functions based upon either incomplete contemporaneous wage indexation or multi-period contracts can clearly be employed, but lead to fruitless complexities at this stage.

Given the presumed absence of transportation and transactions costs, the elimination of profitable arbitrage possibilities necessitates that the domestic currency price of output is determined via a purchasing power parity relationship[9]

$$p_t = s_t + p_t^* \tag{7.2}$$

where p_t^* is the logarithm of the foreign currency price of the (single) commodity; and s_t is defined as the logarithm of the *effective commercial exchange rate*. Because of leakage from the commercial to the financial exchange market, the aggregate exchange rate relevant for commercial trade transactions is not the official commercial rate, but rather the effective commercial rate, where the latter is a function of the commercial and financial rates, i.e. $s_t = F(X_t, \bar{E})$. A logarithmic linear approximation to the unknown function F is given by

$$s_t = \alpha\bar{e} + (1-\alpha)\, x_t \qquad 0 \leqslant \alpha \leqslant 1 \tag{7.3}$$

where $\bar{e}$ and x_t are logarithms of the commercial and financial exchange rates, respectively; and α is an arbitrary linearization point. On a formal level, α is defined as the *initial* share of trade transactions settled in the commercial exchange market.[10] It is this parameter that we identify as the (inverse of) the legally sanctioned degree of leakage. Administrative fiat, however, is not that only reason why certain merchandise trade transactions are settled in the financial exchange market. To the extent that the financial rate is relatively depreciated compared with the commercial rate (Table 7.1 reveals that this is invariably the case), then private exporters have an incentive to circumvent government regulations by *illegally* surrendering export receipts at the financial rate.[11] We turn to a more specific description of the trade balance next.

Note, first, that the total real trade balance in terms of natural units is defined as

$$T_t = Y_t - C_t \tag{7.4}$$

where C_t is real aggregate consumption; Y_t is income; and other components of domestic expenditure such as physical investment have been ignored. In the interest of simplicity, it is assumed that consumption is determined solely by the level of income. It is clearly possible to include other arguments in the consumption function, such as the real interest rate (to capture Barro–Lucas-type intertemporal speculation elements) or real wealth. These extensions complicate the algebra substantially. It is also known from other work that the presence of the real wealth effect in consumption and trade balance functions may lead to structural non-linearities in such stochastic macromodels (see Driskill and McCafferty,

1983). Consequently, we have elected to retain the simplest possible (Keynesian) form of the consumption function. Given this, the trade balance is also determined by the level in income, i.e.

$$T_t = T(Y_t) \qquad 0 < T' < 1 \tag{7.5}$$

Equation (7.5) may alternatively be viewed as the economy's saving function. Since the marginal propensity to spend is less than unity, the trade balance surplus is positively related to income (with T′ as the marginal propensity to save).[12] A logarithmic approximation to Equation (7.5) is assumed to be given by

$$\ln T_t = \bar{T} + \delta_1 y_t \tag{7.6}$$

where $\bar{T}$ represents an autonomous component of the trade balance.[13] Total real exports (T_t have two components; one (denotes T^e) is settled at the commercial exchange rate, while the other (T^x) is settled in the financial exchange market.[14] Component T^x subsumes both legally sanctioned as well as illegal transactions in the financial market. As indicated previously, leakage from the commercial to the financial market is of both varieties. We hypothesize the following functional forms for the logarithms of T^e and T^x

$$\ln T^e = \bar{T}^e + \delta_1^e y_t - \gamma_1^e (\chi_t - \bar{e}) \tag{7.7a}$$

$$\ln T^x = \bar{T}^x + \delta_1^x y_t + \gamma_1^x (x_t - \bar{e}) \tag{7.7b}$$

According to Equations (7.6) and (7.7), an increase in aggregate income increases total exports, which is then allocated to each component as determined by the elasticities δ_1^e and δ_1^x. By contrast, an increase in the spread between the two exchange rates $(x_t - \bar{e})$ has no scale effect upon total exports and leads only to compositional changes. Specifically, private exporters find it more favourable illegally to divert some of their trade transactions to the financial market from the commercial market.[15] The magnitudes of the relevant elasticities γ_1^e and γ_1^x are clearly (inversely) related to the perceived implicit and explicit *penalty costs* of engaging in illegal transactions and to the degree of enforcement of exchange regulations, etc. In the analysis that follows we conduct sensitivity analyses with respect to these penalty cost parameters (in addition to other parameters). Statistically estimated trade balance functions for Belgium do reveal the presence of a strong response to the exchange rate spread (Decaluwe, 1975). Meanwhile, it can be demonstrated that the parameters in Equations (7.6) and (7.7) are interrelated. Since by definition

$$T = T^e + T^x$$

then

$$\ln T = \alpha \ln T^{e} + (1-\alpha)\, T^{x} \tag{7.8}$$

where

$$\alpha \simeq [T^{e}/(T^{e} + T^{x})]^{0}$$

as stated in note 10. From Equation (7.8), it follows that the following 'adding-up' conditions must hold for the parameters of Equations (7.6) and (7.7)

$$\alpha\delta_1^{e} + (1-\alpha)\,\delta_1^{x} = \delta_1 \qquad -\alpha\gamma_1^{e} + (1-\alpha)\,\gamma_1^{x} = 0 \tag{7.9}$$

The next stage in the development of the model involves the specification of asset-market relationships. It can be shown that the logarithm of the *expected* opportunity cost of holding domestic money (as opposed to internationally-issued bonds) is given by

$$i_t = i_t^{*} + (E_t,\, x_{t+1} - x_t) + \bar{i}^{*}\,(\bar{e} - E_t,\, x_{t+1}) \tag{7.10}$$

where i_t is the logarithm of the relevant expected opportunity cost; i_t^{*} is the foreign interest yield payable by foreign securities; and $\bar{i}^{*}$ is its mean value.[16]

We adopt a simple portfolio-balance view with respect to the specification of asset-demand functions. In terms of *natural* units, money demand and demand for foreign assets are given by

$$\frac{M_t^{d}}{P_t} = g[E(1+i_t'),\ Y_t]\,\frac{W_t}{P_t} \tag{7.11a}$$

$$\frac{K_t^{d} X_t}{P_t} = h[E(1+i_t'),\, Y_t]\,\frac{W_t}{P_t} \tag{7.11b}$$

where g and h are positive fractions that add up to unity; Y_t is real income; M_t^{d} and K_t^{d} are nominal stock demands for money and foreign assets, respectively; W_t is nominal wealth; while $E(1+i_t')$ is the expected opportunity cost of holding money (the logarithm of which is i_t; see also note 16). Nominal wealth is defined by

$$W_t \equiv M_t + X_t K_t \tag{7.12}$$

Only one of Equations (7.11a) and (7.11b) is an independent relation and in what follows, we do not utilize Equation (7.11b). The logarithmic form of Equation (7.11a) is assumed to be given by

$$m_t^{d} - w_t = -\lambda i_t + \phi y_t \tag{7.13}$$

while Equation (7.12) can be approximated via the first-order logarithmic Taylor expansion

$$w_t = d_1 m_t + (1 - d_1)(x_t + k_t) \tag{7.14}$$

where

$$d_1 \equiv (M/W)^n > 0$$

is an initial linearization point.

Domestic money supply (in natural units) is given by

$$M_t^s = D_t + \bar{E}R_t \tag{7.15}$$

where D_t denotes domestic credit; and R_t is official reserves, which are evaluated at the commercial exchange rate, as is appropriate. A logarithmic expression for Equation (7.15) is given by

$$m_t^s = d^0 d_t + (1 - d^0)(\bar{e} + r_t) \qquad d^0 \equiv (D/M^s)^0 > 0 \tag{7.16}$$

We now turn to the specification of the *dynamic processes* governing the economy. The model involves two sources of dynamic adjustment – reserve accumulation and foreign asset accumulation. It is to be emphasized that changes in the stock of domestically-held foreign assets are a direct consequence of inter-market leakage. If it is assumed (as in the previous literature) that the two exchange markets are completely segmented, then the floating financial rate ensures that no net movement in foreign asset stocks can occur. Given incomplete segmentation, however, it is the sum of the capital account *plus* the leakage that is now zero. This process has been noted in the descriptive literature – for example, Lanyi (1975, p. 720) writes:

> if the domestic currency is relatively depreciated in the financial market, there will be an incentive for underinvoicing exports, with the difference between the actual and the invoiced export proceeds entering the country in the guise of a capital inflow at the more favorable financial exchange rate.

Thus, the foreign asset accumulation process is formally described by

$$X_t(K_t - K_{t-1}) = P_t^* X_t T^x \tag{7.17a}$$

Note that the real amount of the leakage T^x has been transformed to domestic currency terms by applying the conversion factor $P_t^* X_t$ (rather than the aggregate price level P_t) as is appropriate. The other dynamic process governing the economy involves foreign reserve accumulation. In the absence of the service account, this is the counterpart of T^e, i.e. of that component of total exports that is transacted in the commercial market. Hence,

$$\bar{E}(R_t - R_{t-1}) = P_t^* \bar{E} T^e \tag{7.17b}$$

Equations (7.17) may be transformed into the following logarithmic forms

$$k_t - z^1 k_{t-1} = (1 - z^1)(p_t^* + \ln T^x) \tag{7.18a}$$

$$r_t - z^0 r_{t-1} = (1 - z^0)(p_t^* + \ln T^e) \qquad (7.18b)$$

where z^1 and z^0 are initial linearization points that are bounded between zero and unity and are defined as

$$z^1 \equiv (K_{t-1}/K_t)^0 \qquad z^0 \equiv (R_{t-1}/R_t)^0 \qquad 0 < z^0, z^1 < 1$$

The final step in the formulation of the model involves the specification of the relevant stochastic processes in the economy. In this chapter, we consider only two types of disturbance – foreign price disturbances and domestic credit disturbances. A host of other disturbances (to domestic supply or to various components of the trade balance, for example) can, of course, be incorporated. We leave these extensions to the interested reader. Foreign prices and domestic credit evolve according to the following stationary processes

$$p_t^* = \bar{p}^* + \xi_{1t} \qquad (7.19a)$$

$$d_t = \bar{d} + \xi_{2t} \qquad (7.19b)$$

where $\bar{p}^*$ and $\bar{d}$ are systematic components, while the ξs denote unanticipated disturbances each with zero mean and finite variance.

The description of the model is completed by noting that continuous equilibrium prevails in all markets and that expectations are determined rationally, in the sense of Muth.[17]

THE RATIONAL EXPECTATIONS SOLUTION

The rational expectations solution to the model described above requires that expectations be consistent with available knowledge of the structure of the model itself. Given the linear structure of the model, it is clear that the ultimate reduced-form solution is linear in the vector of all exogenous variables. For convenience we set the anticipated compontents $\bar{d}$ and $\bar{e}$ equal to zero. Thus, the stable components of the solutions to x_t, r_t and k_t are hypothesized to be of the following linear form

$$x_t = \pi_1 r_{t-1} + \pi_2 k_{t-1} + \pi_3 \bar{p}^* + \pi_4 \xi_{1t} + \pi_5 \xi_{2t} \qquad (7.20a)$$

$$r_t = J_1 r_{t-1} + J_2 k_{t-1} + J_3 \bar{p}^* + J_4 \xi_{1t} + J_5 \xi_{2t} \qquad (7.20b)$$

$$k_t = N_1 r_{t-1} + N_2 k_{t-1} + N_3 \bar{p}^* + N_4 \xi_{1t} + N_5 \xi_{2t} \qquad (7.20c)$$

Given the structure of the model, the potentially stable trajectory of the state vector (x_t, r_t, k_t) is fully determined by the vector of predetermined and exogenous variables included in Equations (7.20).

In order to solve for the reduced-form coefficients $\{\pi_i, J_i, N_i\}$, i=1, . . ., 5, it is convenient to use the method of undetermined coefficients popularized by Barro and Lucas. This procedure involves the derivation of three sets of simultaneous relations containing each of the five triples $\{\pi_i, J_i, N_i\}$, $i = 1, \ldots, 5$. Appendix 7A provides details as to the derivation of these three relationships, which are stated in Equations (7A.2), (7A.4) and (7A.6). It is immediately apparent from inspection of these equations that while (7A.2) and (7A.4) involve linear relationships, Equations (7A.6) are intrinsically *non-linear* since they contain product terms. It is possible however to reduce Equations (7A.6a) and (7A.6b) to two non-linear simultaneous equations in π_1 and π_2 by eliminating J_1, J_2, N_1 and N_2 – see Equations (7A.7) and (7A.8). As can be seen, the latter involve both squared and cross-product terms and there are no known analytical methods for solving such systems. Such non-linearities *among reduced-form coefficients* are in fact, fairly common to *structurally linear* rational expectations models that involve time-dependent processes (see, for example, Bhandari, 1982; Flood and Hodrick, 1985). In order to make progress, therefore, we have relied on a variant of the Newton–Raphson search algorithm to isolate numerically the solutions for π_1 and π_2 in Equations (7A.7) and (7A.8), given a plausible parameter grid. This experiment was repeated for several alternative values of α (degree of leakage), γ_1^e (penalty cost) and λ (interest rate responsiveness of money demand). Once the solutions for π_1 and π_2 are obtained, those for the coefficients determining the comparative static properties of the model (i.e. $\{\pi_i, J_i, N_i\}$, $i = 3, 4, 5$) are easily derived in terms of the former, as discussed in Appendix 7A.

Our search procedure isolated four pairs of solutions to (π_1, π_2) in Equations (7A.7) and (7A.8) for every parameter grid chosen. Of these solutions, only a *single* pair was found to be consistent with dynamic stability. Thus, in practice, no potential problems of either non-existence or non-uniqueness of the solution were found to arise.

Our simulation experiments encompassed nine scenarios corresponding to three alternative values of γ_1^e (0.05, 0.5 and 5) and three values of λ (2, 7.5 and 15). Five alternative values of α (0.9, 0.7, 0.5, 0.3 and 0.1) were considered for *each* of these nine cases, i.e. 45 simulations in all were performed. Additional simulations were conducted with respect to b (the slope of the aggregate supply function) when considering the comparative static properties of the model (this parameter is only relevant for static properties). In order to gauge the implications of variations in γ_1^e, λ and b, it is convenient to establish a 'bench-mark case' or 'control case'. Other cases are then compared with the control case for corresponding values of α. The *control case* involves the following parameter grid:[18] $\gamma_1^e = 0.5$; $\lambda = 7.5$; $d_1 = 0.8$; $d^0 = 0.8$; $z^0 = 0.8$; $z^1 = 0.8$; $\phi = 1$; $b = 3$; $\delta_1 = 1.2$; $\delta_1^e = 1$; $\gamma_1^x = [\alpha/(1-\alpha)]\gamma_1^e$; $\delta_1^x = (\delta_1 - \alpha\delta_1^e)/(1-\alpha)$; $\alpha = 0.9$, 0.7, 0.5, 0.3, 0.1. Other scenarios consider in turn, the implications of higher as well as lower

Table 7.3 Reduced-form coefficients for various values of α, γ_1^e and λ

Case 1 $\lambda = 2$, $\gamma_1^e = 0.05$			Case 2 $\lambda = 2$, $\gamma_1^e = 0.5$			Case 3 $\lambda = 2$, $\gamma_1^e = 5$		
α	π_1	π_2	α	π_1	π_2	α	π_1	π_2
0.9	0.0483	−0.2414	0.9	0.0302	−0.1507	0.9	0.0096	−0.0431
0.7	0.0518	−0.2588	0.7	0.0422	−0.2111	0.7	0.0199	−0.0994
0.5	0.0525	−0.2628	0.5	0.0470	−0.2352	0.5	0.0274	−0.1370
0.3	0.0529	−0.2646	0.3	0.0497	−0.2485	0.3	0.0340	−0.1701
0.1	0.0531	−0.2657	0.1	0.0514	−0.2571	0.1	0.0406	−0.2030

Case 4 $\lambda = 7.5$, $\gamma_1^e = 0.05$			Case 5 (*control case*) $\lambda = 7.5$, $\gamma_1^e = 0.5$			Case 6 $\lambda = 7.5$, $\gamma_1^e = 5$		
α	π_1	π_2	α	π_1	π_2	α	π_1	π_2
0.9	0.0180	−0.0899	0.9	0.0136	−0.0680	0.9	0.0058	−0.0289
0.7	0.0186	−0.0929	0.7	0.0168	−0.0838	0.7	0.0101	−0.0505
0.5	0.0187	−0.0935	0.5	0.0177	−0.0887	0.5	0.0128	−0.0636
0.3	0.0188	−0.0937	0.3	0.01821	−0.0911	0.3	0.0147	−0.0736
0.1	0.0189	−0.0940	0.1	0.0185	−0.0928	0.1	0.0164	−0.0819

Case 7 $\lambda = 15$, $\gamma_1^e = 0.05$			Case 8 $\lambda = 15$, $\gamma_1^e = 0.5$			Case 9 $\lambda = 15$, $\gamma_1^e = 5$		
α	π_1	π_2	α	π_1	π_2	α	π_1	π_2
0.9	0.0097	−0.0487	0.9	0.0081	−0.0405	0.9	0.0041	−0.0204
0.7	0.00993	−0.0496	0.7	0.0093	−0.0467	0.7	0.0065	−0.0324
0.5	0.00996	−0.0498	0.5	0.0097	−0.0483	0.5	0.0078	−0.0387
0.3	0.00998	−0.0499	0.3	0.0098	−0.0489	0.3	0.0086	−0.0429
0.1	0.010	−0.050	0.1	0.0099	−0.0495	0.1	0.0092	−0.0460

values of γ_1^e and λ. Thus, $\gamma_1^e = 0.05$ captures a 'high' penalty cost and conversely for $\gamma_1^e = 5$. Further, assuming that the interest rate *elasticity* of money demand is 0.3 (see note 18), $\lambda = 2$ corresponds to a quarterly interest yield of 15 per cent (60 per cent annually), while $\lambda = 15$ implies a quarterly rate of 2 per cent (8 per cent annually).

Tables 7.3 and 7.4 report the computed values of the reduced-form coefficients (π_1, π_2) and associated eigenvalues for each of nine cases for alternative values of α in each of these cases. Tables 7.5, 7.6 and 7.7 list the one-period comparative static implications of anticipated foreign price disturbances ($\bar{p}^*$), unanticipated foreign price shocks (ξ_{1t}) and unanticipated domestic credit innovations (ξ_{2t}) respectively. Thus, the sensitivity of these results to γ_1^e can be assessed by comparing various *rows* in each table for corresponding values of the degree of leakage, while the implications of λ are noted by comparing *columns*. The centre rows and

Table 7.4 Eigenvalues for various values of α, γ_1^e and λ

Case 1 $\lambda=2,\ \gamma_1^e=0.05$			Case 2 $\lambda=2,\ \gamma_1^e=0.5$			Case 3 $\lambda=2,\ \gamma_1^e=5$		
α	S_1	S_2	α	S_1	S_2	α	S_1	S_2
0.9	0.7783	0.79953	0.9	0.6644	0.7970	0.9	0.3671	0.7904
0.7	0.7879	0.79950	0.7	0.7205	0.7962	0.7	0.5151	0.7815
0.5	0.7974	0.79947	0.5	0.7765	0.7953	0.5	0.6630	0.7726
0.3	0.7986	0.79947	0.3	0.7868	0.7951	0.3	0.7202	0.7660
0.1	0.7997	0.79946	0.1	0.7971	0.7949	0.1	0.7774	0.7594

Case 4 $\lambda=7.5,\ \gamma_1^e=0.05$			Case 5 (*control case*) $\lambda=7.5,\ \gamma_1^e=0.5$			Case 6 $\lambda=7.5,\ \gamma_1^e=5$		
α	S_1	S_2	α	S_1	S_2	α	S_1	S_2
0.9	0.7919	0.7998	0.9	0.7387	0.7987	0.9	0.5398	0.7942
0.7	0.7955	0.7998	0.7	0.7817	0.7984	0.7	0.6381	0.7907
0.5	0.7991	0.7998	0.5	0.7911	0.7982	0.5	0.7364	0.7872
0.3	0.7995	0.7998	0.3	0.7961	0.7982	0.3	0.7637	0.7854
0.1	0.7999	0.7998	0.1	0.7990	0.7981	0.1	0.7909	0.7836

Case 7 $\lambda=7.5,\ \gamma_1^e=0.05$			Case 8 $\lambda=7.5,\ \gamma_1^e=0.5$			Case 9 $\lambda=7.5,\ \gamma_1^e=5$		
α	S_1	S_2	α	S_1	S_2	α	S_1	S_2
0.9	0.7956	0.7999	0.9	0.7636	0.7992	0.9	0.6164	0.7959
0.7	0.7976	0.7999	0.7	0.7794	0.7991	0.7	0.6889	0.7941
0.5	0.7995	0.7999	0.5	0.7952	0.7990	0.5	0.7613	0.7922
0.3	0.7997	0.7999	0.3	0.7973	0.7990	0.3	0.7781	0.7915
0.1	0.7999	0.7999	0.1	0.7994	0.7990	0.1	0.7949	0.7908

columns provide comparisons with the control case in each instance. Two other sets of simulations are also reported in Table 7.8 for foreign unanticipated price disturbances and domestic credit innovations. These simulations use the same parameter grid as in the control case, except for the supply curve parameter, which is set at $b=1$ (this parameter is not relevant for the eigenvalues or for anticipated disturbances). The implications of perturbations in b are consequently gauged by comparing Table 7.8 with the relevant control cases in Tables 7.6 and 7.7.

DYNAMIC ADJUSTMENT WITH INCOMPLETE MARKET SEPARATION

It is clear at the outset that the dynamic evolution of the economy is guided by a second-order difference equation system, as expressed by the

Table 7.5 Short-run effects of anticipated foreign disturbances

Case 1				Case 2				Case 3			
α	x_t	r_t	p_t	α	x_t	r_t	p_t	α	x_t	r_t	p_t
0.9	−0.4169	0.2042	0.9583	0.9	−0.1213	0.2121	0.9879	0.9	−0.0162	0.2162	0.9984
0.7	−0.4869	0.2049	0.8539	0.7	−0.2519	0.2252	0.9244	0.7	−0.0574	0.2574	0.9828
0.5	−0.5568	0.2055	0.7216	0.5	−0.3825	0.2383	0.8088	0.5	−0.0986	0.2986	0.9507
0.3	−0.5676	0.2057	0.6027	0.3	−0.4482	0.2449	0.6863	0.3	−0.1742	0.3741	0.8781
0.1	−0.5784	0.2058	0.4794	0.1	−0.5138	0.2514	0.5376	0.1	−0.2497	0.4496	0.7753
Case 4				Case 5 (*control case*)				Case 6			
α	x_t	r_t	p_t	α	x_t	r_t	p_t	α	x_t	r_t	p_t
0.9	−0.4986	0.2049	0.9501	0.9	−0.1331	0.2133	0.9867	0.9	−0.0165	0.2165	0.9984
0.7	−0.5956	0.2059	0.8213	0.7	−0.2951	0.2295	0.9115	0.7	−0.0617	0.2617	0.9815
0.5	−0.6926	0.2069	0.6537	0.5	−0.4570	0.2457	0.7715	0.5	−0.1068	0.3068	0.9466
0.3	−0.7029	0.2070	0.5080	0.3	−0.5432	0.2543	0.6198	0.3	−0.1971	0.3971	0.8620
0.1	−0.7132	0.2071	0.3581	0.1	−0.6294	0.2629	0.4335	0.1	−0.2873	0.4873	0.7414
Case 7				Case 8				Case 9			
α	x_t	r_t	p_t	α	x_t	r_t	p_t	α	x_t	r_t	p_t
0.9	−0.5217	0.2052	0.9478	0.9	−0.1370	0.2137	0.9863	0.9	−0.0167	0.2167	0.9983
0.7	−0.6197	0.2062	0.8141	0.7	−0.3061	0.2306	0.9082	0.7	−0.0632	0.2632	0.9810
0.5	−0.7177	0.2072	0.6412	0.5	−0.4751	0.2474	0.7625	0.5	−0.1096	0.3096	0.9452
0.3	−0.7334	0.2073	0.4866	0.3	−0.5663	0.2565	0.6036	0.3	−0.2041	0.4041	0.8571
0.1	−0.7490	0.2074	0.3259	0.1	−0.6574	0.2656	0.4083	0.1	−0.2986	0.4986	0.7313

Table 7.6 Short-run effects of unanticipated foreign disturbances

Case 1				Case 2				Case 3			
α	x_t	r_t	p_t	α	x_t	r_t	p_t	α	x_t	r_t	p_t
0.9	−1.5900	0.7205	0.8410	0.9	−1.2880	0.8515	0.8712	0.9	−0.6721	1.4318	0.9238
0.7	−1.2497	0.6274	0.6251	0.7	−1.0903	0.7365	0.6729	0.7	−0.6590	1.3224	0.8023
0.5	−0.9093	0.5342	0.5454	0.5	−0.8926	0.6215	0.5537	0.5	−0.6459	1.2130	0.6771
0.3	−0.7907	0.4890	0.4465	0.3	−0.7798	0.5638	0.4541	0.3	−0.6428	1.1536	0.5500
0.1	−0.6720	0.4438	0.3952	0.1	−0.6670	0.5060	0.3997	0.1	−0.6396	1.0942	0.4244

Case 4				Case 5 (*control case*)				Case 6			
α	x_t	r_t	p_t	α	x_t	r_t	p_t	α	x_t	r_t	p_t
0.9	−0.5602	0.7720	0.9440	0.9	−0.4909	0.8196	0.9509	0.9	−0.3964	1.0974	0.9604
0.7	−0.4790	0.7283	0.8563	0.7	−0.4412	0.7707	0.8676	0.7	−0.3735	1.0714	0.8880
0.5	−0.3978	0.6846	0.8011	0.5	−0.3914	0.7217	0.8043	0.5	−0.3505	1.0454	0.8247
0.3	−0.3686	0.6524	0.7420	0.3	−0.3648	0.6865	0.7446	0.3	−0.3387	0.9979	0.7629
0.1	−0.3393	0.6202	0.6946	0.1	−0.3381	0.6512	0.6957	0.1	−0.3269	0.9504	0.7058

Case 7				Case 8				Case 9			
α	x_t	r_t	p_t	α	x_t	r_t	p_t	α	x_t	r_t	p_t
0.9	−0.2994	0.7850	0.9701	0.9	−0.2739	0.8110	0.9726	0.9	−0.2142	0.9825	0.9786
0.7	−0.2621	0.7599	0.9214	0.7	−0.2482	0.7833	0.9255	0.7	−0.2099	0.9633	0.9370
0.5	−0.2248	0.7348	0.8876	0.5	−0.2224	0.7555	0.8888	0.5	−0.2057	0.9440	0.8972
0.3	−0.2138	0.7137	0.8503	0.3	−0.2123	0.7333	0.8514	0.3	−0.2017	0.9175	0.8588
0.1	−0.2027	0.6926	0.8176	0.1	−0.2021	0.7111	0.8181	0.1	−0.1976	0.8909	0.8222

Table 7.7 Short-run effects of domestic credit innovations

Case 1				Case 2				Case 3			
α	x_t	r_t	p_t	α	x_t	r_t	p_t	α	x_t	r_t	p_t
0.9	0.0598	0.0030	0.0060	0.9	0.0525	–0.0021	0.0053	0.9	0.0303	–0.0285	0.0030
0.7	0.0501	0.0073	0.0150	0.7	0.0462	0.0029	0.0139	0.7	0.0301	–0.0248	0.0090
0.5	0.0403	0.0117	0.0202	0.5	0.0398	0.0079	0.0199	0.5	0.0299	–0.0211	0.0150
0.3	0.0353	0.0138	0.0247	0.3	0.0350	0.0106	0.0245	0.3	0.0297	–0.0174	0.0208
0.1	0.0302	0.0160	0.0271	0.1	0.0301	0.0132	0.0271	0.1	0.0295	–0.0136	0.0266

Case 4				Case 5 (*control case*)				Case 6			
α	x_t	r_t	p_t	α	x_t	r_t	p_t	α	x_t	r_t	p_t
0.9	0.0194	0.00097	0.0019	0.9	0.0182	–0.0007	0.0018	0.9	0.0134	–0.0126	0.0013
0.7	0.0181	0.0022	0.0054	0.7	0.0174	0.0013	0.0052	0.7	0.0132	–0.0111	0.0038
0.5	0.0168	0.0034	0.0084	0.5	0.0166	0.0033	0.0083	0.5	0.0129	–0.0096	0.0063
0.3	0.0158	0.0056	0.0111	0.3	0.0156	0.0049	0.0109	0.3	0.0127	–0.0081	0.0088
0.1	0.0147	0.0078	0.0132	0.1	0.0146	0.0064	0.0131	0.1	0.0124	–0.0066	0.0112

Case 7				Case 8				Case 9			
α	x_t	r_t	p_t	α	x_t	r_t	p_t	α	x_t	r_t	p_t
0.9	0.0102	0.0005	0.0010	0.9	0.0098	–0.0004	0.00098	0.9	0.0079	–0.0074	0.0008
0.7	0.0098	0.0016	0.0029	0.7	0.0096	0.0008	0.0029	0.7	0.0078	–0.0066	0.0023
0.5	0.0094	0.0027	0.0047	0.5	0.0093	0.0019	0.0047	0.5	0.0078	–0.0057	0.0039
0.3	0.0091	0.0037	0.0064	0.3	0.0090	0.0029	0.0063	0.3	0.0077	–0.0048	0.0054
0.1	0.0087	0.0046	0.0078	0.1	0.0087	0.0038	0.0078	0.1	0.0076	–0.0039	0.0068

Table 7.8 Short-run effects of domestic credit and unanticipated foreign disturbances for the control case, $b = 1$

Domestic credit shocks (ξ_{2t})			
α	x_t	r_t	p_t
0.9	0.0188	–0.0015	0.0019
0.7	0.0187	–0.00075	0.0056
0.5	0.0185	0	0.0093
0.3	0.0184	0.0008	0.0129
0.1	0.0182	0.0015	0.0164
Unanticipated foreign shocks (ξ_{1t})			
α	x_t	r_t	p_t
0.9	–0.1779	0.4142	0.9822
0.7	–0.1691	0.4071	0.9493
0.5	–0.1602	0.4000	0.9199
0.3	–0.1556	0.3940	0.8911
0.1	–0.1509	0.3879	0.8642

simultaneous system of Equations (7.20b) and (7.20c). This is to be contrasted with the corresponding no-leakage economy wherein there is no net accumulation of foreign assets. In the latter case, the dynamics of the economy are of the first-order variety, being governed entirely by reserve adjustment. This technical point aside, our more immediate concern is the effect of variations in the degree of leakage (α), the penalty cost (γ_1^e) and the interest rate responsiveness of money demand (λ) upon the nature of dynamic adjustment in the present context.

The eigenvalues of the homogeneous part of the dynamic system are given by

$$S_1, S_2 = \frac{(J_1 + N_2) \pm \left[(J_1 + N_2)^2 - 4(J_1 N_2 - N_1 J_2)\right]^{1/2}}{2} \tag{7.21}$$

Tables 7.3 and 7.4 report the stable solutions for π_1 and π_2 as well as associated eigenvalues for various values of α, γ_1^e and λ.[19] A general feature of the (unique) set of stable solutions in every case is that $\pi_1 > 0$, while $\pi_2 < 0$.[20] Such a pattern is readily reconciled with the structure of the model. A positive (negative) sign on π_1 (π_2) implies that a *ceteris paribus* increase in the stock of reserves (foreign assets) leads in the next period, to a depreciation (appreciation) of the financial exchange rate. For example, a decrease in the magnitude of reserve accumulation over the previous period implies a lower trade surplus T^e, via Equation (7.18b). The latter, in turn, is accomplished by a current period depreciation of the financial rate as witnessed by Equation (7.7a). On the other hand, a decline in the magnitude of asset accumulation over the last period necessitates financial appreciation in order to lower T^x in Equation (7.18a).

The implications of changes in the degree of leakage as parameterized by α may now be noted. Specifically, the control case in Table 7.4 reveals that increasing leakage (i.e. declining α) is accompanied by increasing values of one of the eigenvalues (S_1) with a *much smaller* relative increase in the other eigenvalue (S_2). This pattern is also evident in each of the other eight cases reported in this table. Now, the solutions for the paths of, say, reserves and the financial exchange rate are of the form

$$(r_t - \tilde{r}) = A_1 S_1^t + A_2 S_2^t \qquad (x_t - \tilde{x}) = B_1 S_1^t + B_2 S_2^t$$

where a tilde denotes stationary-state values; and the (A_i and B_i) are fixed constants which are determined by initial conditions (i.e. z^0 and z^1). An increase in S_1, unaccompanied by an equivalent offsetting change in S_2, consequently implies that, for the same values of t, the deviations of reserves and the financial exchange rate from their stationary-state levels are correspondingly larger. In this specific sense, therefore, an increased degree of leakage can be regarded as being costly to the economy and can be said to lead to greater 'persistence' in dyanamic adjustment.

Consider now the implications of changes in the penalty cost parameter γ_1^e. A comparison across rows in Table 7.4 reveals that increasing values of γ_1^e (i.e. lower penalty cost) unambiguously lead to lowered values of both roots S_1 and S_2 for corresponding values of α, the larger changes being generally concentrated in the root S_1. Thus, a higher penalty cost implies a greater degree of persistence in the economy (via larger values of S_1 and S_2). These properties suggest the presence of a policy dilemma in the sense that an attempt by the authorities to reduce the extent of illegal transactions, by increasing the penalty costs attributed to the latter, is not without costs of its own.

Table 7.4 also indicates (comparing entries in various columns) that higher values of λ (or lowered nominal interest rates, given a specific value for the elasticity) lead to increased values of both eigenvalues and, hence, to a greater degree of persistence in the economy. This result has implications for 'interest rate liberalization programmes' currently under way in several countries.[21] To the extent that such liberalization results in increased interest rates, the degree of persistence (or serial correlation) in the economy can be expected to decline.

Finally, it may be noted from Table 7.4 that the eigenvalues of the dynamic system are sensitive in varying degrees to the extent of leakage, depending upon the case considered. For example, the combination of high λ and low γ_1^e (i.e. case 7) results in a minimal responsiveness of the roots S_1 and S_2 to α.

We turn now to an examination of the static properties of the model.

INSTANTANEOUS AND STATIONARY-STATE EFFECTS OF STRUCTURAL DISTURBANCES

In this section we consider the first-period and accumulated long-run effects upon the domestic economy of three types of disturbances: anticipated foreign price disturbances; unanticipated foreign price shocks; and domestic credit innovations.

First-period effects

Anticipated foreign price disturbances

The effects of an anticipated foreign price increase (as represented by an increase in the component $\bar{p}^*$) upon the financial exchange rate, on reserves and on foreign asset stocks, are represented by the reduced-form coefficients (π_3, J_3, N_3). Given the effect on the financial exchange rate, the movement in the domestic price level can be calculated by reference to Equations (7.2) and (7.3), i.e. from

$$p_t = (1-\alpha)\,[\pi_1 r_{t-1} + \pi_2 k_{t-1} + \pi_3 \bar{p}^* + \pi_4 \xi_{1t} + \pi_5 \xi_{2t}] + \bar{p}^* + \xi_{1t} \tag{7.22}$$

Thus p_t responds to the extent $[(1-\alpha)\,\pi_3 + 1]$. Furthermore, the anticipated nature of the disturbance implies that domestic output (which responds only to price 'surprises') is unaffected. Table 7.5 reports the computed values of percentage changes in the financial exchange rate, reserves and the price level (following a 1 per cent anticipated increase in foreign prices) for various values of α in each of nine alternative scenarios.

For all values a α and in every case including the control case, the external price increase leads to financial appreciation, domestic price inflation and reserve accumulation. Given a less than proportionate appreciation of the financial exchange rate (and consequently an even smaller appreciation of the effective commercial rate), the price-level increase falls short of a unitary response. Since income is unaffected, the total trade balance is not altered; however, as is clear from Equation (7.7), the volume of exports settled in the commercial market increases at the expense of an equivalent decline in financial market exports T^x. Finally, an increase in the foreign currency value of commercially-settled exports is reflected in accumulation of foreign reserves (see Equation (7.18b)).

Table 7.5 also reveals the implications of changes in the degree of leakage, as parameterized by α. As seen above, decreasing values of α (i.e.

increasing degrees of leakage) are accompanied by increasing financial appreciation and diminishing inflationary effects in every case. The latter can readily be explained. Specifically, as α decreases, the effective commerical rate s_t becomes increasingly flexible, thus providing a greater offset to the increase in $\bar{p}^*$. Consequently, the domestic price level responds to a reduced extent, as is clear from Equation (7.22). Finally, an increased extent of financial appreciation implies a larger increase in the commercially-settled trade balance (see Equation (7.7a)) and, therefore, greater reserve accumulation, as is borne out by Table 7.5

The above properties suggest the presence of a macroeconomic *trade-off* between the severity of domestically-induced effects, in response to changes in the degree of leakage. While increased leakage (i.e. lower α) can be viewed as 'insulating' from the point of view of domestic price effects, this insulation is achieved at the expense of sharper financial exchange rate and reserve stock realignments. Such a trade-off is not present if external unanticipated price disturbances are considered.

The implications of variations in γ_1^e and λ may also be inferred from the results reported in Table 7.5. A comparison across rows (for corresponding values of α) reveals that increasing values of γ_1^e (i.e. lower penalty cost) imply less appreciation but sharper inflationary and reserve accumulation effects for the same degrees of leakage.[22] These properties may be explained as follows. A larger value of γ_1^e implies that a given appreciation leads to a sharper increase in the commercially-settled trade balance T^c and consequently to a greater increase in current reserves (see Equations (7.7a) and (7.18b)). Further, an increase in γ_1^e implies a *ceteris paribus* increase in γ_1^x, so that a given appreciation reduces the financially-settled trade balance, T^x, to a larger extent. By implication (see Equation (7.18a)), the stock of foreign assets and, hence, total wealth, increases less than otherwise. In turn, the demand for money increases less and consequently requires a reduced increase in the domestic opportunity cost, i_t. The latter implies a diminished extent of expected depreciation (see Equation (7.10)) and, therefore, less current appreciation. Finally, reduced spot appreciation implies that the 'offset' to the foreign price increase is reduced (see Equation (7.22)), so that the domestic inflationary effect is enhanced by an increase in γ_1^e. To this extent, then, it is possible to view a higher penalty cost (lower γ_1^e) as providing insulation to the domestic economy against external anticipated inflation.

Unanticipated foreign price disturbances

The domestic implications of unexpected disturbances in the foreign price level are summarized by the coefficients [π_4, J_4, N_4]. Meanwhile, the effect on the domestic price level is obtained from Equation (7.22) and is [$(1 - \alpha)\pi_4 + 1$]. Table 7.6 reports the simulated percentage responses in x_t, r_t and

p_t, following a 1 per cent unexpected increase in the foreign price level, corresponding to several alternative values of α, under alternative scenarios.

Table 7.6 reveals that for all values of α considered and in every case, the domestic economy experiences price inflation coupled with financial appreciation and reserve accumulation, in response to unanticipated increases in the foreign price level. In this respect, these effects are similar to those previously noted in Table 7.5. There are, however, several noteworthy differences between the two cases. First, the unanticipated nature of the disturbance in the present case calls forth an income expansion. The latter, in turn, contributes to a sharper increase in T^e and thus, to stronger reserve accumulation effects. This property is borne out by a comparison of reserve effects in the two cases. Second, while decreasing values of α increase in extent of financial appreciation in Table 7.5, in the present case increasing leakage is unambiguously associated with reduced financial appreciation, along with diminished price and reserve effects. Thus, unlike the previous case, changes in the degree of leakage are not associated with a trade-off in the present instance; a decrease in α is unambiguously beneficial from the point of view of insulation, although substantial exchange rate, price and reserve effects are still found to remain for values of α as low as 0.1. A final comparison between Tables 7.5 and 7.6 that deserves note refers to price effects in the two cases. It is seen that the issue of whether anticipated or unanticipated external disturbances are more detrimental from the point of view of domestic inflation depends upon the existing degree of leakage, as well as upon the existing values of γ_1^e and λ. In the control case, for example, unexpected foreign price disturbances imply sharper domestic inflationary effects than anticipated disturbances, for low values of α and conversely. But, if λ is low, for example (see cases 1, 2 and 3), then anticipated foreign price disturbances lead to sharper domestic price effects than unanticipated innovations, for all degrees of leakage.

Consider now the implications of variations in γ_1^e, λ and b upon the extent of domestically-induced adjustments. Table 7.6 reveals (comparing rows) that as γ_1^e increases (i.e. the penalty cost declines), unexpected foreign price increases lead to less financial appreciation, but to sharper extents of domestic inflation and reserve accumulation, for corresponding degrees of leakage. These properties of γ_1^e are identical to those noted previously for anticipated foreign price disturbances and are similarly explained. Again, a higher penalty cost provides insulation to the economy in the sense of reducing the domestic price impact of external inflation. A higher value of λ is seen in Table 7.6 to lead to reduced financial appreciation coupled with higher inflation.[23] The effects of λ upon reserve accumulation are less clear. Specifically, the reserve effects tend to increase with λ for low values of γ_1^e and conversely for higher values of the latter.

Finally, the implications of the supply curve parameter, b, may be assessed by comparing Table 7.8 with the control case in Table 7.6. As b increases, foreign unanticipated inflation leads to sharper exchange rate and reserve effects upon the domestic economy, along with a lower inflationary impact. These results are readily reconciled with the structural model. A larger value of b implies that a given price level increase leads to a sharper increase in domestic output and consequently to a larger increase in the commercially-settled trade balance T^c. As a result, stronger reserve accumulation effects are observed. The sharper output increase also impinges upon the financially-settled trade balance T^x and thereby upon foreign asset stocks and wealth. In turn, domestic money demand increases to a larger extent and therefore necessitates a sharper expected depreciation or current appreciation, in order to restore equilibrium.

Domestic credit innovations

The effects of domestic credit innovations upon the financial exchange rate and the stock of reserves are given by the coefficients π_5 and J_5, respectively, while the impact upon the domestic price level is $(1-\alpha)\ \pi_5$. Table 7.7 reports the relevant responses. It is seen in all cases that domestic credit innovations are accompanied by generally weak effects upon the financial exchange rate, reserves and the price level. The domestic economy experiences financial depreciation (to an extent that falls well short of a proportionate response) as well as price inflation (to an even smaller absolute degree). The impact upon the level of reserve stocks is more mixed in that reserve stocks may either accumulate or decumulate depending upon the existing degree of leakage and the penalty cost. In every case, however, diminishing values of α (i.e. increasing leakage) are accompanied by reduced depreciation and sharper inflation along with increased (decreased) reserve accumulation (decumulation). To the extent, then, that ξ_{2t} can be interpreted as the unanticipated component of deliberately conducted monetary policy, increased leakage clearly enhances its price–output stabilization rule. This result can readily be explained as follows. As α increases, the effective commercial rate becomes increasingly fixed and the behaviour of the system begins to approximate that of a unified fixed exchange rate regime. As is well known, the combination of purchasing power parity and uncovered interest parity eliminates entirely any stabilizer role for domestic credit policy. Specifically, price, output and interest rate levels are set by world conditions in such circumstances and any domestic credit expansion must be offset by an equivalent reserve loss in order to keep real money supply unchanged. Tendencies towards (sharper) reserve decumulation (or reduced accumulation) and progressively smaller domestic price effects with increasing values of α are evidenced in Table 7.7. Finally, the effect of α upon the extent of financial depreciation may be rationalized in the following manner. At a *given* level of the financial exchange rate, x_t, a decrease in α enhances the resulting output expansion (via p_t) and consequently the increase in T^x. The latter in turn, implies that k_t, and hence w_t, increase more. The result is a reduced excess supply of money which necessitates a lesser expected appreciation in order to restore money market equilibrium. Given the transitory nature of the innovation, this can only be accomplished via a reduced current-period financial depreciation.

Table 7.7 also reveals that a lower penalty cost (high γ_1^e) impairs the effectiveness of domestic credit policy. Thus, increased values of γ_1^e result in reduced price–output effects, reduced financial depreciation, as well as less (more) reserve accumulation (decumulation). An increase in γ_1^e leads, *ceteris paribus*, to an increase in γ_1^x , so that a given financial depreciation now implies a larger increase in financially-settled exports T^x. By implication, the stock of foreign assets, k_t, and hence wealth, w_t, increases more. The resulting increase in demand for money reduces the net excess supply of money (due to the initial increase in domestic credit) so that money market equilibrium necessitates reduced expected appreciation, or reduced current depreciation. Since the price-level effect is linearly proportional to the exchange rate effect, the resulting domestic inflation is correspondingly damped. The source of the ambiguity in reserve adjustment is also now clear. Specifically, to the extent that price and output increase, the commercially-settled trade balance, T^c, tends to increase. On the other hand, financial depreciation tends to offset this effect, by reducing T^c (see Equation (7.7a)). Owing to these conflicting influences, the net movement in T^c and hence stocks, remains unclear. As γ_1^e increases, however, the latter (depressive) effect begins to dominate and reserve stocks decumulate, exactly as witnessed by Table 7.7.

Finally, consider the impact of variations in λ and the supply curve parameter, b, upon the effects of domestic credit policy. Increasing values of λ lead, *ceteris paribus*, to reduced inflation, depreciation, as well as, reduced absolute reserve stock realignments. Higher values of b also imply less financial depreciation and inflation, as may be seen by comparing Table 7.8 with the control case in Table 7.7. As b increases, a given domestic price increase has a larger positive effect (or lower negative effect) upon income and consequently upon the commercially-settled trade balance, T^c. As a result, there is sharper reserve accumulation (or reduced reserve decumulation), as evidenced by the numerical results. In addition, the greater increase in output also stimulates financially-settled exports, T^x. This, in turn, leads to a sharper increase in the stock of domestically-held foreign assets and wealth. As a result, there is reduced net excess supply of money and a reduced financial depreciation is now necessary to restore money market equilibrium.

We turn now to a brief discussion of the long-run or stationary-state effects of these disturbances.

Stationary-state effects

It is clear at the outset that each of the disturbances considered here leads to non-zero effects in the stationary state. A transitory one-period domestic credit innovation, for example, affects current reserve and foreign asset stocks. Since these variables are serially correlated, however (see Equation (7.20)), future reserve and foreign asset stocks are also affected *ad infinitum*. The stationary-state response, therefore, measure the cumulative long-run impact of such innovations.

The stationary state of the economy is attained when all accumulation – of both foreign assets and reserves – has ceased. From the specification of the model, it is clear such a state implies that both components of the trade balance and consequently, the total trade balance as well as the capital account, must each be zero (see Equation (7.17)).[24] Thus, the stationary state is characterized by $r_t = r_{t-1} = \tilde{r}$ and $k_t = k_{t-1} = \tilde{k}$. It is straightforward to derive analytical expressions for the solutions to $\tilde{r}$ and $\tilde{k}$, as well as $\tilde{x}$ and $\tilde{p}$, in terms of their ultimate determinants. First solve Equations (7.20b) and (7.20c) simultaneously as

$$\tilde{r} = \tilde{J}_3\bar{p}^* + \tilde{J}_4\xi_{1t} + \tilde{J}_5\xi_{2t} \tag{7.23a}$$

$$\tilde{k} = \tilde{N}_3\bar{p}^* + \tilde{N}_4\xi_{1t} + \tilde{N}_5\xi_{2t} \tag{7.23b}$$

where

$$\tilde{J}_3 \equiv \frac{[(1-N_2)J_3 + J_2N_3]}{[(1-J_1)(1-N_2) - N_1J_2]} \qquad \tilde{J}_4 \equiv \frac{[(1-N_2)J_4 + J_2N_4]}{[(1-J_1)(1-N_2) - N_1J_2]}$$

$$\tilde{J}_5 \equiv \frac{[(1-N_2)J_5 + J_2N_5]}{[(1-J_1)(1-N_2) - N_1J_2]} \qquad \tilde{N}_3 \equiv \frac{N_1\tilde{J}_3}{1-N_2} + \frac{N_3}{1-N_2}$$

$$\tilde{N}_4 \equiv \frac{N_1\tilde{J}_4}{1-N_2} + \frac{N_4}{1-N_2} \qquad \tilde{N}_5 \equiv \frac{N_1\tilde{J}_5}{1-N_2} + \frac{N_5}{1-N_2}$$

Given these solutions, $\tilde{x}$ can be directly obtained from Equation (7.20a), i.e.

$$\tilde{x} = \tilde{\pi}_3\bar{p}^* + \tilde{\pi}_4\xi_{1t} + \tilde{\pi}_5\xi_{2t} \tag{7.23c}$$

where

$\pi_3 \equiv (\pi_1 \tilde{J}_3 + \pi_2 \tilde{N}_3 + \pi_3) \quad \pi_4 \equiv (\pi_1 \tilde{J}_4 + \pi_2 \tilde{N}_4 + \pi_4) \quad \tilde{\pi}_5 \equiv (\pi_1 \tilde{J}_5 + \pi_2 \tilde{N}_5 + \pi_5)$

Finally, the stationary-state effects upon the price level ($\tilde{p}$) are obtained from Equations (7.2) and (7.3).

In the interests of space we only present the stationary-state effects of the three disturbances $\bar{p}^*$, ξ_{1t} and ξ_{2t} in the control case (i.e. case 5), for various values of α. Table 7.9 reports these results.

It is reassuring to note that the qualitative nature of the effects reported in Table 7.9, as well as their sensitivity characteristics with respect to α, is precisely the same as the corresponding one-period responses. Specifically, both anticipated and unanticipated increases in the foreign price level lead to financial appreciation, reserve accumulation and price inflation. And increasing values of α exacerbate the reserve and price effects in both instances. However, the response of the financial exchange rate to changes in α depends upon the nature of the disturbance, as in the one-period case. The stationary-state implications of domestic credit innovations are also qualitatively identical to those reported in Table 7.7 above.

These qualitative similarities notwithstanding, there are significant quantitative differences between first-period and corresponding stationary-state effects. First, for each value of α and for every disturbance considered (i.e. $\bar{p}^*$, ξ_{1t} and ξ_{2t}), the stationary-state effects upon the reserve level are substantially larger than the analogous first-period responses (the largest reserve effects being, once again, observed for ξ_{1t}-disturbances). Further, for both types of external price disturbance, the extent of stationary-state financial appreciation is larger than the corresponding first-period appreciation for each value of α (compare columns 1 and 4 of Table 7.9 with the relevant columns in Tables 7.5 and 7.6). Since a sharper appreciation for given values of α implies a larger 'offset' in Equation (7.2) to the external price disturbance, it follows that the stationary-state domestic inflation effects are less severe than the analogous short-run (first-period) effects. This property is clearly evidenced by comparison of Table 7.9 with the previous tables. Such a comparison also reveals that, for domestic credit innovations, *both* $\tilde{x}$ and $\tilde{p}$ are smaller, at each value of α, than the effects reported in Table 7.7.[25] For every disturbance considered, then, it is seen that short-run price effects overstate the ultimate stationary-state responses. Finally, domestic credit innovations also imply short-run overadjustment or 'overshooting' of the financial exchange rate, in comparison with the corresponding stationary-state effect.

Table 7.9 Stationary-state effects of various disturbances in the control case

	Change in $\bar{p}^*$		Change in ξ_{1t}				Change in ξ_{2t}		
α	$\tilde{x}$	$\tilde{r}$	$\tilde{p}$	$\tilde{x}$	$\tilde{r}$	$\tilde{p}$	$\tilde{x}$	$\tilde{r}$	$\tilde{p}$
0.9	–0.1429	1.0684	0.9857	–0.8292	4.2605	0.9171	0.0133	–0.0009	0.0013
0.7	–0.3222	1.1516	0.9033	–0.7567	4.0047	0.7730	0.0132	0.0085	0.0040
0.5	–0.5016	1.2488	0.7492	–0.6842	3.7488	0.6579	0.0132	0.0180	0.0066
0.3	–0.5978	1.2981	0.5815	–0.6431	3.5678	0.5498	0.0120	0.0250	0.0084
0.1	–0.6939	1.3473	0.3755	–0.6019	3.3867	0.4583	0.0107	0.0320	0.0096

CONCLUSION

This chapter has constructed and analysed a model of dual exchange markets. A key feature of our model – one that distinguishes the present framework from previous analyses – is the incorporation of the fact that certain current-account transactions are often settled in the financial exchange market. This scenario accords well with prevailing economic reality in the countries engaging in dual exchange rate practices. It was seen that both dynamic and static properties of an economy characterized by such inter-market leakage are quite different from those of a regime in which the two markets are effectively segmented. There is a sense in which cross-transactions impose a dynamic cost upon the economy by leading to a greater degree of 'persistence' in the adjustment of various macro-variables. However, this cost is to be weighed against the potential impact benefits of leakage, where the latter are measured in terms of generally reduced vulnerability of the domestic economy to external disturbances and in terms of the possible rehabilitation of domestic credit policy in stabilization operations. A similar policy dilemma is also present when variations in the penalty cost attributed to illegal cross-operations are considered.

Several extensions of the simplifed framework utilized in this chapter are clearly possible. One fruitful line of future enquiry would seem to be the construction of a two-good model, incorporating both an exportable and an importable commodity. Once this is done, the (presumably) differing implications of assigning certain exports versus imports to the financial exchange market can usefully be investigated.

APPENDIX 7A

The purpose of this appendix is to provide some details of the solution to the reduced-form coefficients (π_i, J_i, N_i), $i = 1, \ldots, 5$. The first step is to rewrite the reserve adjustment equation (7.18b) in reduced form by substituting for p_t^* from Equation (7.19a) and for $\ln T^e$ from Equation (7.7a). These substitutions lead to the following ultimate reduced-form expression for r_t (ignoring $\bar{y}$, $\bar{e}$ and $\bar{d}$, which will subsequently be suppressed with terms involving $\bar{i}^*$ and other constants).

$$r_t = z^0 r_{t-1} + (1 - z^0)(\bar{p}^* + \xi_{1t}) - (1 - z^0)\gamma_1^e [\pi_1 r_{t-1} + \pi_2 k_{t-1} + \pi_3 \bar{p}^* + \pi_4 \xi_{1t} + \pi_5 \xi_{2t}] + (1 - z^0)\delta_1^e b(1 - \alpha)[\pi_4 \xi_{1t} + \pi_5 \xi_{2t}] + (1 - z^0)\delta_1^e b \xi_{1t} \qquad (7A.1)$$

Equating net coefficients to zero in Equation (7A.1) yields the first set of simultaneous relations:

$$J_1 = z^0 - (1 - z^0)\gamma_1^e \pi_1 \tag{7A.2a}$$

$$J_2 = -(1 - z^0)\gamma_1^e \pi_2 \tag{7A.2b}$$

$$J_3 = (1 - z^0) - (1 - z^0)\gamma_1^e \pi_3 \tag{7A.2c}$$

$$J_4 = (1 - z^0) - (1 - z^0)\gamma_1^e \pi_4 + (1 - z^0)\delta_1^e b(1 - \alpha)\pi_4 + (1 - z^0)\delta_1^e b \tag{7A.2d}$$

$$J_5 = -(1 - z^0)\gamma_1^e \pi_5 + (1 - z^0)\delta_1^e b(1 - \alpha)\pi_5 \tag{7A.2e}$$

The next step is to reduce the foreign asset adjustment equation (7.18b) to ultimate reduced form by means of similar substitutions. The result is

$$k_t = z^1 k_{t-1} + (1 - z^1)(\bar{p}^* + \xi_{1t}) + (1 - z^1)\gamma_1^x [\pi_1 r_{t-1} + \pi_2 k_{t-1} + \pi_3 \bar{p}^* + \pi_4 \xi_{1t} \\ \pi_5 \xi_{2t}] + (1 - z^1)\delta_1^x b[(1 - \alpha)(\pi_4 \xi_{1t} + \pi_5 \xi_{2t}) + \xi_{1t}] \tag{7A.3}$$

whence the second set of simultaneous relations:

$$N_1 = (1 - z^1)\gamma_1^x \pi_1 \tag{7A.4a}$$

$$N_2 = z^1 + (1 - z^1)\gamma_1^x \pi_2 \tag{7A.4b}$$

$$N_3 = (1 - z^1) + (1 - z^1)\gamma_1^x \pi_3 \tag{7A.4c}$$

$$N_4 = (1 - z^1) + (1 - z^1)\gamma_1^x \pi_4 + (1 - z^1)\delta_1^x b(1 - \alpha)\pi_4 + (1 - z^1)\delta_1^x b \tag{7A.4d}$$

$$N_5 = (1 - z^1)\gamma_1^x \pi_5 + (1 - z^1)\delta_1^x b(1 - \alpha)\pi_5 \tag{7A.4e}$$

The third fundamental relationship is derived from the money market equilibrium condition. Eliminating all endogenous variables in this condition in terms of predetermined and exogenous components can be shown to lead to

$$\begin{aligned}
&(1 - d_1)d^0 \xi_{2t} + (1 - d_1)(1 - d^0)[J_1 r_{t-1} + J_2 k_{t-1} + J_3 \bar{p}^* + J_4 \xi_{1t} + J_5 \xi_{2t}] \\
&\quad - (1 - d_1)[\pi_1 r_{t-1} + \pi_2 k_{t-1} + \pi_3 \bar{p}^* + \pi_4 \xi_{1t} + \pi_5 \xi_{2t}] \\
&\quad - (1 - d_1)[N_1 r_{t-1} + N_2 k_{t-1} + N_3 \bar{p} + N_4 \xi_{1t} + N_5 \xi_{2t}] \\
&\quad + \lambda \pi_1 [J_1 r_{t-1} + J_2 k_{t-1} + J_3 \bar{p}^* + J_4 \xi_{1t} + J_5 \xi_{2t}] \\
&\quad + \lambda \pi_2 [N_1 r_{t-1} + N_2 k_{t-1} + N_3 \bar{p}^* + N_4 \xi_{1t} + N_5 \xi_{2t}] \\
&\quad - \lambda \pi_1 r_{t-1} - \lambda \pi_2 k_{t-1} - \lambda \pi_4 \xi_{1t} - \lambda \pi_5 \xi_{2t} \\
&\quad = \phi b(1 - \alpha)(\pi_4 \xi_{1t} + \pi_5 \xi_{2t}) + \phi b \xi_{1t}
\end{aligned} \tag{7A.5}$$

Equating net coefficients to zero in (7A.5) yields the third set of simultaneous relations:

$$(1-d_1)\,(1-d^0)J_1-(1-d_1)\pi_1-(1-d_1)N_1+\lambda\pi_1 J_1+\lambda\pi_2 N_1-\lambda\pi_1=0 \quad (7A.6a)$$

$$(1-d_1)\,(1-d^0)J_2-(1-d_1)\pi_2-(1-d_1)N_2+\lambda\pi_1 J_2+\lambda\pi_2 N_2-\lambda\pi_2=0 \quad (7A.6b)$$

$$(1-d_1)\,(1-d^0)J_3-(1-d_1)\pi_3-(1-d_1)N_3+\lambda\pi_1 J_3+\lambda\pi_2 N_3=0 \quad (7A.6c)$$

$$(1-d_1)\,(1-d^0)J_4-(1-d_1)\pi_4-(1-d_1)N_4+\lambda\pi_1 J_4+\lambda\pi_2 N_4-\lambda\pi_4$$

$$=\phi b(1-\alpha)\pi_4+\phi b \quad (7A.6d)$$

$$(1-d_1)\,(1-d^0)J_5-(1-d_1)\pi_5-(1-d_1)N_5+\lambda\pi_1 J_5+\lambda\pi_2 N_5-\lambda\pi_5$$

$$=\phi b\,(1-\alpha)\pi_5-\mathrm{d}^0(1-d_1) \quad (7A.6e)$$

It is evident from inspection of Equations (7A.2), (7A.4) and (7A.6) that the first two involve linear relationships, while Equations (7A.6) are *non-linear* and contain product terms such as $\pi_1 J_1$, $\pi_2 N_1$, $\pi_2 J_2$, $\pi_2 N_2$, etc. In order to make progress it is convenient to eliminate J_1, J_2, N_1 and N_2 in Equations (7A.6a) and (7A.6b) by using Equations (7A.2a), (7A.2b), (7A.4a) and (7A.4b). The result is

$$(1-d_1)\,(1-d^0)z^0-(1-d_1)\,(1-d^0)\,(1-z^0)\gamma_1^e\pi_1-(1-d_1)\pi_1$$

$$-\,(1-d_1)\,(1-z^1)\gamma_1^x\,\pi_1+\lambda z^0\,\pi_1-\lambda(1-z^0)\gamma_1^e\,\pi_1^2+\lambda(1-z^1)\gamma_1^x\,\pi_1\pi_2$$

$$-\,\lambda\pi_1=0 \quad (7A.7)$$

$$-(1-d_1)\,(1-d^0)\,(1-z^0)\gamma_1^e\,\pi_2-(1-d_1)\pi_2-(1-d_1)z^1$$

$$-\,(1-d_1)\,(1-z^1)\gamma_1^x\pi_2-\lambda(1-z^0)\gamma^e\pi_1\pi_2+\lambda z^1\pi_2+\lambda(1-z^1)\gamma_1^x\pi_2^2$$

$$-\,\lambda\pi_2=0 \quad (7A.8)$$

Equations (7A.7) and (7A.8) comprise a simultaneous set of two non-linear equations in π_1 and π_2. There are no analytical methods for solving such non-linear systems. Consequently, values of π_1 and π_2 must be obtained via numerical search methods. Given π_1 and π_2, the coefficients (J_t, N_i), $i=1, 2$, are readily obtained from Equations (7A.2a), (7A.2b), (7A.4a) and (7A.4b).

Consider next the solution to the reduced-form coefficients $\{\pi_i, J_i, N_i\}$, $i=3, 4, 5$. It is apparent from inspection of Equations (7A.2), (7A.4), and (7A.6) that these equations are of a block-recursive nature. Specifically, π_1

and π_2 must first be obtained (numerically) from Equations (7A.7) and (7A.8). Once these solutions are obtained, then those for (π_3, J_3, N_3) follow from simultaneous solution of Equations (7A.2c), (7A.4c) and (7A.6c), and similarly for (π_4, J_4, N_4) and (π_5, J_5, N_5). Further details may be obtained by writing to the authors.

NOTES

1. It is clear that if one includes those countries that have 'black' markets (or 'curb' markets) for foreign exchange, despite officially unified rates, then the number of countries on a *de facto* multiple exchange rate system is far greater than the forty-two reported by the IMF.
2. Parallel exchange markets for limited categories of transactions were reintroduced in France in1982. However, the scope of transactions covered by the parallel market was very narrow, unlike the 1971–4 experience.
3. See also Adam (1982).
4. Italy, for example, witnessed fraudulent imports of gold, allegedly for industrial purposes.
5. Except for Flood and Marion (1982a), none of the previous analyses are conducted in the context of a stochastic rational expectations framework.
6. There is also some 'reverse leakage' in the sense that a limited number of capital account items are required to be settled in the commercial market in some countries. However, these items primarily involve some public sector capital transactions, the actual empirical importance of which does not appear to be significant (see also Lanyi, 1975, in this regard).
7. It is not difficult to extend the model to incorporate two goods, i.e. an exportable one and an importable one. In principle, it is also possible to extend the menu of assets by including domestically-issued bonds. However, in order to focus on the problem at hand (i.e. 'leakage') we have elected to retain the simpler structure utilized in the text.
8. All parameters are defined positively in what follows.
9. Thus, if $p_t < (s_t + p_t^*)$, then domestic consumers purchase only in the home market, bidding up the home currency price, p_t, and conversely.
10. Technically, α represents a value share. However, provided that the initial spread between the two exchange rates is small, α can also approximate the relevant real share (which is, $T^{e0}/(T^e + T^x)^0$).
11. The total extent of actual leakage, which includes both legal and fraudulent trade transactions in the financial market, is endogenous to the economy, since the illegal component of such transactions is itself an endogenous variable. An increase in the exchange rate spread, for example, attracts additional illegal export transactions in the financial market, leading to a greater degree of actual leakage. Our model is fully consistent with this feature. The parameter α, however, represents an initial value and is definitionally exogenous. For expositional purposes, we interpret α as (the inverse of) the policy-controlled extent of legal leakage.
12. If consumption depends upon real wealth, then so does the total trade surplus, as well as its commercial and financial components (to be described below).
13. An equation very similar to (7.6) has been employed by Turnovsky and Bhandari (1982), among others. At this stage it may also be noted that if the

country in question is an importer (so that $T_t < 0$), then it is necessary to replace Equation (7.6) with a function that associates the trade deficit (negatively) with income. Throughout this chapter, we assume without consequence that the domestic economy is an exporter.

14. Note that owing to the one-good nature of the model, the trade surplus ($T_t > 0$) is synonymous with total exports.
15. Thus, the component $\gamma_1^x(x_t - \bar{e})$ in Equation (7.7b) can be associated strictly with fraudulent transactions. The component $\delta_1^x y_t$, however, consists of both legal and illegal transactions (since an increase in total exports legally requires additional settlements in the financial market, as well as encouraging certain traders to underinvoice exports at the *given* spread).
16. A derivation of Equation (7.10) proceeds as follows. One unit of domestic currency purchases $(1/X_t)$ units of capital account foreign exchange which yields (X_{t+1}/X_t) into the next period. During the period $(1/X_t)$ units of foreign exchange earns i_t^* in interest income. Thus, the total interest return is $(i_t^* X_t)$E (we assume in the interest of simplicity that repatriation occurs entirely via the commercial exchange market). Thus, the overall actual yield is

$$(1 + i_t') = \frac{X_{t+1}}{X_t} - \left(\frac{i_t^* \bar{E}}{X_{t+1}}\right).$$

Where we define $(1 + i_t')$ as the actual opportunity cost. Hence the logarithm of the expected opportunity cost may be approximated by

$$\ln(1 + i_t') \equiv i_t = (E_t, x_{t+1} - x_t) + E_t, Z_t \qquad \text{where} \qquad X_t \equiv \frac{i_t^* \bar{E}}{X_{t+1}}$$

One may approximate Z_t as

$$\frac{i_t^* \bar{E}}{X_{t+1}} \simeq [i_t^* + i_t^* (\bar{e} - x_{t+1})].$$

Next, use the approximation $i_t^* (\bar{e} - x_{t+1}) \simeq \bar{i}^* (\bar{e} - x_{t+1})$ when $\bar{i}^*$ is the mean value of i_t^*. Putting all the pieces together results in

$$i_t = i_t^* + (E_t, x_{t+1} - x_t) + \bar{i}^* (\bar{e}\, E_t, x_{t+1})$$

which is identical to Equation (7.10) in the text.

17. In order to focus on the essential issue at hand, i.e. leakage, we do not incorporate the complications of allowing for information gaps. Informational asymmetries in the context of unified exchange rates have been discussed by Bhandari (1982) and Floot and Hodrick (1985), among others.
18. It is assumed that the country in question enjoys a net creditor position in foreign assets and the initial ratios of domestic money to wealth (i.e. d_1) as well as of domestic credit to money (d^0) are each 0.8. It is known that a net debtor position in foreign assets is associated with problems of dynamic instability (see Henderson and Rogoff, 1982). Further, the initial rates of accumulation of both foreign assets and foreign reserves are assumed to be 20 per cent each; hence the chosen values of z^0 and z^1. The income elasticity of money demand (ϕ) is unity, while the interest rate *semi*-elasticity (λ) is 7.5. This value corresponds to an interest rate elasticity of 0.30 and a *quarterly* interest yield of 4 per cent (i.e. a simple annual rate of 16 per cent). The slope of the Phillips curve (b) is assumed to be 3. This value is consistent with the fact the b can be shown to be given by $(\theta/(1-\theta))$ where θ is the share of labour in total output

and θ=0.75, as is the case in most empirical studies. There are virtually no estimates for the elasticity of commercially-settled exports with respect to the exchange rate spread (γ_1^c). We have chosen a value consistent with Decaluwe's (1975) investigation of Belgian trade balance functions in the early 1970s. As indicated previously, γ_1^c is inversely related to the penalty cost of engaging in illegal transactions. The income elasticity of total exports (δ_1) is assumed to be 1.2. This value is in conformity with estimates for most industrial countries (see Goldstein, 1980). There are no estimates at all (that we are aware of) for δ_1^c (income elasticity of commercially-settled exports); we chose $\delta_1^c = 1$. The choice of δ_1^c and γ_1^c *implies* values for δ_1^x and γ_1^x via the 'adding-up' conditions stated in Equation (7.9). The value of β (degree of service account leakage) was fixed in all experiments at 0.5. Finally the value of α is assumed to be given successively by 0.9, 0.7, 0.5, 0.3 and 0.1. The numerical solutions to all coefficients of interest was computed for each of these values.

The initial rate of accumulation of reserves is $(R_t - R_{t-1})^0 / R_t^0 = 1 - (R_{t-1}/R_t)^0 = (1 - z^0)$.

19. In each case, the product term $N_1 J_2$ is less than 10^{-5} so that $S_1 \simeq N_2 \simeq S_2 \simeq J_1$.
20. The other three pairs of solutions for π_1 and π_2 involved the following configurations of signs: (+ +), (– –) and (– +). Each of these pairs was found to be unstable, in the sense that the calculated magnitude of one of the eigenvalues exceeded unity.
21. Interest rate liberalization is frequently an important component of a more general financial reform package that is often recommended by the IMF in such 'financially repressed' economies. In general, financial reform encompasses the dismantling of ceilings on interest rates, thereby allowing the latter to rise to their 'true' market-clearing levels.
22. Higher values of λ, on the other hand, lead to sharper financial appreciation and reserve accumulation, along with diminished inflationary effects for comparable degrees of leakage.
23. A higher value of λ implies that the money market may now be equilibrated by a reduced expected depreciation or a reduced current appreciation (given that the disturbance is transitory).
24. If the service account were incorporated, the description of the stationary state must be modified (see Rodriguez, 1979).
25. For domestic credit innovations, p_t is a linear, positive function of x_t (see Equations (7.2) and (7.3)). Thus, a lesser financial depreciation necessarily implies a reduced extent of domestic inflation.

REFERENCES

Adam, M.-C. (1982) 'Asset markets and foreign exchange intervention: a model of the Belgo-Luxembourg Economic Union', *Journal of Policy Modeling*, vol. 4, no. 2, pp. 223–42.

Abraham, J.P. and Martin, B. (1970) 'Dubbele beligische wisselkoers en internationale renteverschillen 1967–1969', *Economische-Statistische Berichten*, no. 2768, pp. 1007–13.

Abraham, J.P. (1974) 'Recente ervaringen op de belgische dubbele wissel-markt'. *Cahiers du Centre d'Etudes Bancaires et Financieres*, no. 221.

Argy, V. and Porter, M. (1972) 'The forward exchange market and the effect of domestic and external disturbances under alternative exchange rate systems', *IMF Staff Papers*, no. 19, pp. 503–32.

Barattieri, V. and Ragazzi, G. (1971) 'An analysis of the two-tier foreign exchange market', *Banca Nazionele del Lavoro Quarterly Review*, vol. 24, pp. 354–72.

Bhandari, J.S. (1982) 'Informational efficiency and the open economy', *Journal of Money, Credit, and Banking*, vol. 14, no. 4, pp. 457–78.

Cumby, R. (1981) 'Monetary policy under dual exchange rates', unpublished manuscript.

Decaluwe, B. (1974) 'Two-tier exchange markets and other systems: a comparison', *Tijdschrift voor Economie*, no. 1, pp. 55–79.

Decaluwe, B. (1975) '*Le Regime du Double Marché des Changes. Theorie et Practique. L'Experience de l'Union Economique Belgo-Luxembourgeoise*', (Faculté des Sciences Economiques, Sociales et Politiques, Louvain, Nouvelle Serie no. 122), Brussels: Mecaprint.

Decaluwe, B. and Steinherr, A. (1976) 'A portfolio balance model for a two-tier exchange market', *Economica*, vol. 43, pp. 111–25.

Dornbusch, R. (1976) 'The theory of flexible exchange rate regimes and macroeconomic policy', *Scandinavian Journal of Economics*, vol. 78, pp. 255–75.

Driskill, R. and McCafferty, S.M. (1983) 'An equilibrium model of output and relative price movements under flexible exchange rates', mimeograph, October.

Fleming, J.M. (1971) 'Dual exchange rates for current and capital transactions: a theoretical examination', in J.M. Fleming, *Essays in International Economics*, Cambridge, MA: Harvard University Press, pp. 296–325.

Fleming, J.M. (1974) 'Dual exchange markets and other remedies for disruptive capital flows', *IMF Staff Papers*, no. 21, pp. 1–17.

Flood, R. (1978) 'Exchange rate expectations in dual exchange markets', *Journal of International Economics*, vol. 8, pp. 65–77.

Flood, R. and Hodrick, R. (1985) 'Central bank in a rational open economy: a model with asymmetric information', in J.S. Bhandari (ed.), *Exchange Rate Management under Uncertainty*, Cambridge, MA: MIT Press.

Flood, R. and Marion, N. (1982a) 'The transmission of disturbances under alternative exchange rate regimes with optimal indexing', *Quarterly Journal of Economics*, vol. 97, no. 1, pp. 43–66.

Flood, R. and Marion, N. (1982b) 'Exchange rate regimes in transition: Italy 1974', unpublished manuscript.

Frenkel, J.A. and Rodriguez, C. (1981) 'The exchange rate overshooting hypothesis', unpublished manuscript.

Goldstein, M. (1980) 'Have flexible exchange rates handicapped macroeconomic policy?', Princeton University, Special Paper in International Finance, no. 14.

Henderson, D. and Rogoff, K. (1982) 'Negative foreign asset positions and stability in a world portfolio balance model', *Journal of International Economics*, vol. 13, nos 1/2, pp. 85–104.

Kiguel, M. (1982) 'A model of dual exchange rate markets with rational expectations and currency substitution', unpublished manuscript.

Lanyi, A. (1975) 'Separate exchange markets for capital and current transactions', *IMF Staff Papers*, no. 22, pp. 714–49.

Marion, N. (1981) 'Insulation properties of a two-tier exchange market in a portfolio balance model', *Economics*, vol. 48, pp. 61–70.

Mundell, R. (1968) *International Economics*, New York: Macmillan.

Rodriguez, C.A. (1979) 'Short-run and long-run effects of monetary and fiscal policies under exchange rates and perfect capital mobility', *American Economic*

Review, vol. 69, no. 1, pp. 179–82.

Salin, P. (1971) 'Un double marché des changes, est-il justifié?', *Revue d'Economie Politique*, no. 6, pp. 959–74.

Swoboda, A. (1974) 'The dual exchange rate system and monetary independence' in R.Z. Liber (ed.), *National Monetary Policies and the International Financial System*, Chicago: University of Chicago Press, pp. 258–70.

Talent, G. (1970) 'Le Système belge du double toux de change', *Cahiers Economiques de Bruxelles*, no. 46, pp. 161–91.

Turnovsky, S.J. and Bhandari, J.S. (1982) 'The degree of capital mobility and stability of an open economy under rational expectations', *Journal of Money, Credit, and Banking,* vol. 14, no. 3.

8 · RATIONAL EXPECTATIONS AND MONETARY POLICY

Patrick Minford[1]

Not everyone accepts the rational expectations hypothesis, but most now agree that it is worthy of attention, at least as a tractable approximation in an imperfectly understood world. I shall not attempt in this chapter to justify the hypothesis; this would take us too far afield (for discussion and references, see, for example, Begg, 1982; Minford and Peel, 1983a). Rather, I examine its *implications* for monetary policy (in a closed economy, though the arguments are easily extended).

I begin with the reassessment of whether, and if so how, monetary shocks impinge on output. With exogenous or backward-looking expectations this was encapsulated by the Phelps–Friedman Phillips curve. In the equilibrium story, money rose, driving up prices, while wages moved relatively slowly, held in place by sluggishly adjusting expectations; consequently output rose in response to falling real wages and rising profitability. In the disequilibrium version, prices and wages generally were set at levels reflecting expected future prices, quantities being demand-set, and money rises increased demand and so output. Both these stories are undermined by rational expectations – because they respond immediately to available information – and various alternatives have been proposed, none of them without dificulties.

Then, I turn to the definition of monetary policy and its relationship to fiscal policy. The literature on the 'government budget constraint' drew attention to the instability which could arise if monetary and fiscal policy were 'inconsistent' (i.e. if money and bonds grew at different rates), the standard example of this being where a fiscal deficit is permanently bond-financed. Under rational expectations that instability problem, where it occurs, becomes converted to an immediate one: the impossibility of defining an equilibrium path at all. Thus, deficit policy implies bounds on permissible monetary policy. Furthermore, the future possible paths of monetary policy so implied have effects on *current* output and inflation.

Finally, I examine the role of monetary policy in stabilizing output fluctuations (I take its role in controlling inflation through the systematic and long-run growth rate of money as axiomatic). Again, rational expectations has changed the nature of the debate. Previously, there was no question that monetary policy could and should stabilize output, given slowly moving price expectations, provided that the central bank had up to date information at least as good as the private sector's, a good model of the economy with which to forecast its future conditional paths, and was efficient in implementing required policy; the debate revolved around this proviso, the detractors arguing against all three parts of it and concluding that activist policy would be at least as likely to increase as to dampen fluctuations. Now the debate has widened because under rational expectations people incorporate knowledge of the central bank's reactions into their expectations; under certain conditions this can neutralize the effects of monetary policy on output and in general it complicates the economy's responses to stabilization policy in a way which raises questions about its desirability.

DOES MONEY AFFECT OUTPUT?

Under rational expectations the Phillips curve has developed in two main ways. The equilibrium version revolves around a supply curve of labour in which there is intertemporal substitution motivating a sizeable response of labour supply to current expected real wages; other motivations are also possible, e.g. substitution with leisure or unemployment benefits. But there is an information lag for workers with respect to the general price level: they perceive their own nominal wages accurately but they cannot sample all the prices of the many goods they will be buying in a typical year, hence they must form an expectation of the price level, Ep_t, based partly on the prices they do sample and partly on out-of-date general information (Φ_{t-1}) about the economy, including the money supply. Ep_t will therefore incorporate the effect of lagged money supply movements on prices; but current money supply movements that could not be predicted from Φ_{t-1} will only be incorporated in so far as the individual prices sampled can be used to gauge them. These will reflect not only money supply but also individual market influences and economy-wide real shocks; so when the money supply rises unexpectedly and drives up the general price level, the individual price rises will only be partially interpreted as reflecting a money supply change and in general Ep_t will not rise as much as p_t. So expected real wages will exceed any given actual real wages. The supply of labour at period t, L_t^s, can be written, then (treating all variables in natural logarithms and using a loglinear form for simplicity) as:

$$L_t^s = \alpha_1(w_t + p_t - Ep_t) - \alpha_2(w^* - r_t) + \dots \qquad (8.1)$$

where w^* is the expected future real wage and r_t is the real rate of interest (as a decimal rather than a percentage) discounting this to present value. In this set-up, unexpected money supply causes $p_t - Ep_t$ to rise and labour supply to increase.

To complete the picture we add firms' profit-maximizing subject to a production function and a fixed capital stock. We have the demand for labour, L_t^d, given by equating real wages and its marginal product

$$L_t^d = -\beta_1 w_t + \dots \tag{8.2}$$

and output, y_t, depending on labour input through the production function:

$$y_t = \beta_2 L_t^d + \dots \tag{8.3}$$

For firms there is no information problem because they know the prices of their own outputs and inputs from their own factory gate transactions.

Equating L_t^s with L_t^d and substituting into the production function yields the Phillips curve:

$$y_t = \frac{\beta_2 \beta_1 \alpha_1}{\alpha_1 + \beta_1}(p_t - Ep_t) - \frac{\beta_2 \beta_1 \alpha_2}{\alpha_1 + \beta_1}(w^* - r_t)$$

or

$$y_t = \sigma_1 (p_t - Ep_t) - \sigma_2 w^* + \sigma_2 r_t \tag{8.4}$$

To make the link with money supply we can most simply ignore for now the information conveyed by current individual prices (assuming in effect that people think these are dominated by individual market influences); we can write down IS and LM curves

$$y_t = -\gamma_1 r_t + \dots \tag{8.5}$$

$$\bar{m} + \mu m_{t-1} + \epsilon_t = p_t - \delta_1 (r_t + Ep_{t+1} - p_t) + \delta_2 y_t \tag{8.6}$$

The left-hand side of Equation (8.6) is the supply function for money, with a random unanticipated component, ϵ_t, and on the right-hand side we have replaced the nominal interest rate with its real and expected inflation components.

Ep_t can be found by taking expectations of Equations (8.4)–(8.6) (for solution methods, see Minford and Peel, 1983a, chapter 2). The unanticipated price level, $p_t - Ep_t$, which concerns us here, is found by expressing all variables in terms of deviations from expected values (superscript ^{ue}) so we have:

$$-\gamma_1 r_t^{ue} = y_t^{ue} = \sigma_1 p_t^{ue} + \sigma_2 r_t^{ue} \tag{8.7}$$

$$m_t^{ue} = \epsilon_t = p_t^{ue} - \delta_1(r_t^{ue} - p_t^{ue}) + \delta_2 y_t^{ue} \tag{8.8}$$

whence

$$p_t^{ue} = \frac{(\sigma_2 + \gamma_1)}{(1 + \delta_1)(\sigma_2 + \gamma_1) + \delta_1\sigma_1 + \delta_2\gamma_1\sigma_1}\epsilon_t$$

$$y_t^{ue} = \frac{\gamma_1\sigma_1}{\sigma_2 + \gamma_1} p_t^{ue}; \qquad r_t^{ue} = \frac{-\sigma_1}{\sigma_2 + \gamma_1} p_t^{ue} \tag{8.9}$$

A money supply shock therefore raises prices and output and depresses real interest rates in a very familiar way. But only the shock; expected money has no effect on output because it is incorporated into expected prices.

This basic story can be enriched by allowing for people's inferences from their individual market prices to the general price level. These inferences (or 'signal extraction') are based on the past correlation between unforeseen movements in the general price level and these individual prices. If the economy (or regime) is one where monetary shocks dominate all others (e.g. one of high and variable inflation), then the correlation coefficient will tend to unity, people will interpret all local price changes as changes in the general price level and will not alter their supply. At the opposite extreme, when there is monetary stability, Ep_t will respond barely to changes in p_t.

The development of this equilibrium story is mainly due to Lucas (1972), Sargent and Wallace (1975), and Barro (1976) and is often called the 'islands' story because individuals are allocated to local markets and cannot obtain current aggregate (cross-insular) information. The main difficulty with it is its reliance on this information deficiency. Aggregate information on the price level (and the money supply) is routinely made available, at least in developed economies, with a very short delay (a few weeks at most). It is hard to believe that errors in forecasting prices or money are therefore serious enough to mislead workers into significant changes in labour supply. The story seems at its strongest in developing countries where aggregate information is delayed and often corrupted even when available. Indeed Lucas (1973) finds cross-country evidence for his theory from a sample with many such countries in it (their wide inflationary experience giving the expected difference in reactions to inflationary shocks).

The theory has been strengthened somewhat by allowing that people have access to *some* aggregate information such as the nominal interest rate. This complicates the inference problem; people now have an aggregate and a local piece of information from which to infer whether the underlying shocks are local market, or economy-wide real or monetary shocks. The effect on output of money now depends on the variances of all the shocks; but the main point remains as in Lucas's model that as the variance of money rises relative to that of the others, so the response of output to money falls. The model's weakness also remains in its reliance on information delays for aggregate money and prices.

In the major alternative, disequilibrium, version of the Phillips curve (Fischer, 1977; Phelps and Taylor, 1977), it is postulated that workers and firms sign nominal contracts in which labour is supplied at a pre-set nominal wage in whatever quantity firms should require it; typically these contracts will have several periods' duration. (Alternatively, firms may set output prices for several periods; but this is not usually assumed.) To illustrate this replace Equation (8.1) by Equation (8.11), a wage equation in which the nominal wage is set at its expected equilibrium real value, w^*, not adjusted for the expected price level in each period of the contract. Now divide workers into two equal groups settling in alternate periods for a two-period contract, and this period's nominal wages will be an average of expectations of this period's prices formed last period and the period before:

$$W_t = w^* + \tfrac{1}{2}(E_{t-1}\, p_t + E_{t-2}\, p_t) \tag{8.10}$$

where E_{t-1} is the rational expectation formed on the basis of $t–i$ information so that real wages are:

$$w_t = W_t - p_t = w^* - \tfrac{1}{2}(p_t - E_{t-1}\, p_t) - \tfrac{1}{2}(p_t - E_{t-2}\, p_t) \tag{8.11}$$

Putting Equation (8.11) into the rest of the model yields the result that output now is affected by any money supply movements which were not predicted *two* periods before (and in general at the date of the longest-running contract). Because, in effect, the short-term elasticity of labour supply is assumed to be infinite in this disequilibrium version, the response of output to unanticipated money and prices is greater than in the equilibrium version.

These nominal contracts rest on the presence of transactions costs in changing nominal wages; without such costs, contracts signed between firms and risk-averse workers would set both wages and employment, with both varying according to states of the world and wages additionally indexed to prices (i.e. real wages would be the object of the contract). Clearly there may well be transactions costs in such complete indexation, but whether they are significant enough to generate real wage movements of the size required must be in doubt. The experience of European countries such as Italy and Belgium, where formal indexation close to 100 per cent is practised, suggests that real wages are largely impervious to monetary shocks; if so in countries where indexation is formal, why should it be any different in other countries where indexation is informal but presumably no less feasible?

The difficulties with both stories have led, on the one hand, to a search for alternative 'nominal rigidities' which might motivate an effect of money on output, and on the other to a real business cycle theory (Long and Plosser, 1983) under which correlations between output and money are explained by reverse causation (e.g. through a banking system response to higher real balance requirements) and money shocks have no impact on output. It is hard at this stage to say a great deal about this last response other than that it undermines *macroeconomic* explanations of business cycle history to a devastating extent, leaving us with little if anything to say at all (for example, on this theory the Great Depression happened because of some unknown shock to tastes and technology); there is also no clear evidence for or against it since there is no obvious way of distinguishing the directions of causation between contemporaneous shocks. Macro-economists (at least) tend to regard this theory as a last resort.

A natural place to look for other nominal rigidities is asset holdings. Non-indexed government bonds are nominally-denominated assets whose terms were set at various past dates (rather like overlapping wage contracts); they would enter the IS curve (and possibly also the supply and LM curves) provided they are regarded as net wealth because of incomplete discounting of future taxes (reasons could be the partial absence of bequests or incomplete insurance markets across generations combined with a progressive tax system – see Barro, 1974). Money itself may be regarded as a holding asset available as wealth to be spent (rather than a transactions vehicle fully absorbed in the technology of exchange); this is its role in the overlapping generations models of the Minnesota school (see, for example, Wallace, 1980), where its use is underpinned by government regulations restricting the use of alternative assets. This is to be contrasted with money's role when it is an argument of the consumer's utility function, the reason given for this being that more money yields a more smoothly functioning transactions technology.

To see the effect of these assumptions, first change Equation (8.5) to

$$y_t = -\gamma_1 r_t + \gamma_2(\bar{b} - p_t) - \gamma_3 (r_t + Ep_{t+1} - p_t) + \gamma_4(m_t - p_t) \quad (8.12)$$

where $m_t = \bar{m} = \mu m_{t-1} + \epsilon_t$; $\bar{b}$ is the initial (exogenous) nominal value of bonds; and the term in γ_3 represents the effects of capital losses as nominal interest rates rise. Now write Equation (8.4) in its full information form (i.e. where $p_t = Ep_t$) as

$$y_t = \sigma_2(r_t - w^*) \quad (8.13)$$

If the model consisting of Equations (8.6), (8.12) and (8.13) is solved, the correlation between output and monetary shocks is ambiguous. If $\gamma_2 = \gamma_3 = 0$, so money alone is net wealth, then output *is* increased by a monetary shock (so are real interest rates, of course; this is the opposite of the earlier model). But if $\gamma_4 = 0$, so bonds alone are net wealth, the effect of money on output is ambiguous; a permanent monetary shock (i.e. let μ tend to 1) will reduce output, but a temporary shock will increase it provided $\gamma_3 > \gamma_2$.

One may enrich this model with bonds as net wealth if one appeals to a possible confusion not between individual and aggregate price shocks as in the island story but between temporary and permanent monetary shocks. Let $\gamma_4 = 0$ and, first, assume that monetary and real shocks each have a transitory and permanent component between which no distinction can be made in the current period – this emphasis on the transitory/permanent confusion is like that of Brunner *et al.* (1980), though they make a rather different use of it. This assumption places confusions firmly where they can easily enough belong – namely about the *future*. Agents know everything today there is to know; what they *cannot* know is which of today's shocks will endure into the future.

The basis for this confusion is a lack of information but it is not the sort of information that could readily be provided by more surveys; it is not *factual* information, rather it is *interpretative* information. Suppose there is an unexpected rise in the money supply. That is a *fact*, to be established by a statistical recording process. But what one really needs to know is what that fact means for the future: have ministers decided to raise the money supply level once and for all, or the *growth* rate once and for all, or is this a temporary disturbance to the level? How can this be discovered? One may ask the ministers, and discover their intention; that, in turn, may be conditional on how their back-benchers or supporters in the country react to events. One may ask a sample of these their opinions. And so on. There is no *fact* to be discovered at this time, because no one knows what *will* be.

Eventually, it will become apparent what *was* permanent. Reactions will become known as events occur. At some future time $t+k$, we may assume that the permanent money supply at time t is known. We may also assume that the process driving the permanent money supply component is known. For simplicity, we shall assume that $k = 1$ and that the process is a random walk. The transitory component is assumed to be a pure random error.

Take the following model (where also for simplicity γ_1 and γ_2 have been set to zero):

$$y_t = \gamma_3(r_t + Ep_{t+1} - p_t) \tag{8.14}$$

$$y_t = \sigma_2 r_t \tag{8.15}$$

$$m_t = m_t^* + \epsilon_t = p_t - \delta_1(r_t + Ep_{t+1} - p_t) + \delta_3 y_t \tag{8.16}$$

where m_t^* is the permanent monetary shock; and ϵ_t is the transitory shock. Equation (8.15) is the supply curve (see also Equation (8.13)), and

Equation (8.16) is the LM curve (see also Equation (8.6)).

The model is quickly solved to give

$$E_t p_{t+1} = E_t m^*_{t+1} \tag{8.17}$$

$$E_t m^*_{t+1} = \theta_m (m_t - m^*_{t-1}) + m^*_{t-1} \quad \text{where} \quad \theta_m = \frac{\sigma^2_{\Delta m^*}}{\sigma^2_\epsilon + \sigma^2_{\Delta m^*}} \tag{8.18}$$

by the familiar signal extraction formula. Hence

$$y_t = (\gamma_1 + \sigma_2 + \sigma_2\delta_2 \ \gamma_1 + \sigma_2\delta_1)^1 \sigma_2\gamma_1 \left[(1 - \theta_m)(m_t - m^*_{t-1})\right] \tag{8.19}$$

This gives an analogous effect on output to that of Lucas (1983); here the more noisy *permanent* money is relative to transitory money the smaller the effect of a monetary shock on output (in a more general model it could be negative). Real interest rates vary *directly* with output. Notice that it all depends on bonds being net wealth.

This discussion has shown that there are many mechanisms by which under rational expectations monetary shocks *may* affect output but all of them are subject to difficulties of one sort or another, which lead them to appear of limited applicability. Information delays apply most in developing countries, nominal contracts only apply when the transactions cost of indexation are high, money may only have a significant role as wealth when alternative assets are restricted, there may be no money-denominated bonds, and so on; institutional details of the monetary framework will be important in assessing through which channel, if any, monetary shocks work. This judgement may lead us to accept a real business cycle theory for certain situations – e.g. that of a high-inflation country with a weak government incapable of enforcing a currency monopoly; it also suggests that the major (monetary) explanation of the Great Depression due to Friedman and Schwarz (1963) can stand up if we can show that the monetary framework of that time made one at least of these channels operative – not surely a difficult task.

FISCAL CONSTRAINTS ON MONETARY POLICY

Rational expectation models have in principle to be solved into the indefinite future in order to arrive at a determinate solution for the current period. This implies that the model must have a reasonable long-run equilibrium. We now write down the government budget identity in this long-run (steady) state:

$$\dot{H} + \dot{B} = Pg + RB - tPy^* \tag{8.20}$$

where H is high-powered money; B is government bonds at current nominal market value (notice that in steady state interest rates will not be changing so the nominal market value of a bond will not change); $\dot{H}$ and $\dot{B}$ are the rate of change of H and B, respectively; g is government spending (excluding interest); R is the nominal interest rate (the same at all maturities in steady state); t is tax rate minus transfer rate (proportion of GDP); P is price level; and y^* is equilibrium GDP (or GNP).

Now apply the weak condition that in steady state real government debt should be stationary as a fraction of GDP. We will return to this later, but for now let us think of this as ruling out Ponzi financing of government, assuming that the real interest rate is equal to or exceeds the growth rate of GDP and that there is some limit to the tax rate (some 'taxable capacity'). With this condition we have $\Delta \log (B/Py^*) = 0$ or $(\dot{B}/B) - \pi = \gamma$, where π and γ are steady-state inflation and output growth, respectively. Manipulating (8.20), using this, gives the equilibrium growth rate of money:

$$(\dot{H}/H)^* = v^* [(g/y^*) - t + b^* (r - \gamma)] \tag{8.21}$$

where v^* is equilibrium velocity; b^* is the equilibrium government bond to GDP ratio; and r is the real interest rate.

(8.21) says that the steady-state growth rate of money depends upon the ratio to GDP of the steady-state deficit inclusive of real debt interest (sometimes called the 'inflation-adjusted real deficit'), minus an allowance for growth, $b^* \gamma$. We can also note that since in equilibrium $(\dot{H}/H)^* = \pi + \gamma$,

$$(\pi + \gamma)(H + B) = Pg + RB - tPy^*$$

or

$$(\dot{H}/H)^* \left(= \pi + \gamma = \frac{Pg + RB - tPy^*}{H + B} \right) = \left(\frac{PSBR}{Py^*} \right) \left(\frac{Py^*}{H + B} \right) \tag{8.22}$$

which says that money growth equals the public sector borrowing requirement to GDP ratio times the 'velocity' of 'outside money'.

(8.21) and (8.22) are, of course, exactly equivalent, though one uses the inflation-adjusted deficit while the other uses the unadjusted deficit. However, when (8.21) is used to assess what fiscal policy must be used to validate a certain counter-inflationary monetary policy (e.g. one to reduce $(\dot{H}/H)^*$ to γ from some high level), great care must be taken to include in b^* the effects of falling inflation and interest rates on the value of outstanding bonds; this adjustment can be very large when a large proportion of these bonds are non-indexed and of long maturity, so that large cuts in the government deficit excluding interest may be necessary. When (8.22) is used, the implications are more transparent since nominal debt interest will not change except for short-maturity stocks which are rolled over before inflation comes down. These remarks are relevant to the debate on the Thatcher government's Medium Term Financial Strategy, which has not always carefully observed this point (for instance, Buiter and Miller, 1983, incorrectly argue that the fiscal policies were 'unnecessarily' restrictive using a crude adjustment for current inflation on debt at current market value).

Let us now return to the stationarity condition on real government debt. Crucial to this is whether the real interest rate exceeds the rate of GDP growth.[2] Yet, though this has aroused controversy (see, for example, Darby, 1983), as a steady-state proposition it seems quite solid. For consider an economy with constant g/y^* and t, growing at the rate of n (population growth) and τ (technical change resulting from investment in research and development). Assume that money enters the utility function, U, of an infinitely-lived representative consumer as in Sidrauski (1967), but separably, as is appropriate when real balances contribute to the efficiency of transactions technology and real transactions depend on (exogenous) y^*. Then if savings are taxed at the rate t, the consumer's first-order conditions give (see, for example, Drazen, 1985)

$$r = [n + \delta + (\dot{U}_c / U_c)] / (1-t) \qquad (8.23)$$

where δ is the consumer's rate of time preference; and $U_c = \partial U / \partial c$ (c is real consumption). $\dot{U}_c / U_c$ will be negative until satiation occurs where $U_c = 0$; at this point the return on research and development is zero and $\gamma = n$, hence $r > \gamma$. However, even before this stationary stage is reached, the likelihood of $r < \gamma$ is remote if, as seems possible, changing technology brings with it changing tastes to that $\dot{U}_c / U_c$ is positive. Historically the experience of (*ex post*) r and γ has been mixed, largely varying with inflation. In the inflationary post-war period, $r < \gamma$ regularly until the last few years. But from 1924 to 1933, r averaged no less than 4.9 per cent in the UK and 6.6 per cent in the US.

If $r \geq \gamma$, then government must plan to stop its debt to GDP ratio from rising at some point at least if its debt is to maintain its market value; for if it does not so plan, some of its creditors must fail to be paid. If the government were to attempt Ponzi financing, the market would write off the value of its debts (and refuse to lend to it except at most unfavourable terms) until the attempt were called off – a situation familiar from recent LDC 'debt crises'.

Under these conditions, (8.21) implies that in steady state the government may choose three out of $(\dot{H}/H)^*$, g/y^*, t, and b^*; r and γ are exogenously given, and v^* is determined by $(\dot{H}/H)^*$, as a result of consumer optimization and so is a function of the three choice variables.

But there is more to it than this, because b^* and v^* have also to be consistent with past bond and money issues and with the price level. Let us suppose the government chooses a path for money growth up to steady state and also a path for g and t; v^* is given by $(\dot{H}/H)^*$. The price level in steady state must generate v^* given the level of money. Now the government is tied into a terminal b^* and a path for prices and nominal interest rates. It inherits a stock of bonds, some of them (perhaps all) money-denominated; these will be revalued by the new path of prices and interest rates. It must now ensure that the *path* of g and t generates only so many extra bonds as can be accommodated within b^* in steady state. Hence there is a trade-off between history and the steady state; larger deficits along the path require higher terminal inflation or a smaller terminal deficit for a given path of money supply growth, and for a given deficit path lower money growth along the path implies higher terminal debt and so higher terminal inflation.

This trade-off problem was first highlighted by Sargent and Wallace (1981), who argued that it was even possible to have the paradox of lower money growth now (expenditure and tax rates constant) producing higher inflation *now* as well as in steady state. This has given rise to a series of papers examining the status of the paradox – Liviatan (1984) and Drazen (1985) – and confirming that it will hold if the elasticity of demand for money is greater than or equal to unity, in the case of indexed bonds with exogenous output and utility separable in money and consumption. However, one does not need the paradox to appreciate the importance of the general result. Further generalization of the dynamic possibilities is of great interest (Haque, 1984, has explored a number of them).

One way of short-circuiting these complexities, which we will use from now on, is to specify a steady state value for the real deficit to GDP ratio (or equivalently for $(\dot{H}/H)^*$) and either g/y^* or t, letting the other adjust to whatever b^* is thrown up by history. It also leaves the government free to choose the path of g, t and H. This procedure has realism to recommend it in the sense that governments often pursue for protracted periods independent monetary, spending and tax policies and are forced in the end to sacrifice one of these by the implied debt burden. We shall therefore think of monetary policy as 'independent' in the short to medium run but constrained by or constraining the fiscal deficit in the long run (the terminal fiscal deficit in turn fixes the terminal values of either g or t given b^*). This procedure also has the merit that monetary stabilization policy – to which we turn next – can be thought about separately from fiscal policy or long-run monetary growth.

MONETARY POLICY AS AN OUTPUT STABILIZER

Rational expectations leapt to prominence and notoriety in macroeconomics largely because of the policy-ineffectiveness proposition put forward by Sargent and Wallace (1975), thus illustrating the point that for an idea to be noticed and catch on fast in economics it needs to upset strongly-held policy convictions – a point already well understood by Keynes and Friedman. Sargent and Wallace showed that, if you took a standard Keynesian model with an expectations-augmented Phillips curve and merely assumed that expectations were formed rationally, then a monetary authority possessing no better information than that of its private citizens could not affect (at all) the behaviour of output by implementing any planned action; only its monetary 'errors' – i.e. its *deviations* from its monetary plan – would affect output.

This can be seen from the model formed by Equations (8.4)–(8.6), where, to appreciate the shockingness of the story, Equation (8.4) should be rewritten in old Phillips curve form with inflation as the dependent variable:

$$p_t - p_{t-1} = Ep_t - p_{t-1} + (1/\sigma_1)\, y_t + (\sigma_2/\sigma_1)\,(w^* - r_t) \qquad (8.24)$$

Now simply observe that Equations (8.4) and (8.5) solve jointly for y_t and r_t in terms of $(p_t - Ep_t)$ and w^*. We saw on pages 235–6 that $p_t - Ep_t$ is a function solely of t-period shocks (in that case ϵ_t was the only one). It follows that y_t is not affected by $\bar{m}$, μm_{t-1} or any other planned (i.e. in $t-1$ or before for t) component of the money supply one might think up.

This proposition had two main effects, besides pure notoriety. In those committed to monetary stabilization policy, it created an antipathy to rational expectations. In the profession generally it started a massive search for ways of generating policy-effectiveness. Yet, as Lucas and Sargent (1978) emphasized some years later, the proposition was never intended as more than a cautionary tale, designed to illustrate the general point that monetary plans may have effects very different from those supposed to occur under naive expectations hypotheses; 'expectations must be carefully allowed for' is the message.

The ways in which policy-effectiveness may be re-established are numerous and have been surveyed before (see, for example, Minford and Peel, 1983a, chapter 3). If one retains the assumption of government–private sector parity of information,[3] then any nominal rigidity of the sort examined on pages 237–40, where some nominally-denominated asset or contract has a maturity longer than the information lags on nominal variables, will do the trick. The intuition is obvious: if a shock occurs in t whose effects on prices are perceived in $t+1$, then, provided there are some contracts or assets whose value in $t+2$ is affected by the price level in $t+2$, the central bank can, by changing money and so the price level, undo the effects of the shock in $t+2$. Phelps and Taylor (1977) and Fischer (1977) showed this for nominal wage and price contracts, Minford and Peel (1981) showed it for wealth effects of nominal government liabilities. Since we may have to appeal to these very rigidities to motivate an effect of money at all, it is no more or less persuasive to appeal to them to motivate monetary stabilization policy.

If we return to the pure new classical story of information lags – still retaining informational parity across sectors – then it turns out that the basic story of Equations (8.4)–(8.6) – including a serious monetary information content in local prices, which we suppressed in our early exposition – is sufficient to give policy effectiveness. This was first pointed out in a much more complex model by King (1983), where there is also current information on an economy-wide variable, interest rates. However, this is not required. The effectiveness runs off the forward price expectation term that enters interest rates; so the demand for money and so the *current* shock effect. (Turnovsky, 1980, and Weiss, 1980, both noticed the power of this term but used it in a model with asymmetric information, which is also not required. Turnovsky assumed implicitly that agents in bond markets had full current information; Weiss, in the same spirit, assumed that capitalists had full current information but workers could not distinguish nominal from productivity shocks.)

It is worth demonstrating since it is not widely known. Take the model of Equations (8.4)–(8.6) and assume that the innovation in the typical *i*th local price (i.e. $p_{it} - E_{t-1}\, p_{it}$, where E_{t-1} covers information for last period assumed to be generally available but none for this period) is correlated with the general price level's innovations by the parameter ϕ (as $\phi \rightarrow 1$, monetary variance totally dominates, as $\phi \rightarrow 0$ monetary stability is total), so that the *i*th market agent's expectation of the general price level is $E_{(i)}p_t = E_{t-1}p_t + \phi\,(p_{it} - E_{t-1}p_t)$. Aggregating over all local markets gives us the average expectation $Ep_t = E_{t-1}p_t + \phi\,(p_t - E_{t-1}p_t)$, so that $p_t - Ep_t = (1-\phi)(p_t - E_{t-1}p_t)$.

Substituting for y_t and r_t from Equations (8.4) and (8.5) into the LM curve (Equation (8.6)) and dropping constants gives

$$\frac{\epsilon_t}{1-\mu L} = (1+\delta_1)p_t - \delta_1 Ep_{t+1} + \frac{\sigma_1(\delta_2\gamma_1 + \delta_1)\,(1-\phi)}{\sigma_2 + \gamma_1}\,(p_t - E_{t-1}p_t)$$

Using the Muth method of undetermined coefficients (see Minford and Peel, 1983a, chapter 2) write

$$p_t = \sum_{i=0}^{\infty} \pi_i\, \epsilon_{t-i}$$

so that

$$Ep_{t+1} = \pi_1\phi\epsilon_t + \sum_{i=1}^{\infty} \pi_{i+1}\epsilon_{t-i}$$

The solution for π_0 turns out to be

$$\frac{1+\delta_1(1-\mu[1-\phi])}{(1+\delta_1+x)\,(1+\delta_1+\mu\delta_1[2\phi-1])}$$

where $x = (\delta_2\gamma_1 + \delta_1)\sigma_1(1 - \phi)/(\sigma_2 + \gamma_1)$. μ, which represents the effect of planned monetary intervention feeding back off lagged money, thus affects the current output response to monetary and other shocks.

Intuitively what is occurring is that there is an unknown element affecting the real interest rate, namely the response of future expected prices to the current (unknown) monetary shock. People's assessment of how big this element is depends partly on ϕ, the correlation of monetary shocks with local prices, and partly on μ, the authorities' next-period money supply response to today's money. As μ gets more positive future expected prices rise more when the shock occurs, real interest rates fall more, but current prices rise more, and output rises more.

We have written as if there was no possibility for money supply to react immediately to *current* information available to the central bank. Yet such reactions are what most central bankers themselves think of as monetary policy; reserve injections in response to rises in interest rates, exchange rates, and so on. Poole (1970), in a well-known paper, characterized the dilemma for monetary policy as whether to fix interest rates or money supply (or some linear combination); the former, he argued, would stabilize output in response to monetary shocks but destabilize it in response to real shocks (to the IS curve), the latter would do the opposite. The analysis suggests that the central bank should decide on a linear combination (i.e. a rule for money to respond to interest rates) reflecting the relative likelihood of the shocks.

While the Poole approach remains valid for the models with nominal rigidities there is a problem with this approach when interest rates are generally available information since it presupposes that the model is our classical one of Equations (8.4)–(8.6). For people can infer from interest rate changes what the current monetary supply response is; they then incorporate it precisely into Ep_t so that the response is neutralized as far as output is concerned (King, 1983; Minford and Peel, 1983b). This objection would be inapplicable only if the central bank reacts to information only available at a market (micro) level; but this is hard to argue in the case of interest rates, exchange rates, or other asset information the central bank typically uses.

Summarizing overall, in spite of this, our earlier arguments clearly established the effectiveness in general of monetary policy even in the most classical case. But this does not establish its desirability. Three main problems have been identified: the 'Lucas critique' (Lucas, 1976) whereby the system's response can change as policies change; the time-inconsistency or credibility problem (Kydland and Prescott, 1977) whereby announced policies may not be followed through; and the appropriateness of the social welfare functions (e.g. with the output gaps and inflation as arguments) used to weigh up macro policy.

To understand the 'Lucas critique', take the optimal feedback policy in the classical model just reviewed. Suppose ϕ, which is the ratio of $\pi^2_0\sigma^2_\epsilon$ to the sum of $\pi^2_0\sigma^2_\epsilon$ and the variance of the typical local shock, δ^2_η, has been estimated for a sample in which μ was zero. Now we compute the optimal μ based on this ϕ. But then ϕ must be different, depending as it does on the different π_0. If feedback policy is to be done correctly, then allowance must be made for this resulting change in ϕ. This may be possible in a very simple model like the one here (we search for a μ that will minimize the absolute value of π. But in a well-specified model of a real economy it is unlikely to be at all easy to do with any confidence at all. Thus Lucas's critique essentially returns us to Milton Friedman's complaint that policy-makers do not have a good enough model to be sure to improve matters; not good enough because even if good in sample it will shift out of sample with the new policies. The argument is as powerful against using models which rely on nominal rigidities, for these *par excellence* will shift with changes in the policy framework.

Time-inconsistency is a general problem with *any* policy, feedback or no, where the policy-maker is not bound by some external force to stick to his course. It only arises under rational expectations because its essence is that the policy-maker induces certain behaviour in people based on what they expect him to do given his announced policy posture; once he has induced this behaviour, the situation is now a fresh one in which it will generally pay him to renege if this is a one-off episode.

The key example from macroeconomics is announcing tough anti-inflation policy so that people expect low inflation and sign moderate wage contracts, and, once they have committed themselves, expanding the money supply to achieve high output growth as well as not quite so low inflation. (The example can be rigged to give zero inflation by announcing *de*flation.) Unfortunately, this situation degenerates: people in time come to realize in advance that the government will renege, so they expect high inflation (high money growth). The government then finds it has to deliver exactly this amount of money growth and cannot increase output. So the economy winds up merely with high inflation.

The relevance to stabilization policy is that this is in practice discretionary (though it need not be; there are no cases known to me at least where a pre-committed policy rule has been applied). Therefore, the scope for backsliding is greater when stabilization responses are permissible, it is minimized when rules (in practice simple fixed rules) are enforced by some higher authority such as a constitutional court.

Though it may seem attractive to allow the central bank discretion to stabilize, this cost of its abusing the privilege may well outweigh the benefit. Recent research (see, for example, Barro and Gordon, 1983; Backus and Driffill, 1984; and Barro, 1986) has examined whether concern for reputation would be enough to limit or prevent the abuse of discretion; firm answers are not yet available because the nature of the political players, their lifespan (or that of their parties?) and their motivation are not easy to model convincingly. However, it seems likely that, though reputation has an important part to play, it is not enough to solve the problem.

The social welfare functions used for assessing optimal stabilization policy are simple (usually quadratic) functions of what policy-makers appear to worry about – i.e. output (unemployment) and inflation. Yet in a rational expectations world people with the same access to macro information as the government may be presumed to have reacted voluntarily and optimally to it, in the absence of micro distortion. If shocks occur, they *should* react; if oil prices change, for example, certain industries should contract, others should expand, and their respective pace of change may not exactly coincide so that a recession (or boom) occurs. This represents an optimal reaction. To smother it will lower welfare. This argument is put powerfully by Beenstock (1980) and by Sargent (1979, chapter 16). The key qualification to it is the presence of distortions, the most obvious of which are taxes and unemployment benefits that increase desired unemployment. With these, welfare will be raised by reducing unemployment down to and even below the 'natural' (i.e. equilibrium) rate, so justifying stabilization and, in principle at least, the use of unemployment down to and even below the 'natural' (i.e. equilibrium) rate, follow that stabilization is to be preferred to removing the distortions; this will only be so if there is some strong political objection to removal, otherwise on economic grounds removal is preferable.

The case for monetary stabilization policy has not been removed but it has been substantially weakened by rational expectations. The conditions for successful policy are difficult to achieve, and the onus of proof has been shifted onto those who wish to pursue it across all the hurdles we have identified.

CONCLUDING REMARKS

Rational expectations has changed fundamentally the way economists think about monetary policy. The channels through which it works, the constraints upon it, and its stabilization potential all look different in the light of it. But very few of our new perceptions are certain or likely to remain unchanged. Money and the institutions that accompany it – the nominal denomination of contracts and assets – are, if anything, more of a mystery than ever before; for now we find it hard to explain how rational people can bind themselves into arrangements where merely nominal shocks will change their intentions for relative prices and quantities bought and sold about which (to the exclusion of all else) they care. Until we can convincingly unravel some of that mystery, we will not be able to claim a firm foundation for a theory of monetary policy.

NOTES

1. This essay formed the basis of the President's Lecture which I gave to the 1986 Scottish Economic Society Conference. It appears, with minor differences, in the *Scottish Journal of Political Economy*, vol. 33, pp. 317–33, 1986; I am grateful to the Scottish Economic Society for their agreement to reproduce it here.
2. That there is *some* limit on the tax rate is surely non-controversial, because of the allocative effects of taxation. McCallum (1984) discusses the limits on bonds where there is no limit on taxable capacity (on the grounds that taxes are distortion-free so that people are unaffected by higher lump-sum taxes paying for higher transfers). It turns out in this case that real bonds (per capita) can grow as fast as the rate of household time preference; in other words, assuming that GNP growth equals the rate of population growth the debt to GNP ratio can in principle grow without limit. The relevance of this case, however, does not appear to be very great because taxes are not distortion-free.
3. We ignore information superiority on the part of government. In its presence, stabilization is obviously effective. However, it cannot dominate releasing the information, and it will – if the stabilization is not completely efficient – be inferior to releasing it.

REFERENCES

Backus, D. and Driffill, J. (1984) 'Rational expectations and policy credibility following a change in regime', *Review of Economic Studies*, vol. 52, pp. 211–22.

Barro, R.J. (1974) 'Are government bonds net wealth?', *Journal of Political Economy*', vol. 82, pp. 1095–1117.

Barro, R.J. (1976) 'Rational expectations and the role of monetary policy', *Journal of Monetary Economics*, vol. 2, pp. 1–33.

Barro, R.J. (1986) 'Reputation in a model of monetary policy with incomplete information', *Journal of Monetary Economics,* vol. 17, pp. 3–20.

Barro, R.J. and Gordon, D. (1983), 'Rules, discretion and reputation in a model of monetary policy', *Journal of Political Economy*, vol. 91, pp. 589–610.

Beenstock, M. (1980) *A Neoclassical Analysis of Macroeconomic Policy*, Cambridge: Cambridge University Press.

Begg, D.K.H. (1982) *The Rational Expectations Revolution in Macroeconomics –Theories and Evidence*, Oxford: Philip Allan.

Brunner, K., Cukierman, A. and Meltzer, A.H. (1980) 'Stagflation, persistent unemployment and the permanence of economic shocks', *Journal of Monetary Economics*, vol. 6, pp. 467–92.

Buiter, W.H. and Miller, M. (1983) 'Changing the rules: economic consequences of the Thatcher regime', *Brookings Papers on Economic Activity*, no. 2, pp.

305–80.
Darby, M.R. (1983) 'Some pleasant monetary arithmetic', *Federal Reserve Bank of Minneapolis Quarterly Review*, Spring, pp. 328–9.
Drazen, A. (1985) 'Tight money and inflation: further results', *Journal of Monetary Economy*, vol. 15, no. 1, pp. 113–20.
Fischer, S. (1977) 'Long term contracts, rational expectations and the optimum money supply rule', *Journal of Political Economy*, vol. 85, pp. 191–205.
Friedman, M. and Schwarz, A. (1963) *A Monetary History of the United States, 1867–1960*, Princeton, NJ: Princeton University Press.
Haque, B. (1984) 'Monetary policy and its effects on inflation', Centre for Economic Forecasting Discussion Paper no. 135, September, London Business School.
King, R. G. (1983) 'Interest rates, aggregate information and monetary policy', *Journal of Monetary Economics*, vol. 12, pp. 199–234.
Kydland, F.E. and Prescott, E.C. (1977) 'Rules rather than discretion: the inconsistency of optimal plans', *Journal of Political Economy*, vol. 85, pp. 473–91.
Liviatan, N. (1984) 'Tight money and inflation', *Journal of Monetary Economics*, vol. 13, no. 1, pp. 5–15.
Long, J.B. and Plosser, C.I. (1983), 'Real business cycles', *Journal of Political Economy*, vol. 91, pp. 39–69.
Lucas, R.E., Jr (1972) 'Expectations and the neutrality of money', *Journal of Economic Theory*, vol. 4, pp. 103–24.
Lucas, R.E., Jr (1973) 'Some international evidence on output–inflation trade-offs', *American Economic Review*, vol. 68, pp. 326–34.
Lucas, R.E., Jr (1976) 'Econometric policy evaluation: a critique', in K. Brunner and A.H. Meltzer (eds), *The Phillips Curve and Labour Markets*, Carnegie-Rochester Conference Series on Public Policy vol. 1, Supplement to the *Journal of Monetary Economics*.
Lucas, R.E., Jr and Sargent, T.J. (1978) 'After Keynesian macro-economics', in *After the Phillips Curve: Persistence of High Inflation and Higher Unemployment*, Federal Reserve Bank of Boston.
McCallum, B.T. (1984) 'Are bond-financed deficits inflationary? A Ricardian analysis', *Journal of Political Economy*, vol. 92, pp. 123–35.
Minford, A.P.L. and Peel, D.A. (1981) 'On the role of monetary stabilization policy under rational expectations', *Manchester School*, vol. 49, pp. 39–50.
Minford, A.P.L. and Peel, D.A. (1983a) *Rational Expectations and the New Macroeconomics*, Oxford, Martin Robertson.
Minford, A.P.L. and Peel, D.A. (1983b) 'Some implications of partial current information sets in macroeconomic models embodying rational expectations', *Manchester School*, vol. 51, 235–49.
Phelps, E.S. and Taylor, J.B. (1977) 'The stabilizing powers of monetary policy under rational expectations', *Journal of Political Economy*, vol. 85, pp. 163–90.
Poole, W. (1970) 'The optimal choice of monetary instrument in a simple stochastic macro model', *Quarterly Journal of Economics*, vol. 84, pp. 197–221.
Sargent, T.J. (1979) *Macroeconomic Theory*, New York, Academic Press.
Sargent, T.J. and Wallace, N. (1975) 'Rational expectations, the optimal monetary instrument and the optimal money supply rule', *Journal of Political Economy*, vol. 83, pp. 241–54.
Sargent, T.J. and Wallace, N. (1981) 'Some unpleasant monetary arithmetic', *Federal Reserve Bank of Minneapolis Quarterly Review*, vol. 5, Fall, pp. 1–17.

Sidrauski, M. (1967) 'Rational choice and patterns of growth in a monetary economy', *American Economic Review* (Papers and Proceedings), pp. 534–44.
Turnovsky, S.J. (1980) 'The choice of monetary instrument under alternative forms of price expectations', *Manchester School*, vol. 48, pp. 39–63.
Wallace, N. (1980) 'The overlapping generations model of fiat money', in J.H. Karenken and N. Wallace (eds), *Models of Monetary Economies*, Minneapolis, MN: Federal Reserve Bank of Minneapolis, pp. 49–82.
Weiss, L. (1980) 'The role for active monetary policy in a rational expectations model', *Journal of Political Economy*, vol. 88, pp. 221–33.

9 · MONETARY POLICY AND CREDIBILITY

Paul Levine

Notions of 'credibility' and 'reputation' which relate to private sector beliefs regarding future government policy, are now commonplace in the macroeconomic literature. At a more informal level, these ideas frequently enter into discussions of policy effectiveness, especially relating to the disinflationary fiscal and monetary stances pursued by OECD countries in the early 1980s. At the theoretical level there has been much recent progress in developing and clarifying the issues. This chapter presents a survey of this latter work (see also a survey by Persson, 1988, which emphasizes credibility in macroeconomic public finance; and by Levine and Holly, 1989, which focuses on credibility in dynamic models).

What might be called the credibility problem was first highlighted by Kydland and Prescott (1977). They examined models where private agents are forward-looking so that future government policies, if believed, can affect the present. The problem is that optimal policies formulated by minimizing some welfare loss function become, with the passage of time, sub-optimal. The term *time inconsistency* is used to describe this property.

If governments are able to make binding commitments to their *ex ante* optimal policy, time inconsistency would not be a serious problem. In the absence of some institutional arrangements which makes it a 'difficult and time-consuming process to change policy rules', in the words of Kydland and Prescott, an incentive to renege on the time inconsistent policy occurs. This creates the credibility problem – the private sector, with information on the government's optimization problem, can anticipate future reneging so that time-inconsistent policies lack credibility. The only credible policies, or so it would appear, are those which are time consistent. These, unfortunately, can be severely sub-optimal.

The main question posed by the literature is whether the *ex ante* optimal or 'ideal' policy can be made self-enforcing and therefore be sustained in the absence of binding commitments.

The research for this chapter was carried out under ESSRC Grant No. B01250012.

The answer to the question depends on the information the private sector is assumed to have. After summarizing the 'Kydland–Prescott critique' in the next section, the third section of this chapter shows how the problem can be analysed in terms of a complete-information game between the policy-maker and the private sector. By complete information we mean that the private sector knows both the true structure of the model (i.e. can form 'rational' or 'model-consistent' expectations) and the policy-maker's welfare loss function.

In the Barro and Gordon (1983b) policy game with complete information, it is shown that the policy-maker's concern for his/her reputation for precommitment can, in some circumstances, sustain the *ex ante* optimal policy or, at least, policies far superior to those which are time consistent. The fourth section of this chapter discusses some limitations of this analysis. These are: the unravelling problem if the game has a finite time horizon; the multiple equilibria associated with the *ad hoc* character of the private sector's expectations mechanism; the model-specificity of the analysis; and the extreme and unsatisfactory nature of the complete-information assumption.

The fifth section turns to the literature which examines credibility assuming less than full information. Backus and Driffill (1985a; 1985b), Barro (1986) and Vickers (1986) solve finite-time-horizon games using the sequential equilibrium concept due to Kreps and Wilson (1982). The main result which emerges is that uncertainty on the part of the private sector regarding the 'type' of government can be sufficient to sustain the *ex ante* optimal policy for much of the finite time for which the game is played.

In Canzoneri (1985) we return to the Barro–Gordon game and introduce imperfect monitoring of government policy. In his model a stochastic disturbance, for which the policy-maker has a private information, enters the growth rate of the money supply. It is shown that again the *ex ante* optimal policy (zero inflation) can be sustained for most of the time but there will be periodic inflationary episodes.

Finally, Cukierman and Meltzer (1986) combines elements of the previous four studies. Of all the papers, this one allows for the most substantial departure from complete information. It also examines the case where the policy-maker can control the random disturbance entering the instrument. The conclusion is that a low inflation rate, less than the time consistent rate, can be sustained and that it may be in the government's interest to confuse the private sector with loose control of monetary policy.

The chapter concludes with an outline of some areas for future research.

THE KYDLAND–PRESCOTT CRITIQUE

Kydland and Prescott (1977) illustrate the time inconsistency phenomenon and the associated problem of credibility in a simple two-period example. The aim of the policy-maker at time $t=1$ is to minimize some general preference function $W(x_1, x_2, y_1, y_2)$, where x_1, x_2 are policies at $t = 1, 2$ and the model is given by

$$y_1 = f_1(x_1, x^e_{2,1}) \tag{9.1}$$

$$y_2 = f_2(y_1, x_1, x_2) \tag{9.2}$$

with $x^e_{2,1}$ denoting rational expectations of x_2 formed at time $t=1$. In this deterministic model, rational expectations reduces to perfect foresight and $x^e_{2,1} = x_2$. If we assume differentiability and an interior solution, the first-order conditions for the optimality of W are

$$\frac{\partial W}{\partial x_1} + \frac{\partial f_1}{\partial x_1}\left[\frac{\partial W}{\partial y_1} + \frac{\partial W}{\partial y_2} \cdot \frac{\partial f_2}{\partial y_1}\right] + \frac{\partial f_2}{\partial x_1} \cdot \frac{\partial W}{\partial y_2} = 0 \tag{9.3}$$

$$\frac{\partial W}{\partial x_2} + \frac{\partial f_1}{\partial x_2}\left[\frac{\partial W}{\partial y_1} + \frac{\partial W}{\partial y_2} \cdot \frac{\partial f_2}{\partial y_1}\right] + \frac{\partial f_2}{\partial x_2} \cdot \frac{\partial W}{\partial y_2} = 0 \tag{9.4}$$

Solving the four equations (9.1)–(9.4) in x_1, x_2, y_1, y_2 gives the *ex ante optimal* policy.

By contrast, the solution provided by dynamic programming begins in period 2 and proceeds by evaluating x_2 first, given x_1 and y_1 and the constraint (9.2). The first-order condition for x_2 is then

$$\frac{\partial W}{\partial x_2} + \frac{\partial f_2}{\partial x_2} \cdot \frac{\partial W}{\partial y_2} = 0 \tag{9.5}$$

which gives y_2 and x_2 as functions of y_1 and x_1. Comparing (9.4) and (9.5), the dynamic programming algorithm, using backwards recursion, will not correspond to the global optimum unless $\partial f_1 / \partial x_2 = 0$, that is if the model is causal, or unless the direct and indirect effects of y_1 and y_2 on W are exactly offsetting, that is, unless the term in the square brackets of Equation (9.4) is zero.

Kydland and Prescott refer to the policy sequence $\{x_1, x_2\}$ provided by dynamic programming as consistent, a term changed by subsequent literature to *time consistent*.

Definition. A policy sequence $\{x_1, x_2, \ldots, x_T\}$ is time consistent if, for each time period τ, x_τ maximizes $W(y_1, y_2, \ldots, y_T, x_1, x_2, \ldots, x_T)$, taking as given previous decisions, $x_1, \ldots, x_{\tau-1}$, and that future policy decisions, $(x_s, s > \tau)$ are similarly selected.

Clearly, the dynamic programming method does not provide an optimal policy sequence, unless there are no forward-looking expectations, since it cannot satisfy the first-order conditions for the maximization of W.

The possibility of time inconsistency of the *ex ante* optimal policy emerges when we examine policy from the vantage point of a subsequent period. It is found that it is no longer optimal to continue with the *ex ante* optimal policy. In the two-period example, if policy is re-examined, *ex post*, taking x_1 and y_1 as bygones, the first-order condition for maximising W is now given by Equation (9.5). This is the period-by-period optimal decision which involves cheating on the first policy announcement.

On the face of it, then, we have three different policies which have the welfare ranking:

		ex-ante		time
cheating		optimal		consistent
policy	$\succ$	policy	$\succ$	policy

But it is important to observe that the cheating policy is only a feasible option if it is actually believed in the first period that the *ex ante* optimal policy will be implemented in subsequent periods. The scope for achieving a lower cost by reneging in subsequent periods is critically dependent upon this belief.

The main conclusion of the Kydland and Prescott paper is that optimal control is an inappropriate tool for economic planning even when there is a well-defined and agreed-upon fixed social objective function. They advocate instead alternative *fixed*, *simple* policy rules so that it is obvious when a policy-maker deviates from the policy. These should not be chosen optimally but chosen to have 'good operating characteristics'. Finally there should be institutional arrangements which force precommitment on policy-makers and their successors.

An alternative approach to the credibility problem is offered by Barro and Gordon (1983b), who examine whether *reputational considerations* can restore the credibility to policy-makers to pursue seemingly time-inconsistent policies. This is the theme of the next section.

THE BARRO–GORDON POLICY GAME

The model

The model employed by Barro and Gordon (1983b) is the supply curve due to Lucas (1973). This may be derived from the following simple supply-side model.

$$w_t - p_t = \beta l_t^d + u_t \tag{9.6}$$

$$l_t^s = \gamma(w_t - p_t) \tag{9.7}$$

$$l_t = \min(l_t^d, l_t^s) \tag{9.8}$$

$$y_t = \delta l_t \tag{9.9}$$

where w_t is the nominal wage rate; p_t is the prive level; l_t^d is the demand for labour; l_t^s is the supply for labour; l_t is employment; y_t is output; and u_t is a stochastic supply disturbance with zero mean. β, γ and δ are constant parameters. All variables are in logarithms and measured as deviations about the deterministic equilibrium. Thus output and employment are measured as deviations about their natural rates. All parameters are positive.

Equations (9.6) and (9.7) are standard demand and supply curves for labour. According to Equation (9.8), out of equilibrium l_t is given by l_t^d if supply exceeds demand and by l_t^s if demand exceeds supply. In fact we lose nothing by simplifying Equation (9.8) to

$$l_t = l_t^d \tag{9.8a}$$

Finally, Equation (9.9) is a production function.

For labour market equilibrium, $l_t^s = l_t^d$, the money wage is given by

$$w_t = p_t + \frac{u_t}{1 + \beta\gamma} \tag{9.10}$$

We now come to the crucial feature of the model. We assume that the money wage for period t has to be predetermined in period t–1 in a non-contingent manner. In other words, the wage contract is not made contingent on the information that will become available over the period of the contract but must depend only on information available during the previous period. It is further assumed that w_t is chosen in such a way that the expected excess supply in the labour market is zero. Thus, taking expectations of Equation (9.10) at time t–1, w_t becomes

$$w_t = p_{t,t-1}^e \tag{9.11}$$

where $p_{t,t-1}^e$ denotes expectations of p_t formed in period t–1. We assume throughout that the information set in period t includes all current and past observations of endogenous variables, the policy instrument (to be discussed), the disturbances and the true structure of the model.

Thus from Equations (9.6), (9.9), (9.8a) and (9.11) we arrive at the familiar Lucas supply curve

$$y_t = \delta\beta^{-1}(p_t - p^e_{t,t-1} + u_t) \tag{9.12}$$

Barro and Gordon write Equation (9.12) in terms of inflation $\pi_t = p_t - p_{t-1}$, i.e.

$$y_t = \delta\beta^{-1}(\pi_t - \pi^e_{t,t-1} + u_t) \tag{9.13}$$

Monetary policy as a game

We now introduce the game-theoretic ideas which are used throughout the rest of the chapter. The game we describe has five elements. The first element consists of the *players*. There are two players in this game, the policy-maker and the private sector. The latter may be regarded as a unified large player such as a trade union federation or as many atomized but identical individuals. We shall return to this distinction on page 266.

The second element of the game consists of the *moves*. For the policy-maker the moves are adjustments to policy instruments. Monetary policy instruments are normally taken to be the money stock or short-term interest rates. If we were to complete the model with a very crude demand side based on the quantity demand for money then the growth of the money supply would be equal to inflation. Thus inflation may be regarded as the policy instrument. Alternatively, aggregate demand equated to aggregate supply may be taken as the instrument which in turn can be fixed at its desirable level by monetary instruments as before and/or fiscal instruments (taxes and government spending). In terms of the model above this amounts to treating output, y_t, as the instrument.

Turning to the moves of the private sector, in the wage-contracting model above these consist of wage contracts, w_t, formed at time t–1 according to Equation (9.11). The wage-setters move is essentially their prediction of the price level, $p^e_{t,t-1}$, which, given p_{t-1} at time t–1, is equivalent to predicting inflation $\pi_t = p_t - p_{t-1}$.

To summarize, then, the moves of the policy-maker are the inflation rates, π_t, in each period t and those of the private sector are predictions of inflation, $\pi^e_{t,t-1}$, formed in period t–1.

The *welfare criteria* are the third element of the game. For the policy-maker or government Barro and Gordon assume a single-period welfare-loss function of the general form

$$z^g_t = f(\pi_t, y_t) \qquad f_1 > 0, f_2 < 0 \tag{9.14}$$

Thus low inflation and high output are preferred. Barro and Gordon (1983a) discuss in some detail the benefits resulting from $\pi_t > \pi^e_t$ ('surprise inflation') which leads to output above its natural rate ($y_t = 0$). These can occur, for example, if distortions from income taxation, unemployment benefits, etc., reduce the privately chosen supply of labour.

In the Barro and Gordon model the specific form of z_t adopted is

$$z_t^g = (a/2)\pi_t^2 - by_t \qquad a, b > 0 \tag{9.15}$$

Without loss of generality, we may take $a = 1$. The term in output is linear, but as an alternative a quadratic term in output may be chosen of the form

$$z_t^g = \tfrac{1}{2}[\pi_t^2 + b(y_t - \hat{y})^2] \tag{9.16}$$

where $\hat{y}$ is a 'bliss point' for output.

The policy-maker's *intertemporal* optimization problem at time t is to choose a sequence of inflation rates π_t, π_{t+1}, $\pi_{t+2}, \ldots$, writen $\{\pi_t\}$, to minimize the present value of the welfare loss given by

$$W_t = z_t^g + \lambda z_{t+1}^g + \lambda^2 z_{t+2}^g + \ldots \sum_{i=0}^{\infty} \lambda^i z_{t+i}^g \tag{9.17}$$

where $\lambda \epsilon (0,1)$ is a discount factor (i.e. $\lambda = 1/(1+r)$ where r is a discount rate).

The private sector's welfare criteria are more straightforward. Their utility functions lead a rather subterranean existence in this game, lying behind the demand and supply for labour decisions captured by Equations (9.6) and (9.7). These do not need to be made explicit in the Barro–Gordon game. It is sufficient to write the private sector's single-period welfare loss as

$$z_t^p = (\pi_t - \pi_t^e)^2 \tag{9.18}$$

which formalizes the idea that the private sector resists being fooled and aims to forecast accurately.

The fourth element of the game is the *model.* This is given by the Lucas supply curve (Equation (9.13)) and constitutes a constraint for the players' optimization problems.

The final aspect to be considered is the *information set* for both sets of players. As we have mentioned before, we assume that the information available in period t includes all current and past observations of endogenous variables, the moves of the players, the disturbance and the true structure of the model. In the *complete-information* rational expectations case we must add to this information both players' knowledge of the full details of the other player's optimizing calculations, i.e. knowledge of their welfare loss functions. Towards the end of the chapter we shall relax this latter assumption.

The single-shot game

The repeated Barro–Gordon game consists of an infinite number of repetitions of the single-shot game where the policy-maker minimizes z_t^g and the private sector minimizes z_t^p. We shall consider the single-shot game first.

Consider the deterministic version of Equation (9.13) with $u_t = 0$ and, for convenience,

$$y_t = \pi_t - \pi_t^e \tag{9.19}$$

where $\pi_{t,t-1}^e$ is abbreviated to π_t^e. Substituting Equation (9.19) into the first of our welfare loss function for the policy-maker (Equation (9.15)) and with $a = 1$, we have

$$z_t^g = \tfrac{1}{2}\,\pi_t^2 - b(\pi_t - \pi_t^e) \tag{9.20}$$

Suppose the policy-maker minimizes z_t^g given that the private sector forecasts accurately ($\pi_t^e = 0$). Then clearly the optimal policy is zero inflation, $\pi_t = 0$, with $z_t^g = z_t^p = 0$. The alternative policy is to attempt to fool the private sector and to minimize z_t^g for a given expected inflation rate, π_t^e. Then the first-order condition is

$$\partial z_t^g / \partial \pi_t = \pi_t - b = 0$$

which gives $\pi_t = b$. These are, then, two possible moves for the policy-maker: zero inflation and $\pi_t = b$. Consider, next, the private sector choice between $\pi_t^e = 0$ and $\pi_t^e = b$.

If the private sector plays $\pi_t^e = 0$ (i.e. believes in zero inflation) and the policy-maker plays $\pi_t = b$ then z_t^g is lowered to $-\tfrac{1}{2}b^2$, but z_t^p is raised to b^2. If $\pi_t = b$ is anticipated by the private sector, however ($\pi_t^e = \pi_t = b$), then z_t^g becomes $\tfrac{1}{2}b^2$ and z_t^p returns to zero.

Table 9.1 shows the payoff matrix or game in *normal form*. There are two moves for each player and four possible combinations of moves. For completeness the possibility that $\pi_t^e = b$ but $\pi_t = 0$ is included, though this is

Table 9.1 The Barro–Gordon single-shot game in normal form; entries are (z_t^g, z_t^p)

Policy-maker	Private sector $\pi_t^e = 0$	$\pi_t^e = b$
$\pi_t = 0$	(0, 0)	(b^2, b^2)
$\pi_t = b$	($-\tfrac{1}{2}b^2$, b^2)	($\tfrac{1}{2}b^2$, 0)

not an interesting outcome in the subsequent analysis. The entries in the matrix are (z_t^g, z_t^p) for each combination of moves.

Given the payoff matrix of Table 9.1 what is the outcome of the full-information game? Suppose first moves π_t and π_t^e are chosen independently in a *non-cooperative* game. Comparing the two rows of the matrix one can see that whatever the choice of π_t^e, $\pi_t = b$ is the best for the policy-maker. The strategy 'play $\pi_t = b$ whatever the move π_t^e' is said to be a *dominant* strategy. Given $\pi_t = b$ is dominant for the policy-maker, the best move for the private sector is $\pi_t^e = b$. The non-cooperative outcome for this full-information game is then $\pi_t = \pi_t^e = b$ with payoffs $(\frac{1}{2}b^2, 0)$. This is a *Nash equilibrium*, i.e. each player is acting in an optimal way given the move of the other player.

Suppose now the two players can *co-operate* and choose π_t and π_t^e jointly. This amounts to the policy-maker being able to precommit himself/herself in period $t-1$,when π_t^e is formed, to a policy in the subsequent period. Clearly the outcome is now $\pi_t = \pi_t^e = 0$ with payoffs (0, 0) which is Pareto-superior to the Nash equilibrium. The question now is how the cooperative outcome can be reached given that the policy-maker has an incentive to renege on his/her precommitment (or promise) once $\pi_t^e = 0$. To answer this question we must turn to the repeated version of this game.

The repeated game

For the repeated game the players must now solve an intertemporal optimization problem. At each point in time t the policy-maker must choose $\{\pi_t\}$ to minimize W_t given by Equation (9.17). Similarly the private sector chooses $\{\pi_t^e\}$.

Suppose the players were to co-operate at time $t-1$. Given the absence of structural dynamics in the model, the intertemporal problem is simply a repetition of the single-period problem. Thus $\{\pi_t\} = \{\pi_t^e\} = \{0\}$ is the solution. This constitutes the optimal form of precommitment by the government in period $t-1$. Barro and Gordon refer to this outcome as the *ideal policy*. However, in period t, π_t^e is a bygone and the new optimal precommitment solution is $\{\pi_t\}=\{b, 0, 0, \ldots\}$. Thus the ideal policy is *time inconsistent* in the Kydland–Prescott sense.

By contrast, the non-cooperative solution, $\{\pi_t\} = \{\pi_t^e\} = \{b\}$ is *time consistent*. Given $\pi_t^e = b$ in each period there is no incentive for the government to renege on $\pi_t = b$. Barro and Gordon refer to this policy as *discretionary*, since it follows from period-by-period reoptimization.

The problem, then, with the ideal policy is the problem of time inconsistency alluded to by Kydland and Prescott. Zero inflation is the optimal precommitment policy for the future. When the first period arrives, however, it is optimal to renege for one period but to continue to promise zero inflation in the future. Since the private sector has full information it can anticipate this so that zero inflation lacks credibility in the first place. The only credible policy (so it seems) is the time consistent choice $\{\pi_t\}=\{b\}$.

To show how the ideal zero inflation policy can be made credible, an additional feature needs to be introduced into the model. Barro and Gordon postulate a response by the private sector to reneging by the policy-maker which takes the form

$$\begin{aligned} &\text{If } \pi_t=\pi_{t-1}= \ldots 0 && \text{then } \pi^e_{t+i,t}=0;\ i=1,2,\ldots \\ &\text{If } \pi_{t-1}=\pi_{t-2}=\ldots 0 \text{ (but } \pi_t>0), && \text{then } \pi^e_{t+i,t}=b;\ i=1,2,\ldots,P \\ & && \qquad\quad =0;\ i=P+1,\ P+2,\ldots \end{aligned} \tag{9.21}$$

Statement (9.21) can be viewed as a 'threat' or 'punishment' by the private sector. It says that the private sector believes in zero inflation from the time $t+1$ onwards if no reneging has occurred up to time t. Once reneging does occur it believes in the time-consistent policy $\pi_t=b$ for a punishment interval of P periods after which it believes zero inflation will continue indefinitely. A discussion of this expectations mechanism is given on page 265, but for now we accept it uncritically.

Given that statement (9.21) is in place, what, then, is the outcome of the game? Barro and Gordon provide an analysis for $P=1$ which is now generalized to any P. Suppose the ideal policy zero inflation is believed by the private sector. From Table 9.1 given $\pi^e_t=0$, there exists an incentive to renege on $\pi_t=0$ and to play $\pi_t=b$ with a welfare gain of $\frac{1}{2}b^2$. Barro and Gordon call this welfare gain *temptation*.

The policy-maker only enjoys the gains from reneging for one period. From Equation (9.21), having observed $\pi_t>0$, future expectations of inflation are raised to $\pi^e_t=b$ for P periods. Given π^e_t, it is then optimal for the policy-maker to continue to play $\pi_t=b$ for the punishment interval but then to revert to the ideal policy. Compared with zero inflation there is then a deterioration in welfare, which Barro and Gordon term *enforcement*, given by $\frac{1}{2}b^2$ per period or

$$\tfrac{1}{2}b^2(\lambda+\lambda^2+\ldots+\lambda^P)=\frac{b^2\lambda(1-\lambda^P)}{2(1-\lambda)} \tag{9.22}$$

over the P periods.

If enforcement exceeds temptation the punishment mechanism is sufficient to deter the policy-maker from reneging. Since the private sector has full information (including now knowledge of its own punishment mechanism) it can anticipate this and zero inflation is then a credible policy. A sufficient condition for the credibility of zero inflation is then that enforcement, given by Equation (9.22), exceeds temptation, which is $\frac{1}{2}b^2$.

This becomes

$$\frac{\lambda(1-\lambda^P)}{1-\lambda} > 1 \tag{9.23}$$

Thus for $P=1$ (a single-period punishment interval) Equation (9.23) gives $\lambda > 1$, which never holds. At the other extreme, with $P=\infty$ (an infinite punishment period or 'capital punishment' in the words of Barro and Gordon), Equation (9.23) gives $\lambda > 0.5$. If we take the interval of time to be one year this does not seem a strong condition.

For any P the question arises as to what is the *best* enforceable rule, i.e. the one that minimizes expected costs subject to the constraint that enforcement be at least as great as temptation. Following the reasoning above for a general rule $\pi_t = \pi$ we have

$$\text{temptation} = \tfrac{1}{2}(b-\pi)^2 \tag{9.24}$$

$$\text{enforcement} = \tfrac{1}{2}(b^2-\pi^2)\frac{\lambda(1-\lambda^P)}{1-\lambda} \tag{9.25}$$

Thus the credibility condition becomes

$$(b^2-\pi^2)\frac{\lambda(1-\lambda^P)}{1-\lambda} > (b-\pi)^2 \tag{9.26}$$

Ruling out the worst enforceable rule, $\pi = b$, some algebraic manipulation yields

$$\pi > b\left[\frac{1-2\lambda+\lambda^{P+1}}{1-\lambda^{P+1}}\right] \tag{9.27}$$

so the best inflation rule is given by the right-hand side of Equation (9.27). For $P=1$ (the Barro–Gordon case) this gives $\pi = b(1-\lambda)/(1+\lambda) < b$. For $P=\infty$ we have a best rule $\pi = b(1-2\lambda)$ for $\lambda < 0.5$; while for $\lambda > 0.5$, $\pi = 0$ is enforceable (as we have seen).

To summarize, the question posed by Kydland and Prescott on how (in the absence of institutional arrangements) the ideal policy can be reached has been answered by Barro and Gordon. The ideal policy can be sustained by reputational forces provided Equation (9.23) is satisfied, i.e. provided P is large enough and λ sufficiently close to unity. Failing this an outcome superior to the time-consistent inflation rate given by the right-hand side of Equation (9.27) can be enforced. This will be close to zero if b is low (i.e. a high weight is given to inflation in Equation (9.15)), the rate of interest is low (λ close to unity) and the punishment interval, P, is large.

The Barro and Gordon type of repeated game is discussed in Friedman (1977) in the context of games between oligopolies. In what he calls a 'supergame', Friedman postulates a similar mechanism to Equation (9.21) which enables two duopolists to sustain collusion. After arriving at some collusive agreement the 'threat strategy' consists of a permanent switch (i.e. P infinite) to the non-cooperative Cournot–Nash equilibrium in the event of the other party deviating from the agreement. The temptation to renege exists because the threat (as in Equation (9.21)) is not instantaneous but allows a benefit for one period. This benefit must be weighed against the costs of arriving at the Cournot–Nash equilibrium. In the 'balanced temptation theorem' it is shown that collusion can be self-enforcing if the discount factor (λ in Barro and Gordon) is close enough to unity. The balanced temptation theorem is a special case of the general folk theorem for supergames that for a sufficiently low rate of interest (i.e. a discount factor sufficiently close to unity) any outcome Pareto-superior to the Nash equilibrium can be maintained as a non-cooperative or self-enforcing equilibrium (see, for example, Fundenberg and Maskin, 1986).

A stochastic supply disturbance

We conclude this section by briefly considering the case of a stochastic supply disturbance in the Lucas supply curve (Equation (9.13)). The intertemporal optimization problem at time t is now to minimize the expected welfare loss from time t onwards, $E_t\,(W_t)$.

The form of the solution is now $\{\pi_t\}$ where

$$\pi_{t+i} = E_t\,(\pi_{t+i}) + \beta u_{t+i} \tag{9.28}$$

i.e. π_{t+i} consists of a deterministic component plus a stochastic disturbance-contingent component.

The deterministic components for the ideal and time-consistent policies are $E_t(\pi_{t+i}) = 0$ and $E_t(\pi_{t+i}) = b$, respectively. We now consider the stochastic feedback term.

For the ideal policy, substituting $\pi_{t+i} = \beta u_{t+i}$ into z_{t+i} given by Equation (9.15) we have, using Equation (9.13),

$$E_t(z_{t+i}) = E_t\left[\tfrac{1}{2}\beta^2 u_{t+i}^2 - b(\beta u_{t+i} + u_{t+i})\right] = \tfrac{1}{2}\,\beta^2\sigma_u^2 \tag{9.29}$$

where u_{t+i} is assumed to be a white noise disturbance with zero mean and variance σ_u^2. It is now evident that $E_t(z_{t+i})$ and hence $E_t(W_t)$ is minimized at $\beta = 0$. In other words, the ideal policy in the stochastic model is zero inflation with no feedback control.

This result seems to confirm policy prescriptions in the form of open-loop or fixed rules as opposed to feedback or state contingent rules. However, the conclusion is sensitive to the choice of welfare loss function.

If the alternative loss function (Equation (9.16)) is adopted then Equation (9.29) is replaced with

$$E_t(z_{t+i}) = \tfrac{1}{2} E_t\left[\beta^2 u_{t+i}^2 + b(\beta u_{t+i} + u_{t+i} - \hat{y})^2\right]$$

$$= \tfrac{1}{2}\left[\beta^2 \sigma_u^2 + b((\beta+1)^2 \sigma_u^2 + \hat{y}^2)\right] \tag{9.30}$$

Then the first-order condition for a minimum is

$$\frac{\partial E_t(z_{t+i})}{\partial \beta} = (\beta+1)b + \beta = 0 \tag{9.31}$$

Hence $\beta = -b/(1+b)$ and the ideal policy becomes

$$\pi_t = -bu_t/(1+b) \tag{9.32}$$

There is now a role for a stabilization policy in the form of a feedback rule which responds to a positive (negative) supply shock by decreasing (increasing) inflation.

Similar results apply for the time consistent policy. For the Barro–Gordon welfare loss function, $\pi_t = b$ with no feedback component. For the alternative loss function Equation (9.32) becomes

$$\pi_t = b - bu_t/(1+b) \tag{9.33}$$

Thus the feedback component in the ideal and time consistent policies is the same. The importance of the result is that no stochastic elements enter into the sustainability condition since temptation is still $-\tfrac{1}{2}b^2$ and enforcement remains as given by Equation (9.22).

LIMITATIONS OF THE BARRO–GORDON ANALYSIS

In the Barro and Gordon complete-information, infinite-time-horizon game the policy-maker's concern for his/her reputation can sustain the ideal rule provided that two conditions hold: first, in the event of reneging the private sector ceases to believe in the precommitment policy for sufficiently long; and second, the policy-maker is sufficiently farsighted (i.e. the discount factor is close enough to unity). If a combination of a short punishment period and a low discount factor makes reneging beneficial to the policy-maker then all is not lost. In this case there exists a superior credible policy to the time-consistent policy but which is inferior to the ideal policy.

We now turn to the limitations of this framework for analysing credibility. We consider in turn the unravelling problem for the finite-time-horizon game, the multiple equilibria associated with the choice of punishment period, the model specificity of the analysis and, finally, the extreme character of the complete-information assumption.

The Barro–Gordon game with a finite time horizon

The Barro–Gordon result on the credibility of the ideal policy applies only to an infinite time horizon. This can be seen as follows: suppose that the game terminates at some date $t = T$. At the terminal date there are no reputational reasons for the government not to renege on its zero-inflation precommitment so zero inflation lacks credibility. However, under full information the private sector can foresee this so that the optimal policy at $t = T$ turns out to be the non-cooperative Nash outcome, $\pi = b$.

Zero inflation now lacks credibility in the penultimate period T–1 and the same non-zero inflation rate must apply then. The solution then unravels back to $t = 0$, giving the optimal solution as the time-consistent policy $\pi_t = b$, $t = 0, 1, 2, \dots, T$. Hahn (1982) uses a similar argument to show that in a rational expectations full-information world, money cannot exist in an economy of finite duration. If there is a last date no agent will wish to hold paper money at that time. It follows that rational agents will refuse to hold money in the instant preceding the final date. Proceeding in this way, money must be worthless at every date.

To resolve the unravelling problem, Barro and Gordon conclude their paper by suggesting that uncertainty regarding the policy-maker's preferences be introduced into the model. The seminal works of Kreps and Wilson (1982) and Milgram and Roberts (1982) set out to show that reputational effects due to such informational asymmetries can generate co-operative behaviour in supergames even with a finite time horizon. A useful informal treatment is given in Kreps *et al.* (1982). We return to these ideas on page 268.

Multiple equilibria

The punishment mechanism (Equation (9.21)) has two aspects: the switch of expectations from zero inflation to the time consistent inflation rate $\pi_t = b$ and the length of the punishment period. As we have seen, the outcome $\pi_t = \pi_t^e = b$ is a non-cooperative Nash equilibrium for the game. The switch to $\pi_t^e = b$ is in itself rational given that cooperation in the form of $\pi_t = \pi_t^e = 0$ has broken down. (This is analogous to the switch to a Cournot–Nash equilibrium in the duopoly game of Friedman referred to in the previous section.) However, the choice of punishment interval P is entirely *ad hoc*. In fact Barro and Gordon assume for the most part that $P = 1$, whereas Friedman assumes $P = \infty$.

In games with 'large' players one might choose a minimal value for P which is sufficient to enforce co-operation. Players may then choose their punishment as a 'threat' or 'trigger' strategy with the conscious intention of achieving an efficient outcome to the game.

However, if one assumes that the private sector is atomized it makes no sense to talk about strategies. A small player cannot influence the macro-environment by his/her actions. For an atomized private sector the punishment mechanism is an *assumption* which can only be justified as a plausible response which is observed in the real world.

Model specificity

The Barro–Gordon model (Equation (9.13)) is essentially static. For application to macromodels with sluggish adjustment of wages and prices, capital accumulation, and so on, it is necessary to generalize the analysis. For example, consider the structurally dynamic model (taken from Buiter and Miller, 1983)

$$\pi_t = \psi y_t + c_t \tag{9.34}$$

$$c_t = (1 - \mu)(q_{t-1} + \mu q_{t-2} + \mu^2 q_{t-3} + \ldots) \tag{9.35}$$

$$q_t = (1 - \mu)(\pi^e_{t+1,t} + \mu \pi^e_{t+2,t} + \mu^2 \pi^e_{t+3,t} + \ldots) \tag{9.36}$$

where c_t is core inflation; q_t is contract inflation; and the remaining notation is as before.

Equation (9.34) replaces the Lucas supply curve (Equation (9.13)) and is a core inflation Phillips curve. According to Equation (9.35), core inflation is a backward-looking, geometrically declining average of past contract inflation. Equation (9.36) gives contract inflation as a forward-looking geometrically declining average of future expected inflation.

The mean lag in Equation (9.35) is given by $1/(1-\mu)$ which may be interpreted as the expected contract length. In the limit as μ tends to zero, the expected contract length tends to unity, the assumption lying behind Equation (9.11) for the Lucas supply curve. Then $c_t = q_{t-1} = \pi^e_{t,t-1}$ and Equation (9.34) becomes

$$\pi_t = \psi y_t + \pi^e_{t,t-1} \tag{9.37}$$

which is simply Equation (9.19), with $\psi = 1$. In general

$$\mu = 1 - 1/l \tag{9.38}$$

where l is the expected length of contracts. In the Barro and Gordon model $l = 1$, while Equations (9.34)–(9.36) may be considered as a generalization to $l \geq 1$.

The model above may be written in *state-space form* as follows (the less mathematical reader may wish to skip the remainder of this subsection). Let

$$\hat{q}_t = \pi_t + \mu\pi^e_{t+1,t} + \mu^2\pi^e_{t+2,t} + \dots \tag{9.39}$$

Then

$$\hat{q}^e_{t+1,t} = \pi^e_{t+1,t} + \mu\pi^e_{t+2,t} + \mu^2\pi^e_{t+3,t} + \dots \tag{9.40}$$

since $(\pi^e_{t+i+j,t+j})^e_t = \pi^e_{t+i+j,t}$ (see Begg, 1982, p. 72). Hence

$$\mu\hat{q}^e_{t+1,t} - \hat{q}_t = -\pi_t \tag{9.41}$$

It is straightforward to verify that Equation (9.35) may be written as

$$c_{t+1} = \mu c_t + (1-\mu)q_t \tag{9.42}$$

From Equations (9.36) and (9.40),

$$q_t = \mu^{-1}(1-\mu)(\hat{q}_t - \pi_t) \tag{9.43}$$

Equations (9.34) and (9.41)–(9.43) may be written in the form

$$\begin{bmatrix} c_t \\ \hat{q}^e_{t+1,t} \end{bmatrix} = \mathbf{A} \begin{bmatrix} c_t \\ \hat{q}_t \end{bmatrix} + \mathbf{B}y_t \tag{9.44}$$

$$\begin{bmatrix} \pi_t \\ q_t \end{bmatrix} = \mathbf{C} \begin{bmatrix} c_t \\ \hat{q}_t \end{bmatrix} + \mathbf{D}y_t \tag{9.45}$$

where $\begin{bmatrix} c_t \\ \hat{q}_t \end{bmatrix}$ is the state vector; $\begin{bmatrix} \pi_t \\ q_t \end{bmatrix}$ is the vector of outputs; y_t is exogenous; and **A**, **B**, **C**, **D** are fixed matrices. Equations (9.44) and (9.45) are the state-space form of the model.

Levine (1988) shows how the Barro and Gordon analysis may be extended to models of the form of Equations (9.44) and (9.45). In addition, a stochastic extension is considered with exogenous white noise disturbances added to Equation (9.44). Dynamic generalizations of the ideal but time inconsistent policy and the time consistent policies are provided and applied to the model above. The main difference is that the credibility condition corresponding to Equation (9.23) now becomes *time-varying* and must be examined numerically along all possible trajectories corresponding to each initial state and each stochastic realization.

The full-information assumption

Let us recall the meaning of full information. In games of this form the private sector, in forming its expectations, is assumed to know the model and the policy-maker's welfare criteria. More recent literature which relaxes the latter assumption in particular is reviewed in the next section. Some of these studies were motivated by a desire to solve the unravelling problem in finite-horizon games. But, more fundamentally, full information regarding policy-makers' objectives is regarded by many economists as an implausible description of the real world and one which ignores important aspects of the credibility problem.

CREDIBILITY IN GAMES WITH INCOMPLETE INFORMATION

This section reviews five studies which examine the credibility problem in the context of a game with incomplete information. In the first three papers a *finite time horizon* game is considered. The solution concept used to solve these three games is the *sequential equilibrium* due to Kreps and Wilson (1982). This requires of the equilibrium strategy pair that first, it is *subgame perfect*, i.e. the action taken by either player at any point in the game tree is part of a strategy which is optimal for the remainder of the game. Second, each player's beliefs must be consistent with *Bayesian updating* on the hypothesis that equilibrium strategies have been used to date.

Kreps and Wilson used examples from industrial economics. We now turn to the concept of a sequential equilibrium using the Barro and Gordon model, drawing upon Backus and Driffill (1985a; 1985b), Barro (1986) and Vickers (1986).

Backus and Driffill (1985a, b)

Consider the Barro–Gordon policy game with the policy-maker's single-period loss function given by Equation (9.15) and that of the private sector by Equation (9.18). Backus and Driffill suppose there are two types of government. Type 1 ('hard-nosed') attach a zero weight to output in Equation (9.15), $b = 0$, so that there is no incentive ever to deviate from zero inflation. Type 2 ('wet') have $b > 0$ as in the Barro–Gordon game with complete information. At the beginning of the game the private sector does not know whether the government is of type 1 or 2, but everything else is known, i.e. the model, the form of the loss function (9.15) and the value of b if the government turns out to be 'wet'.

Similarly (Backus and Driffill, 1985b), we can suppose there are two types of private sector. Type 1 ('weak') pays an additional fixed cost, c, say if it ever surrenders to zero inflation. This cost captures the idea of resistance to wage disinflation on the part of the private sector. It ensures that a strong private sector never moderates its expectations and always expects $\pi_t^e = b$.

The sequential equilibrium of the Barro–Gordon game is found as follows. Suppose that the government, of type 2, adopts a strategy $\pi_t = 0$ with probability p_t and $\pi_t = b$ with probability $1 - p_t$. The game is played over a finite time horizon $t = 1, 2, \ldots, T$. As we have seen in the discusssion of unravelling on page 265, $p_T = 0$, i.e. type 2 inflates (i.e. $\pi_e = b$) in the terminal period. The private sector does not know whether the government is of type 1 or 2, unless the government turns out to be of type 2 and reveals its identity by playing non-zero inflation. The *reputation* of the government is captured by the private sector's assigned probability α_t that it is of type 1 (committed to $\pi_t = 0$), with $1 - \alpha_t$ being the probability it is of type 2. Suppose that at any time prior to t the government has played non-zero inflation. Then it will have revealed itself as of type 2, since a type 1 government always plays zero inflation, and $\alpha_t = 0$ is thereafter assigned by the public. If, on the other hand, good behaviour (zero inflation) is observed up to time t, then by Bayes's Law, α_t is updated according to

$$\alpha t = \text{prob}(\text{type } 1 \mid \pi_{t-1} = \pi_{t-2} = \ldots = 0)$$

$$= \frac{\text{prob}(\pi_{t-1} = 0 \mid \text{type } 1)\ \text{prob}(\text{type } 1 \mid \pi_{t-2} = \pi_{t-3} = \ldots = 0)}{\text{prob}(\pi_{t-1} = 0 \mid \pi_{t-2} = \pi_{t-3} = \ldots 0)}$$

$$= \frac{\alpha_{t-1}}{\alpha_{t-1} + (1 - \alpha_{t-1})\, p_{t-1}^e} \qquad (9.46)$$

where p_t^e is the private sector's expectation of p_t. The government's reputation is then quantified by the probability α_t,which is a sufficient statistic for past play containing all the relevant information for the players to make optimal decisions.

Similarly, the private sector can adopt a strategy $\pi_t^e = 0$ with probability q_t, say, and $\pi_t^e = b$ with probability $1 - q_t$. The government does not know whether the private sector is weak or strong and must assign a probability β_t, say, which is the private sector's reputation. β_t is updated by Bayes's Law based on the government's expectation of q_t, q_t^e. In a sequential equilibrium $p_t^e = p_t$ and $q_t^e = q_t$.

In the work of Backus and Driffill both the private sector and government act strategically, each player choosing his/her own strategy given the other player's strategy. In Backus and Driffill (1985b) the game is symmetrical in that both players do not know the identity of the other; in

Backus and Driffill (1985a) there is only one type of private sector so that only the government enjoys reputation.

The games described in Backus and Driffill (1985a; 1985b) apply when both the government and private sector act strategically; for example, in a 'social contract' between the government and a trade-union federation. If the private sector is atomistic, however, these two-sided games seem inappropriate. This is the case considered by Barro (1986), to which we now turn.

Barro (1986)

If the private sector is atomistic then only the government chooses a *strategy* (to play $\pi_t = 0$ with probability p_t) and has a *reputation* (summarized by α_t, the private sector's assigned probability that it is of type 1). The private sector must then choose π_t^e. Following Barro we do not assume that π_t^e is a dichotomous variable taking values 0 or b (as do Backus and Driffill) but instead is formed according to

$$\pi_t^e = \alpha_t \cdot 0 + (1 - \alpha_t) \cdot [p_t^e \cdot 0 + (1 - p_t^e) b] = (1 - \alpha_t)(1 - p_t^e) b \tag{9.47}$$

Consider the decision facing a government of type 2. If at any time prior to t it has played non-zero inflation then $\alpha_t = 0$, $\pi_t^e = b$ and the best policy is to play $\pi_t = b$ with probability one from time t onwards. Suppose that $\pi_{t-1} = \pi_{t-2} = \ldots = 0$. Then the expected welfare loss at time t is given by

$$\begin{aligned} V_t = E_t[W_t(\alpha_t)] &= E_t(z_t^g) + E_t(\lambda z_{t+1}^g + \lambda^2 z_{t+2}^g + \ldots + \lambda^{T-t} z_T^g) \\ &= p_t z_t^g(0, \pi_t^e) + (1 - p_t) z_t^g(b, \pi_t^e) + p_t \lambda V_{t+1} + (1 - p_t)(\lambda + \lambda^2 + \ldots + \lambda^{T-t})(b^2/2) \end{aligned} \tag{9.48}$$

We now seek a sequential equilibrium strategy (p_t) for the government. This must be subgame perfect, which implies that V_t in Equation (9.48) must be minimized in the knowledge that a similar procedure will apply to V_{t+1} and so on to the terminal date when $p_t = 0$. In other words, the government must minimize V_t with respect to p_t, taking both V_{t+1} and its reputation, α_t, as given.

From Equation (9.48)

$$V_t = p_t \left(z_t^g(0, \pi_t^e) - z_t^g(b, \pi_t^e) + \lambda V_{t+1} - \frac{\lambda(1 - \lambda^{T-t})}{2(1 - \lambda)} b^2 \right) + z_t^g(b, \pi_t^e) + \frac{\lambda(1 - \lambda^{T-t}) b^2}{2(1 - \lambda)} \tag{9.49}$$

It follows that V_t is minimized at $p_t = 1$, or $0 < p_t < 1$, or $p_t = 0$ according to whether

$$z_t^g(0, \pi_t^e) - z_t^g(b, \pi_t^e) + \lambda V_{t+1} - \frac{\lambda(1-\lambda^{T-t})}{2(1-\lambda)} b^2 \lesseqgtr 0 \tag{9.50}$$

in which case we must have

$$V_t \lesseqgtr z_t^g(b, \pi_t^e) + \frac{\lambda(1-\lambda^{T-t})}{2(1-\lambda)} b^2 \tag{9.51}$$

Using Equation (9.51) to eliminate V_{t+1} in Equation (9.50) we have that $p_t = 1$, $0 < p_t < 1$ or $p_t = 0$ according to whether

$$z_t^g(0, \pi_t^e) - z_t^g(b, \pi_t^e) \lesseqgtr \lambda\,[(b^2/2) - z_{t+1}^g(b, \pi_{t+1}^e)] \tag{9.52}$$

The left-hand side of Equation (9.52) is the *temptation* to cheat in period t by playing $\pi_t = b$ rather than $\pi_t = 0$. The right-hand side is the discounted difference between the $t+1$ welfare loss if cheating is deferred for one period and that if it is not. This constitutes the *enforcement*. If the left-hand side turns out to be less than or equal to the right-hand side then the policy-maker will defer the decision to renege until the next period.

From Equation (9.20), $z_t^g(\pi, \pi_t^e) = \frac{1}{2}\pi_t^2 - b(\pi_t - \pi_t^e)$. Hence, substituting into Equation (9.52), $p_t = 1$, $0 < p_t < 1$ and $p_t = 0$ according to whether

$$\pi_{t+1}^e \lesseqgtr \frac{b(2\lambda - 1)}{2\lambda} \tag{9.53}$$

We shall seek a consistent sequential equilibrium with $p_t^e = p_t$. Then we must have $p_t > 0$ for all $t < T$ and $\lambda > \frac{1}{2}$. For suppose that $p_t = 0$ for some $t < T$. Then, from Equation (9.46), $\alpha_{t+1} = 1$ and, hence, from Equation (9.47), $\pi_{t+1}^e = 0$. But from Equation (9.53) $p_t = 0$ requires $\pi_{t+1}^e > 0$ if $\lambda > \frac{1}{2}$. Thus the assumption $p_t = 0$ for some $t < T$ leads to a contradiction.

We have shown that $p_{T-1} > 0$. It follows now that $p_T = 0$ is preceded by some period of *randomization* $\tau \leqslant t < T-1$, say, in which $0 < p_t < 1$. Then from Equations (9.47) and (9.53) we must have

$$(1-\alpha_t)(1-p_t) = (\lambda/2)(2\lambda - 1), \qquad \tau + 1 \leqslant t \leqslant T \tag{9.54}$$

Combining the Bayesian updating rule (Equation (9.36)) with $p_t^e = p_t$ with Equation (9.45) we now have two equations for α_t and p_t which solve to give

$$\alpha_t = (1/2\lambda)^{T+1-t}$$

$$p_t = [1/2\lambda - (1/2\lambda)^{T+1-t}]/[1 - (1/2\lambda)^{T+1-t}], \qquad \tau + 1 \leqslant t \leqslant T \tag{9.55}$$

To illustrate the solution numerically we take $T = 5$ years and $\lambda = 1/(1+r)$, where $r = 0.05$ (a 5 per cent annual discount rate). Furthermore, suppose that the government enters office at $t = 0$ with a

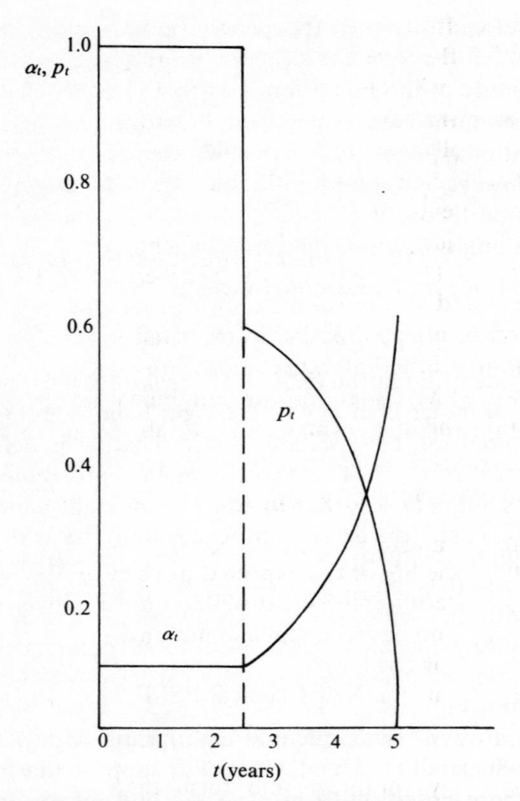

Figure 9.1 Strategy and reputation for type 2 government

reputation $\alpha_0 = 0.1$, the private sector's assigned probability that it is of type 1. Figure 9.1 shows the trajectories for α_t and p_t for a type 2 government.

Working backwards, the period of randomization occurs when α_t, given by Equation (9.55), exceeds $\alpha_0 = 0.1$. This happens at $t = 2.4$. During the time interval $0 \leqslant t \leqslant 2.4$, a type 2 government will play $\pi_t = 0$ with probability $p_t = 1$. During this interval reputation remains at its initial level $\alpha_t = 0.1$. Somewhere between the second and third year the credibility condition for $p_t = 1$ breaks down and a period of randomization begins, with p_t falling from about 0.5 to 0 at the terminal date. Provided $\pi_t = b$ is not chosen, reputation will then rise to its terminal level of around 0.5. During the pre-randomization interval expected inflation π_t^e is zero (from Equation (9.47)); but during the interval $t \epsilon [\tau + 1, T]\ 0 < \pi_t^e \leqslant b$. This applies whether the policy-maker turns out to be of type 1 or type 2 so that with a committed government, which always plays $\pi_t = 0$, the economy suffers from a period of surprisingly high inflation with output below its natural rate.

The main feature of the Barro model is that it shows that, even with a finite time horizon, the ideal policy (zero inflation) can be sustained for a while by reputational forces. This is true whether the government is of type 1 or type 2. However, in the former case the model also shows that the same reputational forces will increase the costs of disinflation by raising expectations of inflation above the actual rate.

Vickers (1985)

The main result arising from Backus and Driffill and Barro is that private sector uncertainty is sufficient to sustain the ideal policy for much of the game. Provided the initial reputation of the government is high enough, no constitutional arrangement is needed in order to achieve the socially efficient outcome except near the end of the game.

However, the results of these papers may be sensitive to some of the restrictive assumptions regarding the objectives of the government. Vickers (1986) generalizes the game by assuming that there are two types of governments with different, but non-zero, weights, b, in the welfare-loss function. This means that the type 1, 'hard-nosed' government with low b is no longer committed irrevocably to the ideal policy of no inflation.

In the terminology of Vickers (1985), assuming the hard-nosed government is always committed to zero inflation leads to a *pooling equilibrium* in which both types of government behave alike for a while. By contrast, if the hard-nosed government cares a little about output (b small, but positive) then Vickers shows that pooling equilibria in a wide class of situations can be ruled out. Instead there are *separating equilibria* in which the hard-nosed government reveals its preferences early during its period in office.

Vickers examines a two-period game with the result that the two types of player take different actions in the first period; but the type is completely revealed in the second period. In the first period the hard-nosed government chooses an inflation rate so low as to reveal its preferences and distance itself from any possible actions of a wet government. This finding contrasts sharply with the Backus and Driffill and Barro pooling equilibria and questions whether the sustainability result of these authors is sufficiently general.

Driffill (1987) shows that if the two possible types of government are sufficiently dissimilar (i.e. b is sufficiently different) then a pooling equilibrium is possible in which both types initially institute a zero inflation rate and the true type is only revealed in the second period of the game.

Driffill also extends the analysis to allow for many types of government with the weight b drawn from a bounded distribution. Again pooling equilibria are possible. Finally, in the spirit of Canzoneri (1985), discussed below, Driffill returns to the simple Backus–Driffill analysis and introduces exogenous noise into the model. The appearance of some inflation can now be construed as the result of some random occurrence with the government still attempting zero inflation. Under these circumstances the incentive for the uncommitted (type 2) government to play zero inflation for a period is considerably weakened.

In both the Vickers and Driffill papers only a two-period game is analysed. A generalization to n periods remains to be done. However, the tentative conclusion is that reputational forces remain effective in sustaining the ideal policy when the objectives of possible governments are generalized; but imperfect monitoring of government policy can weaken these forces considerably.

Canzoneri (1985)

A crucial assumption in the Barro and Gordon, Barro and Backus and Driffill models is that the private sector can observe when the policy-maker has reneged. Canzoneri (1985) analyzes what happens when this assumption is relaxed and the government has private information about money demand. The Barro–Gordon model with an infinite time horizon is now extended with a simple quantity equation for the demand for money

$$m_t - p_t = \bar{y} + u_t \tag{9.56}$$

where m_t and p_t and y are logarithms of the money supply, price level and output respectively, and u_t is a stochastic disturbance following a random walk. Output is approximated by its natural rate $\bar{y}$. First differencing Equation (9.56) we have

$$g_t = \pi_t + \delta_t \tag{9.57}$$

where $g_t = m_t - m_{t-1}$ is the growth rate of the money supply taken to be the government's instruments; and δ_t is a white noise disturbance.

At the end of period t, g_t and π_t are observed and hence δ_t can be calculated by both the government and the private sector. However, suppose the government has a forecast $E(\delta_t) = e_t$ at the beginning of the period and this is private information. The ideal rule in the Barro–Gordon game now becomes $g_t = e_t$. However, there is an incentive for the government to misrepresent its true forecast, e_t, and announce a higher forecast so that in fact it is pursuing a cheating, non-zero inflation policy masquerading as the ideal rule. The consequence of this is that the announced forecast and the rule lack credibility and precommitment would not be possible.

Canzoneri reformulated the Barro–Gordon game to handle private information by modifying the private sector's punishment mechanism. With private information at time t the private sector reverts to expecting inflation if $g_{t-1} > \delta_{t-1} + \bar{\epsilon}$, where $\bar{\epsilon}$ is some appropriately chosen constant. If the policy-maker reneges and sets g_t higher than $\bar{\epsilon}$ then it risks the probability of a breakdown in cooperation. Clearly, if $\bar{\epsilon}$ is small enough, then the ideal rule is enforceable under the same condition as in the Barro and Gordon model.

An interesting feature of the Canzoneri model is that there will still be periodic inflationary episodes associated with large negative prediction errors of δ_t. The private sector will then observe a large g_{t-1} and small δ_{t-1} and trigger off a period of high inflation. It can be shown that if b is high then a large $\bar{\epsilon}$ can be specified; consequently the probability of an inflationary reversion will be small, as will be the frequency of such episodes.

Cukierman and Meldzer (1986)

The final paper examined in this section combines elements of the previous four studies. In Cukierman and Meldzer (1986) noisy control and imperfect monitoring of the monetary instrument (as in Canzoneri) are combined with incomplete information on the part of the private sector concerning the policy-maker's welfare criteria (as in Backus and Driffill and Barro).

Planned inflation π_t^p and actual inflation P_t are related by

$$\pi_t = \pi_t^p + u_t \tag{9.58}$$

where $u_t \simeq N(0, \sigma_t^2)$ is white noise and u_t is not observed at time t (actually the authors conduct their analysis in terms of the growth of the money supply rather than inflation; but we retain inflation as the instrument as in the previous papers in this section).

The weight b on output in Equation (9.15) is now assumed to be time-varying and stochastic and given by

$$b_t = b + \tilde{b}_t \qquad \tilde{b}_t = \rho\tilde{b}_{t-1} + \epsilon_t \tag{9.59}$$

where $\epsilon_t \simeq N(0,\sigma_\epsilon^2)$ is white noise assumed to be distributed independently of u_t and p is a constant parameter. The private sector knows b, σ_u^2, σ_ϵ^2 and ρ but does not observe b_t directly. However, it can draw inferences concerning the policy-maker's objectives from observations of past inflation and its knowledge of the model and the welfare function. Given this learning process of the private sector the policy-maker can calculate his/her optimal decision rule. The result turns out to be a constant planned inflation rate given by

$$\pi_t^p = \left[\frac{1-\lambda\rho}{1-\lambda l} \quad b \right] \tag{9.60}$$

where $0 \leqslant l \leqslant \rho$ is a crucial parameter which measures the degree of sluggishness in expectations. The higher l the longer is the memory of the public and the less important are recent developments. This corresponds to a low punishment period in the Barro–Gordon game. In the upper limit as $l \to \rho$ the discretionary inflation rate, $\pi_t^p = b$, is approached. It can also be shown that l is a decreasing function of σ_ϵ^2 and an increasing function of σ_u^2. The worse the control of the money supply (high σ_u^2) the longer will past policies affect future expectations and the higher the planned inflation rate.

Cukierman and Meldzer proceed to examine the case where the policy-maker can choose the variance of the noise σ_u^2. They find that the politically optimal level of control over inflation is not necessarily the minimum level. It may be in the government's interest to confuse the private sector with loose control of monetary policy.

There are two ways in which the Cukierman–Meldzer treatment of credibility constitutes an advance compared with that of Barro and Gordon. The first is that whereas the crucial learning parameter, l, is derived endogenously assuming optimal least-squares learning, the corresponding parameter in Barro and Gordon – the punishment period – is selected on an *ad hoc* basis. The second improvement is that any relaxation of the extreme complete information is to be welcomed, not just because it prevents unravelling in finite-time-horizon games but, simply, for its own sake.

However, the incomplete-information games surveyed in this section constitute only a very limited departure from full information. In all these games the private sector knows the strategic nature of government behaviour but may be missing some information regarding parameter values. An alternative view of learning is to assume that the public is less well-informed and must estimate the policy or rule by observing data and applying standard econometric techniques. Bray and Savin (1986) exemplify this approach in a paper which examines private sector learning about a cobweb model of price–output behaviour. The adoption of these ideas to credibility and macroeconomic policy is still in its infancy (see, for example, Cripps, 1988; Levine, 1989).

AN AGENDA FOR FUTURE RESEARCH

We conclude by outlining some areas for future research.

Precommitment and punishment mechanisms

The *ex ante* optimal policy assumes a reputation for precommitment which lasts indefinitely. By contrast, in the time consistent policy, precommitment lasts for one period only. Clearly, there may be intermediate cases for which the period of commitment is say, five years, that are more realistic. Even more challenging would be an endogenous determination of the period of precommitment in which reputation would be built up or eroded.

We have commented on the *ad hoc* character of the punishment period in the Barro–Gordon policy game. In the case where the private sector acts strategically another challenge would be the endogenous determination of this punishment period. As we have noted, however, this development would not apply to atomistic agents.

Many policy-makers

There are many aspects to this theme all of which have drawn upon the ideas surveyed in this chapter. A rapidly growing area of research is in international policy co-ordination, where the policy-makers are the different governments in different countries or blocs. In a seminal article Rogoff (1985) shows that gains from international co-ordination between two blocs are crucially dependent on the participants enjoying reputation for precommitment. In the absence of reputation, with policy-makers only able to pursue time consistent policies, cooperation can sometimes be counterproductive, a result confirmed by Miller and Salmon (1985) and Currie *et al.* (1987). In the latter study a complementary result emerged: in the absence of co-ordination, reputation may be counterproductive and it may be better to pursue policies which are time-consistent.

We can understand these results in terms of a three-person game played between the two governments or blocs and the private sector. As in the Barro and Gordon model the ideal rule can be regarded as cooperation between the private sector and the policy-maker. Cooperation between two governments enjoying reputation for precommitment then amounts to cooperation between three players. If the two governments lack this reputation (the Rogoff case) then cooperation is between only two of the three players. This is also the case if governments enjoy reputation but do not cooperate (the Currie *et al.*, 1987 case). It is a standard result from game theory that cooperation between a coalition of players may be counterproductive for the members of the subset. This explains these apparently paradoxical results.

Another example of many policy-makers is where fiscal and monetary policies are independently determined within one country. Thus Alesina and Tabellini (1988a) show how, with uncoordinated policies, reputational policies may be less effective than the time consistent alternative.

Finally, an extra player can be introduced into these games in the form of a competing potential government. The problem of macroeconomic policy design is a democracy with two competing parties is another rapidly growing area of research (see Alesina 1987; 1988; Alesina and Tabellini, 1988b). However, in both the politics of reputation and the international policy co-ordination literature, many of the themes surveyed in the paper for a single policy-maker remain unexplored.

Simple rules

Kydland and Prescott (1977) oppose the use of optimal control and express a preference for rules which are 'simple and easily understood so it is obvious when a policymaker deviates from the policy'. Although we reject the Kydland and Prescott view that the *ex ante* optimal policy is irrelevant, it is clear that its sustainability does require the private sector to be able easily to monitor the policy. If policies take the form of complicated rules then this brings into doubt the ability of the private sector to threaten to 'punish' the government if it reneges.

In the non-stochastic dynamic model examined on page 263, the 'ideal' or *ex ante* optimal policy can be announced and implemented as an open-loop trajectory of instrument values. This in the Buiter (1981) sense is a 'fixed rule' and it is simple. However successful policy design has to cope with uncertainty in the form of stochastic exogenous shocks. It must also deal with the possibility of modelling errors. For both these forms of uncertainty policies in the form of *feedback rules* are required.

For empirical linear models there is a need to design simple rules, parsimonious in character, which come as close as possible to replacing the ideal rule. Vines, *et al.* (1983) use frequency domain techniques to design such simple controllers for a linearized but non-rational expectations model of the United Kingdom. Currie and Levine (1985) derive simple rules by time domain methods for a stylized non-empirical rational expectations model. Christodoulakis *et al.* (1988) design simple rules for a linearized London Business School model which also has rational expectations. Levine *et al.* (1989) examine the use of simple rules in a two-country game.

In all these studies the game is a complete-information game. The idea that simplicity helps the private sector to monitor government policies can be pursued more rigorously by relaxing the information assumption and introducing private sector learning about the rule (Levine, 1989).

Finally, it is standard design criterion in engineering that rules should have the properties of robustness with respect to modelling errors and exogenous shocks. For macroeconomic rational expectations models, following the Kydland–Prescott critique, we must add to robustness the additional criteria of sustainability and simplicity. The design of feedback rules satisfying all these criteria remains a major challenge for macroeconomic policy design.

REFERENCES

Alesina, A. (1987) 'Macroeconomic policy in a two-party system as a repeated game', *Quarterly Journal of Economics*, pp. 651–78.

Alesina, A. (1988) 'Credibility and policy convergence in a two-party system with rational voters', *American Economic Review*, vol. 78, no. 4, pp. 796–805.

Alesina, A. and Tabellini, G. (1988a) 'Rules and discretion with non-coordinated monetary and fiscal policies', *Economic Inquiry*, forthcoming.

Alesina, A. and Tabellini, G. (1988b) 'Credibility and politics' *European Economic Review*, vol 32, nos 2/3, pp. 542–50.

Backus, D. and Driffill, J. (1985a) 'Inflation and reputation', *American Economic Review*, vol. 75, pp. 503–38.

Backus, D. and Driffill, J. (1985b) 'Rational expectations and policy credibility following a change in regime, *Review of Economic Studies*, vol 52, pp. 211–22.

Backus, D. and Driffill, J. (1987), 'The consistency of optimal policy in stochastic rational expectations models', CEPR Discussion Paper, no. 124.

Barro, R.J. (1986) 'Reputation in a model of monetary policy with incomplete information', *Journal of Monetary Economics*, vol 17, pp. 101–22.

Barro, R.J. and Gordon, D.A. (1983a) 'A positive theory of inflation in a natural-rate model', *Journal of Political Economy*, vol. 91, pp. 589–610.

Barro, R.J. and Gordon, D.A. (1983b) 'Rules, discretion and reputation in a model of monetary policy', *Journal of Monetary Economics*, vol. 12, pp. 101–21.

Begg, D.K.H. (1982) *The Rational Expectations Revolution in Macroeconomics*, Oxford: Philip Allan.

Bray, M.M. and Savin, N.E. (1986) 'Rational expectations equilibria, learning and model specification', *Econometrica*, vol. 54, 1129–60.

Buiter, W.H. (1981) 'The superiority of contingent rules over fixed rules in models with rational expectations', *Economic Journal*, vol. 91, September, pp. 647–70.

Buiter, W.H. and Miller, M.H. (1983) 'Costs and benefits of an anti-inflationary policy: questions and issues', Centre for Labour Economics Discussion Paper, no. 178.

Canzoneri, M.B. (1985) 'Monetary policy games and the role of private information', *American Economic Review*, vol. 75, no. 5, pp. 1056–70.

Christodoulakis, N., Gaines, J. and Levine, P. (1988) 'Macroeconomic policy design using large econometric rational expectations models: methodology and application', CEPR Discussion Paper no. 275.

Cripps, M. (1988) 'Learning rational expectations in a policy game', mimeo, University of Warwick.

Cukierman, A. and Meldzer, A.H. (1986) 'A theory of ambiguity, credibility and inflation under discretion and asymmetric information', *Econometrica*, vol. 54, pp. 1099–1122.

Currie, D. and Levine, P. (1985) 'Simple macro policy rules for the open economy', *Economic Journal*, Suppl., vol. 95, pp. 60–70.
Currie, D., Levine, P. and Vitalis, N. (1987) 'International cooperation and reputation in an empirical two-bloc model' in R. Bryant and R. Portes (eds), *Global Macroeconomics: Policy Conflict and Cooperation*, London: Macmillan.
Driffill, J. (1982) 'Optimal money and exchange rate policies', *Greek Economic Review*, vol. 4, December, pp. 261–83.
Driffill, J. (1987) 'Macroeconomic policy games with incomplete information: some extensions', CEPR Discussion Paper, no. 159.
Driffill, J. (1988) 'Macroeconomic policy games with incomplete information: a survey', *European Economic Review*, vol. 32, nos 2/3, pp. 533–41.
Friedman, J.W. (1977) *Oligopoly and the Theory of Games*, Amsterdam: North-Holland.
Fudenberg, D. and Maskin, E. (1986) 'The folk theorem in repeated games with discounting or with incomplete information', *Econometrica*, vol. 54, no. 3, pp. 533–54.
Hahn, F. (1982) *Money and Inflation*, Oxford: Blackwell.
Kreps, D. and Wilson, R. (1982) 'Reputation and imperfect information', *Journal of Economic Theory*, vol. 27, pp. 253–79.
Kreps, D., Milgram, P., Roberts, J. and Wilson, R. (1982) 'Rational cooperation in the finitely-repeated Prisoner's Dilemma', *Journal of Economic Theory*, vol. 27, pp. 245–52.
Kydland, F.E. and Prescott, E.C. (1977) 'Rules rather than discretion: the inconsistency of optimal plans', *Journal of Political Economy*, vol. 85, pp. 473–91.
Levine, P. (1988) 'Does time inconsistency matter?', CEPR Discussion Paper no. 227.
Levine, P. (1989) 'Should rules be simple?' CEF Discussion Paper no. 01–89, London Business School.
Levine, P., Currie, D. and Gaines, J. (1989) 'The use of simple rules for international policy agreements' in R. Portes *et al.* (eds), *Blueprint for Exchange Rate Management*, London: Academic Press.
Levine, P. and Holly, S. (1989) 'The time inconsistency issue in macroeconomics: a survey', *Economic Perspectives*, forthcoming.
Lucas, R.E. (1973) 'Some international evidence on output–inflation tradeoffs', *American Economic Review*, vol. 63, pp. 326–34.
Milgram, P. and Roberts, J. (1982) 'Limit pricing and entry under incomplete information', *Econometrica*, vol. 50, pp. 443–60.
Miller, M.H. and Salmon, M. (1985) 'Policy coordination and dynamic games' in W.H. Buiter and R.C. Marston (eds), *International Economic Policy Coordination*, Cambridge: Cambridge University Press.
Persson, T. (1988) 'Credibility of macroeconomic policy: an introduction and broad survey', *European Economic Reivew*, vol. 32, no. 2/3, pp. 519–32.
Rogoff, K. (1985) 'Can international monetary cooperation be counter-productive?', *Journal of International Economics*, vol. 18, pp. 199–217.
Vickers, J. (1985) 'Signalling in a model of monetary policy with incomplete information', *Oxford Economic Papers*, vol. 18, pp. 199–217.
Vines, D., Maciejowski, J.M. and Meade, J.E. (1983) *Stagflation. Vol. 2, Demand Management*, London: George Allen & Unwin.

10 · DISINFLATION AND WAGE–PRICE CONTROLS

David A. Wilton

Ultimately the rate of monetary expansion determines the rate of inflation ... but the Phillips curve plays a very important role in the adjustment process ... in the downward direction the path of the adjustment process is likely to be tortuous ... If price change expectations are slow to adjust, then the unemployment experience along the adjustment path is likely to be very prolonged and severe ... an incomes policy may well be a useful tool when it is employed together with a restrictive monetary policy to aid in the downward adjustment from an established inflation rate. The incomes policy would then reduce the unemployment burden resulting from the transition to a lower inflation rate ... the Phillips curve is not dead, but ... is in fact a more dangerous device than the simple trade-off approach implies. The danger lies in the costs of reducing inflation, which may not be realized when the economy is moving to higher inflation rates.

(Vanderkamp, 1975, pp. 120–2)

During most of the 1970s and early 1980s the industrialized world was preoccupied with the problem of inflation. Compared to annual inflation rates in the 1–5 per cent range during the 1953–72 period, most countries experienced persistent double-digit inflation during the decade 1973–82.[1] After living with inflation for most of the 1970s, in the early 1980s many countries resorted to very restrictive monetary policies in an attempt to purge inflation out of the system, which in turn led to one of the worst recessions since the 1930s.

The major argument of this chapter can be stated quite succinctly. Assuming that the government wishes to lower the prevailing inflation rate, a restrictive monetary policy, coupled with temporary wage and price controls, may represent the best disinflation policy choice. Without wage and price controls, a disinflationary monetary policy will be likely to impose substantial costs on society in the form of higher interest rates, lower output (income) levels and higher unemployment rates. While wage and price controls exert additional costs on society (mainly government administrative costs and resource misallocation or distortion costs), *temporary* controls have the potential to alleviate some of the macroeconomic costs associated with a disinflationary monetary policy. To the extent that wage and price controls can legislate the inflation rate down to a lower level and break 'high' inflation expectations, the macroeconomic benefits of temporary controls (particularly less unemployment) may exceed their microeconomic costs.

This chapter begins with an analysis of the economic costs of a disinflationary monetary policy under various assumptions about the formation of inflation expectations. This is followed by a presentation of the theoretical case for supplementing a disinflationary monetary policy with temporary wage and price controls. The chapter concludes with a detailed review of the use of wage and price controls in Canada during the 1975–8 period.

A DISINFLATIONARY MONETARY POLICY

Virtually all economists would agree with the monetarist proposition that in the long run inflation is a monetary phenomenon. To lower the long run equilibrium inflation rate, the government must restrict the growth rate of the nominal money supply. Unfortunately, the short-run adjustment costs of such a long-run disinflationary monetary policy may be very painful. Gearing the economy down from a high inflation rate to a low inflaton rate may entail a prolonged period of high unemployment and high interest rates. In this section we analyse the costs of a disinflationary monetary policy. We begin our analysis by considering a conventional IS–LM model augmented by a price-expectations-augmented Phillips (PEP) curve in which inflation expectations are formed in an adaptive manner. After reviewing the costs of a disinflationary monetary policy in an adaptive expectations IS–LM–PEP macroeconomic model, we then consider the disinflation implications of a rational expectations New Classical model.

An IS–LM–PEP model with adaptive expectations

Suppose that an economy can be represented by the following three equations:

$$Y = f(A; R - \dot{P}^{e}) \qquad \text{(IS curve)} \tag{10.1}$$

$$Y = g(M/P; R) \qquad \text{(LM curve)} \tag{10.2}$$

$$\dot{P} - \dot{P}^{e} = h(Y - Y^{*}) \qquad \text{(PEP curve)} \tag{10.3}$$

where Y is the level of output; Y^* is the natural rate level of output; R is the nominal interest rate; P is the price level; $\dot{P}$ is the inflation rate; $\dot{P}^e$ is the expected inflation; M is the nominal money supply; and A is autonomous demand forces (such as fiscal policy). To complete the model we assume that inflation expectations are formed adaptively and are therefore some function of past inflation rates ($\dot{P}_{lag}$):

$$\dot{P}^e = j(\dot{P}_{lag}) \tag{10.4}$$

Our four-equation adaptive expectations IS–LM–PEP model determines the values for the four endogenous variables Y, R, $\dot{P}$, and $\dot{P}^e$, assuming given values for the exogenous (predetermined) variables A, M, Y^* and $\dot{P}_{lag}$.

Given the dynamic and non-linear form of this conventional IS–LM–PEP model, a two-panel diagram (first suggested by Lipsey, 1978) is employed to trace out the adjustment path following the implementation of a monetary disinflation policy. In the upper IS–LM panel of Figure 10.1, the economy is initially assumed to be in equilibrium at the natural rate of output Y^* (position A). In the lower PEP curve panel this initial equilibrium position A is characterized by a 10 per cent inflation rate which is validated and fully expected. Now suppose that the government decides to reduce this 10 per cent equilibrium inflation rate to 5 per cent and restricts the growth rate of the nominal money supply accordingly. Assuming adaptive inflation expectations, the adjustment path following the implementation of a monetary disinflation policy will be cyclical in nature, beginning with a recession.

Initially when the growth rate of the nominal money supply is lowered to 5 per cent, individuals will still (adaptively) base their inflation expectations on previous inflation rates, assumed to be 10 per cent. Consequently in the initial period inflation expectations will remain at 10 per cent and the original IS and PEP curves corresponding to inflation expectations of 10 per cent will remain in force. The new lower growth rate of the *nominal* money supply will cause a reduction in the *real* money supply and the LM curve will begin to shift upwards (to LM_B). The economy will move from position A to position B. Higher real interest rates will reduce investment expenditures and lower output levels (from Y^* to Y_1), which in turn will lead to a moderation in the inflation rate (to $\dot{P}_1$ in the lower panel of Figure 10.1).

In the second period the LM curve will again shift upwards (to LM_C), although by a smaller amount than in the first period (because the inflation rate is now less than 10 per cent). Given adaptive inflation expectations, in the second period inflation expectations will begin to moderate, with the extent of the moderation depending upon the weight assigned to the previous inflation rate (compared to other lagged values) in the adaptive

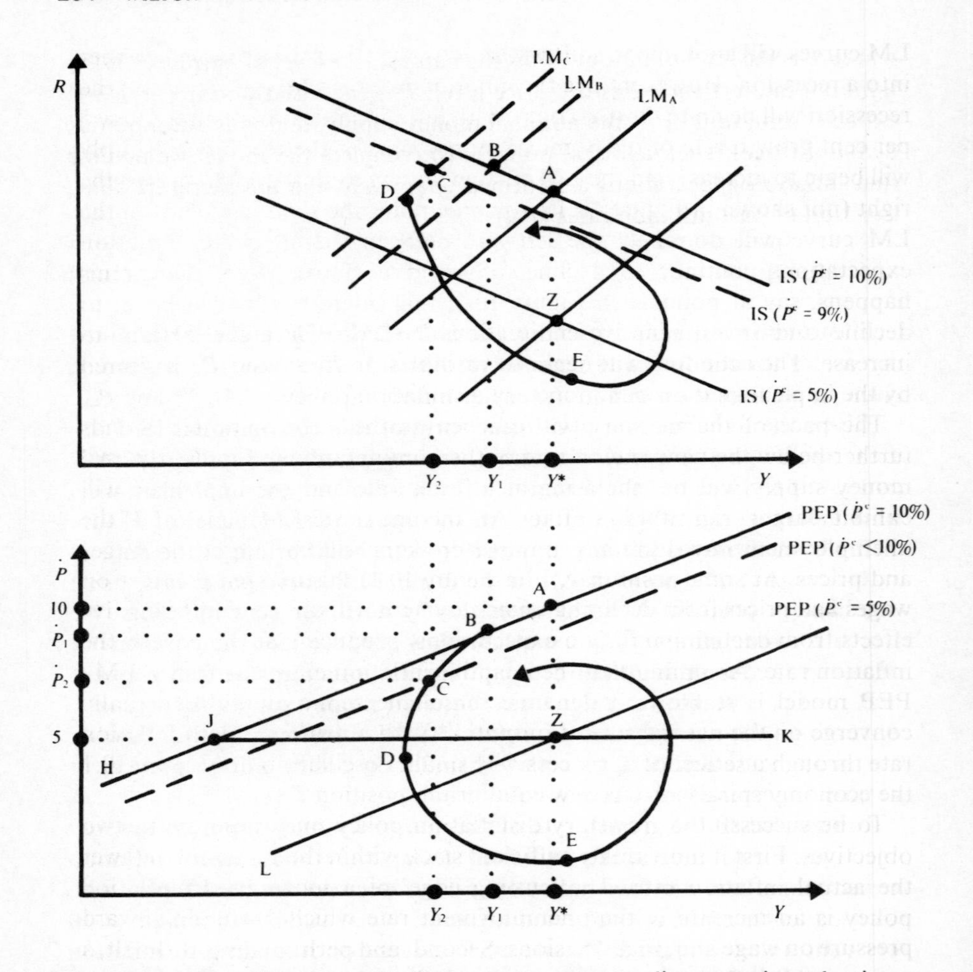

Figure 10.1 The effects of a disinflationary monetary policy assuming adaptive inflation expectations

expectations forecasting equation. The decline in inflation expectations will cause both the PEP and IS curves to shift downwards in period two and the economy will move to position C. Output levels further decline (to Y_2), as both the LM and IS curves are shifting to the left. The assumption of adaptive inflation expectations accelerates the downward adjustment of the inflation rate (to $\dot{P}_2$). Not only is the economy moving downwards along the PEP curve (because output levels are declining), the PEP curve is also shifting downwards (because inflation expectations are declining).

As long as the declining inflation rate remains above 5 per cent (the assumed new growth rate of the nominal money supply), both the IS and

LM curves will continue to shift to the left, propelling the economy further into a recession. However once the inflation rate falls below 5 per cent, the recession will begin to 'bottom out'. With inflation rates less than the new 5 per cent growth rate of the nominal money supply, the real money supply will begin to increase and the LM curve will start to shift downwards to the right (not shown in Figure 10.1). At some point the rightward shift in the LM curve will dominate the leftward shift in the IS curve (inflation expectations continue to decline, albeit at a slower pace). Once this happens, say at point D in Figure 10.1, real interest rates will begin to decline and investment expenditures and income levels will start to increase. The economy will begin to recover from the recession triggered by the implementation of a monetary disinflation policy.

The pace of the recovery will quicken as the inflation rate descends further below the new growth rate of the nominal money supply (the real money supply will be increasing at a faster rate and the LM curve will exhibit larger rightward shifts). As income levels increase and the unemployment rate decreases, upward pressure will be exerted on wages and prices. At some point (say, E in Figure 10.1) this upward pressure on wages and prices from declining unemployment will outweigh the negative effects from declining inflation expectations, producing an increase in the inflation rate. Assuming that the adaptive inflation expectations IS–LM–PEP model is stable in a dynamic sense, the economy will eventually converge on the natural rate of output Y^* with a new 5 per cent inflation rate through a sequence of successively smaller oscillations (in Figure 10.1 the economy spirals into its new equilibrium position Z).

To be successful, a monetary disinflation policy must accomplish two objectives. First it must create sufficient slack within the economy to lower the actual inflation rate. The 'cutting edge' of a monetary disinflation policy is an increase in the unemployment rate which exerts downward pressure on wage and price decisions. Second, and perhaps more difficult, a monetary disinflation policy must lower inflation expectations. Under the assumption of adaptive inflation expectations, inflation expectations decline following the recession-induced reduction in the actual inflation rate. In the framework of a conventional macroeconomic model with adaptive inflation expectations, the term *disinflationary* monetary policy should be understood as an euphemism for reduced nominal aggregate demand, higher interest rates and higher unemployment rates. In the words of former Canadian Finance Minister, John Crosbie, society must endure 'short-term pain for long-term gain'. Both neo-Keynesians and monetarists agree on this fundamental, but discouraging, point.[2]

The magnitude and duration of this 'painful' recession depend on how quickly wages and prices adjust to a monetary disinflation policy. Three factors tend to prolong this 'tortuous' short-run adjustment to a lower inflation rate. First, the labour market is not an auction market where wages are renegotiated every day. In North America, long-term overlapping union contracts (two to three years in length) prevent wages from being immediately adjusted to reflect a change in economic conditions. In the non-union sector, most workers have their wages adjusted once a year (an annual performance review), not each time the monthly unemployment rate or consumer price index changes. Since most workers are 'locked into' existing wage contracts (be they explicit or implicit), the 'cutting edge' of a new disinflationary monetary policy can only take effect as existing wage contracts expire.

Second, wage rates, when they are adjusted, may not be very sensitive to current labour market conditions, particularly excess supply conditions. Employed workers (and their unions) strenuously resist a reduction in wages, particularly if it is believed that the existing recession is only temporary. It is not easy for unemployed workers to obtain a job by offering to work at a lower wage rate than the existing workforce. In short, the Phillips curve tends to be rather flat, reflecting a limited degree of downward wage flexibility. Relatively large increases in unemployment tend to generate only small decreases in wage inflation. After reviewing six US Phillips curve studies, Okun (1978) found that

> For an extra percentage point of unemployment maintained for a year, the estimated reduction in the ultimate inflation rate at equilibrium unemployment ranges between one-sixth and one-half of 1 percentage point, with an average estimate of 0.3. Or, to put it another way, the average estimate of the cost of a 1 point reduction in the basic inflation rate is 10 per cent of a year's GNP.

Third, the extent of the short-run recession also depends on how quickly labour market participants lower their inflation expectations. Labour market participants about to sign long-term wage contracts are likely to be very reluctant to lower their inflation expectations simply because the government has announced a new restrictive monetary policy. People may not believe that the new policy will work or that the government is willing (if necessary) to tolerate a recession to purge inflation out of the economic system. Several painful years of recession may be necessary to convince people that the monetary disinflation policy is indeed working and that the government is committed to reducing the inflation rate. Despite the growing popularity of the rational inflation expectations hypothesis among academic economists (see below), it is conceivable that labour market participants may prefer to formulate their expectations of the future inflation rate by adapting to past actual inflation rates rather than by believing the predictions of economists and the assurances of politicians.

All factors considered, the short-run adjustment period following the implementation of a monetary disinflation policy may be prolonged and

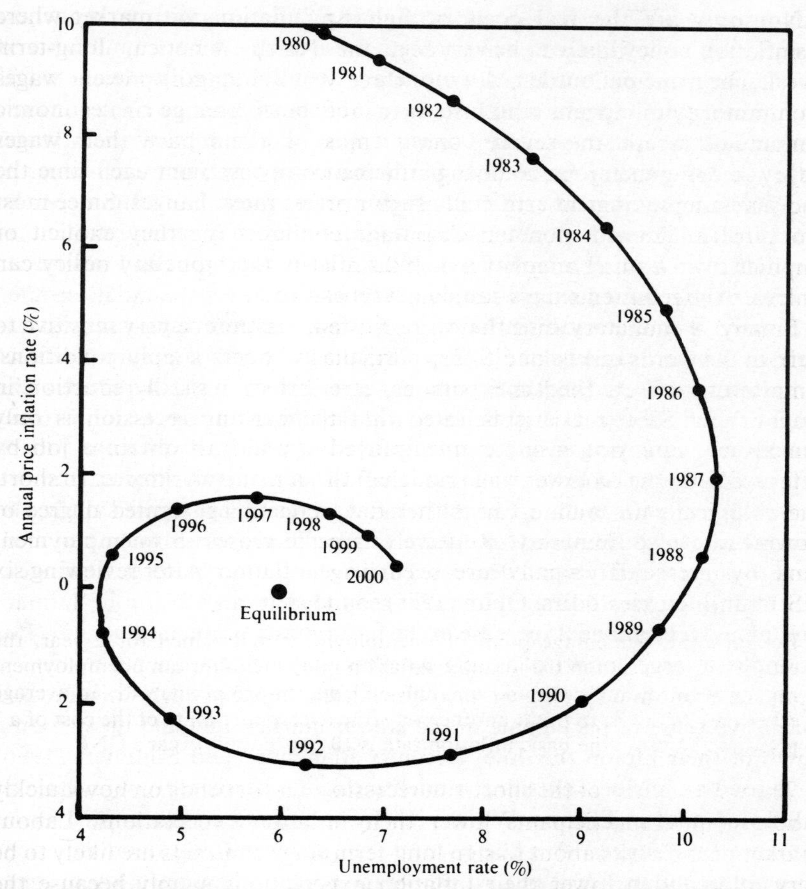

Figure 10.2 Simulated effects of monetary disinflation on unemployment and inflation, 1980–2000 (reproduced from Tobin 1980, p. 67)

painful. James Tobin (1980) simulated the effects of a *gradualist* monetary policy designed to lower the inflation rate from 10 per cent to zero using a 'stylized' version of a 'consensus' macroeconomic model.[3] As shown in Figure 10.2 (reproduced from Tobin's original paper), such a gradualist monetary disinflation policy produces a deep and protracted recession. For seven consecutive years the unemployment rate continues to rise, reaching a peak of 10.3 per cent, and exceeds the natural rate of unemployment (assumed to be 6 per cent) for almost thirteen years (the first half cycle of the dynamic adjustment path analysed in Figure 10.1).

Not only are the real costs of fighting inflation with a monetary disinflation policy likely to be very high, these costs are not equally shared by all. The principal burden of a monetary disinflation policy tends to fall on a minority of citizens who lose their jobs, businesses or homes. Many individuals escape the severe consequences of a monetary disinflation policy, keeping their jobs, receiving inflation-compensating wage increases, and investing savings at artificially high interest rates. Unfortunately, the blunt instrument of a monetary disinflation policy may require maximum sacrifice from a small minority who must give up their jobs and businesses to create the required excess supply conditions to lower the inflation rate.

Finally, a monetary disinflation policy may impose long-run costs as well. In the words of Phelps (1972, p. 78), 'the live hand of history produces a hysteresis effect: the time path to equilibrium partially shapes the equilibrium'. Since real interest rates will be higher during the adjustment period accompanying a monetary disinflation policy, investment will be depressed and the economy will find itself with a relatively smaller, and less technologically up-to-date, capital stock. As a result, aggregate supply, the natural rate of output and/or future economic growth may be reduced. Such hysteresis effects may also occur in the labour market. Persistent short-run increases in unemployment may lead to an erosion in 'human' capital and a permanent increase in the natural rate of unemployment. For example, a large cohort of young workers may be permanently excluded from the economic system, never requiring the necessary job skills in their formative years to participate in the labour market, and end up spending much of their life on the dole. Recently Blanchard and Summers (1986) have used an 'insider–outsider' model to explain persistently high rates of unemployment in Europe. While such hysteresis effects are controversial (because they suggest that the natural rate of output and unemployment may not be independent of past monetary policy), the possibility of long-run, supply-side effects of a monetary disinflation policy should not be ignored.

Rational expectations and the New Classical macroeconomics

In recent years many economists have rejected the assumption of adaptive inflation expectations, primarily because it is backward-looking, mechanistic and characterized by systematic forecasting errors (see, for example, Begg, 1982). Building on the concept of rational expectations as originally articulated by Muth (1961), a new school of macroeconomics emerged in the late 1970s. Led by Lucas, Sargent and Barro (among others), the New Classical macroeconomic model provided the startling conclusion that perfectly anticipated monetary policy will have absolutely *no* effect on output or employment levels in any relevant time period (the policy ineffectiveness proposition). In terms of the subject matter of this chapter, the New Classical model predicts that a disinflationary monetary policy will be entirely *costless*. Under New Classical assumptions, the short-run adjustment period associated with a monetary disinflation policy collapses to zero and the economy will move instantaneously to the new lower inflation rate without any short-run increase in unemployment.

While the New Classical model retains a conventional IS and LM curve (Equations (10.1) and (10.2) above), the price-expectations-augmented Phillips curve is replaced by a Lucas price surprise supply function (PSSF) and the assumption of adaptive inflation expectations is replaced by the assumption of rational inflation expectations. To simplify the following algebra, the IS and LM equations are combined into the following aggregate demand schedule, where all variables are expressed in logarithms:

$$P_t = M_t + aA_t + b(P_t^e - P_{t-1}) + cY_t + u_t \qquad (10.5)$$

where a, b and c are parameters.

In Equation (10.5), the log of the expected price level minus the log of the lagged actual price level represents the effects of expected inflation on investment (the distinction between real and nominal interest rates) and u_t represents a random error term.

Equation (10.6) presents the New Classical PSSF:

$$Y_t = Y^* + d(P_t - P_t^e) \qquad (10.6)$$

While individuals always optimize and form their expectations in a rational manner, the New Classical model assumes that individuals possess incomplete information. In particular, it is assumed that each individual has very good information concerning the price of the product which he or she is producing or selling, but has incomplete information about all other prices (information which is costly to collect). Thus an optimizing agent with incomplete information may mistake an unexpected general price increase for an increase in the relative price of the good which he is producing, leading him to increase aggregate supply. Output will deviate from the natural rate Y^* whenever prices move in an unexpected manner (a price surprise). Unlike the disequilibrium underpinnings of the price-expectations-augmented Phillips curve, the PSSF assumes that markets always clear. Any discrepancy between actual output and the natural rate of output is the result of an unanticipated price movement, not disequilibrium in the goods or labour market.

Invoking the assumption of rational expectations, the expected price level can be obtained by substituting Equation (10.6) into Equation (10.5) and taking expected values:

$$P_t^e = M_t^e + aA_t^e + b(P_t^e - P_{t-1}) + cY^* \qquad (10.7)$$

Substituting Equations (10.5) and (10.7) into the PSSF equation (10.6), the following reduced-form income equation for the New Classical model is obtained: where $k = d/(1 - dc)$:

$$Y_t = Y^* + k(M_t - M_t^e) + ak(A_t - A_t^e) + ku_t \qquad (10.8)$$

where $k = d/(1 - dc)$. Given rational expectations and a PSSF, output will deviate from the natural rate of output only if there is an unanticipated change in monetary policy or an unanticipated change in A (or a non-zero value for the random error u). Anticipated monetary policy will have absolutely no effect on output levels. Thus the New Classical model predicts that a publicly announced monetary disinflation policy should produce a lower inflation rate without any increase in the unemployment rate or reduction in output.

Given the very strong policy ineffectiveness conclusions of the New Classical model, it is important to identify the key assumptions which generate such strong conclusions. If one retains the PSSF but replaces the assumption of rational expectations with adaptive expectations, then a change in monetary policy, be it anticipated or not, will affect output levels.[4] While rational expectations is a *necessary* condition for the policy ineffectiveness proposition, it is *not* a *sufficient* condition. In addition to rational expectations, the policy ineffectiveness proposition also requires that prices instantly adjust to clear the goods market. As shown by Buiter (1980), if prices do not instantly adjust (i.e. markets do not always clear), then the level of output will systematically deviate from the natural rate. In the presence of sluggish price adjustments or contractual wage–price rigidities, monetary policy will have systematic output effects even if expectations are formed in a rational manner.[5] The New Classical policy ineffectiveness proposition requires the joint assumptions of rational expectations and continual market clearing.[6]

How seriously should one take the New Classical proposition that monetary disinflation imposes no unemployment costs on society? With respect to the necessary and sufficient conditions for the policy ineffectiveness proposition, a number of studies have questioned the empirical validity of the assumption of rational inflation expectations (see, for example, Figlewski and Wachtel, 1981). Despite the theoretically appealing nature of the assumption of rational expectations, some economists view the assumption of rational expectations with considerable scepticism (see, for example, Pesaran, 1982). However, the most damaging criticism levelled against the New Classical macroeconomic model concerns the assumption of perfectly flexible prices and continuous market clearing. For many economists, the double-digit unemployment rates of the early 1980s are difficult to square with the notion of continuous labour market equilibrium. Critics of the New Classical school of macroeconomics argue that the widespread use of contracts (both explicit and implicit) in product and labour markets impedes the adjustment of wages and prices. Prices are not perfectly flexible in the short run and the economic system can be characterized by quantity adjustments, not just price adjustments.

As Benjamin Friedman (1983) has argued,

> experience has belied the most significant policy implication of the new classical macroeconomics ... the tight monetary policy during this period [1980–82 in the United States] was probably about as well anticipated as such policy is ever likely to be ... economic events suggest anything but costless inflation. Instead they are strikingly in line with the conventional estimates of disinflation surveyed by Okun some years before the fact.

In Friedman's view, the New Classical macroeconomic model failed the 'decisive' test of the early 1980s; a deliberate policy of monetary disinflation did not achieve a lower inflation rate without a deep and protracted recession.

THE THEORETICAL CASE FOR A SUPPLEMENTARY POLICY OF TEMPORARY WAGE AND PRICE CONTROLS

Rather than waiting for the economy slowly (and painfully) to gear down to a new lower inflation rate, the government could impose temporary wage and price controls to expedite its monetary disinflation policy. By directly controlling the size of wage and price increases, the government could quickly force the inflation rate down to a new lower rate (consistent with the new lower rate of monetary expansion). Wage and price controls would attempt to legislate the inflation rate down to its new lower target level and then hold the inflation rate at this new lower level until inflation expectations have been lowered. Once inflation expectations have been reduced to the new lower target rate, the government could then terminate its temporary controls programme.

To illustrate the theoretical case for imposing temporary wage and price controls along with a monetary disinflation policy, we again assume that the economy is initially in equilibrium (at Y^*) with a validated and expected inflation rate of 10 per cent (position A in Figure 10.1). In addition to restricting the growth rate of the nominal money supply to 5 per cent, suppose that the government also imposes temporary wage and price controls, placing a 5 per cent ceiling on the inflation rate. Given the imposition of wage and price controls, the PEP curve (corresponding to $\dot{P}^e$ at 10 per cent) will now be represented by the kinked line HJK in Figure

10.1. While wage and price controls are assumed to have no effect if the inflation rate is below 5 per cent, inflation rates above 5 per cent are now illegal under the new controls programme.

With wage and price controls limiting the inflation rate to 5 per cent, the economy will move directly from point A to point Z in the lower panel of Figure 10.1. Since the nominal money supply has been restricted to a 5 per cent growth rate (equal to the 5 per cent controlled inflation rate), the real money supply will be constant, the LM curve will be stationary and output levels will remain at Y^*. The economy has at least temporarily achieved a new lower 5 per cent inflation rate without a recession. However the economy is not yet in long-run equilibrium. While the new legally enforced 5 per cent inflation rate is validated by a 5 per cent growth rate in the nominal money supply, inflation expectations remain at 10 per cent. To achieve their desired results, wage and price controls must remain in force until inflation expectations are lowered to 5 per cent. Once inflation expectations have been lowered to 5 per cent, the PEP curve will shift down to PEP ($\dot{P}^e = 5$ per cent) and the kink in the controlled PEP curve (LZK) will now appear at point Z. With inflation expectations now at 5 per cent, point Z represents the long-run equilibrium position for the economy. The 5 per cent inflation rate is fully expected and validated, and the economy is at the natural rate of output, Y^*.[7]

As soon as inflation expectations are lowered to 5 per cent, wage and price controls become redundant. Given the lower PEP curve corresponding to $\dot{P}^e = 5$ per cent, the inflation rate will be 5 per cent at Y^* without the need for wage and price controls. Wage and price controls are only required until inflation expectations are lowered to 5 per cent. If wage and price controls are removed before inflation expectations are lowered, then the economy would revert back to its original 'high' inflation rate and would have to rely on the recession generated by the monetary disinflation policy to bring the inflation rate down to 5 per cent. The success of a temporary wage and price control programme depends crucially on whether inflation expectations are lowered to the new target inflation rate (consistent with the new lower rate of monetary expansion).

It is important to point out that the use of temporary wage and price controls does *not* remove the necessity of reducing nominal aggregate demand by monetary and fiscal restraint. If wage and price controls are implemented along with an expansionary monetary and/or fiscal policy (as occurred on numerous occasions in the United Kingdom and during President Nixon's US control programme in 1971–3), controls will obviously not work. However, if controls are successful in reducing the size of both wage and price inflation, are left in place until inflation expectations have been lowered, and are accompanied by monetary and fiscal restraint to maintain nominal aggregate demand at a level consistent with the new lower inflation rate, there should be no post-controls wage and price explosion. With no erosion in the real wage rate and no additional aggregate demand stimulus, there is no economic reason for a price explosion when controls are removed.

Wage and price controls represent one potential government policy which might be implemented in conjunction with a monetary disinflation policy.[8] The sole purpose of temporary wage and price controls would be to speed up the disinflation process and lessen the 'short-term pain' associated with a monetary disinflation policy. As such, the economic benefits of temporary wage and price controls are measured in real opportunity cost terms: less unemployment, fewer bankruptcies, lower interest rates, more output, etc. Temporary wage and price controls, implemented in conjunction with a monetary disinflation policy, are best thought of as a recession analgesic and not as an inflation cure.

Whether governments should implement temporary wage and price controls is a highly controversial issue. Citizens generally favour wage and price controls and economists oppose them.[9] While much of economists' opposition to wage and price controls stems from their ideological belief in the free market system, there are indeed costs to controls. As Lipsey (1977) has noted:

> The obvious costs are the administrative costs, and they are borne both by the public and private sectors. The less obvious costs concern the distortions that are introduced into the economy by any centrally administered set of prices and wages. These costs, of course, get larger the longer the controls are in place ... There is also a further set of hidden costs that concern quality changes that occur when prices are effectively controlled ... This leads me to the general conclusion that wage–price controls should be opposed under virtually all peacetime circumstances since they produce at best small and transitory short-term benefits in return for large and persistent long-run costs.[10]

Besides the standard set of microeconomic arguments against wage and price controls, there is also a general consensus among macroeconomists that UK and US controls programmes during the 1960s and 1970s did not work.[11] While US and UK wage and price control programmes may have had a temporary restraining effect on inflation while controls were in place, any restraining effects tended to be offset by 'catch-up' wage and price explosions following the removal of controls. At best, UK and US controls programmes influenced the timing of wage and price movements, but achieved no permanent reduction in the price level. However, it must be noted that the US controls programme of 1971–3 and most UK applications of incomes policy were accompanied by monetary and/or fiscal expansion. To be effective, wage and price controls must be accompanied by policies which restrain nominal aggregate demand, not expand it.

THE CANADIAN ANTI-INFLATION BOARD

In October 1975 the Canadian government introduced a three-year programme, entitled *Attack on Inflation, a Program of National Action.* Its two major elements were a prices and incomes policy to be administered by the Anti-Inflation Board (AIB), and fiscal and monetary policy aimed at increasing total aggregate demand at a rate consistent with declining inflation. For the first time in Canadian peacetime history, mandatory wage and price controls were imposed.

The ceiling for wage increases was determined by the following three part formula: an inflation protection factor which was set at 8, 6 and 4 per cent for the three respective years of the programme; a 2 per cent annual national productivity factor; and an inflation catch-up factor which varied between –2 per cent and +2 per cent. While all Canadians were expected to comply with these wage guidelines, major employee groups (500 employees or more) and all government workers were legally bound by these guidelines. In addition to restraining wages, the AIB monitored and controlled profit margins. Price increases were permitted but limited to recovering cost increases, excluding discretionary cost increases for such things as advertising. If profit margins exceeded base period target margins, firms were ordered to divest themselves of the excess revenues (typically by reducing prices). By monitoring and controlling wage increases and profit margins, the AIB hoped to control the rate of price inflation.[12]

The AIB was given a three-year mandate to 'halt and reverse the spiral of costs and prices that jeopardizes the whole fabric of our economy and our society' (*Attack on Inflation, a Program of National Action*, p. 24). The economic rationale given for the imposition of wage and price controls was very similar to the argument presented in the previous section of this chapter. In the words of the Governor of the Bank of Canada:

> It is useful to supplement financial discipline by direct action to restrain increases in incomes and prices ... This approach can bring about the needed adjustment at less cost in terms of unemployment and lost output, and with less serious inequities, than would result from sole reliance on monetary and fiscal policies. (*Bank of Canada Annual Report*, 1975, p. 11)

The Canadian AIB was a temporary (three-year) wage and price control programme used in conjunction with 'consistent monetary and fiscal policies'. It was never intended as the permanent solution to the inflation problem and in October 1977 the Canadian government announced that the AIB would be phased out during 1978, slightly ahead of schedule.

Before reviewing the empirical evidence pertaining to the AIB's effect on wage and price inflation, several important exemptions to the Canadian wage and price controls programme should be noted. First, the AIB was not given the power to control existing wage contracts. Only as pre-AIB wage contracts expired did workers come under the effects of controls. Given the prevalence of two- and three-year wage contracts in Canada, very few workers actually had their wages controlled in the first year of the controls programme and many workers continued to receive inflationary deferred wage increases contained in long-term contracts signed prior to the creation of the AIB. Second, food prices at the farm gate and energy prices were excluded from the controls programme. With respect to energy prices, Canada (a net exporter of oil during this period) decided to phase in the 1973–4 OPEC oil price shock. As a consequence, Canadian domestic oil prices were rising quite rapidly in the late 1970s as Canada tried to catch up with world oil prices (which doubled in 1978).[13]

The moderating effects of the AIB on Canadian wage inflation are obvious when one reviews the pattern of new wage settlements in the second half of the 1970s. During the eighteen months prior to the imposition of wage controls in October 1975, new wage settlements were averaging more than 18 per cent per annum (over the life of the contract). Against this backdrop of 18 per cent annual wage settlements in the period immediately preceding controls, average annual wage settlements declined to 10.7 per cent in 1976 and to less than 8 per cent in 1977 and 1978. While much of this ten percentage point decline in average Canadian wage settlements can be attributed to economic factors other than the controls programme, a number of econometric studies have concluded that the AIB exerted a significant negative effect on Canadian wage increases.[14] In quantitative terms these studies suggest that annual wage settlements were about 2.5–3 percentage points lower than they would have been in the absence of the AIB. For example, Fortin and Newton (1982) conclude 'that after three years of operation the AIB was able to "shock" wage inflation down, cumulatively by about 7.5 [percentage] points'. Given the prevalence of long-term contracts, however, the aggregate wage inflation effects of the AIB were slow in building up as most workers were locked into inflationary pre-AIB contracts for much of the early life of the AIB. Based on the existing bargaining cycle, Christofides and Wilton (1979) estimated that 'the cumulative impact of the AIB on private sector wage rates was only about 0.8 per cent after one year and 3.2 per cent after two years, but rose quite dramatically to 6.1 per cent after three years and 7.2 per cent after four years.'

In summary, all empirical evidence suggests that the Canadian AIB exerted a significant moderating influence on the rate of wage inflation, with a total cumulative effect of seven or eight percentage points on wage levels. Despite predictions of a post-controls wage-rebound effect (to recapture 'lost' wage increases during the controls period), there were no obvious signs of such a post-controls wage explosion. New wage settlements negotiated during the first two years after the AIB was terminated barely kept pace with the inflation rate, which was running at approximately 9 per cent in 1978–9. In this initial two-year period after controls were lifted, 80% of all wage settlements were for less than 10 per cent per annum and only 4% of all wage settlements exceeded 13 per cent per annum. Not only were there no obvious signs of a post-controls wage explosion (to recapture the seven or eight percentage point controls effect), post-AIB wage settlements were extremely moderate in comparison to the very large real wage gains negotiated in the pre-AIB period. Econometric evidence presented by Christofides and Wilton (1985), based on micro wage contract data, confirms the absence of any post-controls wage explosion and also points to a less inflationary structure for wage settlements in the post-AIB era.

Since there is no evidence that aggregate profit margins rose during the AIB period,[15] one would surmise that this AIB-induced moderation in wage settlements must have produced a significantly lower rate of price inflation. Unfortunately this was not the case, as a number of supply–price shocks prevented the Canadian inflation rate from falling. As mentioned above, farm food prices and energy prices were exempt from the controls programme. Canadian food prices increased by 8.3 per cent in 1977 and 15.5 per cent in 1978; and energy prices increased by 15.4 per cent, 12.1 per cent and 9.3 per cent in the three years 1976–8. If one excludes food and energy prices from the Consumer Price Index, then the inflation rate was clearly falling during the life of the AIB (from 9.6 per cent in 1975 to 6.1 per cent in 1978). In a simulation study, Wilton (1984) has shown that without the food, energy and foreign price shocks which occurred during the AIB period, wage and price controls likely would have lowered the rate of price inflation to about 5 per cent, very close to the government's 4 per cent target. However, the presence of these large supply–price shocks produced an upward trend in the actual inflation rate during the 1977–8 period, with the Canadian inflation rate reaching 8.9 per cent in 1978 (compared to a 10.8 per cent inflation rate when controls were implemented in 1975).

Even though controlled wages and domestic costs were more or less on target during the AIB period, exogenous food price increases and the government's energy policy (allowing heavily subsidized domestic oil prices to move towards world prices) shocked this underlying inflation by almost three percentage points. Since most people form their inflation expectations in terms of expected price increase for all goods, Canadian wage and price controls probably had very little impact on reducing inflation expectations, the *raison d'être* of the AIB. Entering the 1980s, the actual and expected Canadian inflation rate remained stubbornly at about

10 per cent (its 1975 level). Even though the AIB may have won the battle on the wage front, it lost the war against inflation expectations and failed to achieve its major objective – a lower inflation rate.

Nevertheless, the AIB should not be deemed a complete failure. Without wage and price controls in place, the aforementioned supply–price shocks would have pushed the Canadian inflation rate to 11 per cent in 1978, despite the existence of a restrictive monetary policy. With controls in force, the 1978 inflation rate was just under 9 per cent, about two percentage points lower than it would have been in the absence of controls (see Wilton, 1984). Furthermore, in the absence of any supply–price shocks (including energy price increases), the Canadian AIB would likely have lowered the actual inflation rate to about 5 per cent. While the AIB failed to achieve its overall inflation targets (and was consequently considered by many to be a failure), it at least halted and prevented any further acceleration of the inflation rate which would have occurred because of rising energy prices and the food-import price shocks of 1977–8. In the words of Wilson and Jump (1979), 'we could have done far worse' without the AIB.

In conclusion, all empirical studies agree that the Canadian AIB significantly reduced the annual rate of wage inflation (by about three percentage points) and there is no evidence of a 'catch-up' wage and price explosion following the removal of controls in 1978. As discussed earlier in this chapter, the major benefits of a temporary wage and price controls programme implemented in conjunction with a monetary disinflation policy are measured in real opportunity cost terms. Disinflation can be accomplished without having to endure a severe painful recession with high unemployment rates, high real interest rates and a substantial loss in output. Assuming that the slope of the Canadian Phillips curve is about one-half, to achieve the same degree of wage restraint (three percentage points per year) without controls should have required an additional six percentage points of unemployment (i.e. unemployment rates of approximately 13 per cent for 1976–8). The economic benefits of imposing temporary wage and price controls were equivalent to approximately 600,000 more jobs (for three years). While the AIB undoubtedly imposed some administrative and resource distortion costs on the Canadian economy, such microeconomic costs are likely to have been much smaller than the substantial macroeconomic costs associated with a major recession engineered to generate the same degree of wage restraint as produced by the AIB.

As a final postscript to this chapter, the Canadian government rejected the use of temporary wage and price controls in 1981–2 when it again decided to fight inflation with a restrictive monetary policy. During this two-year period, the Bank of Canada reduced the real money supply (as measured by M1 deflated by the CPI) by over 16 per cent, as the nominal money supply grew by only 3.9 per cent in 1981 and 0.6 per cent in 1982. Given this highly restrictive monetary policy, our earlier analysis of a conventional IS–LM–PEP model with adaptive inflation expectations would have suggested a substantial rise in both interest rates and unemployment rates above their equilibrium values as the economy slowly geared down to a lower inflation rate. This is precisely what happened. During 1981–2 the prime lending rate of Canadian chartered banks averaged over 17 per cent and the unemployment rate jumped from 7.5 per cent in 1981 to 11 per cent in 1982. In output terms, real Canadian GNP fell by 4.4 per cent in 1982. This severe recession, aided and abetted by a very restrictive monetary policy, had the predicted effects on the inflation rate. The 12.5 per cent inflation rate of 1981 was driven down to 5.8 per cent in 1983 (and 4.4 per cent in 1984). A monetary disinflation policy will indeed lower the long-run inflation rate, but at a very high short-run cost.

NOTES

1. For example, during the years 1962–72, the average annual inflation rate in Canada, France, West Germany, Italy, Japan, the United Kingdom and United States was only 4.1 per cent. In contrast, during the 1973–82 period the average annual inflation rate for these seven major industrialized countries was 9.3 per cent, reaching 13.3 per cent in 1974 and 12.2 per cent in 1980.
2. 'I don't believe our policy of so-called monetary gradualism will bring down the inflation rate without a major recession' (R.G. Lipsey, *Financial Post*, 6 December 1980); and 'I know of no example of a country that has cured substantial inflation without going through a transitional period of slow growth and unemployment' (M. Friedman, *Newsweek*, 12 November 1979).
3. The slope of Tobin's Phillips curve is two-thirds and a two-year lag on inflation is included to proxy inflation inertia (a variant of adaptive inflation expectations).
4. To demonstrate this point, simply substitute the aggregate demand equation (10.5) into the PSSF equation (10.6) and then substitute a price-level version of the adaptive expectations equation (10.4) for P^e.
5. See, for example, Fischer, 1977.
6. For further discussion of the New Classical macroeconomic model, see Wilton and Prescott (1987).
7. There is one additional complication. When inflation expectations are lowered to 5 per cent, the IS curve will also shift downwards (see Figure 10.1), which will produce an output level below Y^* and an inflation rate below 5 per cent (a mini-recession). Given a 5 per cent increase in the *nominal* money supply, the *real* money supply will increase, the LM curve will shift downwards to the right and the economy will (eventually) return to Y^* with a 5 per cent inflation rate.
8. Rather than imposing wage and price controls, the government could consider using a tax-based incomes policy (see, for example, Seidman, 1978).
9. In a 1979 survey of US economists, 72 per cent were generally opposed to

wage and price controls and only 6 per cent were generally in favour of wage and price controls (see Kearl *et al.*, 1979). On the other hand, Hibbs (1982) notes that 57 per cent of Americans participating in a 1979 Gallup poll were in favour of having the government bring back wage and price controls, while only 31 per cent were opposed.

10. It should be noted that three years after rousing Canadian economists to 'stand up and be counted' against wage and price controls, Lipsey (1979) conceded to Australian economists that 'wage and price controls might be used to force the inflation rate down' and that if he were Prime Minister he would 'cut the rate of monetary expansion ... slap on a six month wage–price freeze followed by a flat modest percentage increase for a further transitional period ... and wear a bullet proof vest every time I showed myself in public.' Lipsey's dramatic about-face on the use of controls was motivated by the difficulty in 'breaking inflationary expectations ... [which] is easier said than done.'
11. For a review of UK and US wage and price control programmes, see Parkin *et al.* (1972); Henry (1981); Fallick and Elliott (1981); Sumner and Ward (1983); Pencavel (1981); Reid (1981); Blinder and Newton (1981); Frye and Gordon (1981).
12 For further details concerning the nature and implementation of the Canadian wage and price control programme, see, for example, Christofides and Wilton (1979, chapters 1 and 2).
13. In fact Canadian domestic oil prices were only deregulated in June 1985, as world oil prices fell back towards the lower Canadian domestic oil price.
14. See, for example, Auld *et al.* (1979), Christofides and Wilton (1979; 1983), Cousineau and Lacroix (1978), Fortin and Newton (1982), Reid (1979), Riddell and Smith (1982) and Wilson and Jump (1979).
15. In fact, the ratio of corporate profits to net national income at factor cost fell from 15.2 per cent in 1975 to 13.0 per cent in 1977 and 14.3 per cent in 1978.

REFERENCES

Auld, D.A.L., Christofides, L.N., Swidinsky, R. and Wilton, D.A. (1979) 'The impact of the Anti-Inflation Board on negotiated wage settlements', *Canadian Journal of Economics*, vol. 12, no. 2, May.

Begg, D.K.H. (1982) *The Rational Expectations Revolution in Macroeconomics*, Oxford: Philip Allan.

Blanchard, D.J. and Summers, L.H. (1986) 'Hysteresis and the European unemployment problem' in S. Fischer (ed.), *NBER Macroeconomics Annual 1986*, Cambridge, MA: MIT Press.

Blinder, A.S. and Newton, W.J. (1981) 'The 1971–1974 controls program and the price level: an econometric post-mortem', *Journal of Monetary Economics*, July.

Buiter, W.H. (1980) 'The macroeconomics of Dr. Pangloss, a critical survey of the New Classical economics', *Economic Journal*, vol. 90, March.

Christofides, L.N. and Wilton, D.A. (1979) *Wage Controls in Canada (1975:3–1978:2): A Study of Their Impact on Negotiated Base Wage Rates*, Ottawa: Anti-Inflation Board.

Christofides, L.N. and Wilton, D.A. (1983) 'Incomes policy reconsidered', *Journal of Macroeconomics*, vol. 5, Winter.

Christofides, L.N. and Wilton, D.A. (1985) 'Wage determination in the aftermath

of controls', *Economica*, vol. 52, February.
Cousineau, J.-M. and Lacroix, R. (1978) 'L'Impact de la politique canadienne de contrôle des prix et des revenus sur les ententes salariales', *Canadian Public Policy*, vol. 4, no. 1 March.
Fallick, J.L. and Elliott, R.F. (eds) (1981) *Incomes Policies, Inflation and Relative Pay*, London: George Allen & Unwin.
Figlewski, S. and Wachtel, P. (1981) 'The formation of inflationary expectations', *Review of Economics and Statistics*, vol. 63, February.
Fischer, S. (1977) 'Long-term contracts, rational expectations and the optimal money supply', *Journal of Political Economy*, vol. 85, February.
Fortin, P. and Newton, K. (1982) 'Labour market tightness and wage inflation in Canada' in M.N. Baily (ed.), *Workers, Jobs and Inflation*, Washington, DC: Brookings Institution.
Friedman, B.M. (1983) 'Recent perspectives in and on macroeconomics', NBER Working Paper no. 1208, September.
Frye, J. and Gordon, R.J. (1981) 'Government intervention in the inflation process: the econometrics of "self-inflicted wounds"', *American Economic Review, Papers and Proceedings*, vol. 71, May.
Gordon, R.J. (1982) 'Why stopping inflation may be costly: evidence from fourteen historical periods', in R.E. Hall (ed.), *Inflation: Causes and Effects*, Chicago: University of Chicago Press.
Henry, S.G.B. (1981) 'Incomes policy and aggregate pay', in J.L. Fallick and R.F. Elliott (eds), *Incomes Policies, Inflation and Relative Pay*, London: George Allen & Unwin.
Hibbs, D.A. Jr (1982) 'Public concern about inflation and unemployment in the United States: trends, correlates, and political implications' in R.E. Hall (ed.), *Inflation: Causes and Effects*, Chicago: University of Chicago Press.
Kearl, J.R, Smith, C.L., Whiting, G.T. and Wimmer, L.T. (1979) 'A confusion of economists', *American Economic Review*, Papers and Proceedings, vol. 69, May.
little good', *Canadian Public Policy*, vol. 3, no. 1 March.
Lipsey, R.G. (1978) 'The place of the Phillips curve in macroeconomic models' in A.R. Bergstrom (ed.), *Stability and Inflation,* Chichester: John Wiley & Sons.
Lipsey, R.G. (1979) 'World inflation', *Economic Record*, December.
Lipsey, R.G. (1981) 'The understanding and control of inflation: is there a crisis in macroeconomics?', *Canadian Journal of Economics*, vol. 14, no. 4, November.
Muth, J.F. (1961) 'Rational expectations and the theory of price movements', *Econometrica*, vol. 29.
Okun, A.M. (1978) 'Efficient disinflationary policies', *American Economic Review*, Papers and Proceedings, vol. 68, May.
Parkin, M., Sumner, M.T. and Jones, R.A. (1972) 'A survey of the econometric evidence of the effects of incomes policy on the rate of inflation' in M. Parkin and M.T. Sumner (eds) *Incomes Policy and Inflation*, Manchester: Manchester University Press.
Pencavel, J. (1981) 'The American experience with incomes policies' in J.L. Fallick and R.F. Elliott (eds), *Incomes Policies, Inflation and Relative Pay*, London: George Allen & Unwin.
Pesaran, M.H. (1982) 'A critique of the proposed tests of the natural rate-rational expectations hypothesis', *Economic Journal*, September.
Phelps, E.S. (1972) *Inflation Policy and Unemployment Theory*, New York: Norton.
Reid, F. (1979) 'The effect of controls on the rate of wage change in Canada',

Canadian Journal of Economics, vol. 12, no. 2, May.
Reid, F. (1981) 'Control and decontrol of wages in the United States: an empirical analysis', *American Economic Review*, vol. 71, March.
Riddell, W.C. and Smith P. (1982) 'Expected inflation and wage changes in Canada', *Canadian Journal of Economics*, vol. 15, no. 2, August.
Seidman, L.S. (1978) 'Tax-based incomes policies', *Brookings Papers on Economic Activity*, no. 2.
Sumner, M.T. and Ward, R. (1983) 'The reappearing Phillips curve', *Oxford Economic Papers*.
Tobin, J. (1980) 'Stabilization policy ten years after', *Brookings Papers on Economic Activity*, no. 1.
Vanderkamp, J. (1975) 'Inflation: a simple Friedman theory with a Phillips twist', *Journal of Monetary Economics*, vol. 4, January.
Wilson, T.A. and Jump, G. (1979) *The Influence of the Anti-Inflation Program on Aggregate Wages and Prices*, Ottawa: Anti-Inflation Board.
Wilton, D.A. (1984) 'An evaluation of wage and price controls in Canada', *Canadian Public Policy*, vol. 10, no. 2, February.
Wilton, D.A. and Prescott, D.M. (1987) *Macroeconomics, Theory and Policy in Canada*, 2nd edn, Toronto: Addison-Wesley.

11 · MONETARY GROWTH MODELS: THE ROLE OF MONEY DEMAND FUNCTIONS

Taradas Bandyopadhyay and Subrata Ghatak

INTRODUCTION

In the growing literature on money and economic growth, money is usually regarded as *superneutral* when steady-state real variables are independent of the rate of growth of money supply. Writers on monetary growth models have focused attention on the relationships among the capital intensity, real rate of return and the steady-state rate of inflation. In a dynamic context, the stability of monetary growth models has also received attention. However, as Barro and Fischer (1976) point out that 'since the steady state results have themselves been a matter of controversy, it is not surprising that there is a little agreement on appropriate dynamic analyses'.

The basic neo-classical monetary growth models, as developed by Tobin (1965) in his seminal contribution and Sidrauski (1967) assume only one commodity and two assets – money and capital. Since new issues are introduced in the economy as lump-sum transfers, all money is regarded as 'outside' money. Accordingly, disposable income comprises transfer payments from the government. Savings are a fixed proportion of disposable income. It has been shown that in the steady state the rate of inflation is equal to the rate of growth of nominal money supply net of the rate of growth of population. The main conclusion of the Tobin model is that capital intensity rises with the rate of inflation; this conclusion depends on both savings and portfolio effects. If we assume a portfolio effect, then a rise in the steady-state rate of inflation will reduce the real balances for a given stock of capital. This implies lower savings from disposable income. Since savings are assumed to be a fixed proportion, a larger form of savings must comprise a rise in capital intensity.

Levhari and Patinkin (1968), however, have shown in their important contribution that in a non-optimizing model, the steady-state impact of inflation on capital intensity can be either positive or negative. Indeed, if we assume, along with Dornbusch and Frenkel (1973), a direct relationship between *consumption* and inflation (anticipated), then the Tobin–Sidrauski result ceases to follow (see Barro and Fischer, 1976).

Brock (1974) has shown that in an extended Tobin–Sidrauski model where labour–leisure choice is *endogenous*, the steady-state values of the capital–labour ratio and the real rate of return remain unaffected by the rate of inflation. However, the steady-state ratios of capital and labour to *total population* are influenced via induced alterations in the participation rate of the labour force.

Further extensions of the Tobin model have been made by Levhari and Patinkin (1968), Johnson (1967), Dornbusch and Frenkel (1973), and Stein (1970; 1971) where money enters the utility function as a consumer good or production function as a producer good. The main result that has followed from this class of models is that although the steady-state real rate of return is independent of the rate of inflation, the ratio of capital to labour changes if real balances influence the marginal productivity of capital and labour differently. Clearly, money will no longer be superneutral under such circumstances.

In this chapter we examine the monetary growth model as developed by Tobin. The crux of this analysis lies in the conclusion that, in a monetary economy, savings can consist of capital (physical) goods and/or real cash balances. Hence, the equilibrium value of capital intensity (and, therefore, production per head) is a function of the composition of the portfolio. Now it is easy to see that in a money economy (where money can be held as an extra asset in a portfolio) the equilibrium capital intensity will be lower than in a real economy. But an increase in the rate of growth of money supply leads to a fall in real cash balances and a *higher* capital intensity.

We then analyse the two major changes of Tobin's analysis by Johnson (1967) and Levhari and Patinkin (1968). Both consider the services emanating from the holding of real money balances as influencing individuals' disposable income. They show that when money is introduced as a consumer good in a single-sector neo-classical growth model, the effect of inflation upon the degree of capital intensity in a steady-state equilibrium is ambiguous. Levhari and Patinkin argue that 'it is this dropping of the assumption of [a] constant [saving ratio] rather than the different definition of disposable income' which yields qualitatively different results from those of the Tobin model.

In this chapter we argue that it is neither the dropping of a constant saving ratio nor the different definition of disposable income, but the *form of the demand-for-money function* which produces the fundamentally different results (Bandyopadhyay, 1982). Introducing money as a consumer good, as suggested by Levhari and Patinkin, it will be shown that with a general functional form of the money demand function, the effect of inflation on steady-state capital intensity remains ambiguous as in a neo-classical monetary growth model where money is neither a consumer good nor a producer good. In a portfolio approach to the money demand function, it is shown that the steady-state capital intensity rises with the rate of inflation. These results are actually independent of the definition of disposable income. In a Harrodian growth model, even with a general functional form of the money demand function, equilibrium capital intensity is lower in the monetary model and the effect of inflation on the steady-state capital intensity is determinate and positive.

As a special case, we then introduce a Kaldorian 'pseudo-classical' savings function. This extended framework with a variable savings function does not diminish the significance of the role of the money demand function or the policy implications of a monetary growth model. In another special case, we distinguish between money as a consumer good and money as a producer good and analyse some of its implications for capital intensity. It is shown that the introduction of money as a producer good validates the neo-classical result that the steady-state capital intensity is lower in a monetary economy than in a barter economy. Furthermore, we show that an increase in the steady-state rate of inflation raises the steady-state capital intensity unambiguously if the nominal interest rate is greater than some critical value. A casual empirical observation suggests that the restriction on the nominal interest rate is very realistic. In other words, with the portfolio approach to the demand for real balances, one can obtain various unambiguous results in different monetary growth models. However, with other forms of the demand-for-money function this unambiguity disappears even in the context of a very simple monetary growth model.

INFLATION AND REAL RETURN: THE BASIC MODEL

Our basic model consists of the following equations:

$$Y = F(K, L) = Lf(k) \tag{11.1}$$

$$f'(k) > 0, \quad f''(k) < 0, \quad \lim_{k \to 0} f'(k) = \infty, \quad \lim_{k \to \infty} f'(k) = 0$$

$$k = K/L \tag{11.2}$$

$$S = s[Y + (M/P)(\mu + r)] \tag{11.3}$$

$$S = s[Y + (M/P)(\mu - \pi)] \tag{11.3a}$$

$$I = S - [(M/P)(\mu - \pi)] \tag{11.4}$$

$$\dot{K} = I \tag{11.5}$$

$$r = f'(k) \tag{11.6}$$

$$\dot{L}/L = n \tag{11.7}$$

$$M/PL = m = h(i, f(k)) \tag{11.8}$$

$$i = r + \pi \tag{11.9}$$

$$\dot{M}/M = \mu \tag{11.10}$$
$$\dot{P}/P = \pi = \mu - n - \dot{m}/m \tag{11.11}$$

where Y is output; K is capital; L is labour; P is the price level; n is the growth of labour supply; M is the nominal money supply exogenously given; S is savings; I is investment; μ is the rate of growth of money supply; π is the rate of change of price level; i is the nominal interest rate or 'expected' opportunity cost of holding money; r is the real rate of return on capital; and $\dot{U}$ denotes the rate of change of the variable.

Equation (11.1) describes the standard neo-classical production function where output (Y) is related to capital (K) and labour (L). The relation is homogeneous of degree one and thus output per head (y) is a function of capital per head k or K/L. In Equation (11.3), savings (S) is a constant fraction of disposable income. Disposable income is defined as output, plus the real value of government transfer payment ($\mu M/P$), less the loss in real value of existing cash balances due to inflation ($\pi M/P$), plus the opportunity cost of holding money which is $[(r+\pi)M/P]$. This opportunity cost needs some explanation.

Since money is a consumer good in our model, people derive utility from money holdings, and hence the imputed value from the holding of cash balances is included in disposable income. These imputed services must clearly be valued at the alternative cost at the margin of holding money balances. There are two different prices that are relevant to the holding of money balances: one is the goods that are given up to acquire a dollar; and the other is the number of cents per dollar per year that the money holder must spend to keep his real balances constant. Thus, the opportunity cost of holding money is the money rate of interest (i), which is the real return on capital (r) plus the loss of value through inflation at the rate of π. If we consider the 'non-sophisticated' definition of disposable income, i.e. do not take into account the utility yield of holding money balances, then Equation (11.3a) is our savings function. Not all of these savings can go into investment. The rate of change of real balances $(\mu - \pi)M/P$ cannot be held in the form of physical assets; accordingly, equilibrium in capital market is defined by Equation (11.4).

We write the demand for real balances as

$$M^d/PL = h(i,y), \quad h_i < 0, \quad h_y > 0.$$

If the real return on capital or the rate of inflation increases then the opportunity cost increases and, therefore, the demand for real money balances decreases, *ceteris paribus*. Unless otherwise specified, the partial interest elasticity of demand for real balances is assumed to be less than unity in absolute value.[1] Total money supply in the economy consists only of outside money (M^s) which is growing exponentially at the rate of μ.

Clearly, $M^s_{(t)} = M_0\exp(\mu t)$. Thus, the expected cost of holding money balances is equal to $r + \mu - n - \dot{m}/m$. We assume rational expectations about the rate of inflation, which is equal to $\mu - n - \dot{m}/m$. The symbols m_d and m_s will be used to denote the variables M^d/PL and M^s/PL, respectively. One of the most important characteristics of the neo-classical monetary growth model is that the money market is always assumed to be in equilibrium. At any point in time, k is predetermined. Only the price level adjusts instantaneously in such a way that the money market is always in equilibrium. Thus, $m_d = h(i, y) = m_s = m$, and relation (11.8) ensures equilibrium in the money market.

The excess demand in the commodity market is the gap between the planned investment and the planned savings in goods. By Walras's Law

$$(I/L - S/L) + \omega\,(m_d - m_s) = 0$$

Since money is the stock variable, we introduce an adjustment factor, ω, and assume that excess demand for asset flows is a constant proportion to excess demand for asset stocks. Since instantaneous adjustment in price always clears the money market, planned investment must always equal planned savings. So there is no place for an independent investment function in the neo-classical model. We assume that actual investment always equals planned savings in goods. Therefore, $\dot{K} = S - [(M/P)(\mu - \pi)]$.

It is readily shown that $\dot{K}/L = \dot{k} + nk$ and, making use of this relationship, we can substitute Equations (11.3), (11.5), (11.7) and (11.8) into (11.4), divide by L and rearrange terms to obtain the following expression for the dynamic path of capital intensity:

$$\dot{k}/k = \phi(k) - n$$

where

$$\phi(k) = \frac{sf(k)}{k} - (1-s)n\frac{m}{k} + si\frac{m}{k} \quad (11.12)$$

Under the specification of the model above, an explicit solution (for the steady-state capital intensity) will exist if $\phi'(k) < 0$. In fact, this is a necessary condition for the existence of a unique and stable steady-state solution.[2] Differentiating $\phi(k)$ with respect to k, after some rearrangement, we get

$$\phi'(k) = s\,\frac{kf'(k) - f(k)}{k^2} - [(1-s)n - si]\frac{d(m/k)}{dk} + (sm/k)\frac{di}{dk} \quad (11.13)$$

where the first and the last terms of the right-hand side are unambiguously negative. We have to determine the sign of the second term. We assume that $[(1-s)n - si] > 0$; we will provide its justification towards the end of the chapter. Differentiating Equation (11.8) with respect to k, we obtain

$$\frac{d(m/k)}{dk} = \left(h_i f''(k) + h_y \frac{f'(k)}{k} \right) - \frac{h}{k^2}$$

where the first term is positive and the second term is negative. Substituting Equation (11.14) into Equation (11.13) one can easily check that $\phi'(k) \gtreqless 0$. Hence, there does not necessarily exist an explicit solution for steady-state capital intensity, or a unique equilibrium solution under the specification of the model.

Following Tobin now, we assume the portfolio approach to the money demand function which requires that the community will hold the real money in proportion to the stock of capital, and the proportions depend on their real yields. The yield on capital is equal to the rental on capital, which, under perfect competition, is equal to its net marginal product. The yield on money is equal to the negative of the rate of change in prices. Therefore, the demand function for real cash balances can be written as follows:

$$\frac{M^d}{PK} = \lambda[f'(k) - (-\pi)] = \lambda(i), \qquad \lambda_i < 0. \tag{11.15}$$

Using Equation (11.15), the equilibrium condition in the money market can be written as

$$m = \lambda(i)k. \tag{11.8a}$$

Differentiating Equation (11.8a) with respect to k we obtain,

$$\frac{d(m/k)}{dk} = \lambda_i f''(k), \tag{11.16}$$

which is positive. Substituting Equation (11.16) into Equation (11.13), we can write, after some rearrangement

$$\phi'(k) = s\,\frac{kf'(k) - f(k)}{k^2} - (1-s)n\lambda_i f''(k) + s\lambda\left(\frac{i\lambda_i}{\lambda} + 1\right) f''(k).$$

The first term and the second term of the right-hand side are clearly negative. Since the partial elasticity of the demand for money with respect to nominal interest rate is less the unity in absolute value, $[i(\lambda_i/\lambda) + 1]$ is positive and the third term is negative. Hence, $\phi'(k) < 0$.[3]

The economic interpretation of $\phi'(k) < 0$ is straightforward. An increase in the capital stock lowers the average product of capital and as a result capital accumulation declines. Furthermore, it reduces the marginal product of capital which is the real rate of interest. This in turn will increase the per capita demand for real money if the increase in the stock of real money produces an increase in privately disposable real income, consumption is stimulated, and the rate of capital accumulation is further reduced.

Now to show that $dk^*/d\pi^* > 0$, we differentiate the equation for the dynamic path of capital intensity at the steady state with respect to the rate of inflation, and obtain

$$\frac{\partial(\dot{k}/k^*)}{\partial \pi^*} = -(1-s)n\lambda_i + s\lambda[i(\lambda_i/\lambda) + 1].$$

where k^* and π^* refer to the steady state values. Since the interest elasticity, $i(\lambda_i/\lambda)$, is less than unity in absolute value, and $\lambda_i < 0$,

$$\frac{\partial(\dot{k}/k^*)}{\partial \pi^*} > 0.$$

Hence, by the implicit function rule,

$$\frac{dk^*}{d\pi^*} = \frac{\partial(\dot{k}/k^*)\partial \pi^*}{\partial(\dot{k}/k^*)/\partial k^*} > 0.$$

Equivalently, the real interest rate falls with the rate of inflation. An intuitive explanation for this result is as follows. Consider an increase in the steady-state inflation rate. For a given stock of capital, portfolio behaviour implies that the real money balances will be reduced, which implies that less disposable income has to be saved to provide the growing population with real money balances. Since the savings rate is constant, a larger fraction of savings takes the form of capital, thus raising capital intensity.

We observe that if we consider the portfolio approach to the demand-for-money function in a monetary growth model, which incorporates the imputed value of holding cash balances in the measurement of disposable income, the effect of the rate of inflation on steady-state capital intensity would remain unambiguous. This shows the role of the money demand function in a monetary growth model. To clarify this point further, consider a non-sophisticated definition of disposable income, which does not include the utility yield from the services of holding cash balances; then, using Equation (11.3a), instead of (11.3), Equation (11.12) becomes

$$\phi(k) = s\frac{f(k)}{k} - (1-s)\frac{h[i, f(k)](\mu - \pi)}{k}. \qquad (11.12a)$$

Once again, we have $\phi'(k) \gtreqless 0$. But if we replace the money demand function specified in Equation (11.15) then the equilibrium condition in the money market would ensure $\phi'(k) < 0$.[4] Thus, we can conclude that it is not the definition of disposable income that causes the ambiguity of the effect of the rate of inflation on steady-state capital intensity, but it is the form of the demand-for-money function that leads to a qualitatively different result.

We now examine the implications of the demand-for-money function. Given the specification of the model, the sufficient condition for the existence of a unique equilibrium or the existence of an explicit solution in our model is that

$$\frac{\mathrm{d}m}{\mathrm{d}k}\frac{k}{m} - 1 \geqslant 0. \tag{11.17}$$

We have shown that though the money demand function of the form of Equation (11.12) does not satisfy condition (11.17), it is satisfied by the portfolio approach to the money demand function specified in Equation (11.15). Let us examine now the implications of considering the quantity theory version of the money demand function.

From the demand-for-money function (Equation (11.8)) we observe,

$$\frac{\mathrm{d}m}{\mathrm{d}k}\frac{k}{m} = \psi_i \frac{\mathrm{d}i}{\mathrm{d}k}\frac{k}{i} + \psi_y k \frac{f'(k)}{i(k)}$$

where ψ_i and ψ_y are the interest elasticity and the income elasticity of the demand for money, respectively. Assume, without loss of generality, the rate of inflation to be zero. Then, Equation (11.17) may be written in alternative form as

$$\frac{\mathrm{d}m}{\mathrm{d}k}\frac{k}{m} = (-\psi_i)\frac{\rho}{\theta} + \psi_y(1-\rho), \tag{11.18}$$

where ρ and $1-\rho$ are, respectively, the share of labour and the share of capital in total output; and θ is the elasticity of substitution. Rearrangement of Equation (11.18) shows the condition (11.17) holds if the elasticity of substitution is not bigger than the interest-elasticity of money demand. Thus, under the assumption of the quantity theory of the demand-for-money function, the elasticity of substitution should have to be very close to zero.

In a barter economy model, we know that the fixed-coefficient technology production function leads to the well-known Harrodian instability problem, an instability which, among other things, the neo-classical model was designed to overcome by introducing an infinitely substitutable production function. Besides the neo-classical solution to the Harrodian instability problem, another escape route was offered by Kaldor (1956) and Pasinetti (1962), who introduced a 'pseudo-classical' savings function which consequently makes the overall savings–output ratio a variable. But in our monetary model, though aggregate savings is a constant proportion to the total disposable income, the overall savings–output ratio,

$$\Phi = s + [s(i+n) - n]\,\frac{h[i, f(k)]}{f(k)} = \Phi(k, \pi)$$

is a variable; and in general it is a function of capital intensity and the rate of inflation. Thus in a growth model of Harrod–Domar variety, under the assumption of a generalized money demand function, there exists a unique and stable steady-state solution; and the effect of an increasing inflation rate is to increase steady-state capital intensity. This conclusion would remain valid in a neo-classical growth model if we assume a portfolio approach to the money demand function; otherwise the effect of an increasing inflation rate on steady-state capital intensity would be ambiguous.

VARIABLE SAVING RATIO: AN EXTENSION OF THE MODEL

It would now be interesting to examine whether the introduction of a variable savings ratio (s) would make a qualitatively different result. Following Kaldor (1956) we introduce a 'pseudo-classical' savings function where the propensity to save differs between workers and capitalists, and consequently the overall savings ratio varies with the distribution of income. Accordingly, total savings in the economy is

$$S = s_p Y_p^d + s_w Y_w^d \qquad 0 \leqslant s_w < s_p < 1,$$

where Y_p^d and Y_w^d are the disposable income of the profit earners and wage earners, respectively. Assume that the government distributes the money supply in proportion to the share of income of two classes. In that case, the savings ratio

$$s = S/Y^d = (s_p rK + s_w wL)/Y \tag{11.19}$$

and a change in the distribution of income will change s. Since the real return on capital and wage rate are, respectively, $r = f'(k)$ and $w = f'(k) - kf'(k)$, we can write equation (11.9) as

$$s = \frac{(s_p - s_w)kf'(k) + s_w f(k)}{f(k)} \tag{11.20}$$

As k increases the rate of return on capital and wage rate will change and make s to vary. Notice that, since $0 \leqslant s_w < s_p < 1$, s lies between 0 and 1.

Now substituting Equations (11.3), (11.4), (11.8) and (11.20) into Equation (11.12), the fundamental differential equation of the system is found, after a little manipulation, to be

$$\dot{k}/k = \phi(k) - n,$$

where at the steady state,

$$\phi(k) = (s_p - s_w)f'(k) + s_w \frac{f(k)}{k} + (n+i)\left((s_p - s_w)\frac{f'(k)}{f(k)} h[i, f(k)] + s_w \frac{h[i, f(k)]}{k}\right) - \frac{nh[i, f(k)]}{k}.$$

Differentiating $\phi(k)$ with respect to k at the steady state, we obtain

$$\phi'(k) = \left((s_p - s_w)f''(k) + s_w \frac{kf'(k) - f(k)}{k^2}\right) + (s_p - s_w)\left((n+i)\frac{h[i, f(k)]}{f(k)} f''(k) + f'(k)\frac{\mathrm{d}\{h[i, f(k)]/f(k)\}}{\mathrm{d}k}\right)$$

$$- [(1 - s_w)n + s_w i]\frac{kh_k - h}{k^2} + \left((s_p - s_w)\frac{f'(k)}{f(k)} h[i, f(k)] + s_w \frac{h[i, f(k)]}{k}\right) f''(k).$$

Once again in the general case $\phi'(k^*) \gtreqless 0$. Now in addition to $[(1 - sw)\, n - s_w^i\,] > 0$, if we assume that the income elasticity of demand for money is not greater than unity and the money demand increases proportionately more than capital stock per head, $\phi'(k) < 0$.

An increase in the expected rate of inflation lowers private disposable income in two ways, by increasing expected capital losses on the stock of money balances, and by lowering the amount of real money balances that the individual (and the community) desires to hold. Differentiating once again the equation for the dynamic path of capital intensity with respect to π, we obtain

$$\frac{\partial(\dot{k}/k)}{\partial\pi} = (n+i)\left((s_p - s_w)\frac{f'(k)}{f(k)} h_i - (1 - s_w)\frac{h_i}{k}\right) - i\left(\frac{h_i}{k}\right)$$

$$+ \left((s_p - s_w)\frac{f'(k)h(i, f(k))}{f(k)} + s_w\, h[i, f(k)]\right)$$

$$= -(n+i)\{(s_p - s_w)[f(k) - kf'(k)] + (1 - s_p)f(k)\}\frac{h_i}{kf(k)}$$

$$- \frac{ih_i}{k} + \left((s_p - s_w)\frac{f'(k)}{f(k)} h[i, f(k)] + s_w \frac{h[i, f(k)]}{k}\right).$$

Since $h_i < 0$,

$$\frac{\partial(\dot{k}/k)}{\partial \pi} > 0.$$

Now we use the implicit function rule and obtain $dk^*/d\pi^* > 0$, which means that an increasing rate of inflation increases steady-state capital intensity in the economy or, equivalently, decreases the real return on capital. Hence, dropping the assumption of constant s does not yield a qualitatively different result.

To summarize the results of this section: we have shown that, in a neo-classical economy (see, for example, Solow, 1956) in which money is treated as a consumer good, the effect of inflation on capital intensity is determinate and positive if we consider a portfolio approach to the money demand function; otherwise, the effect is ambiguous. This ambiguity can be removed under the assumption of a generalized money demand function if we replace the neo-classical infinitely substitutable production function with a production function of fixed-coefficient technology. We have also shown that neither the variability of the overall saving to disposable income ratio nor the variability of the overall saving to output ratio on its own causes a qualitatively different result in a neo-classical growth model, contrary to the argument put forward by Levhari and Patinkin (1968). The ambiguity of the effect of a change in inflation rate on steady-state capital intensity arises from the specification of the demand-for-money function.

MONEY AS A CONSUMER OR PRODUCER GOOD

Next we examine the implications of introducing money both as a consumer good and as a producer good. We postulate that, during a given interval, perceptive real money balances (m) are being held by both producers and consumers. We write

$$m = m_f + m_h \tag{11.21}$$

where m_f represents per capita real money balances held by producers, and m_h represents per capita real money balances held by consumers.

Money as a producer good becomes an argument in the production function. Accordingly, we write,

$$y = g(k, m_f), \qquad g_k > 0, \qquad g_m > 0. \qquad [11.1']$$

Note that $r = g_k(k, m_f)$ and $r + \pi = g_m(k, m_f)$. Thus, the profit-maximizing behaviour of a producer determines the demand for real money balances which in general depends on i and k. We assume

$$m_f = \lambda_f(i)k, \qquad \lambda_{fi} < 0. \tag{11.22}$$

Since total real balances are part of wealth, the growth in total real balances should be added to real income. In addition, only the part of real money balances held by consumers renders utility. Thus

$$S/L = s[g(k, m_f) + m(\mu - \pi) + (r + \pi)m_h]. \qquad [11.3']$$

The household demand for real money balance comes from the utility-maximizing behaviour and once again in general depends on i and k. We assume,

$$m_h = \lambda_h(i)k, \qquad \lambda_{hi} < 0. \tag{11.23}$$

The total demand for money balances, m^d, is equal to its supply $m^s (= m)$ by instantaneous adjustment to the price level. Thus $m = [\lambda_f(i) + \lambda_h(i)]k$.

With these in mind we now write the dynamic path of capital intensity in this economy as

$$\dot{k}/k = \phi(k) - n, \tag{11.24}$$

where

$$\phi(k) = s[g(k, m_f)/k] - (1 - s)(\mu - \pi)[\lambda_f(i) + \lambda_h(i)] + si\lambda_h(i).$$

Differentiating $\phi(k)$ with respect to k at the steady state, we obtain

$$\phi'(k) = s\left[\frac{k\{g_k + g_m[(\lambda(i)/k) + \lambda_{fi}]\} - g}{k^2}\right] - (1 - s)n[(\lambda_{hi} + \lambda_{fi})]\, g_{kk}$$

$$+ s\lambda_h\left(i\frac{\lambda_{hi}}{\lambda_h} + 1\right) g_{kk}.$$

Now, under the assumption of diminishing marginal productivity of capital, $g_{kk} < 0$, the second term is clearly negative. Since the partial elasticity of the household's demand for real money balances with respect to nominal interest rates is less than unity in absolute value, the third item is also negative. Next consider the first term. The term $k\{g_k + g_m[\lambda_f(i)/k + \lambda_{fi}]\}$ is the direct and the indirect effect of an increase in capital on output. The marginal productivity of labour is positive therefore, the first term is obviously negative. Hence, $\phi'(k) < 0$. Thus, $\partial(\dot{k}/k)/\partial k < 0$. To examine the effect of an increase in the rate of inflation on the steady-state capital intensity, we set $\mu - \pi - n = 0$ and differentiate (11.24) with respect to π^* and we get

$$\frac{\partial(\dot{k}/k)}{\partial \pi} = sg_m\lambda_{fi} - (1 - s)n[\lambda_{fi} + \lambda_{hi}] + s\left(i\frac{\lambda_{hi}}{\lambda_h^{(i)}} + 1\right)(i).$$

Since $g_m = i$, we can alternatively write,

$$\frac{\partial(\dot{k}/k)}{\partial \pi} = [s(i+n)-n]\lambda_{fi} - (1-s)\lambda_{hi} + s\left[i\frac{\lambda_{hi}}{\lambda_h^{(i)}} + 1 \right] \lambda_h(i).$$

Clearly, the second and third term is positive. Since $\lambda_{fi} < 0$, $\partial(\dot{k}/k^*)/\partial\pi^* > 0$ if $[s(i+n)-n] > 0$, i.e. if $i > [(1-s)/s]n$. During the period of increasing rate of inflation, a casual observation about the values of s and n in the western industrial economy suggests that this is a plausible condition. Now, using the implicit function theorem, at the steady state,

$$\frac{dk^*}{d\pi^*} > 0 \quad \text{if} \quad i > \left(\frac{1-s}{s}\right) n.$$

Once again, under the assumption of a portfolio approach to the money demand function, the effect of an increasing rate of inflation on steady-state capital intensity is positive whenever $i > [(1-s)/s]n$. It is left to the reader to check that, even under the assumption of $i > [(1-s)/s]n$, if one considers a general form of a money demand function, then that would lead to ambiguity as before. Thus, in a world where money is used for both production and consumption, the essential conclusions of Tobin remain unaffected.

NOTES

1. We have made this assumption in accordance with most empirical studies. See, for example, De Leeuw (1965); Laidler (1966; 1985).
2. This is a necessary condition for the existence of a unique and stable solution in the neighbourhood of equilibrium.
3. Johnson (1967) and Levhari and Patinkin (1968) considered a 'quality theory version' of the money demand function, $M^d/PL = \lambda(i)f(k)$, $\lambda_i < 0$, and obtained $\phi'(k) \lesseqgtr 0$.
4. This result is due to Tobin (1965). Introducing, alternatively, $M^d/PL = \lambda(i)f(k)$, one can check that in this case $\phi'(k) < 0$.

REFERENCES

Bandyopadhyay, T. (1982) 'The role of money demand function in one-sector growth models', *Journal of Macroeconomics*, vol. 4, no. 2, pp. 225–31.

Barro, R. and Fischer, S. (1976), 'Recent developments in monetary theory', *Journal of Monetary Economics*, vol. 1, no. 2, pp. 133–67.

Brock, W. (1974) 'Money and growth: the case for long-run perfect foresight', *International Economic Review*, vol. 15, pp. 750–77.

De Leeuw, F. (1965) 'A model of financial behavior' in J.S. Duesenberry *et al.* (eds), *The Brookings Quarterly Model of the United States*, Chicago.

Dornbusch, R. and Frenkel, J. (1973) 'Inflation and growth: alternative

approaches', *Journal of Money, Credit and Banking*, vol. 5, pp. 141–56.
Fischer, S. (1972) 'Keynes – Wicksell and neo-classical models of money and growth', *American Economic Review*, vol. 62.
Johnson, H. G. (1967) *Essays in Monetary Economics*, London: Allen & Unwin.
Johnson, H.G. (1969) 'Inside money, outside money, income, wealth and welfare in contemporary monetary theory', *Journal of Money, Credit and Banking*, vol. 1, pp. 30–45.
Kaldor, N. (1956) 'Alternative theories of distribution', *Review of Economic Studies*, vol. 23, pp. 94–100.
Laidler, D. (1966) 'The rate of interest and the demand for money: some empirical evidence', *Journal of Political Economy*, vol. 74.
Laidler, D. (1985) *The Demand for Money: Theories, Evidence and Problems*, 3rd edn, New York: Harper and Row.
Levhari, D. and Patinkin, D. (1968) 'The role of money in a sample growth model', *American Economic Review*, vol. 58, pp. 713–53.
Pasinetti, L. (1962) 'Rate of profit and income distribution in relation to growth', *Review of Economic Studies*, vol. 29, pp. 267–79.
Sidrauski, M. (1967) 'Rational choice and patterns of growth in a monetary economy', *American Economic Review*, vol. 57, May, pp. 534–44.
Sijben, J. (1977) *Money and Economic Growth*, Leiden: Martinus Nijhoff.
Solow, R. (1956) 'A contribution to the theory of economic growth', *Quarterly Journal of Economics*, vol. 70, pp. 65–94.
Stein, J. (1971) 'Monetary growth theory in perspective', *American Economic Review*, vol. 60, pp. 85–106.
Stein, J. (1971) *Money and Capacity Growth*, New York/London: Columbia University Press.
Tobin, J. (1965) 'Money and economic growth', *Econometrica*, vol. 33, pp. 671–84.

INDEX

Entries are in word-by-word alphabetical order (in which spaces are taken into account); 'Bank rate' therefore comes before 'bankers' deposits'. Hyphens are treated as spaces. Abbreviations, such as 'EMS', are treated as words. References to chapter notes are indicated by 'n'.